Backstories: The Kitchen Table Talk Cookbook

2021 The Digital Press @ The University of North Dakota

Book Design: William Caraher
Cover Design: Paul Forest

Library of Congress Control Number: 2021937519
The Digital Press at the University of North Dakota, Grand Forks, North Dakota

ISBN-13 (paperback): 978-1-7364986-2-0
ISBN-13 (PDF): 978-1-7364986-3-7

Cover Image: Stephen Sylvester Main collection, University of Guelph Library, Archives, and Special Collections, Agricultural History (XA1 MS A230 #214)

Backstories

The Kitchen Table Talk Cookbook

Edited by
Cynthia C. Prescott
and
Maureen S. Thompson

The Digital Press at the University of North Dakota
Grand Forks, ND

Cover Image: Stephen Sylvester Main collection, University of Guelph Library, Archives, and Special Collections, Agricultural History (XA1 MS A230 #214)

—Contents—

Introduction: Kitchen Table Talk
Cynthia C. Prescott & Maureen S. Thompson xv

Part I: Studying Rural Women through Cookbooks

1. Introduction
Cynthia C. Prescott 3

2. A Little History of the Rural Women's Studies Association (RWSA)
Joan Jensen, Katherine Jellison, Pamela Riney-Kehrberg, and Cynthia C. Prescott 5

3. Rural Women, Rural Words: Recipes and History
Rebecca Sharpless 11

4. Quantity Cooking: Cabbage Salad for Sixty
Catharine Wilson 19

5. Three Centuries of Scottish Cookery
Kathryn Harvey 21

6. Mustard Plaster
Catharine Wilson 37

7. Curry Powder
Catharine Wilson 39

8. Cookbooks: Exploring Economic(s) Themes
Erna van Duren 43

9. Buckaroo Stew and Before: Four Generations of Kurtz Family Recipes
Mazie Hough 61

10. Let Them Eat [Pound] Cake
Maureen S. Thompson 65

Part II: Community Cookbooks

11. Introduction
Cynthia C. Prescott 69

12. Banana Bread, Pineapple Pudding, Cocoanut Dainties, and Date Bars: Favorite Recipes as a Window into Women's Lives in Early-Twentieth Century Downeast Maine
Rachel Snell 71

13. Kitchen Joy
Cherisse Jones-Branch 83

14. "Hospitality was their byword": Food, Tradition, and Creativity in Borderlands Kitchens
Mary Murphy 87

15. Kent Family Recipes
Sarah Kesterson 97

16. The Montana Rural Home: A Community Cookbook
Amy McKinney 103

17. Tamales in the UTSA Mexican Cookbook
Steph Noell 123

18. Brains, Skill, and Butter: Sample a Feast of History in Century-Old Cookbooks
Katie Mayer 135

Part III: Nostalgia and Foodways

19. Introduction
Cynthia C. Prescott with contributions by Maureen S. Thompson 145

20. The Bradley Women and The Delmarva Farmer
Sara E. Morris 151

21. Lady Baltimore Cake
Sara E. Morris 159

22. Morris Family Recipes
Elizabeth H. Morris 163

23. Bischoff Family Coffee Cake
Katherine Jellison 167

24. Grandmama's Cooking Traditions
Joseph Cates 169

25. Chicken and Noodles
Pamela Riney-Kehrberg 175

26. Sauerbraten mit Oscar, Gerhardt, Fredrich und Freunde
Joan Speyer 177

27. At Mam-Maw's Table
Tracey Hanshew 181

28. Hanshew Family Recipes
Tracey Hanshew 193

29. Sour Cream Pie and Nana's Buns
Diane McKenzie 201

30. Spanish Buns
Catharine Wilson 205

31. Zucchini Bread
Cynthia C. Prescott 209

32. Blackberry and Apple Jelly
Margaret Thomas-Evans 213

33. Harvest Photographs
Pamela Riney-Kehrberg 215

34. Mom's Rhubarb Relish
Marie Kenny 217

35. November Mincemeat
Pamela J. Snow Sweetser 219

36. Two Cakes and Three Generations
Sara Egge 225

37. Grammie Botsford's Molasses Cookies
Rachel Snell 229

38. Chocolate Pudding
Eli Bosler 231

Part IV: Politics and Authority

39. Introduction
Cynthia C. Prescott 233

40. Cake and Politics
Sara Egge 239

41. Domecon Cake
Lynne Byall Benson 249

42. Photographic Essay: Hunger During the Great Depression and World War II
Cynthia C. Prescott 251

43. Soup for Dessert? My Mother's "Secret" Cake Recipe
Linda M. Ambrose 259

44. 3,000 Tons to Lose: Farm Women and Weight Control
Jenny Barker Devine 263

45. Teaching Food History
Pamela Riney-Kehrberg 275

46. Federal Writers' Project Slave Narratives
Pamela Riney-Kehrberg and Cynthia C. Prescott 283

47. Pavlova
Cynthia C. Prescott 287

Part V: Twenty-First-Century Foodways

48. Introduction
Cynthia C. Prescott 293

49. Putting the Little Town on the Prairie on Culinary Maps
Cynthia C. Prescott 299

50. Convenience Cooking: Seven-Layer Casserole
Catharine Wilson 311

51. Kalua Pork
Cynthia C. Prescott 313

52. Breadfruit Stew
Diana Chen 317

53. Doing the Heavy Lifting: Gender Roles and Consumption in the Age of COVID-19
Virginia Scharff 319

54. North Fareway Visit, March 23, 2020
Pamela Riney-Kehrberg 331

55. Pam's Pandemic Soup
Pamela Riney-Kehrberg 333

56. COVID Reflection
Sara Egge 335

57. Life Amid a Pandemic
Cynthia C. Prescott 337

58. Clay, COVID, and Matzah Balls:
An [Im]Perfect Passover in a New Home
Rebecca Stoil 345

59. Quarantine Baking
Nikki Berg Burin 353

60. ". . . Time enough for that":
A Recipe for Comfort in the Pandemic
Pamela J. Snow Sweetser 355

61. Recipes for the Pandemic
Dee Garceau 359

62. Labor, Loss, and Joy:
COVID-19 and Food among Faculty Parents
Samantha K. Ammons and Krista Lynn Minnotte 363

Conclusion: Community Potlucks and Global Markets
Cynthia C. Prescott 367

Contributors 379

—Recipes—

Part I: Studying Rural Women through Cookbooks

Mrs. Chiswel's Receipt for a Cake, very good 12
To Prepare Rennet 13
English Curd Pie 13
Raspberry Peek-a-Boos 14
Cabbage Salad for Sixty 20
Mustard Plaster 38
Curry Powder 40
Buckaroo Stew Waquoit 62
Chocolate sauce 62
Gamma's Orange Cakes 63
Egg Nog 64
Pound Cake 66

Part II: Community Cookbooks

Swiss Lettuce Roll Salad – Mrs. Martha Richardson 74
Cocoanut [sic] Dainties 78
Blueberry Muffins – Margaret Richardson 78
Blueberry Cake – Mrs. Heath 78
Date Bars 79
Pineapple Fluff – Mrs. L.P. Somes 81
Crab Cakes 84
Spoon Bread 84
Okra Soup 84
Wild Rice Fried Shrimp 85
Frogmore Stew 85
Hard Times Pudding 88
Fattigmand No.1 89
Ginger Cordial 90
Raw Oysters on Ice 92
An Apple Sea Serpent 92
Coffee Mousse 93
Dream Sandwiches 94
Huckleberry Pudding 97
Pickled Peaches 99
Brown Bread 100
Mince Meat 102

Strawberry Jam ... 107
Canned Cherry Pie ... 108
Cousin Mabel's Good Crabapple Pickles ... 108
Chocolate Pixie ... 110
Pow Wow Buns ... 110
Ribbon Icebox Dessert ... 111
Rhubarb Custard Pie ... 112
Rhubarb Marlow ... 112
Baked Pheasant ... 112
Braised Venison ... 113
Boiled Tongue ... 113
Pavatica ... 113
Salmon Casserole with Parsley Biscuits ... 114
Parsley Biscuits ... 114
Baked Eggs in Macaroni Nests ... 114
Fish Pie ... 116
Brownie Mix ... 117
Biscuit Mix ... 118
Spaghetti Casserole ... 119
Rosy Red Cookies ... 119
Tamales ... 125
Curd Tamales ... 128
Coconut Tamales ... 128
Minced Tamales ... 129
Chicken Tamales ... 129
Tamal Casserole ... 131
Rice Tamales (Version 1) ... 134
Rice Tamales (Version 2) ... 134
Milk to Fill the Tamales ... 134
Common Tamales ... 134
Never-Fail Sponge Cake ... 136
Pork Cake (Original) ... 138
Scripture Cake ... 138
Devil Cake ... 139
White Mountain Cake ... 139
Bran Gems ... 139
Brains on Toast ... 139
Macaroni and Cheese ... 140
Corn mustard ... 140
Mayanoise [sic] ... 140
Pigeons in Casserole ... 140
Peanut Sandwiches ... 141
Beef Steak Balls ... 141
Scrambled Eggs ... 141

Part III: Nostalgia and Foodways

Squash Casserole ... 155
Company Beef Steak ... 156
Pop-Pop's Raisin Cookies ... 157
Lady Baltimore Cake ... 160
Quick Caramel Frosting ... 161
Easy Apple Cake ... 163
Easy Crab Soup ... 164
Harvestore Bars ... 164
Granny's Lemon Snowflake Sugar Cookies ... 165
Applesauce Deluxe ... 165
Bischoff Family Coffee Cake ... 167
Chicken and Noodles ... 176
Sauerbraten mit Kartoffelkloesse und Rotkohl ... 178
Kartoffelkloesse (Potato Dumplings) ... 179
Rotkohl (Red Cabbage) ... 179
Chess Cake ... 193
Mam-maw Weathers' Buttermilk Pie ... 194
Tea Cakes ... 195
Lemon Meringue Pie ... 196
Peanut Patties ... 198
French Cream Pie (Sour Cream Pie) ... 202
Nana's Buns ... 202
Cinnamon Rolls ... 203
Spanish Buns ... 207
Culver Family Zucchini Bread ... 210
Hayes Family Zucchini Bread ... 211
Blackberry and Apple Jelly ... 214
Mom's Rhubarb Relish ... 217
November Mincemeat ... 222
Applesauce Cake ... 227
Brown Sugar Frosting ... 227
Sour Cream Scratch Cake ... 228
Grammie Botsford's Molasses Cookies ... 229
Chocolate Pudding ... 231

Part IV: Politics and Authority

War Cake ... 246
Domecon Cake ... 249
White Mountain Frosting for Domecon Cake (7-Minute Frosting) ... 250
Tomato Soup Cake ... 261
Pavlova ... 290
Chocolate Sheath Cake (Texas Sheet Cake) ... 291
Chocolate Frosting ... 291

Part V: Twenty-First Century Foodways

Seven-Layer Casserole 312
"Kalua" Pork 315
Hawaiian Fried Rice 316
Breadfruit Stew 317
Pam's Pandemic Soup 333
Maztah Ball (Kneidlach) Soup 350
Tzimmes (Slow-Baked Fruit Compote) 351
Parker House Rolls 357
Banana-Chocolate-Chip Muffins 361
Vegetable Mayhem 361
Pandemic Safety Sandwich 361

—Introduction—

Introduction: Kitchen Table Talk

Like rural women around the world, members of the Rural Women's Studies Association (RWSA) rise early in the morning and squeeze tasks into already busy schedules to plan our upcoming conferences. Also like our rural sisters worldwide, we often accomplish RWSA business by gathering together around a shared meal. Bleary-eyed at early morning business meetings held in a campus dining hall at our 2018 conference and over exorbitant continental breakfasts in hotel meetings rooms at other academic conferences, we crafted a theme for our 14th Triennial Conference in Guelph, Ontario, Canada, in 2021 that captures that sense of gathering. "Kitchen Table Talk to Global Forum" emphasizes how conversations, relationships, and food shape rural communities, and how local interactions influence global processes.

In keeping with that theme, one of our members suggested that RWSA produce a cookbook to accompany our 2021 conference. Members assembled at an RWSA breakfast meeting held in conjunction with the 2019 centennial meeting of the Agricultural History Society in Washington, DC, endorsed the idea, and volunteers gathered for lunch at a nearby French bistro to explore what that might look like. Over quiche, exquisite pastries, and lots of coffee, a vision took hold that we could produce a community cookbook in the tradition of those published by many rural women over the past two centuries for women's church- and auxiliary-group fundraising. Like those cookbooks, we imagined a volume that would bring together members' cherished recipes. But while most community cookbooks simply collect tried-and-true or aspirational recipes, we wanted to capture the food culture that those recipes represent. We therefore chose to collect not only member-contributed heirloom recipes, but also the family histories, cultural heritages, and personal memories that make those heirloom recipes meaningful.

Just as we gathered over shared meals to dream about this collection, we seek to gather recipes and stories in this volume that contribute to virtual gathering centered around food. According to Pria Parker, author of *The Art of Gathering: How We Meet and Why it Matters*, "Gathering—the conscious bringing together of people for a reason—shapes the way we think, feel, and make sense of our world."[1] Because eating is an essential act of wellbeing, activities have been de-

[1] Pria Parker, *The Art of Gathering: How We Meet and Why it Matters* (New York: Penguin Books, 2018), 4.

veloped around mealtimes. Food brings people to the table and dialogue ensues. While sharing food we exchange information and ideas, but also elements of our personal lives. We nourish each other with sustenance and knowledge.

Sharing recipes that produce our favorite dishes is a form of intimate conversation. Recipes are more than a list of ingredients and accompanying directions. They are often handed down through generations and include backstories of the people—typically women—who produced them through countless hours of trial and error. In fact, Yale professor Maria Trumpler, who teaches a "Women Food and Culture" course considers cookbooks "female literary genre."[2] *Backstories: The Kitchen Table Talk Cookbook* seeks to honor female tradition while producing a volume that engages cookbooks on a scholarly level, reflecting the themes associated with the 2021 RWSA conference including food production, preparation, rituals, hospitality, etiquette, and display. By telling the stories behind the recipes, we seek to uncover rural people's gatherings around kitchen tables. It considers how recipes transmit significance, meaning, and culture, appealing to an audience that craves a serving of knowledge alongside their food.

This cookbook furthers RWSA's efforts to honor and preserve rural traditions. But as our small group of cookbook creators returned from Washington, DC, to our daily lives as academics and activists, we began to ponder ways that this nascent cookbook project might also further RWSA's efforts to promote scholarship about rural women in diverse settings, and to build bridges to bring together academics, activists, and rural residents. We looked for ways to integrate storytelling and recipes with more scholarly content. Rather than adhering to long-standing divisions between (often male-dominated) formal academic publishing and more personal writing, what if we united research with storytelling, and memory with analysis?

What emerged is so much more than a cookbook. It contains beloved recipes and records oral traditions about how and when those recipes should be enjoyed, and how they have been passed down through generations. Many of these stories are steeped in nostalgia, celebrating family traditions. But because many of these stories have been recorded by feminist scholars, the accompanying narratives also uncover diverse themes such as the daily realities of farm labor and ethnic and social class differences. The more academic essays teach us many lessons about changing foodways over the past three centuries, all presented in an approachable style that is accessible to general audiences. Thus, this volume recovers the stories of rural women, and others, as women's historians have sought to do for the past half century. But the narratives included in *Backstories* are not just stories. These backstories are crucial because understanding these conversations and memories centered around food changes the way we understand women's lived experiences, and reveals crucial community dynamics. Unearthing these memories highlights

---

[2] Maria Trupler, "Women Food and Culture" syllabus, https://summer.yale.edu/sites/default/files/files/Syllabi/2018/WGSS%20S120%20-%20Women%2C%20Food%20and%20Culture.pdf Accessed 09/10/2019.

rural women's central roles in their families and communities. It also uncovers their crucial economic and cultural contributions to the larger societies in which they lived.

Women are often tasked with food preparation. We nostalgically remember our mothers and grandmothers preparing food on a daily basis or creating special dishes for holiday meals, especially the kitchen's aromas. Olfactory memory is authentic and plays a substantial role in how information is processed. The reason odors trigger strong reminiscences is because the olfactory bulb relays messages to the hippocampus and amygdala, which are regions of the brain associated with memory and emotion. Food odors can transport us to childhood and beyond, as we associate scents with people, feelings, locations, and occasions.

Eating is often associated with emotion and memory, while scholarly research is typically associated with very different parts of the mind. Uniting the two can produce powerful results. In his interpretation of Claude Levi-Strauss's *The Raw and the Cooked*, Dr. Ouzi Elyada surmises, "While nature is perceived as emotional–instinctual, culture is perceived as intellectual." Furthermore, "the evolution of cooking techniques and rules, and the transformation of cooking [is] a cultural process . . ." Based on Elyada's reasoning, the process of cooking can be regarded as an intellectual activity that humans developed over the course of millennia.[3] Similar to Levi-Strauss's anthropological study, this project was predicated upon seemingly binary oppositions, in this case scholarly analysis and nostalgia. *Backstories: Kitchen Table Talk to Global Forum* seeks to bridge that divide. This volume reflects a form of collaboration that is traditionally associated with cookbooks produced by women's organizations including personal anecdotes shared alongside recipes. Additionally, it also features peer-reviewed articles examining the transformation of cooking manuals over the course of centuries, food history and culture, and how both the government and the processed food industry educated rural women about food preparation and nutrition.

Scholars tend to question *everything*. Social scientists study people to understand why they behave in particular ways. Often, customs, religious ideology, and geography play a role in the foods we eat or reject. Historians typically rely on primary sources to analyze notable trends. While cookbooks might initially appear as a list of ingredients with instructions describing how to prepare them, cookbooks offer evidence of the past including what types of food were available in a certain geographic location, traditional cuisines immigrants brought to America, and how indigenous foods were substituted for customary ingredients in recipes. Within these pages, we share heart-felt memories associated with family recipes and local foodways. Yet we also apply a scholar's perspective on those memories, mining those nostalgic anecdotes for perspectives on the place of food within culture and society.

As we gathered these recipes, stories, and essays in spring 2020, a pandemic swept through our homes, communities, and nations. COVID-19, a highly infectious and too-often deadly respiratory virus, transformed our lives overnight.

[3] Ouzi Elyada, "The Raw and the Cooked: Claude Levi-Strauss and the Hidden Structures of Myth," art-gallery.nalfa.ac.il. n.d.

Schools and restaurants closed. Social distancing required us each to remain in our own homes. Store shelves were picked bare of hand sanitizer, toilet paper, and food staples. Many suddenly had to work from home, accompanied by children struggling to learn, while food service and grocery employees suddenly became front-line workers. We were told to stay at least 6 feet away from anyone outside our immediate household unit, and to don a mask whenever venturing outside our homes (which had to be homemade to save surgical masks for front-line health workers). Many of us responded to shortages and social barriers by embracing baking, celebrating our triumphs with sourdough bread and elaborate desserts on social media and bemoaning homemade hamburger buns that failed to rise like those picture-perfect buns displayed on recipe websites.

In these unprecedented times, our contributors did what rural women have always done: they worked harder and made do. We sewed masks for ourselves and others. We snuck in a few minutes of writing between attempting to understand the new fourth-grade math and maintaining dramatically increased housework demands. (Who knew how much of our food had previously come from restaurants and the school cafeteria?) And we also sought to capture these experiences for posterity. We gathered reflections from RWSA members and friends recording how their lives—and particularly their relationships with food—had changed as a result of the pandemic. We offer these stories and reflections here as a collection of primary sources documenting a dramatic period in our lives, and as a first draft of a new history of early-twenty-first-century foodways.

Backstories: The Kitchen Table Talk Cookbook draws on a long tradition of women's clubs producing cookbooks as fundraisers for their organizations. As Rachel Snell (Snell, Ch. 12, this volume) and Mary Murphy (Murphy, Ch. 14, this volume) document in this volume, cookbooks were a common way for women's clubs and auxiliaries to raise funds for charitable causes; some three thousand community cookbooks were published between the US Civil War and World War I. Just as rural communities have generously shared to support one another and enrich each other's lives, so RWSA chooses to make electronic copies of this volume available free of charge. And like fundraising cookbooks of old, hard copies of *Backstories* will be sold to raise funds for RWSA's Jensen-Neth Fund, which provides scholarships for students, activists, and international scholars to attend RWSA conferences. As such, it supports and enables the kinds of global conversations that make RWSA conferences so valuable.

But *Backstories* is much more than just another fundraising cookbook. RWSA is an international association founded in 1997 to promote and advance farm and rural women's/gender studies in a historical perspective by encouraging research, promoting scholarship, and establishing and maintaining links with organizations that share these goals. As an organization that unites historians, sociologists, anthropologists, and community activists, within this volume we seek to unite those recipes and stories with interdisciplinary scholarship that explores the social, cultural, and economic relationships fostered by food production, preservation, and consumption. In so doing, we seek to elevate and promote scholarship on rural peoples and processes that are all too often overlooked. In this volume, we open windows onto the kinds of conversations that traditionally occurred over hot stoves or in parlor circles. At the same time, we unpack scholarly analysis to make it approachable to non-specialists. We weave together recipes, memories, and analysis. We probe memories and consider popular culture.

Our cookbook presents diverse regional foodways across centuries. They range from simple eighteenth-century "receipts" to contemporary dishes. While current cookbooks often focus on one category of food, this volume reflects the RWSA's aspiration to be a global forum. Our triennial conferences attract participants from Africa, Asia, Europe, and Oceania, but our membership still largely reflects the organization's North American roots and origins in academic conferences. We had hoped that this volume could reflect our organization's growing geographic and cultural diversity. Unfortunately, though perhaps not surprisingly, the recipes and scholarship that our members contributed to this volume come primarily from longtime members, most of them European-descended academics residing in North America. But that does not mean that they lack diversity. Our members' contributions of both recipes and scholarship reflect the regional and community-level specificity that RWSA's approach emphasizes.

The first section of this volume, "Studying Rural Women through Cookbooks," explores different approaches to studying rural women. RWSA co-founder Joan Jensen and other longtime RWSA members provide a brief history of the Rural Women's Studies Association (Jensen at al., Ch. 2, this volume). We then introduce various ways that RWSA scholars and others use cookbooks as primary sources. Rebecca Sharpless (Sharpless, Ch. 3, this volume) provides a historical introduction to how North American recipe books have changed over time, and how they can be mined by scholars to learn about changing foodways and women's work. Across the Atlantic, Kathryn Harvey (Harvey, Ch. 5, this volume) explores changes in cookbooks over three centuries in Scotland. And Erna van Duren (van Duren, Ch. 8, this volume) highlights varied economic themes revealed in those changing recipe books. Recipes submitted by RWSA members demonstrate the research value of these recipes, and amplify the economic themes explored in van Duren's essay.

The second section of this volume, "Community Cookbooks," applies those lessons to studying cookbooks and recipe collections in specific times and places within North America. Together, these essays explore relationships of production, consumption, and community production. Rachel Snell (Snell, Ch. 12, this volume) focuses on rural foodways in early-twentieth-century Downeast Maine, and Mary Murphy (Murphy, Ch. 14, this volume) examines foodways in the US-Canada borderlands. Amy McKinney (McKinney, Ch. 16, this volume) demonstrates that women's columns in a rural Montana newspaper constituted their own form of community cookbook. And Steph Noell (Noell, Ch. 17, this volume) shares historic tamale recipes from an invaluable archive of cookbooks from the US-Mexico borderlands. Representative recipes appear throughout these essays, serving as illustrations of this scholarship and offering cooks an opportunity to experience a taste of these varied places and time periods.

Katie Mayer's (Mayer, Ch. 18, this volume) exploration and revisiting of Oregon community cookbooks in her archive serves as a bridge to our more personal third section. "Nostalgia and Foodways" takes a more intimate look at the ways that recipes operate within families. Sara Morris (Morris, Ch. 20, this volume) reflects on the women in her family and their participation in a local rural newspaper's recipe contest. Tracey Hanshew (Hanshew, Ch. 27, this volume) reviews her family's kitchen table as an epicenter for honing domestic skills and addressing the challenges of rural life. Joseph Cates (Cates, Ch. 24, this volume) records oral traditions of his Grandmama's cooking. Throughout this section, RWSA members share beloved heirloom recipes, exploring many lessons that we can learn from their varied food memories.

Section Four, "Politics and Authority," investigates the various ways that foodways have been taught and demonstrates that they are valuable window into agrarianism. Sara Egge (Egge, Ch. 40, this volume) explores wartime adaptations in foodways, and the ways that early-twentieth-century American women used food and recipes to bridge political and cultural divides. Jenny Barker Devine (Barker Devine, Ch. 44, this volume) examines the ways that government agencies sought to influence farm women's relationships to food in the mid-twentieth century. And Pamela Riney-Kehrberg (Riney-Kehrberg, Ch. 45, this volume) suggests ways that we engage our twenty-first-century students around foodways to help them think critically about agriculture and rural life. Recipes in this section highlight the ways that cooks were introduced to new products and explored new flavors.

Our final section explores contemporary "Twenty-First-Century Foodways." Cynthia Prescott (Prescott, Ch. 48, this volume) examines the role of the media in shaping constructions of rural womanhood in the early twenty-first century. Just as our lives changed suddenly in March 2020 as a result of the COVID-19 virus, so this volume shifts gears substantially in this section. We close this volume with both scholarship and informal reflections on how a global pandemic affected our relationships to food and domestic labor as we prepared this volume for press in Spring 2020. Through these short pieces, we seek to document a dramatic period in our daily lives and offer reflections on what COVID-19 revealed about our place within an increasingly global food chain.

Throughout this volume, we integrate formal scholarship with informal reflections, analyses of recipe books with heirloom recipes, and text with images to emphasize the ways that economics, politics, and personal meaning come together to shape our changing relationships with food. By embracing elements of history, rural studies, and women's studies, *Backstories: The Kitchen Table Talk Cookbook* offers a unique perspective relating food history with social dynamics. It is sure to inspire eclectic dining and conversations.

Cynthia C. Prescott and Maureen S. Thompson, editors
March 2021

PART I

Studying Rural Women through Cookbooks

—1—

Introduction

Cynthia C. Prescott

When the field of women's history emerged in the 1970s, most studies focused on relatively privileged urban white women who had left relatively ample documentation of their lives. Scholars were hesitant to examine rural women due to the shortage of sources. A few stalwart feminist scholars embraced the challenge, finding new ways to mine existing archival sources and identifying new kinds of sources. Historians Joan M. Jensen, Deborah Fink, and Elizabeth Jameson, and sociologist Katherine Jensen (Scharff, Ch. 53, the volume) were among the first to investigate rural women's work. Their groundbreaking scholarly research yielded fertile ground in which a second generation of scholars, including Katherine Jellison, Valerie Grim, Nancy Grey Osterud, Pamela Riney-Kehrberg (Riney-Kehrberg, Ch. 45, this volume), and many others grew to prominence, furthering our understanding of rural women's lives. Jensen, Susan Armitage, and Sarah Albert initiated the first of several conferences to share their discoveries, eventually leading to the formation of the Rural Women's Studies Association (RWSA) in 1998 (Jensen et al., Ch. 2, this volume). Over the past two decades, the RWSA has nurtured new generations of feminist scholars (https://ruralwomensstudies.wordpress.com/2019/03/20/grandmothers-and-granddaughters-of-the-rwsa-what-generation-gap/) exploring rural gender and sexuality.

We begin this volume—as many community cookbooks historically have done—with a brief history of the organization that produced it. Joan Jensen offers her recollections of RWSA's early days, supplemented by contributions from other RWSA leaders to carry our group's story up to the present (Jensen et al., Ch. 2, this volume). It highlights the efforts of pathbreaking scholarship and also, like much of the volume, points to the importance of gathering and sharing both food and ideas.

Feminist scholars today carry on the work that Jensen and others began a half century ago, continuing to pioneer new research methods. In the twenty-first century, some turned to cookbooks to uncover not only what people were eating, but how those foods were produced and consumed. We begin with Rebecca Sharpless' introduction to the use of recipes as historical sources, which highlights the many ways that feminist scholars can mine these primary texts to uncover otherwise hidden aspects of rural work and community life (Sharpless, Ch. 3, this volume).

Her essay provides a foundation for the scholarly work that follows, introducing both research methodologies and themes that are central to this volume, including women's labor and cultural expertise, production, and consumption.

The scholarly essays and brief interludes that follow Sharpless' overview demonstrate the different ways that these research methods can be applied. Catharine Wilson's brief contribution (Wilson, Ch. 4, this volume) to this section models this approach at work. Wilson shares a recipe and photograph that she discovered in her historical research that reveals farm wives' work feeding crowds at neighborhood work "bees," and highlights how changing labor patterns affected food consumption. Kathryn Harvey's detailed survey of "Three Centuries of Scottish Cookery" (Harvey, Ch. 5, this volume) uncovers changing foodways and economic systems within one nation. We pair it with a twentieth-century Canadian medicinal recipe (Wilson, Ch. 6, this volume) and British-Canadian immigrant Hannah Peters Jarvis' 1840s curry recipe (Wilson, Ch. 7, this volume) shared by Catharine Wilson to highlight ways that medicinal knowledge and exotic tastes traveled through the British Empire. We turn next to Erna van Duren's examination of economic themes in cookbooks (Van Duren, Ch. 8, this volume), accompanied by Mazie Hough's (Hough, Ch. 9, this volume) and Maureen Thompson's (Thompson, Ch. 10, this volume) as examples of economic decision-making at work in the twentieth-century United States.

As the essays and recipes in this section highlight, cookbooks represent valuable primary sources that uncover gendered divisions of labor, the impact of technology on women's work, the economic decisions underpinning rural foodways, and much more.

—2—

A Little History of the Rural Women's Studies Association (RWSA)

Joan Jensen, Katherine Jellison, Pamela Riney-Kehrberg, and Cynthia C. Prescott

When the Rural Women's Studies Association (RWSA) was formally established in Waco, Texas, in 1997, it had already existed informally for over a decade. The scholars who originally came together in the 1980s to study rural women were concerned that American historians had devoted little attention to these women, although they were the majority of the female population for the greater part of American history. The Agricultural History Society sponsored only one symposium each year, with no general conference where a wide assortment of historical issues could be discussed. The Social Science History Association had a rural section that presented a small forum for rural studies. What scholarship did exist at the time barely discussed rural women or gender issues. Regular conferences in history were unlikely to address the general lack of scholarly interest in rural history.

Sometime in late 1982 or early 1983, historians Sue Armitage, Sarah Elbert, and Joan Jensen decided that scholars interested in expanding the field of rural women's studies should do something about this situation. In 1981, Jensen had published an anthology of women's writing, *With These Hands: Women Working on the Land*, which sketched out the broad scope of rural women's work. But there was no place where interested scholars could meet to discuss the vast undertaking of documenting women's role in rural life. These three historians felt that they could not start a separate group at that time, but they might be able to organize an interdisciplinary conference to bring American scholars together with rural women and policy makers to engage in a conference addressing the needs of contemporary rural women.

Armitage, Elbert, and Jensen planned the first "American Farm Women in Historical Perspective" conference for February 1984 at New Mexico State University, a land grant institution where Jensen was teaching women's history. The deans of the colleges of Arts and Sciences and Agriculture pledged support with a grant and funding from several outside agencies, including the New Mexico Endowment for the Humanities and the S & H Foundation. About 125 people attended, and the response was so enthusiastic that a second conference was immediately planned. No proceedings from this first conference were published, but Jensen summarized the research in "Rural Women in American History," the introduction to her 1991 book *Promise to the Land: Essays on Rural Women.*

Wisconsin rural sociologists Wava Haney and Jane Knowles, who attended the first conference, volunteered to host a second conference in Madison at the University of Wisconsin. This second "American Farm Women in Historical Perspective" conference, held in October 1986, was larger and even more successful than the first. The Kellogg Foundation funded the participation of a number of representatives of rural women's organizations, and agricultural policy makers were particularly visible at this conference. In 1988, Westview Press published *Women and Farming: Changing Roles, Changing Structures*, a selection of papers from this conference edited by Haney and Knowles.

Originally, planners hoped land grant universities in different regions of the country would host conferences. That proved to be impractical as few land grant universities had a core group of scholars large enough to arrange such conferences. A third conference, held in December 1988 at Tuskegee University in conjunction with their annual Agricultural Work Conference, moved into the American South for the first time but proved to be less successful because only a small group of scholars attended. Those who did were particularly impressed by the way in which Alabama scholars linked their research directly to the needs of rural people.

In 1991, Jensen contacted the Agricultural History Society to ask if they could focus their next annual symposium on rural women. Mort Rothstein, then editor of the organization's journal, *Agricultural History*, immediately supported the plan. He helped raise funds within the University of California at Davis and community and made local arrangements. This fourth conference, held at UC Davis, occurred in June 1992. Several hundred people attended, including many members of the Agricultural History Society and representatives of rural women's organizations whose attendance, once again, was sponsored by the Kellogg Foundation. Cornelia Flora, now director of the North Central Regional Center for Rural Development, was especially active in coordinating support with the Kellogg Foundation. Jensen and Nancy Grey Osterud edited a group of papers presented at this conference for a special issue of *Agricultural History* (Spring 1993, 67.2), titled "American Rural and Farm Women in Historical Perspective." The following year the Agriculture History Society published this issue in book form.

The success of the fourth conference at UC Davis left people anxious to have yet another. Anne Effland, of the Economic Research Service of the USDA, offered to coordinate the "Fifth Conference on Rural and Farm Women in Historical Perspective," at the National 4-H Conference Center in Chevy Chase, Maryland, that was held in December 1994. This conference was particularly important for the number of international scholars who attended. Jensen and Margreet van der Burg, from the Wageningen Agricultural University in The Netherlands, worked with a group of international scholars who asked to participate in the conferences. At this time, no other country had hosted a similar conference devoted entirely to historical study of the role of women in rural society. Scholars from Europe, Canada, Australia, and New Zealand attended. The conference was also rich in the number of non-governmental organizations which sent representatives to the conference. Jensen and Anne Effland edited a selection of papers from this conference with additional invited papers for a special issue of *Frontiers* (2001, 22.1).

Almost three years passed before the "Sixth Conference on American Rural and Farm Women in Historical Perspective" was held at Baylor University in Waco, Texas, in September 1997. Debra Reid handled the local arrangements. A selection of papers from the sixth conference in Waco appeared in the Spring 1999 issue of *Agricultural History* (73.2), edited by Deborah Fink, Valerie Grim, and Dorothy Schwieder. Participants at this conference decided to establish a formal organization to host the conference every three years. Attendees chose the name Rural Women's Studies Association (RWSA), contributed membership dues to help begin RWSA, and accepted an invitation from Debbie Miller to host the seventh conference at the Minnesota Historical Society in St. Paul, Minnesota, in 2000.

Among those who established the formal RWSA structure in Waco were a number of scholars who had attended all six conferences over the previous thirteen years, and many who had attended four or five. Members selected Mary Neth and Joan Jensen to serve as co-coordinators until 2000. Mary Neth offered to continue to serve until 2003 with a new co-chair, Barbara Steinson, who would then serve for six years. After the Waco conference, the group adopted by-laws, applied for non-profit status, created and mailed its first newsletter, found an official home with Barbara Steinson at DePauw University, set up a website, and established local arrangements and program committees for the upcoming seventh conference in Minnesota.

Over 170 people attended the June 2000 conference of the Rural Women's Studies Association at the Minnesota History Center in St. Paul. One highlight of the conference was a field trip to the Oliver H. Kelly historical farm and museum in nearby Elk River, Minnesota. At the meeting, participants accepted the invitation of the New Mexico Farm & Ranch Heritage Museum and New Mexico State University to host the 2003 conference in Las Cruces to mark the "nearly" twentieth anniversary of the first rural women's conference. Jensen and Cameron Saffell, Historian at the New Mexico Farm & Ranch Heritage Museum, served as local arrangements co-chairs. The Mountain/Plains and Western Regions of the Association for Living History, Farm and Agricultural Museums (ALHFAM) soon agreed to hold their conference jointly with RWSA.

The 2003 RWSA conference took place in Las Cruces, New Mexico, in February 2003 and was a joint conference with the Mountain/Plains and Western Regions of the ALHFAM. The New Mexico Farm and Ranch Heritage Museum and New Mexico State University co-hosted the event, and Joan Jensen and Cameron Saffell were the local arrangements co-chairs. The conference included hands-on workshops on such activities as cast iron cooking and cheese making at the Farm and Ranch Heritage Museum and a tour of exhibits by and about rural women at the Las Cruces Cultural Complex.

The RWSA conference went to Pennsylvania Amish country in autumn 2006. Millersville University played host to the conference, and Diane Zimmerman Umble was among the Millersville faculty who organized local arrangements. The conference included a visit to the Landis Valley Museum, where participants could view many farm and household crafts, including hog butchering and processing. Unfortunately, the conference took place on the heels of a local tragedy, the mass murder of Amish schoolgirls at the Nickel Mines schoolhouse.

Indiana University was the setting for the autumn 2009 RWSA meeting. Valerie Grim was in charge of local arrangements. The theme of the Indiana meeting was "Health, Healing, and Rural Life." Tours included visits to two Bloomington-area farms, and the Bloomington Farmer's Market. At the conference business meeting, attendees approved Katherine Jellison's offer to become the RWSA web site manager, and her institution, Ohio University, became host for the organization's web site. The organization also created new positions to better distribute the work required by the growing organization, including a fundraising chair.

When the Agricultural History Society began holding yearly meetings in 2006, the Rural Women's Studies Association started to hold business meetings in conjunction with the AHS meetings during the off-years between triennial conferences. Additionally, the AHS meetings provided an opportunity to hold sessions in honor of various RWSA members. At AHS meetings, RWSA members held a "festschrift" for founder Joan Jensen, and memorial sessions for both Mary Neth and Dorothy Schwieder.

In July 2012, the RWSA triennial conference took place outside the United States for the first time. RWSA co-chair Deborah Stiles, director of the Rural Research Centre at Nova Scotia Agricultural College, was instrumental in arranging for a Maritime Province setting for the 2012 meeting, which took place in Fredericton, New Brunswick, co-hosted by the Rural Social Justice Centre for Research at St. Thomas University and the University of New Brunswick. Among the excellent program sessions was a multi-generational panel of scholars who discussed the history and future goals of the RWSA (https://ruralwomensstudies.wordpress.com/2018/04/25/past-present-future-rwsa/). Other conference highlights included a goodie bag filled with local agricultural products for each participant and tours of nearby Village of Gagetown and the Kings Landing Historical Settlement.

San Marcos, Texas, was the setting for the February 2015 RWSA meeting. Texas State University, the home base of RWSA co-chair Rebecca Montgomery, was the host institution. The 2015 meeting welcomed a diverse group of international attendees, including filmmakers, scholars, and activists. Off-campus conference highlights included a tour of a nearby urban farm and a visit to Texas wine country. Much of the discussion at that year's business meeting centered around choosing a site for the 2021 triennial conference. In the end, the University of Guelph emerged as the strongest contender. RWSA embraced electronic media, launching a blog and social media presence.

The 2018 triennial meeting took place in May at Ohio University in Athens, with RWSA co-chair Katherine Jellison heading up the local arrangements. The conference program included a plenary session in which rising scholars discussed the origins of their own research in the work of long-time RWSA members. Other highlights included comments by Chief Glenna Wallace of the Eastern Shawnee Tribe, museum tours of contemporary art quilts and of Navajo women's weavings, music and poetry by Appalachian women, and a pre-conference tour of Appalachian company towns. RWSA co-chair Catharine Wilson closed the conference with a preview of plans for the 2021 conference to be hosted by her home institution, the University of Guelph in Ontario, Canada.

As the COVID-19 pandemic spread around the globe in spring 2020, RWSA members gathered virtually to plan for that 2021 conference and for this cookbook. Meeting participants readily embraced co-chair Catharine Wilson and the local arrangements committee's recommendation that RWSA pivot to planning its first-ever virtual conference, which will be hosted by the University of Guelph in May 2021.

—3—

Rural Women, Rural Words: Recipes and History

Rebecca Sharpless

In publishing *Backstories: The Kitchen Table Talk Cookbook*, the Rural Women's Studies Association (RWSA) joins a long and proud tradition of women's organizations producing cookbooks with recipes contributed by their members. As long as humans have been preparing food, they have passed down formulas for cookery orally and, later, in writing. It doesn't take much imagination to picture a Native American woman showing her young daughter exactly when the cornmeal and water reached the right consistency to place the mixture on a flat rock to bake. Such a demonstration would be valuable information to the younger woman as she became responsible for her own family's meals.

As women gained literacy, recipes sometimes became written sets of instructions, a combination of directions and ingredients. Perhaps they included a few notes of explanation, but most recipes were simple. They did not seek to explain why the recipes were done a certain way, and they definitely didn't try to show why the recipes had social significance. Like much of women's work, the recipes existed in a domestic realm where their importance was taken for granted.

By giving context to recipes, this volume seeks to redress that lack. In looking both at recipes and scholarly analysis of foods, the RWWA breaks new ground. Recipes matter in and of themselves, but they also can be examined and set into the framework of scholarly discourse to tell the reader much about the setting in which they came about and, hence, their significance.

In the twenty-first century, historians have begun to recognize the usefulness of cookbooks as sources for research. Humble, homely volumes, stained and tattered, speak of meals prepared, sometimes as demonstrations of love, sometimes shows of cooking prowess, frequently acts of practicality because the family needed supper—and sometimes combinations of all three. In addition to gracing the bookshelves of innumerable homes, thousands of cookbooks have become part of library collections across the US and elsewhere, ready for research and interpretation, and more are appearing on the Internet every day in both organized and unorganized fashion.

The historical questions that a cookbook answers are often stronger on dailiness—the recurrent, mundane tasks of women's work in caring for their families—than on geopolitical questions, although each is an artifact of time and place, and the volumes carry important evidence about people's interactions with their environment and the society around them.[1] Most cookbooks are heavily gendered: produced by women, for women, giving insight into household work as few other sources can. And although most printed cookbooks are products of urban environments, they can still be useful for examining rural life. Rural women read city-published cookbooks, and numerous rural churches and clubs produced their own volumes. Home demonstration club members especially showed their prowess in the kitchen.[2]

Cookbooks have been a part of European cookery since the early modern period, and they showed up in early America in two ways: as European imports and as household cookery books. In the British colonies, cookbooks such as *The English Hus-Wife* by Gervase Markham (1615) became a part of the repertoire of well-to-do households in the seventeenth century. They were integrated into American foodways as women diligently copied recipes from them into their so-called household books. These household books might incorporate both family recipes and some from print sources, all transcribed in longhand and passed from generation to generation throughout the eighteenth century.[3] Jane Bolling Randolph's household book from the 1740s, now housed in the Virginia Museum of History and Culture, shows the basic nature of many of these books. She carefully attributed this cake recipe to a Mrs. Chiswel, who may have been her sister-in-law. But following her directions takes more than a bit of guessing.

Mrs. Chiswel's Receipt for a Cake, very good

To half a peck Flour put 2 lb. Butter, 1 ¼ lb. Sugar, ½ an oz: Nutmegs, ½ an oz: Mace, ¼ an oz: Cloves ¼ an oz: Cinnamon, 16 Eggs, ½ the Whites, a pt Cream, ½ pt. Sack a qt. Yest, & 5: lb Currants. Let it stand all Night to rise.

The amounts are enormous: a half peck of flour is about a gallon, or five pounds. Sack was a white wine, often mixed with brandy, imported from Spain, similar to sherry. "Yest" is yeast, typically made from the leftovers from brewing ale. Currants are a small berry that thrives and is well loved in England and not so much in the colonies. Their presence clearly marks this recipe's European influences.

[1] This essay contains material previously published in "Cookbooks as Resources for Rural Research," Agricultural History 90, No. 2 (Spring 2016), 195-208. Important and recent works interpreting cookbooks include *Recipes for Reading: Community Cookbooks, Stories, Histories*, ed. Anne L. Bower (Amherst: University of Massachusetts Press, 1997); Janet Theophano, *Eat My Words: Reading Women's Lives through the Cookbooks They Wrote* (New York: Palgrave, 2002); David A. Davis and Tara Powell, editors, *Writing in the Kitchen: Essays on Southern Literature and Foodways* (Jackson: University Press of Mississippi, 2014); Megan J. Elias, *Food on the Page: Cookbooks and American Culture* (Philadelphia: University of Pennsylvania Press, 2017); and Rafia Zafar, *Recipes for Respect: African American Meals and Meaning* (Athens: University of Georgia Press, 2019).

[2] Bettina Aptheker, *Tapestries of Life: Women's Work, Women's Consciousness and the Meaning of Daily Experience* (Amherst: University of Massachusetts Press, 1989), 44.

[3] An excellent example of a household book is an edited, published household book is Karen Hess, editor, *Martha Washington's Booke of Cookery* (New York: Columbia University Press, 1981). A partial bibliography of manuscript cookbooks is The Manuscript Cookbooks Survey, https://www.manuscriptcookbookssurvey.org/ (accessed May 26, 2020).

And Randolph says absolutely nothing about how to bake this monumental piece of work. One would know what kind of pan to use, how to prepare it, how hot to have the oven, and how long to bake it.[4]

As the American colonies moved toward independence from England, so did their food and the texts from which they cooked. The first cookbook produced in the colonies was a reprint of an English cookbook, *The Compleat Housewife* by Eliza Smith, printed in Williamsburg in 1742. Amelia Simmons is considered the first American cookbook writer, with her *American Cookery* published in 1796 in Hartford, Connecticut. Almost nothing is known about Simmons, who was either from New England or New York. Her recipes display not only a loyalty to the old ways brought from England but also liberal use of ingredients first found in North America such as corn, cranberries, and pumpkin.

Following Simmons, a veritable explosion of cookbooks appeared in the Northeast in the first quarter of the nineteenth century. Authors such as Susannah Carter, Maria Rundell, and the feminist-turned-abolitionist Lydia Maria Child published tomes containing hundreds of recipes for dishes from woodcock to "fried artichoak." The cuisine still had English roots but American elements as well. African culinary influences first appeared in *The Virginia Housewife* by Mary Randolph, published in 1838, in recipes such as okra gumbo.

Cookbooks such as those by Carter, Rundell, Child, and Randolph—and hundreds of others—speak with the authoritative voice of one woman. To ordinary housewives, such women became like friends in the kitchen. Catharine Beecher and her famous sister, Harriet Beecher Stowe, provided such guidance. Writing in the 1840s, Beecher assumed that her readers would still be involved in caring for and perhaps even slaughtering animals. She included recipes for preparing rennet, an enzyme that causes milk to coagulate into cheese, and then for using rennet in a pie.

To Prepare Rennet

Take the stomach of a new-killed calf, and do not wash it, as it weakens the gastric juice. Hang it in a cool and dry place five days or so, then turn the inside out and slip off the curds with the hand. Then fill it with salt, with a little saltpeter mixed in, and lay it in a stone pot, pouring on a teaspoonful of vinegar, and sprinkling on a handful of salt. Cover it closely and keep for use.

English Curd Pie

One quart of milk. A bit of rennet to curdle it. Press out the whey, and put into the curds three eggs, a nutmeg, and a tablespoonful of brandy. Bake it in paste, like custard.[5]

---

[4] Randolph's cookery book has been published in Katherine E. Harbury's masterful study, *Colonial Virginia's Cooking Dynasty* (Columbia: University of South Carolina Press, 2004).

[5] Catharine Beecher, *Miss Beecher's Domestic Receipt-Book*, 3rd ed. (New York: Harper & Brothers, 1856), 35, 106.

In the late nineteenth century, American women spoke of authors such as Sarah Tyson Rorer and Maria Parloa as though they were neighbors down the block.

As the field of home economics developed in the late nineteenth and early twentieth centuries, recipes became more standardized, with precise measurements and step-by-step instructions. Cooking experts were determined to make their work more of a science and less of an art. With the growth of American consumer products, from stoves to egg beaters, corporations hired professional food writers to assemble cookbooks that would best showcase their products. Thousands of those ephemeral corporate cookbooks reside in archives, with countless more hidden in kitchen drawers and shelves. The home economist speaks with a voice of authority, often a teacher more than a friend. Firmly and sometimes kindly, they advised American cooks on just how to prepare the foods that would keep their families healthy and happy.

These nationally distributed cookbooks may seem far afield for the researcher on rural foodways, for they are highly prescriptive and didactic, more a model than a reality for many. They should not be overlooked, however, for they were wildly popular and reached broad audiences. And they were freely plagiarized in other cookbooks. General Mills spread its recipes through the voice of Betty Crocker on radio beginning in the 1930s, and many prosperous rural women heard those cheery though authoritative broadcasts in their homes. Corporations created other friendly voices on the radio, and even the US Department of Agriculture got into the act with Aunt Sammy, a radio character whose cookbook first appeared in 1927.[6]

Betty Crocker is of course still a major player in US cooking. As General Mills developed mixes and shortcuts, Betty Crocker showed home cooks how best to use them. In 1964, for example, General Mills published a cookbook devoted to its Bisquick mix. Home economists developed tasty recipes such as "Raspberry Peek-a-Boos":

Raspberry Peek-a-Boos

Muffins

1 to 1 ¼ cups fresh raspberries
4 tablespoons granulated sugar
½ teaspoon nutmeg
½ teaspoon ground cinnamon
2 teaspoons lemon juice
2 cups Original Bisquick™ mix
¼ cup softened butter
⅔ cup milk

Glaze

1 cup powdered sugar
½ teaspoon vanilla
Pinch of salt
1 ½ tablespoons milk (or enough to make it easy to drizzle)

---

[6] Justin Nordstrom, editor, *Aunt Sammy's Radio Recipes* (Fayetteville: University of Arkansas Press, 2018) is an annotated version of the original 1927 publication.

Steps

1. Heat oven to 450°F. Place paper baking cup in each of 12 regular-size muffin cups, or grease muffin cups.
2. In small bowl, toss raspberries, 2 tablespoons of the granulated sugar, the nutmeg, cinnamon and lemon juice. Set aside.
3. In medium bowl, mix Bisquick mix, remaining 2 tablespoons granulated sugar and the butter. Add milk all at once; stir with fork into soft dough. Beat 20 strokes.
4. Spread a tablespoonful of dough in bottom of each muffin cup. Top each with 1 tablespoon raspberry mixture. Drop slightly less than 1 tablespoonful of dough onto berries.
5. Bake 10 to 15 minutes or until golden brown. Remove from muffin pans immediately after baking. Cool slightly.
6. Meanwhile, in small bowl, stir together Glaze ingredients until easy to drizzle. Drizzle over muffins.[7]

Likely more interesting for the historical researcher are locally published community cookbooks, artifacts of one particular place and time, as Katie Mayer points out in "Brains, Skill, and Butter" in this volume (Mayer, Ch. 18, this volume). These well-loved publications came into being during the American Civil War, when Ladies Aid Societies gathered favorite recipes of members and sold collections at bazaars in the North. A community cookbook was an ingenious idea that allowed women to raise money for causes they cared about while staying well within the gender conventions of the day. From churches and clubs, the books of donated recipes began to pour forth, and more than two thousand had been published by the end of the nineteenth century.[8] A thorough search of the twentieth century would undoubtedly turn up many thousands more.

The question inevitably arises about the extent to which community cookbooks actually reflect people's foodways. Sometimes the recipes are favorites that people actually eat, and sometimes they're recipes designed to show off, with fancy foods and elaborate recipes. Cookbooks and recipes, like every other aspect of human existence, are subject to fads and fashions. A newly available ingredient or cooking tool might spawn a slew of recipes from cooks wanting to appear au courant. In the late nineteenth century, chafing dishes were all the rage, while pressure cookers, fondue pots, and other such impedimenta appeared periodically in American kitchens with accompanying recipes. New foods, such as sweetened condensed milk and flavored gelatin, resonated with American cooks, who then wrote them into recipes. A 1925 Texas cookbook, for example, revealed a peculiarly strong fascination with dates, as the chewy goodies appeared in more than 10 percent of the recipes, both for entrees and desserts. That remarkable turn of events is because of clever marketing by date growers in California. In 1912, botanists from the US Department of Agriculture imported date palms from pres-

[7] From the 1964 "The Bisquick Cookbook," https://www.bettycrocker.com/recipes/vintage-betty, accessed May 26, 2020.

[8] Margaret Cook, *America's Charitable Cooks: A Bibliography of Fund-raising Cook Books Published in the United States (1861-1915)* (Kent, Ohio, 1971), is an early checklist of community cookbooks.

ent-day Iraq and set up orchards in the Coachella Valley of California. The dates thrived, and growers made sure that the sweet treat became the must-have ingredient for bakers in the 1920s.[9] Fashionable housewives wanted to make sure they appeared to be in the know about the latest ingredients.[10]

Some works, on the other hand, showcased the tried and true, the standby formulas that a cook had returned to time and again. The Presbyterian women of Augusta, Georgia in 1880 were adamant about the commonness of their recipes: "This is a book of home cookery—the savory dishes of our infancy. . . ."[11] The reader of such a cookbook could be confident that the recipes reflect the true dietary practices of middle- to upper-class white families in Augusta fifteen years after the Civil War. In general, a community cookbook can provide a bounty of insights into the group that produced it.

Often cookbooks are just straightforward compilations of recipes, sometimes with the ingredients listed before the directions, sometimes not. (Fannie Farmer of the Boston Cooking School in the 1880s was one of the first cookbook writers to introduce the innovation of an ingredients list.) Sometimes recipe writers included anecdotes with their recipes, and the editors allowed them to stand. Some cookbook writers had strong voices of their own. But, if the contributors and writers of the cookbooks don't usually give us the background stories of their recipes, what are we to learn from them?

We can understand the time and the place. When a recipe is formulated or published matters. Tastes, ingredients, and technology all change over time. And in some places and at various times, African American or immigrant domestic workers, not the farm wives, provided much of the labor in preparing food for farm families. The influence of the home demonstration service, part of the extension service of the US Department of Agriculture, becomes evident after World War I. Sara Egge, in "Cake and Politics" in this volume (Egge, Ch. 40, this volume), clearly shows the impact of the woman suffrage movement on cooking, and vice versa.

As transportation networks grew, so did the array of goods available to a rural cook. Many farm families prided themselves on their self-sufficiency: growing their own food—cows, chickens, pigs, grains, vegetables, fruits—was a mark of distinction for a self-sufficient farm. No matter how industrious the family, however, some items still had to be bought, including coffee, sugar, and flavoring extracts. In the early twentieth century, traveling salesmen from companies such as Rawleigh and Watkins made sure that rural cooks had access to those good things, taking eggs and butter in trade.

---

[9] "Forbidding Fruit: How America Got Turned on to the Date." https://www.npr.org/sections/thesalt/2014/06/10/320346869/forbidding-fruit-how-america-got-turned-on-to-the-date, accessed September 13, 2019.

[10] *50 Selected Recipes by 50 Denton Women* (N.p., n.d. [ca. 1925]), 8, 16, 28, 42.

[11] Augusta, Ga., Second Presbyterian Church, Choice Recipes of Georgia Housekeepers by the ladies of the Second Presbyterian Church, Augusta, Ga. (New York: Trow's Printing and Bookbinding co., 1880), iii-iv. Unpublished personal recipe collections can also be extremely revealing. For a project documenting heavily used recipes (revealed by virtue of the stains on them), see http://www.dirtypages.org/ (accessed April 3, 2020).

A family with some cash income and a way to get to town could buy an ever-growing variety of foods. Trade for food was, after all, one of the reasons for global exploration in the fifteenth century. Through the decades, the wealthiest Americans had been able to purchase almost anything as long as they were close to a seaport, even as their poor compatriots continued to subsist on corn and pork. But again, technology had its impact. Improved sea transportation allowed the importation of items such as oranges from Sicily and, eventually, bananas from Central America. The growth of the railroad allowed cattle to be shipped up from Texas, slaughtered in Chicago, and served in New York, just as oysters appeared on the northern Plains, as Mary Murphy points out in "Hospitality Was Their Byword" (Murphy, Ch. 14, this volume). The American diet became more standardized with the creation of giant corporations such as Nabisco and General Mills. Industrial products, like Jell-O and Hershey bars, became parts of recipes.

The technology available to cooks also shifted over time. In the US, almost all cooking was done in an open fireplace until the 1820s or so. The most affluent had separate baking ovens, either built into the side of the fireplace or outside of the kitchen. In the early nineteenth century, stoves fueled by wood or coal became available. Ironically, the middle-class cook was more likely to have a stove than an upper-class matron, who had servants to cook and rarely invested in the latest technology for them. Some Americans, however, continued to cook on open hearths until the early twentieth century. Electric and gas-powered stoves came about in the early twentieth century for the most part, although some people cooked on wood stoves until the 1970s.

While more affluent farm people could buy appliances, they still had to have power sources to make them run. As late as the 1930s, few rural Americans had electricity, and indoor plumbing with fresh, pure water often came at a premium as well.[12] Cooks had to adjust: A recipe that specified a "slow oven," for example, indicates that the cook was used to working without either a thermostat or a thermometer on her oven. She was likely familiar with the various ways of testing the heat of an oven, which included throwing flour on the bottom of the oven or sticking her hand into the oven chamber.

Refrigeration lagged behind cooking technology. First were natural springs for cooling foods, particularly dairy. Then came iceboxes, literally wooden boxes that could hold commercially made or harvested ice. Mechanical refrigerators, usually run by electricity, came about in the early twentieth century, although they were still enough of a novelty in the 1950s that "icebox cake" and "icebox cookies" became a trend. Small appliances evolved too: the split stick gave way to the wire whisk, which yielded to the rotary egg beater and finally the electric mixer, beginning about 1915. But as late as the 1950s, some housewives still considered an electric mixer a luxury and continued to beat their batters by hand.

Before World War I, region mattered more than it did later. Although trade in food has existed as long as there have been people, for most of human existence, people ate locally out of necessity. As the food supply changed, regional tastes

---

[12] David Danbom, *Born in the Country: A History of Rural America* (Baltimore: Johns Hopkins University Press, 1995), 220-22.

persisted nonetheless—for example the Midwestern attachment to hotdish, the casserole made of ground meat, a starch (usually potatoes), and canned soup, that sometimes eludes people from other parts of the country. See Cynthia Prescott, "Putting the Little Town on the Prairie on Culinary Maps" (Prescott, Ch. 49, this volume) for a discussion of regional specialties including hotdish. People in cooler climates had readier access to milk products, including butter and cheese, than did residents of warmer climates, where milk spoiled easily and summer temperatures made butter making difficult if not impossible. Ethnicity sometimes mattered in determining what a farm family ate. German families, for example, treasured recipes for sausage that were different from those of their Anglo neighbors. Families from Bohemia ate different types of bread than did their neighbors from Mexico, who had special formulas for *pan dulce* and tortillas.

For many rural Americans, change happened at slower rates than for their urban sisters. But happen it did, and with good roads, the increase of work in town, and the turn toward specialized crops, the self-sufficient family farm has become rare. Rural people, nonetheless, in the past and now, have loved food and thought about food and cooked good food: as the essays in this volume show.

—4—

Quantity Cooking: Cabbage Salad for Sixty

Catharine Wilson

Ontario, Canada, 1920s

Across the province of Ontario up until the 1960s, families that engaged in mixed agriculture (crops and livestock) held "bees," where they worked together at a neighbor's farm like bees in a hive. Together they cleared fields, raised barns, threshed grains, cut wood, and filled silos. Farm women played an essential role at these events by providing food. The promise of a good meal attracted workers and fueled their energy and enthusiasm for the job. The meal, moreover, was the host's first installment in the payback system, an immediate, material, and symbolic expression of reciprocity. Through food, women demonstrated their culinary skill and exercised the esteemed twin qualities of thrift and generosity. They did their best even if their family could only afford a modest affair because generosity was the mark of neighborliness. They sought a delicate balance of meeting what others expected of them *without* overstepping neighborhood standards. To deliberately show-off promoted rivalry, unnecessary expense, and bad feelings. It struck at the heart of neighborliness, at notions of fair exchange and economy.

I remember my aunt feeding the threshers in the 1960s, hungry, dirty men in from the fields who crowded around her harvest table laden with food. At a threshing bee, women might feed twenty-five men. At a barn raising they might feed one hundred or more.

In the process of writing a book about "Bee-ing Neighbours," I have found the following recipe for Cabbage Salad which comes from *The Farmer's Wife* magazine, June 1924. Quantity cooking was not as simple as converting a recipe for two people into a recipe for two hundred by multiplying ingredients; the proportions of ingredients needed adjusting. In addition, one had to predict the quantity of food necessary so as not to run out. Appetites were hearty. Whereas today experts in quantity cooking recommend a half-pound of raw meat per man and a three-inch wedge of pie, hosts at bees in the nineteenth century calculated one pound of raw meat and one whole pie per man with each slice being a seven-inch wedge! A very popular *Mennonite Community Cookbook* (1950) reprinted an old menu for "Food for a Barn Raising" for 175 men. The list included such things as fifty pounds roast beef, sixteen chickens, three hams, three-hundred rolls, ten gallons of potatoes, nine gallons of various puddings, 115 lemon pies and various other desserts. Men wanted tasty, filling, familiar, and easily handled food. They had little interest in

Figure 4.1: Image of Photograph of a barn raising feast, Stephen Sylvester Main Collection, Archival and Special Collections, University of Guelph.

urban status foods such as hot-house celery or salads. In the early twentieth century, however, women transformed the sturdy cabbage into coleslaw which benefited from sitting in its brine days in advance, an attractive quality when women had so much other cooking and baking to do on bee-day. This recipe serves sixty people.

Cabbage Salad for Sixty

4 lbs. cabbage
½ c chopped pimento
1 ½ c chopped pickle
3 c salad dressing

The pickles and salad dressing would have been homemade in 1924 but you'll be able to purchase them when you try this for your next family gathering.

—5—

Three Centuries of Scottish Cookery

Kathryn Harvey

According to literary scholar Susan J. Leonardi, writing in 1989, "Like a story, a recipe needs a recommendation, a context, a point, a reason to be."[1] More than 220 years earlier Hannah Robertson had similarly stated that "The Receipts contained in the following treatise are founded on many years experience, and are calculated for the improvement or amusement of young Ladies as well as for the use and advantage of those who may have the care of childrens education, who, though properly instructed themselves will find it an advantage to have receipts at hand to put them in mind of what they had formerly learnt."[2] If one precept is deducible from the history of cookbooks, or receipt books as they were called in the early modern period, it must be that the author(s) have a story to tell rendered from a position of authority. Furthermore, such culinary works have a firm place in social history as they reveal contemporary mores and even health concerns.[3]

My selection of the seven cookery books discussed here is an interesting story. Originally, I planned to look at three: one each from the 18th (Hannah Robertson's *School of Arts for Young Ladies*), 19th (Mrs Dalgairns' *The Practice of Cookery*)[4] and 20th (*Scottish Women's Rural Institutes Jubilee Cookery Book*)[5] centuries housed in Archival and Special Collections at the University of Guelph. And then the library closed due to COVID-19. Without access to these rare books, I had to change course. Fortunately, various editions of two works (Robertson's and Mrs Dalgairns') are available online, and I was able to purchase the third (*SWRI Jubilee Cookery Book*) on eBay! Then, in the course of my now exclusively online research, I became aware of four others equally worthy of examination. Facsimile editions

[1] Susan J. Leonardi, "Recipes for Reading: Summer Pasta, Lobster à la Riseholme, and Key Lime Pie," *PMLA* 104, no. 3 (1989): 340.

[2] Hannah Robertson, *The Young Ladies School of Arts; Containing a Great Variety of Practical Receipts*, 2nd ed. (Edinburgh: Walter Ruddiman Jr, 1767), Eighteenth Century Collections Online, vi.

[3] Janet Mitchell, "Cookbooks as a Social and Historical Document. A Scottish Case Study," *Food Service Technology* 1, no. 1 (Spring 2001): 13, https://doi.org/10.1046/j.1471-5740.2001.00002.x.

[4] Mrs Dalgairns, *The Practice of Cookery : Adapted to the Business of Every Day Life* (Edinburgh: Cadell & Co., 1829), http://archive.org/details/b21530701.

[5] SWRI Housewives Committee and Sheila Lumsden, *SWRI Jubilee Cookery Book* (Glasgow: McCorquodale & Co., 1967).

of the two earliest Scottish cookery books were available through Amazon.ca (*Mrs McLintock's Receipts for Cookery and Pastry-work*[6] and *Mrs Johnston's Receipts for All Sorts of Pastry...*[7]) and the two others from the 19th century (Christian Isobel Johnstone's *The Cook and Housewife's Manual*[8] and *The Cookery Book of Lady Clark of Tillypronie*[9]) are available online. These seven works well represent the development of published Scottish recipes over three centuries moving from collections of individual recipes by a single author in the 18th century to complete systems of cookery by a single author in the 19th century to compilations of recipes from many individuals in the 20th.

From the earliest cookbooks published in Scotland in the 18th century to ones appearing in the 20th century, the influence first of French cuisine, then (as mobility and international travel increased) the influence of other European and Asian cuisines is apparent. But throughout the centuries, what remains constant is the rootedness of the recipes in the available local ingredients—from oysters to calves and oats to onions. A tour of these seven recipe books spanning three centuries of Scottish cookery shows that their authors had tapped into the spirit of the time and—as seen by the enormous success of all the books—recognized what their audiences wanted.

The 18th Century and the Earliest Scottish Cookbooks

The first Scottish cookery book appeared in the 1730s,[10] though English counterparts had an almost two-hundred-year head start.[11] Written during a tumultuous time when Scotland was suffering the fall-out of the Jacobite rebellions of 1715 and 1719 and rioting across the country over the imposition of the English malt tax on Scotland,[12] *Mrs. McLintock's Receipts for Cookery and Pastry-work* (1736), published in Glasgow, distinguished itself from its English cousins by, as Catherine Brown notes, "a distinctively Scottish stamp in its measurements, language and content."[13] Not only does the work contain a large number of Scots words and

---

[6] Mrs McLintock, *Mrs McLintock's Receipts for Cookery and Pastry-Work*, ed. Iseabail Macleod (Aberdeen: Aberdeen UP, 1986).

[7] Mrs Johnston, *Mrs Johnston's Receipts for All Sorts of Pastry, Creams, Puddings, Custards, Preserves, Marmalets Sauces, Pickles and Cookery, after the Newest and Most Approved Method* (Edinburgh, 1740).

[8] Christian Isobel Johnstone, *The Cook and Housewife's Manual Containing the Most Approved Modern Receipts for Making Soups, Gravies, Sauces, Etc*, 1st ed (Edinburgh, 1826), http://access.bl.uk/item/viewer/ark:/81055/vdc_100027400241.0x000001.

[9] Charlotte Coltman Clark, *The Cookery Book of Lady Clark of Tillypronie*, ed. Catherine Frances Frere (London: Constable, 1909), http://archive.org/details/b21530130.

[10] Catherine Brown, "Scottish Cookery," in *The Edinburgh History of the Book in Scotland*, ed. Warren McDougall and Stephen Brown, vol. 2 (Edinburgh: Edinburgh University Press, 2012), 407.

[11] Glyn Hughes, "Foods of England - Cookbooks," The Foods of England Project, April 10, 2020, http://www.foodsofengland.co.uk/references.htm.

[12] Iseabail Macleod, "Introduction," in *Mrs McLintock's Receipts for Cookery and Pastry-Work* (Aberdeen: Aberdeen University Press, 1986), xx.

[13] Brown, "Scottish Cookery," 407.

spellings,[14] but it also shows the Scottish manner of using "as much of the animal (or fish) as possible—head, tongue, lights, lure (udder)" as well as using local ingredients such as oysters.[15] Interestingly, though, common foods such as oats and "kail"[16] do not appear often in the recipes, suggesting perhaps that some of the more common dishes that cooks would routinely make from memory are not included.[17] Although only one recipe appears with oysters being the "star" of the dish ("CLXXXIV: To frigasie Oysters"), many of the fricassees, soups, and ragouts, call for oysters as well as mussels and cockles. Indeed, one recipe ("To dress a Neats [cattle] Tongue and Lure") calls for two tongues, one lure, and 100 oysters. Far from being expensive delicacies, oysters—like lobsters—were plentifully abundant and not solely the food of the rich.

In terms of organization, McLintock's cookery book contains only loosely ordered individual recipes such as one might find in a manuscript collection rather than a "complete system" of cookery that outlines the manner of preparing a proper meal, sometimes of several courses. For instance, she begins with a series of cake, biscuit, loaf, bread, pie, and pasty recipes (both sweet and savory), followed by a series of cream, syllabub,[18] curd, cheesecake, custard, pudding, and posset,[19] and tart recipes. These constitute the first seventy recipes. The next sixty-two are for preserves, syrups, jellies, and a variety of chips and tablets[20] (all containing liberal amounts of sugar), wines, and pickles. The remaining recipes are primarily meat and seafood dishes (including soups) for beef, pork, rabbit, chicken, lobster, lamb, fowl, and mutton, followed by various sauces. To round out the cookery book, she includes a miscellany of recipes such as "CLXVI: To dress a Calf's Head sweet," "CLXVII: To dress a Calf's Head savoury," "CXXVI (sic): To make a shoulder of Mutton eat like Venison," and "CLXXVIII: To boil Ducks the French Way." Interestingly, they demonstrate a variety of techniques—making a dish two ways, presenting one dish as another, and using the French culinary style to make duck.

Traditional Scottish dishes such as haggis and barley broth do not make an appearance; however, what is apparent in the collection is that approximately half the book is devoted to preserves, clearly indicating that food preservation was a predominant concern for the author. This fact can hardly be surprising since iceboxes did not make an appearance in history until the middle of the next century. Furthermore, unlike several of the other early receipt books, it contains no medicinal recipes; again, suggesting the real focus of the work is to provide its readers with a sizable collection of functional household recipes.

Nothing is really known about the sales and reception of this cookery book, but four years after its appearance another work called *Mrs. Johnston's receipts for all sorts of pastry, creams, puddings, custards, preserves, marmalets sauces, pickles*

[14] Macleod, "Introduction," xxi.

[15] Macleod, xiv.

[16] This is an alternate spelling of kale but can also refer to cabbage.

[17] Macleod, "Introduction," xvi–xvii.

[18] Syllabub is a sweet cream-based drink or dessert with wine or claret in good quantity.

[19] Posset is a hot drink made of milk curdled with wine or claret.

[20] Chips are basically dried candied fruit. Tablets are akin to fudge.

and cookery, after the newest and most approved method was published in Edinburgh, and of the 221 recipes in it, the first 186 are direct transcriptions of McLintock's, presented in the same order. As Catherine Brown notes, we do not know whether "it was copied from Mrs McLintock or written by her under a different name."[21] The additional recipes include some sweet and several savory with most focusing on meat and fish—pork, veal, mutton, beef, Westphalia ham, turbot, lobster, salmon, lamprey, and mackerel. Several of these recipes, as did those in McLintock's collection, deal with various preparations of offal, including sheep's head (1 recipe), calf's head (2 recipes), nolt (ox) head (3 recipes), nolt feet (2 recipes), hog's feet and ears (1 recipe). Also, like McLintock's volume, Johnston's does not include any medicinal recipes, choosing instead to focus on the immediate needs of feeding the family.

A Very Different Later 18th Century Receipt Book

Whereas the earlier receipt books have no medicinal recipes, Hannah Robertson's *The Young Ladies School of Arts; containing a Great Variety of Practical Receipts* (1767) contains many. It was published during a period in Scotland's history known as the Highland Clearances, a period known for its forced eviction of people from the Highlands and Islands to make way for agricultural production. With many people settling in unfamiliar new areas, the necessity for entrepreneurialism and self-sufficiency would have been great, thus a volume containing medicinal remedies and profitable skills would find a ready market. Robertson's book sets itself apart from the previously discussed ones in that it is really more a compendium of instructions for a wide variety of arts than explicitly a cookery book. Robertson clearly knew her audience well, and the book was hugely popular, going through 10 editions by 1806. Her second edition contained several additions, and as she notes in her introduction "As the former was bound under one, for the conveniency of the buyer, I have made this in two parts: the first to contain the nice arts for young Ladies; the second to contain the receipts for Cookery, &c. As many mistresses of families, house-keepers, and others, may have occasion for the Cookery part that have no occasion to purchase that containing the nicer Arts."[22]

Although a granddaughter of Charles II, she did not lead a charmed upper-class life. At many times in her marriage and as a widow raising not only her own children (she outlived all nine) but also some of her grandchildren, she was the primary breadwinner. Most of her jobs had to do with the practice and teaching of the arts of which she wrote—making gum-flowers, filigree, japanning, shell work, gilding, and painting, all skills she learned on her own as a child. As she explains in the preface to the second edition, she arranged descriptions of the different arts in order of difficulty, in the order which children should be taught them. She also deliberately arranged her cookery recipes: first come the ones for "Cosmetics &c.": e.g., "a water to take away Pimples," "Powder for taking off Freckles," "To take off Warts," "To make Teeth white," "To wash Silk Stockings, Gloves, and

[21] Catherine Brown, *Scottish Cookery* (Edinburgh: Mercat Press, 1999), 261.

[22] Robertson, *The Young Ladies School of Arts*, v.

Mitts," "Painting Rooms, Rails, &c.," "White Varnish," and "To bleach Bees-wax." Next are her recipes for jellies, preserves, and creams. Cakes, candying, pickling, and wine-making follow, and she completes the book with what she calls "Various Receipts in Physick, &c." which include a diverse assortment of recipes most of which are medicinal. She provides "An Antidote against the poison of Toads," "Cure for the bite of a Mad Dog," "Cure for Barrenness," "To Cure Deafness," and "For the Gout or Rheumatism" to name a few.

What is notable in this volume, unlike McLintock's and Johnston's is that Robertson's is very much aimed at the upper class as this is the audience she catered to in her shop and teaching; however, she also suggests in her introduction that the work would be valuable to "young women who have no fortunes, or may be left in low circumstances," a situation she knew intimately. "It is too well known how small the value is set on womens work, so that the cleverest at the needle can scarcely earn subsistence; but a knowledge of the curious branches mentioned in this treatise, will greatly make for their advantage."[23] Also, unlike McLintock's and Johnston's volumes, Robertson's does not contain any main course recipes, so if her readers were hoping to feed their families based on the recipes, they would be going hungry. Thus, the *Young Ladies School of Arts* may not be a complete system of cookery—or even a partial one—but it is an extensive catalogue of the decorative arts of the day, right down to the complex art and science of taxidermy[24] ("To preserve Birds with their Plumage unhurt")[25] and a useful assortment of medicinal remedies.

"A complete system of cookery" in the 19th Century

The Cook and Housewife's Manual (1826)

If the previous authors from the 18th century did not attempt to propose a "complete system of cookery," Meg Dods, the pseudonym of Christian Isobel Johnstone, did in *The Cook and Housewife's Manual containing the most approved modern receipts for making soups, gravies, sauces, etc.* (1826). Written during Scotland's Industrial Revolution—as the middle-class expanded, a new skilled working class formed,[26] and the population exploded[27]—this cookery book aims to satisfy the

[23] Robertson, *The Young Ladies School of Arts*, ix.

[24] Beth Fowkes Tobin discusses the exquisite detail that Robertson goes into explaining the harmfulness of the chemicals and how to handle them properly ("Bluestockings and the Culture of Natural History," in *Bluestockings Now!: The Evolution of a Social Role*, ed. Deborah Heller (Farnham, Surrey: Ashgate Publishing, Ltd., 2015), 63), and she argues that Robertson's process of preparing a bird for taxidermy is very similar to "the techniques for stuffing and preserving a bird are not that far removed from those used in cooking and in needlework" ("Women, Decorative Arts, and Taxidermy," in *Women and the Material Culture of Death* (Routledge, 2016), 318–19.)

[25] Robertson, *The Young Ladies School of Arts*, 35.

[26] Michael Lynch, *Scotland: A New History* (Random House, 2011), 394.

[27] "Scotland - The Industrial Revolution," Encyclopedia Britannica, accessed May 25, 2020, https://www.britannica.com/place/Scotland.

urban home cooks who are eager to prepare fine meals for their families while at the same time taking advantage of the famed Scottish literacy rates[28] to interweave some playful sections of fiction.

Pam Perkins has called the book "something of a Scottish literary in-joke as well as a practical book on cookery, but more than that, it offers readers today a quirky example of the early nineteenth-century literary marketplace at work."[29] The in-joke comes from the fact that Johnstone took her pseudonym, Meg Dods, from the inn hostess in Sir Walter Scott's *St. Ronan's Well* (1824); one of her characters, Peregrine Touchwood, from that same book; and another of her characters, Dr. Redgill, from *Marriage* (1818) by Susan Ferris. And in so doing, as Andrew Monnickendam argues, she "makes a valuable contribution to Scottish literature and culture through her investigation into the importance of food in our sense of identity."[30] Johnstone was already quite a name in Scottish literary circles as the publisher of novels, and she went on to become the first female editor of a major Victorian periodical when she assumed the helm as working editor of *Tait's Magazine* in 1834. It was under her leadership the magazine changed its focus to literature.[31] *The Cook and Housewife's Manual* published in 1826, however, was her first and only attempt at a domestic manual. A spirited blend of fiction (see the Part 1 section, "History of the Institution of St Ronan's Culinary Club") and serious discourse on the processes of cookery, this work was called almost a century after it was written "one of the soundest and most trustworthy of cookery books, and combines technical usefulness with a quaint narrative and many apposite quotations, evidence of wide reading and research."[32]

While the first edition page count came in at 366, the subsequent editions all revised and enlarged the work. The third edition included more than 200 additional recipes, (bringing the total number of recipes to around 1200), and by then she had greatly reorganized her presentation not only of national Scottish dishes but her collection of recipes from other national cultures. The first edition included in the general Part I a section devoted to "Scottish National Dishes" and another to "Miscellaneous National Dishes," but the latter did not specify (except in two cases) the countries of origin. By the third edition, she had moved these sections to Part III, which laid out in much more detail "Made-dishes,"[33] "French Cookery,"

[28] R. K. Webb, "Literacy among the Working Classes in Nineteenth Century Scotland," *The Scottish Historical Review* 33, no. 116 (1954): 100.

[29] "A Taste for Scottish Fiction: Christian Johnstone's Cook and Housewife's Manual," *European Romantic Review* 11, no. 2 (March 1, 2000): 248, https://doi.org/10.1080/10509580008570114.

[30] Andrew Monnickendam, "Eating Your Words: Plate and Nation in Meg Dods's the Cook and Housewife's Manual (1826)," *Scottish Studies Review* 6, no. 1 (May 2005): 34.

[31] Susan Brown, Patricia Clements, and Isobel Grundy, eds., "Christian Isobel Johnstone Entry: Writing Screen," in *Orlando: Women's Writing in the British Isles from the Beginnings to the Present* (Cambridge: Cambridge University Press Online, 2006).

[32] Frank Schloesser, "Meg Dods and 'The Cook and Housewife's Manual.'" *Notes and Queries* s11-III, no. 64 (March 18, 1911): 210, https://doi.org/10.1093/nq/s11-III.64.209j.

[33] "Made-dishes" typically require some combination of cooking techniques (e.g., boiling, frying, roasting) as well as several different ingredients. For instance, stews, ragouts, fric-

"Dishes of Fish," "National Dishes—Scottish, Irish, Welsh, German, Spanish, and Oriental," as well as two more sections on pastries, pies, pancakes, etc. and on creams, jellies, trifles, custards and others. Both the Scottish dishes and the other national dishes sections almost doubled in size, and Johnstone clearly took reviews of her first edition to heart by including in the recipes an indication of their country of origin. By the eighth edition the Scottish and other national dishes sections expanded even further (31 Scottish recipes, including two more preparations of haggis and 25 other national recipes).

In the preface to the first edition, Johnstone refers (as Hannah Robertson did) to the tried, tested, and true nature of her recipes:

> Many of them are original, the result of observation in various quarters; and, with few exceptions, they have all stood the test of experiment among skilful cooks and intelligent mistresses of families, and been approved for the judicious combination of what is elegant and what is healthful, economical, and agreeable to the palate.[34]

And as she continued to revise and enlarge her manual, she included additional instructions and whole new sections as asked for presumably by readers. For instance, by the third edition, she included an "Explanation of Culinary Terms" and her "Directions for Carving" now contained illustrations that show the various cuts. By the eighth edition she had added a new appendix on domestic brewing as well as chapters on "Preparations for the Sick and the Convalescents, Of Coffee, Chocolate, &c., best mode of making, Preparations for the Dressing-room, Cheap Dishes, and Cookery for the Poor" and "Miscellaneous Receipts for Cleaning and Preserving Furniture, Clothes, &c."

Despite *The Cook and Housewife's Manual* being so thoroughly infused with Scottish literary culture and cuisine, Monnickendam proposes that "Johnstone is not fenced in by patriotic concerns, as many eighteenth-century cookbooks were, but bases her recipe for success on economy."[35] This is apparent in two ways: Johnstone, like Robertson, without question had "higher society" in mind as her readers; however, she (also like Robertson) did not want to put her work out of the realm of usefulness to those of less means. As Johnstone said in the Preface to her first edition: "as a general principle, the total omission of all costly ingredients is recommended to the young housekeeper, as more commendable than the adoption of the paltry substitutes resorted to by spurious economy united with the desire to be genteel."[36] And secondly, despite—or perhaps because of—Johnstone's considerable attention to French influences on Scottish cookery, she exhibited the same attention to using all parts of the animals and fish that McLintock and Johnston did by including recipes making use of tongue, tripe, heads, feet, hearts, lungs, sweetbreads, brains, etc. That sense of economy also appears in Johnstone's

assees, and curries are "made-dishes."

[34] Johnstone, *The Cook and Housewife's Manual*, 8.

[35] "Eating Your Words," 34.

[36] Johnstone, *The Cook and Housewife's Manual*, 9.

section on "Miscellaneous Recipes for the Sick and Convalescent, and Cheap Dishes." While Robertson had many medicinal recipes for specific illnesses, Johnstone's are primarily preparations of meals and broths for non-specified illnesses, and she also presented, like Robertson, preparations of cosmetics and recipes for cleaning a wide variety of products from furniture to dresses to japanned goods, helping make housewives very self-sufficient in most aspects of household management.

Johnstone's cookery book provides, through its introductions to chapters, plenty of rich detail about the social milieu and practices around meal preparation. For instance, the chapter on vegetables references the profound improvements in agriculture and market access to produce by noting

> Much, however, has been judiciously done, of late years, both to, improve the quality, and to spread the cultivation of vegetables.... The vegetable markets of most towns have within the same period undergone a wonderful improvement. The number and quantity of articles are more than doubled, and the price, except for early vegetables, has diminished at least half, so that this healthful and harmless luxury is now within the reach of all classes.[37]

Similarly, in her introduction to soups, she observes they have been called "the vestibule to a banquet" and the "only true foundation to the principal repast of the day"[38] and, furthermore, that it is widely acknowledged that the French make the best soup with Scots ranking second. She additionally stipulates that "*beef* is the only foundation of a good *soup*" (her emphasis).[39] These details give 21st century readers a glimpse into early 19th century foodways and suggest a development in cookery books from a composition of individual recipes to an expansive approach to multi-dish meal preparation.

The Practice of Cookery (1829)

A mere three years after the publication of Christian Isobel Johnstone's *The Cook and Housewife's Manual*, Mrs. Dalgairns' *The Practice of Cookery: Adapted to the Business of Every Day Life* appeared. Also printed in Edinburgh and with stiff competition from Johnstone, Mrs. Dalgairns[40] nonetheless was tremendously successful with her own cookery book. (Interestingly, her book was published by Cadell and Company, Sir Walter Scott's publisher.) Both works are remarkably alike in terms of content: they each profess to present "a Complete System of Practical Cookery"[41]; they each include a large number of specifically Scottish dishes but

[37] Johnstone, *The Cook and Housewife's Manual*, 141–42.

[38] Johnstone, *The Cook and Housewife's Manual*, 64.

[39] Johnstone, *The Cook and Housewife's Manual*, 64.

[40] Although Mrs. Catherine Emily Dalgairns published her book in Scotland and, indeed, lived there at the time, she was originally from Prince Edward Island, Canada, and had married into the Scottish gentry. See Mary Williamson, "The Publication of 'Mrs. Dalgairns' Cookery': A Fortuitous Nineteenth-Century Success Story,'" *Papers of the Bibliographical Society of Canada* 45, no. 1 (2007): 45.

[41] Dalgairns, *The Practice of Cookery*, iii.

also branch out to include international cuisine; both provide a miscellany of recipes for cleaning walls, making ink, washing lace, etc.; and both contain no medicinal recipes. According to Mary Williamson, that was not a decision that Mrs. Dalgairns made. It was that of her mentor Captain Basil Hall, who had introduced her to her publisher. Williamson states:

> Unexplained delays held back the cookbook until March 1829. By that time Captain Hall had made sure that the chapter on Medicine was excised. He recognized that cookery books often ended with such a chapter, but he was convinced it was out of place, even though he suspected the author had a "hankering" after it. "Some other cookery books have it," he wrote to Cadell, "but really I don't think that a sufficient reason for keeping it in - however well done. Surely nothing can be worse than encouraging people to do without medical advice in such a country as this."[42]

As Williamson goes on to explain, the removal of the section on medicine is indicative of the intended audience: the upper classes which had access to medical advice.

Williamson, through extensive research, learned that, although no mention is made in the work itself, the Preface was not written by Mrs. Dalgairns but by her mentor, Captain Basil Hall,[43] and in it he states:

> A perfectly original book of Cookery would neither meet with, nor deserve, much attention ; because what is wanted in this matter, is not receipts for new dishes, but clear instructions how to make those already established in public favour.... Every receipt, therefore, has either been actually tried by the author, or by persons whose accuracy in the various manipulations could be safely relied upon.[44]

A busy time it must have been trying all 1434 recipes included in the volume! The cookery book takes the reader through chapters on soups, fish, beef, mutton, lamb, veal, pork, poultry, curries, game, gravies and sauces, vegetables, puddings and pies and tarts, creams and custards, cakes, preserves, vinegar and pickles, and domestic wines. Most of these chapters begin with "Preparatory Remarks" which provide some general directions to preclude the need to repeat in each recipe or with information about how to recognize freshness and high-quality ingredients, as well as the various cuts of meat and their best uses. The final chapters are devoted to the miscellany, poultry yard, dairy, brewing, kitchen garden, bees, and pigs. The Appendix contains direction on how to break the total annual income into categories to properly finance the household; a note on when the meat, fish, and

---

[42] Williamson, "The Publication of 'Mrs. Dalgairns' Cookery,'" 53.

[43] Williamson, "The Publication of 'Mrs. Dalgairns' Cookery,'" 54.

[44] Dalgairns, *The Practice of Cookery*, v.

vegetables are in season; and an equivalency of measures for those not familiar with Scots measures which had only been standardized in 1824 through an Act of Parliament.[45]

The major difference in Johnstone's and Dalgairns' works shows in their organization. The former is organized around putting together complete courses of dishes for a meal, on processes (boiling, roasting, etc.), and then individual recipes; the latter takes a different approach by organizing around the food type and presenting at the end of the work tips useful to those raising their own bees and animals and farming their own land, something which would not have been out the realm of possibility given the increased emphasis on developments in farming since the founding of the Society of Improvers in the Knowledge of Agriculture in Scotland in 1723. The society included among its numbers many members of the nobility and led the way by the 1820s, as T. C. Smout argues, to a wider rural middle-class involvement.[46]

20th Century Community Cookbooks

Lady Clark of Tillypronie

The Cookery Book of Lady Clark of Tillypronie was compiled and edited by Catherine Frere (1909) at the request of Lady Clark's husband. His late wife had gathered recipes throughout her life as she travelled with her own family and then with her husband (a diplomat) throughout Europe, in particular to France and Italy; however, the collection also includes recipes from "Switzerland, Denmark, Russia, Spain, Germany, Portugal, Holland, Austria, as well as England, Scotland, Wales, and Ireland, with some Turkish and Indian dishes thrown in, which give an Oriental flavour."[47] Drawn from about 3000 manuscript pages,[48] the cookery book reads like a community cookbook in that it is filled with recipes from others noted by name and sometimes by location and date: for example, "Barm—Australian. (Mrs. Penrose Rogers, Falmouth. 1881.)," "'Haggis.' (Lady Login.)" and "Birch Wine. (Mrs. Farquharson. July, 1855.)." Many recipes come from Sir John and Lady Clark's servants over the years, but some are "names well known in the social and historical life of England and of Europe in the nineteenth century."[49] Frere's Preface actually goes into detail about several of the individuals and the recipes they contributed.

Frere had difficult decisions to make about how to organize the collection. As she explains in the Preface:

> Lady Clark had evidently no idea of publication in collecting recipes—they were therefore not arranged for printing—nor did she set herself to compile

[45] Macleod, "Introduction," xxx.

[46] "A New Look at the Scottish Improvers," *Scottish Historical Review* 91, no. 1 (April 2012): 134, https://doi.org/10.3366/shr.2012.0074.

[47] Clark, *The Cookery Book of Lady Clark of Tillypronie*, xiv.

[48] Clark, *The Cookery Book of Lady Clark of Tillypronie*, ix.

[49] Clark, *The Cookery Book of Lady Clark of Tillypronie*, xi.

> an exhaustive book on cookery. It is essentially her own collection, for home use, of such dishes as struck her as worthy of record, useful, or specially good and uncommon ; the manuscript interspersed with amusing individual comments, some of which are left where they occurred, in the text.[50]

So why did Sir John Clark ask Catherine Frere to prepare the collection? First, he was aware of her previous work assisting another author, Hilda Duckitt, with her culinary manuscripts, and secondly, because Frere and his wife were well known to each other. Further, he stated, it was "at the earnest request of several friends who know their value, to give these records of my wife's labour of love to the public."[51]

The book is arranged by food type, and each chapter organized alphabetically by recipe title. The first chapter is "Baking Powder, Barm and Yeast," and the collection continues with the usual suspects of beverages, breads, cakes, cheese, confectionaries, curries, eggs, fish, meats, jellies, preserves, and so on. Two chapters of note are "Domestic Recipes" and "Invalid Cookery." The former is a hodge-podge of instructions about how to clarify butter, clean metal, make an Indian chutney, clean cooking pots, kill flies, fatten fowls, make mushroom catsup, make pot pourri, bottle tomato sauce, and clean white paint, etc. Why some of the food recipes are not included in other sections is something of a mystery, but the household tips fall into the same genre as we saw in Robertson's, Johnstone's, and Dalgairns'. Likewise, the section on "Invalid Cookery" has some similar traits to Johnstone's in that several recipes do not specify what illness or disease they are supposed to treat; however, there are a few entries that do, for instance, "Colds. *See* Gruel. *See also* Sloe Jam, under Jams and Jellies" or "Sleeplessness. *See* Hop Tea." And, as with all but Robertson's cookery books, Lady Clark's contains a healthy number of recipes for all parts of the animal, a particularly Scottish and French fashion. Again, there are recipes for brains, heads, heart, lungs, etc. Indeed, the chapter on pork begins with a section titled "How to Use a Whole Pig. (Mrs. Thomas.)"

One interesting addition to the book, inserted by Frere herself, provides a window to late 19th and early 20th century Scotland with respect to treatment of animals. In both England and Scotland, attention to animal cruelty and the unsanitary conditions of slaughterhouses and meat markets was on the rise with societies such as the Scottish Society of the Prevention of Cruelty to Animals founded in 1839 and the Humanitarian League in London in 1891 taking up the causes. Frere wrote in an appendix a discourse on animal cruelty arguing that "animals and birds necessary for food should be spared all possible suffering ; to help towards this result I subjoin a few notes by authorities on the subject."[52] She then provides instructions by the Royal Society for the Prevention of Cruelty to Animals for the humane slaughter of crabs, lobsters, rabbits, and birds. With regard to calves, cattle, and sheep she refers readers to a report by the Admiralty Committee to "Consider the Humane Slaughtering of Animals, 1904." Such information was clearly

50 Clark, *The Cookery Book of Lady Clark of Tillypronie*, xvi.

51 Clark, *The Cookery Book of Lady Clark of Tillypronie*, viii.

52 Clark, *The Cookery Book of Lady Clark of Tillypronie*, 545.

dear to her heart since she explains that she has used it before in a previous work, *Hilda's Diary of a Cape Housekeeper* (London: Chapman and Hall, 1902), though her hand in that publication is not credited.

The cookery book contains many variations of individual recipes. There are, for example, five recipes for pressed beef, six for orange marmalade, ten for mushrooms, eleven for cutlets and for carrots. As Catherine Brown argues, "the strong hidden implication [is] that if you give fifty different chefs the same recipe, they will all produce a different dish."[53] For this very reason, Lady Clark's cookery book presents a compelling study in the personality of food. Certainly, the question may come up why one would publish a cookery book for recipes everyone knows how to make. One answer provided here is that recipes speak to their creators' attitude to food and to the availability of certain ingredients. Another is that cookery books can expand their audience's repertoire and show home cooks that dishes from other countries are within reach in Scotland.

Scottish Women's Rural Institutes

If *The Cookery Book of Lady Clark of Tillypronie* reads like a community cookbook, the *SWRI Jubilee Cookery Book* (1967) most certainly is of that genre. This Golden Anniversary edition is an update of the first cookbook the Scottish Women's Rural Institutes published in 1925. Sheila Lumsden, preface author of the 1967 edition, looks back at the book's origin observing that the recipes are all provided by SWRI members and that "An S.W.R.I. Cookery Book should certainly have our old Scots recipes in it," but "the inclusion of the old does not mean the exclusion of the new."[54] She notes that the first edition included "name and Institute of the member supplying the recipe"[55] and sold out its 10,000 copies in three years. By 1934, a further 22,000 copies of subsequent editions sold out. As Lumsden explains, "No two editions of this book are the same, as to every edition new recipes were added and alterations made as necessary."[56] With regard to the current volume she says,

> Now once again in 1967 the Housewives Committee have added new sections: one at the request of many younger members on joints of meat, and another, for which they are indebted to Miss Jean Butchart, Mrs. Mitchell and Mr. Wilson, on deep freezing, with the hope of keeping the S.W.R.I. Cookery Book, as always forward looking.[57]

Unfortunately, over the course of 50 years, one feature that was lost was the name and Institute of each contributor, making this version of the work seem less like a community cookbook and more like one by an individual author.

---

[53] Brown, *Scottish Cookery*, 264.

[54] SWRI Housewives Committee and Lumsden, *SWRI Jubilee Cookery Book*, v.

[55] SWRI Housewives Committee and Lumsden, *SWRI Jubilee Cookery Book*, v.

[56] SWRI Housewives Committee and Lumsden, *SWRI Jubilee Cookery Book*, vi.

[57] SWRI Housewives Committee and Lumsden, *SWRI Jubilee Cookery Book*, vi.

Before the recipes, the SWRI presents a page of its mottoes and some rhyming quotations (including the Selkirk Grace) that demonstrate the generosity, spirit, and economy of Scottish women. The general notes on meal-planning "the four-group way" (the body-building foods, energy foods, and two groups of protective foods) and on methods of cooking clearly reveal the mid-20th century Scottish approach to diet and food choices. After that follow sections illustrating the joints of meat, information on keeping food fresh, standard measurements, and "catering for numbers." The subsequent arrangement of recipes is by now quite standard with sections on soup, fish, meat, made-up dishes (i.e., "made-dishes"), vegetables and sides, puddings, pastries, baking, cheese, Scottish national dishes, egg, sandwiches, fruit bottling, chutneys and sauces, beverages, sweets, and deep freezing.

Each chapter typically contains an introduction that provides a quotation or motto and general tips. For instance, the introduction of the section on "Traditional Dishes" starts off with a nod to Scottish nationalism: "The destiny of nations depends on their diet."[58] The section contains many recipes we have seen before: haggis, sheep's head pie, cock-a-leekie, and others. Overall, the cookery book includes (as do all others except Robertson's) recipes using many animal parts—including sweetbreads, sheep's head, tripe, and tongue—however, these are less in evidence than in earlier centuries, perhaps indicative of changing tastes and availability of products as Sarah Skerratt shows in her study of food availability and choice in mid-1990s rural Scotland.[59]

Community cookbooks are quickly becoming a popular area of study with scholars looking to them for examples of how women navigate between the public and private spheres and define their national identity,[60] what rural community cookbooks from the late 19th through mid-20th century tell us about changing foodways,[61] how they construct their own stories about community,[62] what the publishing history of community cookbooks tells about the work's relationship to kitchen practice and local significance,[63] and how they can assist genealogists in

[58] SWRI Housewives Committee and Lumsden, *SWRI Jubilee Cookery Book*, 131.

[59] "Food Availability and Choice in Rural Scotland: The Impact of 'Place,'" *British Food Journal* 101, no. 7 (January 1, 1999): 543–44, https://doi.org/10.1108/00070709910279009.

[60] Jill Nussel, "Heating Up the Sources: Using Community Cookbooks in Historical Inquiry," *History Compass* 4, no. 5 (2006): 956–61, https://doi.org/10.1111/j.1478-0542.2006.00342.x.

[61] Elizabeth Ransom and Wynne Wright, "Constructing Culinary Knowledge," *Food, Culture & Society* 16, no. 4 (December 1, 2013): 669–89, https://doi.org/10.2752/17517441 3X13758634981895.

[62] Anne L. Bower, "Our Sisters' Recipes: Exploring 'Community' in a Community Cookbook," *The Journal of Popular Culture* 31, no. 3 (1997): 137–51, https://doi.org/10.1111/j.0022-3840.1997.3103_137.x; Anne Bower, "Cooking Up Stories: Narrative Elements in Community Cookbooks," in *Recipes for Reading : Community Cookbooks, Stories, Histories* (Amherst, Mass: University of Massachusetts Press., 1997), 29–50; Lisa Mastrangelo, "Community Cookbooks: Sponsors of Literacy and Community Identity," *Community Literacy Journal* 10, no. 1 (December 30, 2015): 73–86, https://doi.org/10.1353/clj.2015.0021.

[63] Elizabeth Driver, "Cookbooks as Primary Sources for Writing History: A Bibliographer's View," *Food, Culture & Society* 12, no. 3 (September 2009): 257-.

reconstructing not just family histories but "long-lost family recipes."[64] Although the *SWRI Jubilee Cookery Book* may be valuable in studies of food availability in the rural areas of Scotland or of kitchen practices or of favourite local recipes, the removal of the personalization of individual recipes renders the cookery book more akin to a commercial one. We don't, in this edition, see the character of the recipes coming from the thirty-three branches whose crests are all printed on the inside front cover. We don't learn anything about the women who contributed. We do know that the various editions of the *SWRI Cookery Book* show, like the many editions of the other writers mentioned here, a sensitivity to the reception of the work and the demands of readers. However, it would be productive to do a study of the evolution of all the various editions from 1925 through 1967 to understand more about the decision-making that removed much of the personality that usually shines through in community cookbooks.

General Observations

The French influence on British and Scottish cookery is well-known, dating back to the Middle Ages with the forging of the "auld alliance" and picking up its pace after the French Revolution.[65] We can see some of the influences in Mrs. McLintock's and Mrs. Johnson's recipes. For instance, the "To dress Scots Collops" recipe calls for thin slices of veal, where "collops" comes from the French "escalope" meaning thin slices of meat usually veal. The "To make a Ragou of Veal or Lamb" comes from the French "ragoûter" and the etymology of "frigacy" is also of French origin, the compounding of "frire" (to fry) and "casser" (to break). By the 1820s Johnstone and Mrs. Dalgairns included many dishes with "à la" in their titles, and such influences continue into the 20th century.

Spices (cinnamon, black pepper, caraway, nutmeg, ginger, and cloves) had been available in Europe since the Middle Ages, but as international trade increased in the 18th and 19th centuries, obtaining these spices became much easier for the average home cook, so their use became more fully integrated into Scottish cookery. Improved travel mobility prompted more of an interest in international cuisines as is evident particularly in Johnstone's, Mrs. Dalgairns' and Lady Clark's cookery books.

The seven works discussed in this article represent three centuries of the evolution of Scottish cookery. Although most are single-authored works published in and probably came from urban rather than rural authors, most reveal their authors' desire to appeal not only to the upper-class household but also to the less well-off. No recipes track through all the cookery books—largely because Robertson's recipes contain no meal recipes—however, there are a small number of recipes which appear in most: seed cake, Scotch Shortbread and dressed, stewed or boiled tongue appear in six, and cock-a-leekie soup and haggis crop up in four (Mrs. Dalgairns, Johnstone, Lady Clark, and SWRI), and mulligatawny soup ap-

[64] Alison P. Kelly, "Choice Receipts from American Housekeepers: A Collection of Digitized Community Cookbooks from the Library of Congress," *The Public Historian* 34, no. 2 (2012): 31, https://doi.org/10.1525/tph.2012.34.2.30.

[65] Brown, "Scottish Cookery," 408.

pears in three (Johnstone, Lady Clark, and SWRI). Despite this lack of uniformity of overlapping recipes, some conclusions, I believe, can be drawn. As Catherine Brown notes of McLintock's and Johnston's collections from the 18th century, the authors had "clearly been influenced by the need for preservation of food since more than half the book is taken up with recipes for pickling, potting, preserving, and making wines."[66] Although preserves, pickles, and wine recipes do continue to appear throughout, they take less prominence as we move into the 20th century. Indeed, the *SWRI Jubilee Cookery Book* takes the progress of food storage to the next level with its whole section on deep freezing. McLintock's and Johnston's cookery books focused on meals and preserving foods. The others presented to varying degrees tips for household management, medicinal recipes, and more complete "systems" of cookery, excepting Robertson's which incorporated extensive instructions on the decorative arts. What the diversity of approaches to the presentation of these cookery books provides readers is a window into their authors' contemporary society, its needs, interests, and health concerns.

[66] Brown, *Scottish Cookery*, 261.

—6—

Mustard Plaster

Catharine Wilson
Recipe of Jean Wilson
Kemptville, Ontario, Canada, 20th Century

Old cookbooks often include recipes for home remedies for complaints such as piles, asthma, coughs, and constipation. This recipe is for loosening up a tight chest when you have a cold. I know first-hand that it works. It has been in our recipe box in Ontario, Canada, for years; I've used it on my children, my mother used it on me, and her mother used it on her. In fact, mustard plasters go back to ancient times. They were already popular in ancient Egypt and in Babylonian medicine around 3000 BCE, and Hippocrates, the father of medicine, advocated their use around 300 BCE.

A mustard plaster or poultice is made of a mixture of mustard seed powder and water. The mixture is applied to a cloth and placed on the body to warm sore muscles that come with pulmonary illness and rheumatism. The heat from the mustard penetrates the body and increases blood circulation to the pained area, helping to break up congestion and/or relieve soreness. It works in a similar way to heat treatments such as VapoRub.

Versions of mustard plasters were sold in pharmacies in the nineteenth century, but they fell from favor in the twentieth century. Today people think it is the latest thing to acquire medicines through the skin via medicated adhesive patches, but people in rural and isolated areas who still practice home remedies have relied on transdermal remedies such as mustard plasters for a long time. My Mother gave me this recipe when I left home in the 1980s.

Mustard Plaster

Mix together: 1 part [about 1 tablespoon] mustard powder and 6 parts flour for an adult. (For a child: 1 part [about ½ tablespoon] mustard powder and 8 parts flour; for an infant: 1 part mustard powder and 12 parts flour).

Combine with water until the mixture spreads easily but water will not soak into cloth. The consistency you're aiming for is like peanut butter or tahini.

Cut a piece of cotton or flannel that when folded will cover the area of the chest. My mother comically added (this varies!).

Use the mustard mixture to butter one half of the fabric, pressing it out almost to the edges. This layer should be about ¼ to ½ thick.

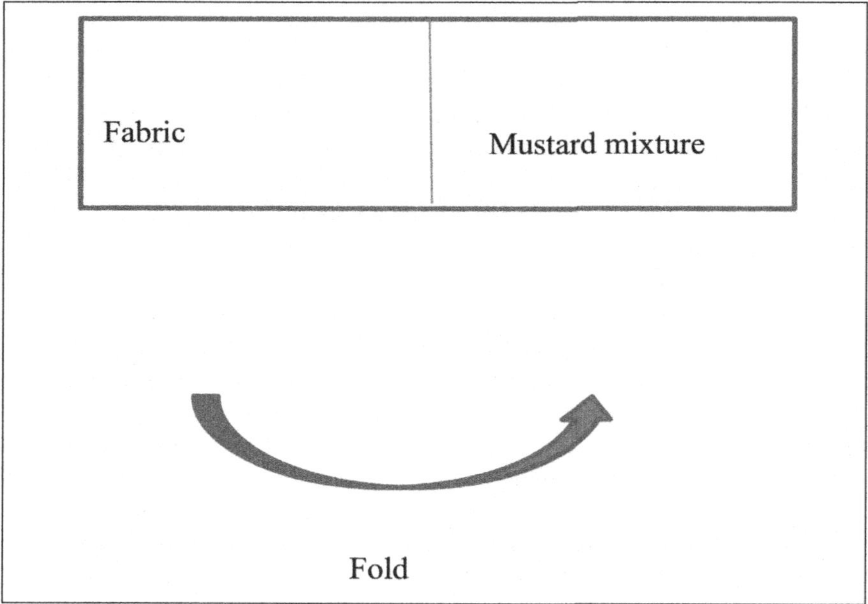

Figure 6.1: Mustard Plaster

Fold the unbuttered half of the fabric over the half that is spread with mustard and tuck in the edges, so the mustard won't ooze out.

Place on the chest. Cover with a towel and place heat on top, either a hot water bottle or heating pad.

Check the chest skin every two minutes and remove the plaster when skin begins to turn pink, or after ten to twenty minutes, whichever comes first.
Gently wash the chest with soap and water. Rub with oil or cream and keep warm.

Do not go outside for a few hours as you will chill very easily. Instead, snuggle up and relax.

—7—

Curry Powder

Catharine Wilson

Recipe of Hannah Peters Jarvis

Queenston, Ontario, Canada, 1840s

I find there is something deliciously sensual, exotic, and deeply satisfying (yes, I'm talking about food) when making my own curry powder. As the spices toast, their pungent aroma fills the kitchen and soon calls are emanating from other parts of the house "What smells SO good?" The product is far superior to the standardized, purchased, spice blend and adds a unique, personalized flavor to recipes. Making my own spice blend fits nicely into the Slow Food Movement that has emerged since the 1980s with its emphasis on preserving traditional cuisine, taste education, doing things from scratch, and gastronomic pleasure.

This recipe comes from the household compendium of Hannah Peters Jarvis (1763-1845). Hannah's original diaries and recipes are in the Archival and Special Collections, University of Guelph, which is well known for its Culinary Collection. Her transcribed diaries written during her declining years in the 1840s can be read at the Rural Diary Archive website (https://ruraldiaries.lib.uoguelph.ca/home). Hannah emigrated from England in 1792 to Toronto with her husband, a loyalist exile. There she mingled with the elite and had servants and slaves, but by the 1840s, she was reduced to poverty. She was caring for her daughter and nine penniless grandchildren who resided in their home called Willowbank in the rural village of Queenston. In this decaying mansion home, she scrubbed, mended, and cooked. Her recipes reflect her DIY attitude and her desire to keep up appearances: recipes such as soft soap, shoe blacking, biscuit, salve, durable ink, pickled and potted beef, currant wine, furniture varnish, black dye for silks, and eau de cologne.[1] I think of Hannah every time I flavor a dish with her Curry Powder.

[1] Elizabeth Oliver-Malone, compiler, *Recipes & Remedies in Upper Canada by Hannah Peters Jarvis* (Queenston, Ontario: Elizabeth Oliver-Malone, 2015).

Curry Powder

9 oz coriander	5 d (Pence. Halifax Currency was in use at the time.)
9 oz Turmerick	3 d
1 oz each black pepper,	6 d
Mustards and Ginger	8 d
½ oz each Alspice and	
Cardamums	6 d (Cardamom)
¼ oz Cumin seed	

Thoroughly pounded and mixed together—to be kept close stopped in a bottle

I like to toast the spices for a few minutes in a cast iron pan, and then grind them. The mix keeps well for several weeks in a glass bottle.

Figure 7.1: Spice in pan. Photo by C. Wilson. Photo courtsey of C. Wilson.

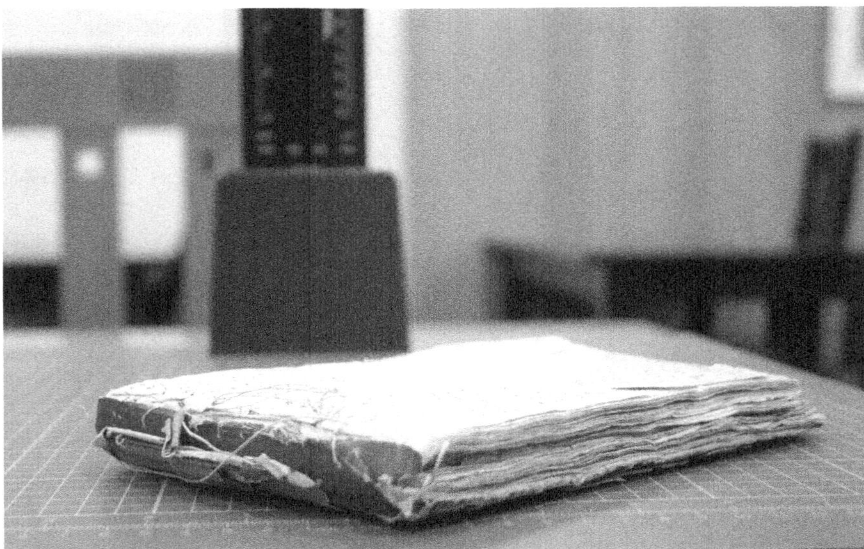

Figure 7.2: Diary of Hannah Peters Jarvis, Archival and Special Collections, University of Guelph. Photo courtesy of Jacqui McIsaac. Diary is in the public domain.

—8—

Cookbooks: Exploring Economic(s) Themes

Erna van Duren

During a telephone conversation with my 84-year-old mother amidst the ongoing COVID-19 crisis, she recounted how my father had given her C.J. Wanneé's *Kookboek van de Amsterdamche Huishoudschool Samengesteld* (the official cookbook of the Dutch Household School)[1] on Mother's Day 1960. Lovingly inscribed with a handwritten message from my dad, she thought the book in safe hands when she loaned the book to a friend, who apparently had never owned a cookbook. When the book was finally returned it wasn't my mother's treasured copy since the borrower had spilled coffee on the book, destroyed the personalized message from my father, damaged the book, and felt a clean, new copy was the best way to make amends. C.J. Wanneé's book was the only cookbook that my mother took with her when our family moved from the Netherlands to Canada in the summer of 1969, and for much of my childhood I remember learning how to make family favorites from this book.

During the 1970s, my mother, who was always an avid cook and keenly interested in food, accumulated recipes from magazines, newspapers, recipe cards, and handwritten notes from friends, some of whom were also of Dutch origins and many of whom were members of the United Church Women. My father's workplace injuries and frequent layoffs from construction work during the economically turbulent 1970s required my mother to work part-time. So as the eldest daughter, I learned to cook. During this time our family's food fare expanded in variety due to living and making friendships within a vibrant community with German and Mennonite roots, which also housed two rapidly growing universities that attracted students and faculty from all over the world. However, these experiences meant that a focus on economizing, nutrition, and avoiding food waste had been imprinted, deeply, within me. After earning a B.A. in Applied Economics and Political Science, I won a scholarship to study Agricultural Economics and earned an M.Sc. and PhD at the University of Guelph, where I continue to work to this day.

My research interests in international business, food policy, and value chains and experiences in teaching economics, business, and food courses have affected how I interpret and use a cookbook. In this essay I attempt to make some of my experience explicit. Cookbooks can be understood through many perspectives.

---

[1] C. J. Wannee, *Kookboek van de Amsterdamsche Huishoudschool Samengesteld* (Amsterdam: H.J.W. Becht, 1959).

Those oriented to understanding economics cannot be neatly separated from cultural, historical, gender, technological, and other perspectives.[2] This essay explores economic themes in cookbooks using three perspectives and their interplay.

The first is a *cookbook-perspective* that focuses on the cost of preparing a dish using a given recipe within a cookbook. While this perspective seems simple, it is far from straightforward since the cost of producing a recipe is influenced by far more than the prices of ingredients, which by themselves can vary considerably due to differences in unit or packaging size, retailing format as well as when and where they are purchased. From an economic perspective, we must also consider available cooking skills, access to equipment and time requirements, all of which can result in significant variations in the cost of a dish. Applying a cookbook-perspective requires examining the whole cookbook since information on how to organize and stock a kitchen, buy ingredients and equipment, and cooking techniques is more often discussed in the preface, introduction, special sections, or specific chapters of cookbook, and not the recipes themselves.

The second approach this essay utilizes is a *household-perspective*, which involves applying economic theory to understand how households relate to cookbook use as well as their development. Household production theory was developed over fifty years ago[3] and has been widely applied in analyzing food policy issues such as the Supplemental Nutrition Assistance Program, also known as SNAP or by its old name "Food Stamps,"[4] as well as understanding household level food demand using economic data modelling.[5] Household production theory can be simplified by focusing on key drivers of households' concerns and behaviors. Many cookbooks offer a great deal of insight into household production and management, both practical and aspirational.

The third is a *food-context-perspective,* which encompasses economic, social, cultural, physical, political, and technological factors as well as their institutions, relationships, and dynamics. All these jointly determine the food context in which people make production, purchasing and consumption decisions about food. As well, all of us have food philosophies, either explicit or perhaps hidden and unchallenged, about how to interact with food. These are reflected in concerns about sustainability, food waste, and treatment of animals, but also our choices and behaviors relating to how we buy, prepare, and consume foods. Some of us support

---

[2] Jeffrey M. Pilcher, "Cultural Histories of Food," in *Oxford Handbook of Food History*, ed. Jeffrey M. Pilcher (Oxford University Press, 2012).

[3] Gary S. Becker, "A Theory of the Allocation of Time," *The Economic Journal* 75, no. 299 (1965), https://doi.org/10.2307/2228949, 10.2307/2228949.

[4] Julie Caswell, "Individual, Household, and Environmental Factors Affecting Food Choices and Access," in *Supplemental Nutrition Assistance Program: Examining the Evidence to Define Benefit Adequacy*, ed. Yaktine AL Caswell JA (Washington, DC: National Academies Press (US), 2013).

[5] Wallace E. Huffman, "Household Production Theory and Models," in *Oxford Handbook of the Economics of Food Consumption and Policy* (Oxford University Press, 2012).

local value chains and niche products while others prefer the products and service of the modern food system. Cookbooks reflect aspirational and practical aspects of food context.[6]

Cookbooks and Primary Research Approach

Several universities have excellent culinary collections that include contemporary publications along with rare and archival materials. These collections provide plentiful and diverse primary source materials for the exploration of economic themes in cookbooks. However, many readers will not have access to such a collection, and alas I did not have access to the excellent collection at my academic home at the University of Guelph, since the library remained closed due the COVID-19 pandemic while preparing this essay. To adapt, I selected cookbooks that were easily accessible at the Internet Archive (https://archive.org/). The Internet Archive is a non-profit organization that houses archived versions of internet sites and a large, growing collection of digital artifacts. I used the Internet Archive to create a digital collection of cookbooks.[7] With the exception of a few books, all the cookbooks used in this essay are available online in digital format to anyone with internet access and can be downloaded, or borrowed for online reading by creating an account at the Internet Archive.

In March 2020, the Internet Archive contained just over 5,600 entries for cookbooks. Over 1,000 of these can be downloaded onto one's own computer or tablet, while over 4,500 can be borrowed for two weeks at one time. The cookbooks chosen for this essay were selected to obtain a mix of commercial, advertising, community, and other types of cookbooks; at least one book from each decade from the 1890s to the 2010s; and a variety of topic emphases such as general interest, ingredient-specific foci, cooking on a budget, lifestyle, health, and more. The resulting collection of cookbooks that was used in this essay contained 100 books, most of which are listed in the references.[8] This collection reflects my necessity of having to work from home but wanting to provide readers access to the source materials. Hopefully, this approach will provide convenience and additional value for readers of the essay.

The composition and size of the cookbook collection used in this essay uses saturation sampling logic of qualitative research. Saturation sampling means that the researcher continues to add sources of information to one's sample until analysis of further sources does not add new insights. In terms of this essay, this means that although there were other cookbooks available at the Internet Archive that could be added to the analysis, they did not appear to add new data or provide new

---

[6] Phyllis L. Fleming, "From Scullion to Gastronome: A Journey through the American Cookbook," *Journal of American Culture* 1, no. 3 (1978), https://doi.org/10.1111/j.1542-734X.1978.0103_554.x, 10.1111/j.1542-734X.1978.0103_554.x.

[7] Readers who are interested in using any of these books can create an account at Internet Archive.

[8] A summary is available at my University of Guelph website at https://www.uoguelph.ca/lang/people/erna-van-duren.

insights that were relevant to assessing economics themes.[9] Three perspectives on economic themes, which were briefly discussed in the introduction, were used in the analysis. This involved looking for the answers to the following sorts of questions, simultaneously.

For the cookbook-perspective the following sort of questions guided the analysis: Did the cookbook provide advice on how to buy ingredients, store food so it does not spoil or waste, use of the ingredients in more than one dish or meal as well as how to prepare food that is valuable to those who eat it based on characteristics such as tastiness, nutrition, and other elements that shape the appeal of food? Did chapter introductions or recipes provide information on the per serving cost or total cost of preparing a recipe, how to substitute lower priced ingredients, or other advice on how to save money?

Applying a household-perspective to understanding how cookbooks relate to economic themes and other aspects of household management requires some explanation of the relevant economic theory. According to household production theory, households buy, make, consume, and provide a mix of products and services for sale in markets. For example, households buy, make, and use food, shelter and housing, cleaning, education, entertainment and other products and services depending on their composition, income and wealth, and needs and wants. Households differ across these factors in important ways. For example, households with children generally put considerable focus on meeting children's nutritional needs, and therefore would be characterised by a healthy children driver. When applied to food decisions, drivers are interrelated attitudes and behaviours that help to understand how households make decisions about food buying, preparation and consumption.

As suggested above, factors of particular importance in understanding household food concerns and behaviour can be labelled as key drivers of that household's food behaviours. Food marketers, and increasingly those who develop and implement food policy, aim to understand these drivers to influence people's food consumption choices and patterns. The healthy children driver has been quite important since the 1960s. Since then many new cookbook offerings have been aimed at this driver of household food activity. Just a few examples include *The Natural Baby Food Cookbook*, *The Baby Cookbook: Tasty and Nutritious Meals for the Whole Family and Babies and Toddlers will also Love* and *The Baby and Toddler Cookbook* which are available at the Internet Archive, but there are many other print and online cookbook and resources focused on this driver.[10]

Drivers of household food concerns and behavior encompass demographic, lifestyle, and other variables that represent a household. A household can be one person or an extended family spanning several generations. Some households are focused on using time effectively, others on minimizing grocery shopping trips

[9] This approach has been used in other cookbook-based studies. For an example relating to American cookbooks and ethnicity, see Liora Gvion, "What's Cooking in America?: Cookbooks Narrate Ethnicity: 1850-1990," *Food, Culture & Society* 12, no. 1 (2009), https://doi.org/10.2752/155280109X368660.

[10] Margaret Kenda and Phyllis S. Williams, *The Natural Baby Food Cookbook* (New York: Avon Books, 1973). Karin Knight and Jeannie Lumley, *The Baby Cookbook: Tasty and Nutritious Meals for the Whole Family that Babies and Toddlers will Also Love* (New York: Quill, 1992).

or food preparation time, while others are driven by health issues and concerns and specific lifestyle constraints or choices. There are cookbooks geared to the interests and needs associated with all of these drivers, along with many others. For example, during the last 50 years we have seen cookbooks focused on vegan athletes,[11] people who want to eat like famous vegans,[12] and an increasing number of cookbooks and resources for those interested in a plant based diet for a mix of personal and environmental reasons.[13] Income, age, ethnicity, and other demographic variables along with work-life balance, health, and other lifestyle related concerns can be important drivers of food concerns and behavior. In this essay, the focus is on economic drivers.

Last, cookbooks, recipes, and a household's food concerns and behaviors exist with a food-context-perspective. Economic factors are an important part of this context. Most households participate in a market economy to meet all or part of their food needs. The tradition, and in today's world a proactive decision, to grow a garden and preserve some of its bounty requires choosing to remove part of the household's food production and consumption from the market economy.[14]

Economic factors interplay with social, cultural, physical, political, and technological factors. For example, social pressure affects food decisions; politics affects the prices and availability of foods; technologies affect the costs at which foods are produced, processed, and distributed. Some households have sufficient incomes to devote to selecting food products and services available through food value chains that offer differentiated attributes. These may be fairly simple such as organics, foods that are fully or partly prepared, or foods that are more complex and based on premium lifestyle preferences, such as fair trade or year round fresh fruit, most of which is now imported by the United States, as well as Canada.[15]

Economic Themes

Many food studies scholars categorize cookbooks into sub-genres such as commercial cookbooks, advertising cookbooks, community cookbooks, household manuals, government publications, manuscripts, and other types that increasingly include cookbooks prepared by celebrity chefs and self-published materials.[16] These sub-genres encompass a wide range of subject foci. Among the more

---

[11] See as an example Nicolas Benfatto, *The Vegan Cookbook for Athletes* (Open Source, 2019).

[12] See as an example Ingrid Newkirk, *The PETA Celebrity Cookbook* (New York: Lantern Books, 2002).

[13]An early example is Frances Moore Lappé, *Diet for a Small Planet*, ed. Friends of the Earth (New York: Friends of the Earth, 1974). Among bestsellers in this sub-genre, see Mollie Katzen and Moosewood Restaurant, *The New Moosewood Cookbook* (2000); Rachel Smith, *Vegan Cookbook, Vegan Food and Living, Spring, 101 Plant Based Recipes*, ed. Rachel Smith (Vegan Food and Living, 2019).

[14] Danille Elise Christensen, "Simply Necessity? Agency and Aesthetics in Southern Home Canning," Southern Cultures 21, no. 1 (2015), https://doi.org/10.1353/scu.2015.0004.

[15] David Karp, "Our New Global Garden: Most of America's Fruit Is Now Imported. Is That a Bad Thing?" *New York Times*, March 14, 2019 2018, D, https://www.nytimes.com/2018/03/13/dining/fruit-vegetables-imports.html.

[16] Elizabeth Driver, "Cookbooks as Primary Sources for Writing History: A Bibliographer's View," *Food, Culture & Society* 12, no. 3 (2009), https://doi.org/10.2752/175174409X431987, 10.2752/175174409X431987.

common subjects are general interest cookbooks that discuss cooking basics and include the full range of recipes[17] and ethnic or regionally specific cookbooks that often provide historical and geographic information along with recipes that represent that cuisine.[18] Health focused books that provide scientific information and advice about medical or nutrition issues along with eating guidelines and recipes that can be prepared to follow the advice are also popular.[19] Other subjects for cookbooks include, but are not limited to, lifestyles (local food,[20] farm, or own grown produce[21]), food philosophies (no meat/plant only[22]), specific types of ingredients (chocolate,[23] vegetables[24]) or dishes (cookies[25]) and use of a specific appliance (microwave[26]) and combinations of any or many of these (for example, using milk in microwave cooking[27]). The new combinations of subjects continue to amaze me!

These next sections of this essay are based on a selection of cookbooks that reveal key economic themes. Each section has a subheading that aims to capture key economic ideas along with a discussion of the relevant theory, the practical constraints in the application of that theory along with examples from selected cookbooks. The discussion is organized by themes that build on each other and is followed by some concluding thoughts. The four economic themes explored below are reducing costs, budgeting money and time, making quality food, and finally economic and social value created through cookbooks. In many instances there are several excellent examples of cookbooks that illustrate one or more economic themes. To provide a greater variety of examples, nearly all the referenced cookbooks are used only in the discussion of one theme although many cookbooks provide excellent examples for more than one theme.

---

[17] A very early example is Lillian C. Masterman, *The Common Sense Cook Book* (Minneapolis: The Swinburne Printing Company, 1894). The Internet Archive contains the 1965 edition of a book that has been updated and reprinted many times is Fannie Merritt Farmer and Wilma Lord Perkins, *The Fannie Farmer Cookbook* (Boston: Little, Brown, 1965). An update by a new author of a popular book from 1941 is Kimberly Beeman and Lily Haxworth Wallace, *Big Basic Cookbook* (New York: Mud Puddle Books, 2007).

[18] Some excellent examples that vary in their approach include Calvin B. T. Lee and Audrey Evans Lee, *The Gourmet Chinese Regional Cookbook* (Secaucus, N.J.: Castle Books, 1981). A reprint of the 1968 classic is available online. See Edna Staebler, Wayson Choy, and Rose Murray, *Food That Really Schmecks* (reprint, accessible e-book) (2009).

[19] A relatively early example of a disease specific book is Collin H. Dong and Jane Banks, *The Arthritic's Cookbook* (New York: Kensington Books, 1980).

[20] Books aimed at eating local continue to proliferate. An excellent example is Janet Fletcher, Sur La Table, *Eating Local: The Cookbook Inspired by America's Farmers* (Kansas City: Andrews McMeel Pub., 2010).

[21] Again, there are many excellent books aimed at this topic. See Susan Herrmann Loomis, *Farmhouse Cookbook* (New York: Workman Publishing Company, 1991).

[22] Smith, *Vegan Cookbook.*

[23] Hershey's, *Cocoa Cookbook* (Hershey Chocolate Company, 1979).

[24] Paul Mayer, *Vegetable Cookbook* (Concord, CA: Nitty Gritty Productions, 1975).

[25] Publications International, *The Great American Cookie Cookbook* (2001).

[26] Anne Marshall, *Microwave Cookbook* (London: Tiger Books International, 1986).

[27] Ontario Milk Marketing Board, *Milk's Microwave Cookbook* (Ontario Milk Marketing Board, 1989).

Reducing Costs

All recipes explain how to combine ingredients using processes to obtain a desired dish. Reducing costs means that one starts with the desired output and determines what ingredients and processes can be used to reduce, or minimize, the cost of creating that output. This approach requires locating and buying the appropriate ingredients at the lowest prices and using the most efficient cooking processes. Of course, there are all sorts of practical problems associated with this approach. In some households, someone has good cooking skills thereby supporting efficient processes to prepare the recipe. In other households, this level of cooking skill or access to certain kitchen equipment may not exist. As well, obtaining ingredients at the lowest prices can be a challenge, both at the household level and within the broader food context. Having to walk or bus to a grocery store, lack of appropriate storage, or a low budget all limit buying in the volumes often required to obtain the lowest price.

For many households, cookbooks support reducing household food costs. A general plan for the types of dishes that are appealing, or acceptable, to the household shapes the types of ingredients that will be purchased from grocery stores, sourced from one's garden or obtained elsewhere over a given period of time. The cost of the "basket of food" used by the household can then be minimized. Information about cooking and the associated food knowledge found in cookbooks support minimizing household food costs.

The food context determines how well households can reduce food costs. The modern food system relies extensively on large scale production, processing, distribution, retailing, and food services. On average, this system drives down costs, but it does not make it easier for all or some households to minimize costs. Living in a food desert[28] and other elements of a household's "food environment" (see the "USDA's Food Environment Atlas"[29]) such as fewer food buying choices increase this challenge.

The Practical Cookbook,[30] written over 100 years ago by Margaret Howard who was the Head of the Domestic-Science Department of the High School of Practical Arts in Boston, is organized to help its readers develop the cooking, shopping, and other practical skills to manage a household with cost-consciousness. The book comprises sections that are organized by the type of ingredient, such as water (tea, coffee), mineral salts (fruit, vegetables), starch (potatoes, corn and more), sugar, proteids (milk, meats, nuts and more), fats and oils, and more. Within each of these sections, discussions of sets of ingredients such as winter

---

[28] U.S. Department of Agriculture Economic Research Service, "Access to Affordable and Nutritious Food-Measuring and Understanding Food Deserts and Their Consequences: Report to Congress" (2009), https://www.ers.usda.gov/publications/pub-details/?pubid=42729.

[29] "Food Environment Atlas," updated August 27, 2019, 2020, accessed April 20, 2020, https://www.ers.usda.gov/data-products/food-environment-atlas/go-to-the-atlas/.

[30] Margaret W. Howard, *The Practical Cookbook: A Book of Economical Recipes* (Boston: Ginn and Company, 1917).

vegetables, dried fruits, breakfast cereals, cheese, poultry, and more, are organized to provide information of the sources, value, costs and cooking methods for these ingredients. Variations for specific ingredients are organized into charts that aid in calculating the cost of preparing any given recipe. As with many cookbooks, and indeed many discussions about food prices and costs, the terms price and cost are used incorrectly or interchangeably. Prices are the dollar amount paid for a specified package size or unit of a product at a specified quality of that product or service, while costs account for the amount purchased, expenses incurred in locating, transporting, using, and disposing of the unused portion of a product or service. Margaret Howard's logic and approach are admirable in teaching the reader how to think about ways of reducing food costs.

Reducing food costs is an important element of many cookbooks, and many cookbooks provide advice on how to buy ingredients, stock a pantry and equip a kitchen. In Mrs. Beeton's book *Household Management*, she attempts to give "an intelligible arrangement to every recipe, a list of the *ingredients,* a plain statement of the *mode* of preparing each dish, and a careful estimate of its *cost*, the number of people for whom it is *sufficient* and the time when it is *seasonable.*"[31] In chapter 3, she provides advice on the "Arrangement and Economy of the Kitchen." Although the distribution of a kitchen "must always depend so much on local circumstances," there are some general principles such as good lighting and ventilation, being sufficiently far removed from other rooms so that people don't "perceive the odor incident to cooking," and having plenty of fuel and water.[32] Kitchens should also be "well supplied" with a good range, various utensils, storage and scales.[33] Knowing "times when things are in season is one of the most essential pieces of knowledge which enter into the 'Art of Cookery.'" Mrs. Beeton's detailed list, organized by month and food type, provides this information.[34] In practice, reducing costs is part of household food budgeting, the next theme to be discussed.

Budgeting: Money and Time

The concept of budgeting refers to planning the amount of money that one spends over a given period of time on certain goods and services. Time spent managing food and cooking is an important aspect of budgeting. Cookbooks aim to help with budgeting by explaining how to cook with lower priced ingredients, the time that will be needed to prepare a food, advice on using ingredients in more than one dish so that they are not wasted, buying ingredients at lower prices, knowing how to buy ingredients at various quality levels, advising on what not to buy, how to store food so it does not spoil and thereby waste money, as well as how to create a variety of dishes from one or a few ingredients.

---

[31] Isabella Beeton, *Mrs. Beeton's Household Management: A Guide to Cookery in All Branches: Daily Duties, Menu Making, Mistress & Servant, Home Doctor, Hostess & Guest, Sick Nursing, Marketing, the Nursery, Trussing & Carving, Home Lawyer* (London: Ward, Lock, 2007, 1899).

[32] Beeton, *Mrs. Beeton's Household Management*, 25.

[33] Beeton, *Mrs. Beeton's Household Management*, 26-33.

[34] Beeton, *Mrs. Beeton's Household Management*, 33-27.

Most cookbooks written over the last 150 years aim to stretch the food budget through providing generally relevant knowledge and advice, but more recent books increasingly focus on specific aspects of budgeting. The preface to *Southern Living's Low Cost Cookbook* from 1972 captures praise for this skill superbly. The preface provides the following anonymous quotation" "My wife is a great manager!" The text then goes on to emphasize that "certainly an important part of being a good manager is getting the most for your food dollar ... the art of seasonal buying, thrifty cooking methods, and other ways to trim [the] food budget without sacrificing either quality of flavor ... shopping advice, innovative substitutions ... [are] certain to save you precious food dollars."[35] A much earlier book from 1911, *The Cookbook of Leftovers,* aimed "to be simply a practical handy book for the average housekeeper, who cannot afford to waste food which has been leftover from her table, and who nevertheless desires to serve the best and most attractive dishes."[36] The Browns, who as a family comprised writers and teachers who wrote short stories and travel non-fiction and authored cookbooks, created the *Most for Your Money Cookbook* in 1938. This book contains advice gleaned from international travels during the 1930s advises on how to create "the tastiest and most nourishing dishes at the lowest cost," and is organized by the "best value in terms of cost and time."[37]

Books aimed at a certain demographic segment who might need to budget became increasingly popular in the last fifty years. Phyllis MacDonald's 1967 *Cookbook for the Leisure Years* suggests that bargain buying is an "exciting hobby" and provides ample advice on how to organize a shopping list to save time and money, and to store and prepare foods so one is not wasting time or money on food.[38] Books such as *The Starving Students' Cookbook*[39] and the *Student Pasta Cookbook*[40] were also popular into the 1990s. Of course, much of the advice provided in these books is now freely available on a proliferation of websites.

Some budget-oriented cookbooks aim to meet the needs of households receiving food assistance. Susan Irby's *$7 a Meal* books[41] and Brown's Kickstarter-funded book *Good and Cheap: Eat Well on $4*[42] provide advice such as don't buy drinks, buy fresh bread later in the day, buy produce in season, try to build a pantry, don't buy at delis, avoid fresh fish since it has often already been frozen, learn to com-

---

[35] Southern Living, *The Low Cost Cookbook* (Birmingham, AL.: Oxmoor House, 1972).

[36] Helen Carroll Clarke and Phoebe Deyo Rulon, *The Cook Book of Left-Overs: A Collection of 400 Reliable Recipes for the Practical Housekeeper* (New York: Harper & Bros., 1911).

[37] Cora Brown, Rose Brown, and Bob Brown, *Most for Your Money Cookbook* (New York: Modern Age Books, Inc., 1938).

[38] Phyllis MacDonald, *A Cookbook for the Leisure Years with Dividends for You of Money, Time, and Energy* (Garden City, NY: Doubleday, 1967).

[39] Dede Hall Napoli, *The Starving Students' Cookbook* (New York: Grand Central Publishing, 1982).

[40] Sarah Freeman, *The Student Pasta Cookbook: Eating Well without Mixer, Microwave or Money* (London: Collins & Brown, 1993).

[41] Chef Susan Irby, *The $7 a Meal Healthy Cookbook: 301 Nutritious, Delicious Recipes That the Whole Family Will Love* (Cincinnati: F+W Media, 2010).

[42] Leanne Brown, *Good and Cheap: Eat Well on $4* (2014).

pare prices, understand the cost per recipe and per serving, buy ingredients with which you can do more (i.e. bone-in chicken breasts, eat the meat and use the rest for soup), understand how ingredients contribute to the cost of recipe (i.e. butter versus more expensive oils), and finally learn to eat lower on the food chain (i.e. less processed). Each of these books, along with many other budget focused cookbooks provide advice on how to use coupons effectively. *The Frugal Foodies: Waste Not Recipes for the Wise Cooks* warns that coupons are for overprocessed food.[43] However, coupons can also extend a household's food budget as per the focus of *The Money-Savers Cookbook*, which explains how to organize coupons and advises "don't use them for what you don't need."[44]

Other books aim at different budgets, needs and wants. The *Ideals Ground Meat Cookbook* explains how a single pound of ground meat can be used to make dishes of American, Italian, Chinese, Mexican and many other origins that can feed six people.[45] Altman's 2005 *Big Food: Amazing Ways to Cook, Store, Freeze and Serve Everything You Buy in Bulk*[46] assumes its readers have a large enough budget to buy in bulk, own freezers, and most likely own cars as well. To counter the food waste that often comes with this budget and food philosophy, the cookbook explains how to use heavy Ziploc© bags to freeze food properly, cook multiple meals from one bulk purchase in order to save time and money and avoid waste and what not to buy at all, which can be understood through diagnosing one's "buying style."[47] *The Ultimate Bulk Buying Cookbook: 120 Money Saving, Family Recipes*[48] offers similar advice and promotes the Food Saver© system along with sharing bulk meat purchases across families.

Time pressure and needing fewer ingredients are also important in cooking within budget constraints. Advertising cookbooks often aim at solving these problems, both those for appliances and ingredients. Books aimed at how to use toaster ovens,[49] stand mixers,[50] slow cookers, and more recently the Instant Pot® all tend to stress how the user will save money by learning how to cook food with the newly acquired appliance. Advertising cookbooks have provided advice on how to cook within a budget for over 100 years. Gunns' 1919 *Recipes: Wholesome, Nutritious, Economical* demonstrates how its Easifirst shortening will "produce better, more economical and healthful foods than either lard or butter." Being able to use less

[43] Lara Starr and Lynette Rohrer Shirk, *The Frugal Foodie Cookbook: Waste-Not Recipes for the Wise Cook* (Waterville, ME: Thorndike Press, 2010).

[44] Jody Cameron, *The Money-Savers Cookbook* (New York, NY: Avon Books, 1992).

[45] Naomi Arbit and June Turner, *Ideals Ground Meat Cookbook* (Milwaukee, WI.: Ideals Pub. Corp., 1981).

[46] Elissa Altman, *Big Food: Amazing Ways to Cook, Store, Freeze, and Serve Everything you Buy in Bulk* (Emmaus, PA: Godalming: Rodale; Melia [distributor], 2005).

[47] Altman, *Big Food*, 15-20.

[48] Jan Muller and Bob Warden, *The Ultimate Bulk Buying Cookbook: 120 Money Saving, Family Pleasing Recipes* (Philadelphia, PA: Dynamic Housewares, 2010).

[49] Diane Yanney, *Better Homes and Gardens Toaster Oven Cookbook* (Better Homes and Gardens 1981).

[50] Sunbeam Corp., *Sunbeam Mixmaster Cooking Guide* (1950).

shortening compared to lard or butter relaxes the budget constraint. Campbell's Soups can be added to many combinations of staples, vegetables and meats to save time, and money for those who don't have a well-stocked pantry.[51] *Betty Crocker's Quick & Easy Cookbook: 30 Minutes or Less to Dinner* explains how to save time by preparing some ingredients ahead of time, using disposable supplies such as tin-foil, cooking-sprays, adding convenience foods to recipes, and keeping ingredients to eight or fewer.[52]

The No-Time-to-Cook Cookbook[53] and JoAnna Lund's *Fast, Cheap and Easy*[54] offer similar and additional advice such as using cooking basics for fewer ingredients, how to stock a pantry, buying ingredients that will make more than one meal at a time or even aiming for the occasional cooking marathon that results in meals that take only the time required to reheat them.

Making Quality Food

Most people prefer food that tastes good and has certain quality characteristics. Desired quality characteristics vary immensely and include ensuring certain ingredients are used (e.g. plants, brand name product) or not used (e.g. meat, dairy, gluten), contributing to a desired nutritional outcome (e.g. cancer friendly, low carbs), and creating a specific style or taste of food associated with a ethnic or regional heritage (e.g. Italian, Mennonite, etc.). There are seemingly countless commercial, advertising, community, and other types of cookbooks that aim to help their readers make quality food that tastes good.

For many cookbook readers and users, making quality food that tastes good is the main practical and aspirational reason for browsing, reading, trying selected recipes, and using a cookbook. In economic theory, this approach to food production is termed maximizing output at a desired quality. One decides what combination of characteristics one wants to consume,[55] buys the ingredients, prepares and cooks them, and then consumes them at the time and place one chooses. Cookbooks provide recipes and other information that explain the knowledge one needs to prepare, exactly and precisely, the quality of food one chooses.

There are many types of knowledge. Several types are particularly important to cooking, eating and cookbooks. The distinction between codified and tacit knowledge assists in organizing those most relevant to food including sensory, procedural, scientific, general, and applied knowledge. Codified knowledge, also often referred to as formal or explicit knowledge, can be articulated, stored in text

---

[51] Company Campbell Soup, *Most-for-the-Money Main Dishes: Recipes Developed and Tested by Home Economists of Campbell Kitchens* ([n.p.]: Campbell Soup Company, 1975).

[52] Betty Crocker, *Betty Crocker Quick & Easy Cookbook: 30 Minutes or Less to Dinner* (Hoboken, NJ: Wiley Pub., 2009).

[53] Joanne Abrams and Marie Caratozzolo, *The No-Time-to-Cook Cookbook* (Garden City Park, N.Y.: Avery Pub. Group, 1999).

[54] JoAnna M. Lund, *Fast, Cheap, and Easy: 100 Original Recipes that Make the Cooking as Much Fun as the Eating*, Healthy Exchanges Inc (New York: Berkley Pub. Group, 1999).

[55] Kelvin J. Lancaster, "A New Approach to Consumer Theory," *Journal of Political Economy* 74, no. 2 (1966), https://doi.org/10.1086/259131.

or other media, and transferred to others. Tacit knowledge is more difficult to transfer, through text or other media, because it is difficult to explain and generally requires experience or context to understand and apply.

Cookbooks have evolved in how knowledge is communicated, as has the economic value of this information. Although some early cookbooks assume that their users have a certain amount of general knowledge about food and cooking, many of the most popular and best-selling cookbooks published since about 1900 aimed to provide economic value to their readers by codifying that knowledge. Fannie Farmer's 1896 *Boston Cooking School Book* excelled in this goal with its introduction of standardized measures and equipment, detailed descriptions of food preparation and cooking procedures, explanations of nutrition and food sources along with practical suggestions on equipment and suitable ways to serve foods.[56]

Mass market cookbooks became more popular over the next 70 years.[57] The number of new cookbooks and the variety of subject emphases show the expanding interest, increased literacy and expanding markets for food and cooking related knowledge. Although data on cookbook sales are of uncertain quality, don't reflect resales, and cannot capture actual use or popularity, they certainly include comprehensive cookbooks such as *Better Homes and Gardens New Cookbook* (1930; sales estimate 40 million copies), *Betty Crocker's Picture Cookbook* (1950; sales estimate 65 million copies) and Irma Rombauer's *Joy of Cooking* (1931; sales estimate 18 million copies).[58]

Cookbooks with specific topic foci such as ethnic cuisine also became more popular. Ethnic and regional cuisines are not a focus of this essay, except to provide just a few examples of how cookbooks provide the knowledge to prepare foods with very specific qualities. These are often based on specific, localized ingredients, food preparation and cooking techniques. Specific ingredients may require substitutes either because they are not generally available at grocery stores or due to particular preferences. In fact, very specialized qualities in food could be prepared using the right cookbook, including foods of Italian, Chinese, and French origin that were also kosher[59] and specific regional cuisines such as Waterloo, Ontario's Mennonites.[60]

---

[56] Fannie Merritt Farmer, *The Original Boston Cooking-School Cook Book, 1896* (New York: H.L. Levin Associates: Distributed by Crown Publishers, 1896). The original edition of my mother's *Wannee kookbook,* published in 1910, was also written by a director of a domestic or household school. Like Farmer's cookbook it aimed to make knowledge about cooking, but also managing a household, more widely accessible, particularly to women of lower and middle classes along with those serving or part of the upper class.

[57] The year 1970 was used as an ending point for this cookbook era since it was 50 years ago, coincided with a sustained increase in the amount and diversity of information published.

[58] Data on sales were obtained from the Daily Meal, "25 Best-Selling Cookbooks of All Time (slideshow)," (2011). https://www.thedailymeal.com/cook/25-best-selling-cookbooks-all-time-slideshow.

[59] Among the myriad ethnic and regionally focused cuisine books published a few exceptionally interesting books include Ruth Grossman and Bob Grossman, *The Kosher-Cookbook Trilogy* (New York: Galahad Books, 1965).

[60] Another example is Edna Staebler, *Food That Really Schmecks* (1968), which has been updated and is accessible online at Staebler, Choy, and Murray, *Food That Really Schmecks*

Books that provide knowledge about preparing food with health-enhancing or disease-prevention or amelioration characteristics started to become more widely available from the 1970s. Although health advice and medical "receipts" were part of many manuscript cookbooks and early cookbooks (as demonstrated by Rebecca Sharpless (Sharpless, Ch. 3, this volume) and Kathryn Harvey (Harvey, Ch. 5, this volume),[61] those that focused solely on health goals that also provide scientifically created knowledge along with practical advice and recipes gained popularity in the 1970s. Such books, and websites, are part of the food environment today, but were novel in the 1960s and 1970s. Weight Watchers,[62] founded in 1963 by Jean Nidetch, published its first cookbook in 1966 with program information, menu plans, 550 recipes.[63] The book became a best-seller, selling more than 1.5 million copies, and spawned a new industry. Other books aimed at the same market started to appear more and more rapidly.[64]

The *American Heart Association's Cookbook*, now in its 9th edition, was first published in 1973. This cookbook stressed that it was not a diet book, but rather a "fun book for people who like to cook and eat." It provided plentiful information on fats and cholesterol along with a large variety of appropriate recipes.[65] Other books aimed at providing information about the qualities of food that could help with arthritis, cancer, and increasingly more specific health conditions have followed.[66]

Today information on how to cook with or without certain ingredients is easy to locate. New cookbooks focused on specific ingredients, dietary needs, and particular tastes and preferences appear on an almost daily basis. Search engines like Amazon's make these easy to locate, and too easy to buy! There are also many websites that offer food and cooking advice that allow the user to filter for the presence or the absence of an ingredient.[67] Some of these surged in popularity during the COVID-19 pandemic as people looked to cook with what they already

(reprint, accessible ebook).

[61] *The Common Sense Recipe Book: Containing All the Latest Recipes On Cooking With Economy: And Also Very Valuable Medicinal Recipes* (Montreal: unknown, 1895).

[62] Weight Watchers, "Evolution & History of WW Program," (2020), https://www.weightwatchers.com/nz/wellbeing/evolution-of-ww.

[63] The 1973 version of the book is available at Jean Nidetch, *Weight Watchers Program Cookbook* (Great Neck, NY: Hearthside Press, 1973).

[64] See as one example, Robert C. Atkins, *Dr. Atkins' Diet Revolution: The High Calorie Way to Stay Thin Forever* (1972).

[65] American Heart Association, *Cookbook*, 2nd ed. (New York: McKay, 1975).

[66] Today there are plethora of cookbooks aimed at those who have celiac disease. Until recently, people with the disease generally had to learn and adapt from existing cookbooks. An early example of a book that recognized the need for information, advice and appropriate recipes is June Roth, *The Troubled Tummy Cookbook* (1976).

[67] SuperCook, My FridgeFood, Allrecipes Dinner Spinner, BigOven, Epicurious, CookPad, Tasty, America's Test Kitchen are among a few examples. Some of these require a membership, while others are free.

had on hand or were able to acquire online or at their usual grocery stores (see the reflections on COVID-19 foodways at the end of this volume (Riney-Kehrberg, Ch. 54, this volume)).

Economic and Social Value

Early cookbooks include many works written by cooks at "magnificent and wealthy courts" so that cooks in other courts can aspire, and with some practice, acquire culinary knowledge to further their own careers. Of course, people of slightly lower classes and merchants could also acquire this knowledge.[68] Clearly, food's social significance has always had economic dimensions.

The modern food system, which is based on large scale production, mass marketing, just-in-time distribution, and offering food products differentiated for nearly all income groups, is often decried in contemporary cookbooks by chefs, celebrities, food experts, and assorted foodies. However, knowing how to use processed food and owning modern appliances were important indicators of socio-economic class and aspirations. Advertising cookbooks tapped into that trend early. Duke University's Nicole Di Bona Peterson Collection of Advertising Cookbooks allows one to search, by company and product, to explore early examples of such books.[69] Plainly, people who could afford to buy the products in such books could have better lives through better time management, more predictable cooking results, and better health and living.

Cookbooks that celebrated modern technology through new products and new appliances had several economic impacts. Cookbooks, which were generally provided for free, that explained how to use new appliances such as electric ranges,[70] stand mixers,[71] and CrockPots©[72] (now known more generically as slow cookers[73]), ensured that foods prepared with the new appliances turned out well, could be shown off to family and friends, and often became the preferred type and brand of kitchen equipment. The current popularity of Instant Pots®, and the seemingly countless cookbooks and online information available on what to cook with them, is the most current example of this phenomenon.

Cookbooks that use processed ingredients have some of the same impacts. Being able to cook a recipe that appeals to popular taste, predictably, easily, reliably, and quickly has a lot of economic value in many households since members with less cooking skills or inclination to learn them can produce a predictable

---

[68] Ken Albala, "Cookbooks as Historical Documents," in *The Oxford Handbook of Food History*, ed. Jeffrey M. Pilcher (Oxford University Press, 2012), p. 7.

[69] Duke University, "Nicole Di Bona Peterson Collection of Advertising Cookbooks," (2020). https://library.duke.edu/rubenstein/findingaids/petersoncookbooks/, https://repository.duke.edu/

[70] General Electric, *Tempting Recipes for Your General Electric Pushbutton Range*, (1950), https://www.ge.com/.

[71] Sunbeam Corp., *Sunbeam Mixmaster Cooking Guide*.

[72] Marilyn Neill, "Rival Crock-Pot Cooking," (1975).

[73] America's Test Kitchen, *Healthy Slow Cooker Revolution: One Test Kitchen, 40 Slow Cookers, 200 Fresh Recipes* (2015).

dish. Cookbooks that made use of product innovations and product line extensions helped to create value in the household and the food industry. *The Can Opener Cook Book*, offered the can opener to "brave young women ... who are engaged in frying as well as bringing home the bacon" ... as a magic wand to becoming the "artist-cook, the master, the creative chef."[74] The *Frozen Cookbook*—first published in 1948 and updated in 1962[75]—explained how households, food service, and restaurants could save time and money and improve the quality of foods consumed through the purchase and storage of the increasing diversity and amounts of frozen foods that were becoming available. From the 1960s to date, more and more advertising cookbooks were published, either for sale or for promotional distributions. Some of these are now easily accessible online. These have enabled home cooks, of all skill levels and time constraints, to prepare predictably tasty and attractive baked and other foods. The introduction to Ceil Dyer's *Best Recipes from the Backs of Boxes, Bottles, Cans and Jars*[76] praises the great economic value created by the food processing industry. Ceil Dyer wrote several popular cookbooks during the 1970s and 1980s. However, the *Best Recipes from the Backs of Boxes, Bottles, Cans and Jars* is my all-time favorite cookbook because it made it possible to prepare food with my two young children on many occasions after becoming a widow in my early forties. For many busy parents Dyer's statement "In compiling this book I have come to appreciate how really lucky we are in this country; not only do we have an abundance of food, we are rich in the variety and quality of food produced and distributed to us by our food companies" is true most days, although it has particular resonance today.

Community cookbooks have a long tradition in North America. They are part of the social fabric in many communities and are widely recognized for their importance. Volunteerism and contributing to a community cause have resulted in uncountable numbers of cookbooks to raise money for one's church, local hospitals or social organizations, political causes, victims of disasters, and other causes. The economic value of such cookbooks is clear. Volunteers provide their recipes, writing and organizational skills, and hopefully most of the money raised by sales of the cookbooks goes to the intended beneficiaries and not printers or other contributors. Community cookbooks also enable distribution and sharing of socio-economically appropriate recipes and food knowledge, although elevated and aspirational recipes also tend to appear in these collections.[77]

Concluding Thoughts

Cookbooks are changing along with the digital media now available to share food knowledge. Websites, eBooks, phone-based apps, multimedia and social media

---

[74] Excerpts from the introduction of Poppy Cannon, *The Can-Opener Cookbook* (New York: Crowell, 1952).

[75] Jean Irwin Simpson, *The Frozen Food Cookbook* (Westport, CT: Avi Pub. Co., 1962).

[76] Ceil Dyer, *Best Recipes from the Backs of Boxes, Bottles, Cans and Jars* (New York: Galahad Books, 1981).

[77] Due to the literally countless number of community cookbooks that have been created in North America, only one reference is provided from the U.S. Midwest: Ann Seranne, *The Midwestern Junior League Cookbook* (New York: D. MacKay, 1985).

can provide the same, as well as real-time and interactive, content as traditional cookbooks. Consumers, businesses and anyone or any organization with a stake in the food and agricultural system can produce the information that was traditionally found in cookbooks. To start winding-down this essay, it seems sensible to explore the positive and negative economic and social value created through this trend. This value encompasses using food knowledge to support changing roles within a family,[78] changing food buying choices to support local agriculture,[79] promoting food experiences, encouraging better nutrition, and many other aspects of food production to consumption.

Celebrity chefs, food activists, celebrities, and others who have, or hope they are perceived to have, important knowledge to share about cooking, food or the food system increasingly share that knowledge through combining cookbooks, cooking shows, interviews and testimonials, and websites that share a variety of digital content. Many chefs provide exceptional knowledge of cooking processes, ingredients and their variations and uses, as well as inspiring better cooking and eating. However, readers, viewers, and those who browse through online food content offered by chefs may get an incomplete or misleading view of cooking, appropriate foods, and the food system. It takes time, effort, and—depending on the recipe—also money, to buy ingredients and learn how to cook like a celebrity chef, and can result in frustration, anxiety and wasted time and money.[80] Of course, aspiring to cook well can produce practical skills with real economic and social value. Fortunately, there are many excellent resources that build food knowledge and cooking skills including Samin Nosrat's recent *Salt, Fat, Acid, Heat.*[81] Unfortunately, the entertainment and knowledge provided by other chefs are much more variable and controversial in terms of their impacts on economic and social value.

Although cookbooks written by food activists have a long history, digital media have improved their reach and impact. Food activism can be focused on improving the food system, the uses of food in achieving social justice, as well as other causes. Assessing the economic, social and political value of their publications, speeches, webpage and cookbooks continues to get more serious academic attention but is far beyond the scope of this essay.[82] However, cookbooks are often effective vehicles for food activism, and range from the subtle and seductive to the direct and jarring.[83] Many of these are beautiful cookbooks that explain how to eat healthy, local foods and thereby promote lifestyles that are far from practical or af-

---

[78] John Donohue, *Man with a Pan: Culinary Adventures of Fathers Who Cook for Their Families* (Chapel Hill, NC: Algonquin Books of Chapel Hill, 2011).

[79] John Peterson and Lesley Littlefield Freeman, *Farmer John's Cookbook: The Real Dirt on Vegetables* (Angelic, Organics) (Salt Lake City, Utah: Gibbs Smith, 2006).

[80] This is part of the story told in *Julie and Julia* (2009) starring Amy Adams and Meryl Streep. See Nora Ephron, *Julie and Julia*, (2009). https://www.imdb.com/title/tt1135503/

[81] Nosrat, Samin. *SALT, FAT, ACID, HEAT* (Simon and Schuster: Crown Books, 2017).

[82] For an excellent book on the topic see Warren J. Belasco, Appetite for Change: How the Counterculture Took on the Food Industry (2014)., https://doi.org/10.7591/9780801471278; One of the more recent treatments includes Jasmine Lorenzini, "Food Activism and Citizens' Democratic Engagements: What Can We Learn from Market-Based Political Participation?" *Politics and Governance* 7, no. 4 (2019), https://doi.org/10.17645/pag.v7i4.2072.

[83] Newkirk, *The PETA Celebrity Cookbook.*

fordable for many people.[84] It all depends on how households use the information: Does it inform better food decisions, or does it spur spending on more expensive ingredients that are out-of-season or sold at premium food boutique prices at the expense of staples for a well-rounded diet?

Celebrities' pronouncements on their diets along with food ideologies and food system perspectives seem to be everywhere and appear on various websites and in cookbooks. An impressive lineup of actors, models, and media personalities provide advice on how to eat, and more often than not, the ingredients are expensive, specialized, or hard to locate. Many of the same issues that pertain to advice from food activists apply to celebrity cookbooks and their food advice, but with one important addition. The body images promoted, sometimes deliberately but almost certainly subconsciously, through celebrity cookbooks and online food information promote certain body types. The social and economic impacts of the celebrity food phenomenon are just beginning to be assessed.

Low-cost and easy access to creating an online, digital food personality makes it possible for just about anyone to self-publish the content that has traditionally been found in cookbooks. Nutrition specialists, food activists, wellness bloggers, doctors, health organizations, and ordinary people with food knowledge, experience or advice that they want to share all compete to get our attention on the World Wide Web. Most readers of this essay will likely have enough knowledge of cooking, food systems and nutrition to be able to sort through these websites and place the information into categories such as correct, misleading, or harmful.[85]

Instagram, Facebook, Pinterest, Twitter, Tumblr, Snapchat, and YouTube appear to be the most popular social media for sharing food interests, concerns about sustainability, and consumption experiences. TV, magazines, websites, social media, and cookbooks remain popular for finding recipes.[86]

Information on recipes, ways to solve household level food challenges—as well as the broader food system—has moved outside the confines of the traditional cookbook. Today it is possible to find specific recipes or meals, get ideas on how to create or serve a meal with specific ingredients within a budget, as well as an informed understanding of how those choices are possible within the modern food system. In the mid-1960s among Americans who cooked, men spent an average of 37 minutes on cooking per day, and women an average of 113 minutes. Fifty years later, men who cooked spent 45 minutes per day compared to 66 minutes for women.[87] During the last 10 years, economic pressure on the middle and

---

[84] See as examples Herrmann Loomis, "Farmhouse Cookbook" and Fletcher, *Eating Local.*

[85] An increasing amount of research in this area is being published. For a very recent contribution see Lily K. Hawkins, Claire Farrow, and Jason M. Thomas, "Do perceived norms of social media users' eating habits and preferences predict our own food consumption and BMI?" *Appetite* 149 (2020), https://doi.org/10.1016/j.appet.2020.104611.

[86] For a good report on food and social media in the United Kingdom, see *Social Chain Media, The Flavour of Social: An Exploration into the World of Food and Social* (2019), https://www.thedrum.com/, https://media.socialchain.com/insights/.

[87] Lindsey Smith, Shu Ng, and Barry Popkin, "Trends in US Home Food Preparation and Consumption: Analysis of National Nutrition Surveys and Time Use Studies from 1965-1966 to 2007-2008," *Nutrition Journal* 12, no. 1 (2013), https://doi.org/10.1186/1475-2891-

working classes seem to have increased the time devoted to grocery shopping and in-home food preparation. For these households, the accessibility of information traditionally associated with cookbooks, which is now easily obtained online, has considerable economic and social value. However, being able to locate a recipe for the ingredients one has on hand or watch a video that teaches how to cook something provides different economic and social benefits for different households. For some households, the knowledge provides a valued culinary skill, produces a great dinner, and increases its food production capabilities, while for others it may provide a second-best solution to a specific problem that does not always seem to be important. However, COVID-19's impact on food consumption habits and the food system suggest that all households just might want to pick up a cookbook!

12-45.

—9—

Buckaroo Stew and Before: Four Generations of Kurtz Family Recipes

Mazie Hough

Pennsylvania and Massachusetts, USA, 20th Century

These recipes were collected in my Aunt Belle's handwritten cookbook—that she photocopied for all of us. They are all from another era or two. My great grandmother, wife of a prosperous merchant in York, Pennsylvania, taught her children to bake orange cakes—possibly the only thing she knew how to cook. I am sure my grandfather, who took a bottle of whiskey to visit all his neighbors to celebrate Victory in Europe Day, had no hesitation putting a quart of whiskey in his Christmas eggnog. My aunt and her three sisters were not affluent but learned how to cook on a limited budget. Many of my aunt's recipes are highlighted with: "good" and "cheap!!" My aunt taught at a girls' school and worked hard, but loved having people to dinner where they would invariably argue politics over her good cooking. Her chocolate sauce was famous. Every summer all of us cousins, 15 in total, would gather at my grandmother's summer cottage in Waquoit, Massachusetts—dubbed by my aunt "Camp Carefree." There we would play baseball, swim, put on musicals written by my Aunt Belle, and eat the filling, easy, and cheap buckaroo stew.

Buckaroo Stew Waquoit

Waquoit, Massachusetts, 1950s

(6 servings)
1 ½ lbs ground beef
1 garlic clove, minced
1 t. salt
¼ t. pepper
4 T. shortening
1 large onion chopped (one cup)
1 T. chili powder
2 cans (1 lb. each) tomatoes
1 can (about 1 lb.) red kidney beans
1 can (about 1 lb.) white kidney beans
1 can (12 or 16 oz.) whole kernel corn
1 pk. (4 oz.) shredded cheddar cheese
2 T. chopped parsley

1. Set oven at 350
2. Combine ground beef, garlic, salt and pepper in large bowl. Mix lightly until blended. Shape into 36 balls.
3. Brown meatballs, part at a time, in shortening. In large pot or Dutch oven, stir in onion and chili powder. Cook slowly until onion is soft.
4. Stir in tomatoes, beans, corn, and the liquids in their cans.
5. Simmer 15 minutes.
6. Bake 2 hours at 350.
7. Mix cheese and parsley.
8. Spoon stew into soup plates—serve cheese mixture separately to spoon on top.

Serve with French bread or buttered toasted hard rolls & salad.

Chocolate sauce

2 oz. unsweetened chocolate
2 cup sugar
1 c. heavy cream

Melt cream & choc slowly; pour in sugar gradually, stirring all the time. Cook slowly (stirring) for about 5 minutes.

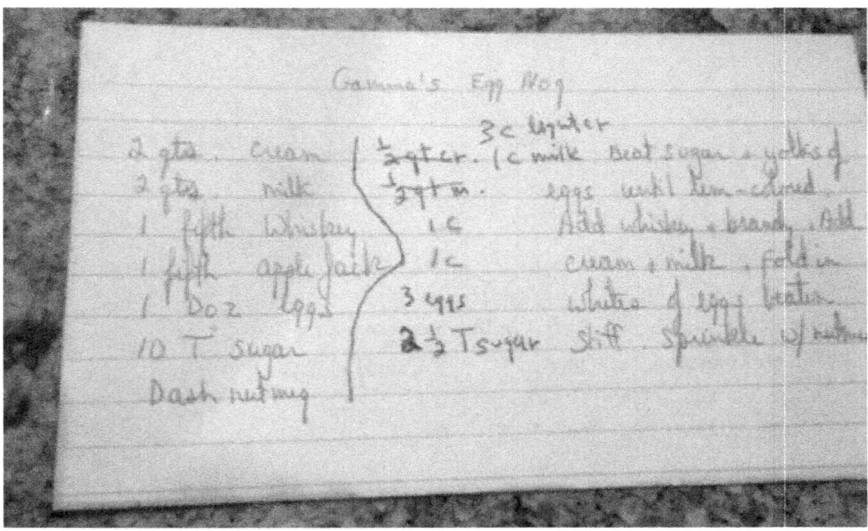

Gamma's Egg Nog

3c liquor

2 qts. cream ½ qt cr. 1c milk Beat sugar & yolks of
2 qts. milk ½ qt m. eggs until lem-colored.
1 fifth Whiskey 1c Add whiskey & brandy. Add
1 fifth apple jack 1c cream & milk. Fold in
1 Doz eggs 3 eggs whites of eggs beaten
10 T sugar 2½ T sugar stiff. Sprinkle w/
Dash nutmeg

9.1: Grandma's Egg Nog.

Gamma's Orange Cakes

York, Pennsylvania, 20th century

1 doz. eggs
4 lemons
2 c. sugar
6 oranges
2 c. flour

Beat 12 egg yolks until lemon colored, adding sugar gradually. Add juice and rind of 2 oranges and 1 lemon. Fold in 2 c. flour and then 10 whites of eggs beaten stiff. Grease and flour muffin tins for cup-cake pans, fill ¾ full with batter, and bake in a 350 oven for 12 minutes until golden brown on top. Cool. Dip in icing made of 2 egg whites whipped to a froth and combined with the juice and rind of 4 oranges and 3 lemons and sugar to taste (rind must be grated).

Egg Nog

2 qts. cream
1 doz. eggs
2 qts. milk
10 T/ [Tbsp] sugar
1 fifth whiskey
dash of nutmeg
1 fifth apple jack

Beat sugar with yolks of eggs until lemon colored
Add whiskey and apple jack
Add cream and milk
Fold in white of eggs beaten stiff.

—10—

Let Them Eat [Pound] Cake

Maureen S. Thompson

Greenville, South Carolina, USA, 1950s

In November 1954, my seventeen-year-old mother married my father during his brief leave from military service. Like many other couples in the Cold War era, they wed young and planned to contribute to the ongoing baby boom. While anxiety surrounding nuclear weapons loomed large, the mid-1950s featured full employment, rising wages, and more consumer goods than ever imagined. Memories of the Great Depression and World War II's lean rationing years faded into history's rearview mirror. Traditional gender roles were reasserted as Rosie the Riveter transformed into Harriett the Housewife.

In *Homeward Bound,* historian Elaine Tyler May explains, "The self-contained home held the promise of security in an insecure world. It also offered a vision of abundance and fulfillment."[1] Under the sway of capitalism American consumers were juxtaposed with Soviet Communists who seemingly had little respect for private property or God. Church attendance increased post-war and in 1954, the year my parents married, the words "under God" were added to the Pledge of Allegiance.

Against this backdrop my devout Irish Catholic mother embraced her role as housewife while establishing a domain at Donaldson Air Force Base in Greenville, South Carolina. Perhaps sensing a young woman's inexperience, my mother's neighbor gifted her the 1943 version of *The Boston Cooking School Cookbook,* authored by Fannie Merritt Farmer. Because my father was frequently away on assignments, my mother didn't cook that much, opting instead to open a can of Campbell's soup purchased from the commissary.

While raising five children in the 1960s and 1970s, my mother took advantage of prepared convenience foods, but *The Boston Cooking School Cookbook* appeared on the kitchen counter whenever our family was preparing food for special occasions. Birthdays were always celebrated with pound cake, which according to the Fanny Merritt Farmer recipe required—literally— several pounds of ingredients. The cake my mother baked was moist and delicious and could stand alone but was often paired with homemade vanilla frosting.

---

[1] Elaine Tyler May, *Homeward Bound: American Families in the Cold War Years* (New York: Basic Books, 1988), 3.

The cookbook was passed down to me, and although I don't prepare many of the antiquated recipes, I'm pleased to share the pound cake recipe with readers. Enjoy!

Pound Cake

1 pound butter
10 eggs, separated
1 pound sugar
2 tablespoons brandy
1 pound flour
½ teaspoon mace

Cream butter, add sugar gradually, and continue beating; then add egg yolks beaten until thick and lemon-colored, egg whites beaten until stiff, flour, mace, and brandy. Beat vigorously 5 minutes. Bake in deep pan 1 ¼ hours in slow oven (300 degrees F) or, if to be used for fancy ornamented cakes, bake 30 to 35 minutes in shallow pan.[2]

[2] Fannie Merritt Farmer, *The Boston Cooking-School Cook Book* (Boston: Little, Brown and Company, 1943), 642.

PART II

Community Cookbooks

—11—

Introduction

Cynthia C. Prescott

As we saw in Part I (Prescott, Ch. 1, this volume), cookbooks have been published in Europe and North America for centuries. While the earliest cookbooks were attributed to individuals, they were never truly an individual accomplishment. Instead, these cookbook authors compiled expertise that had been shared orally, and perhaps informally in written form, for generations. In the second half of the nineteenth century, as Rebecca Sharpless pointed out in "Rural Women, Rural Worlds" (Sharpless, Ch. 3, this volume), female voluntary organizations began to publish their own cookbooks. Often produced as fundraisers for philanthropic projects (just like this volume), they featured recipes collected from members of that organization or the larger community. Like the nationally-known cookbooks analyzed in the previous section (Van Duren, Ch. 8, this volume), studying these local community cookbooks reveals women's labor, the impact of trade networks, and changing culinary tastes. But, because they are products of specific local communities, comparing these small-scale publications and the recipes shared within them also reveals a great deal about rural culture.

In this section, contributors drill down to focus on individuals' manuscript recipe collections and community cookbooks drawn from different regions within North America in the nineteenth and twentieth centuries. We move from Maine, USA, and its maritime culture to South Carolina's Lowcountry featuring foods that migrated with the African slave trade. We then move west, looking at foodways on the North American grasslands in the US and Canada from earliest white settlement through the mid-twentieth century. From the US's northern border we leap to its southern border to examine Mexican tamale recipes drawn from the University of Texas at San Antonio's Mexican Cookbook Collection. Finally, we turn north once more to the Pacific Northwest in an attempt to reproduce the flavors of these community cookbooks in a modern kitchen.

Comparing community cookbooks uncovers the flavors of different places and time periods. It also reveals common experiences of women's labor and sociability. Rachel Snell's examination of community cookbooks from Downeast Maine reveals that a desire for social connections beyond the domestic sphere motivated women to embrace new food products (Snell, Ch. 12, this volume). Recipes sampled from a South Carolina church cookbook, by contrast, emphasize the persistence of locally available ingredients and point to the persistence of African foodways among African Americans (Jones-Branch, Ch. 13, this volume). Mary

Murphy's study of women in the western US–Canadian borderlands (Murphy, Ch. 14, this volume) highlights frontier women's notions of hospitality and their social class aspirations as they hosted others in their homes and shared recipes for social occasions in their cookbooks. The Kent family's manuscript cookbooks, kept by a couple that migrated from Ontario in eastern Canada to Wyoming Territory, USA (Kesterson, Ch. 15, this volume), also highlight the importance of hospitality to that region, as well as the practical demands for preserving farm produce in the late nineteenth century. Amy McKinney (McKinney, Ch. 16, this volume) demonstrates that a rural newspaper such as the Montana Rural Home section of the *Montana Farmer-Stockman* could serve as a community cookbook. Examining its contents reveals much about the realities of rural women's lives in the mid-twentieth century.

As many of these essays make clear, food preservation and preparation were skills that were passed down and shared. The final two contributions to this section draw on rare cookbooks in archival collections held by the University of Texas at San Antonio and the Oregon Historical Society. UTSA's cookbooks (Noell, Ch. 17, this volume) reveal how tamales were made and highlight the range of sweet and savory fillings once enjoyed in different regions of Mexico. Technical Services librarian Katie Mayer (Mayer, Ch. 18, this volume) then shares her exploits attempting to reproduce a recipe from a 1904 cookbook from Baker City, Oregon.

—12—

Banana Bread, Pineapple Pudding, Cocoanut Dainties, and Date Bars: *Favorite Recipes* as a Window into Women's Lives in Early-Twentieth Century Downeast Maine

Rachel A. Snell

In 1929 and 1936, two women's organizations in Downeast Maine produced collections of recipes titled *Favorite Recipes*.[1] These community cookbooks compiled by the members of the Mount Desert Chapter No. 20 of the Order of the Eastern Star (O.E.S.) and the Young Ladies Guild (Y.L.G.) of the Centre St. Congregational Church in Machias paint a portrait of a community, preserving a record of the food items available within rural municipalities along the eastern coast of Maine.[2] The two recipe collections examined here represent the communities of Somesville, a village located on prosperous and connected Mount Desert Island, and Machias, a small urban center in more rural and isolated Washington County. Located at the easternmost section of coastal Maine, Hancock, and Washington counties were one of the last sections of coastal Maine to be settled. Agriculture and fishing dominated this rural region, while industries such as tanneries, pulp and paper, granite, and sardine canneries also flourished. Like much of the state in the early twentieth century, the inhabitants of Downeast Maine comprised northern European immigrants, French and English Canadian migrations, and a dwindling Native population. With the notable exception of Mount Desert Island, the home of Acadia National Park and opulent summer cottages, these counties remained

---

[1] "Cocoanut" was an alternate spelling of the term "coconut" that has fallen out of use over the past century. The term "downeast" refers to parts of coastal eastern Maine and the Canadian Maritimes. The term originated in sailing terminology, from Boston one would sail downwind and east to reach this area. Within the state of Maine, "downeast" frequently refers specifically to the eastern most section of the state composed of coastal Hancock and Washington counties. This specific terminology is used in this essay.

[2] Mount Desert Chapter No. 20, Order of the Eastern Star, *Favorite Recipes* (Ellsworth, ME: The American Print, c. 1929), Mount Desert Island Historical Society, Mount Desert, ME; The Young Ladies Guild of the Congregational Church, *Favorite Recipes* (Machias, ME, 1936), Schrumpf (Brownie and William E.) Papers, 1905-1990s, Special Collections, Raymond H. Fogler Library, University of Maine.

sparsely settled and less prosperous compared to the southern coast throughout their history. This region was among the last places in the state to enjoy electricity and the connections provided by railroads and automobile roads.[3]

The recipes collected by women in Somesville and Machias provide a window into the eating and socialization habits of the early twentieth-century inhabitants of rural Downeast Maine at a critical juncture as rural reliance on local and homemade food products was giving way to nationalized, commercialized, and industrialized food choices. Ingredients representing local resources and nationally available commercial brands comingle within the pages, sometimes within the same recipe, and hint at the types of food available and used within these communities. The utilization of these new products and the types of recipes contained within the cookbook's pages reveal the priorities women in Downeast Maine placed on their foodwork. When properly contextualized, these sources suggest one reason rural women embraced new food products was a desire for socialization outside the home.

Recipes are powerful sources for women's history because they are "a peculiarly female form of writing," and as such, they allow "an opportunity for women to creatively record and inscribe individual lives."[4] As historians increasingly seek to understand women in their own words, the preservation of ordinary acts and everyday forms in recipe collections provides one of the best sites for understanding women's work, roles, and relationships. Susan Leonardi first introduced recipes as "embedded discourse," representative of relationships between friends, neighbors, relatives, and wider communities.[5] She persuasively argued that recipes are much more than lists of ingredients and methods for combining them into dishes. Rather, the intertextuality of recipes engages the reader or the cook in a conversation with context and relationships that should not be ignored. Therefore, the recipe "besides being a narrative itself, offers us other stories too: of family sagas and community records, of historical and cultural moments or changes, and also personal histories and narratives of self."[6] Recipes not only reveal human relationships but, as historian Rebecca Sharpless argued, also "important evidence about people's interactions with their environment and the society around them."[7] Recipes provide a sense of the tools and materials available, dining customs, identity formation, expectations, food system transitions, the development of unique food cultures, and much more. Recipe collections such as the two examined in this essay offer one of the best sources for understanding women's work, roles, and

---

[3] Stephen J. Hornsby and Richard W. Judd, Eds., *Historical Atlas of Maine* (Orono, ME: University of Maine Press, 2015).

[4] Janet Floyd and Laurel Forster, "The Recipe in its Cultural Contexts" in Janet Floyd and Laurel Forster, eds., *The Recipe Reader: Narratives – Contexts – Traditions* (Burlington, VT: Ashgate, 2003), 5.

[5] Susan J. Leonardi, "Recipes for Reading: Summer Pasta, Lobster àla Riseholme, and Key Lime Pie," *PMLA* 104, no. 3 (1989): 340.

[6] Floyd and Forster, "The Recipe in its Cultural Contexts," 2.

[7] Rebecca Sharpless, "Cookbooks as Resources for Rural Research," *Agricultural History* 90, no. 2 (Spring 2016): 195.

Figure 12.1: Masonic Lodge, Somesville. This undated photograph shows the two and one-half story Somesville Masonic Hall built in the early 1890s that provided the impetus for the Mount Desert Chapter's founding. Courtesy of the Mount Desert Island Historical Society.

relationships. These two collections of favorite recipes offer a glimpse into associational life in the early twentieth century, and some of the means women used to support their endeavors outside the home.

In the United States, women's formalized activity outside the home began with charities, benevolent societies, and other women-dominated organizations. Women's organizations have sustained communities throughout the United States through charitable projects, opportunities for socialization, political organization, and more since women formalized conventional female charity into formal associations in the decades following the American Revolution.[8] The reform spirit of the nineteenth century produced thousands of women's organizations in urban and rural areas that provided American women with the opportunity to participate in their communities, albeit collectively and in ways firmly connected to their domestic roles.

The women's organizations represented by the cookbooks in this study exemplify women's desire for social interaction and the role of foodwork in these organizations. Like numerous other women's organizations of this period, the Mount Desert Chapter of O.E.S., a co-ed organization open to Master Masons and their adult female relatives (but membership rolls indicate was overwhelmingly dominated by women), compiled two cookbooks, a 1903 edition separate from the cookbook discussed here. The impetus for their founding, as their history plainly states, was sociability. A brief history of the Mount Desert Chapter of O.E.S. opines, "the ladies of Somesville, desirous of enjoying more frequent opportunities of meeting together, held a number of meetings during the fall and winter of 1894, taking preliminary action toward the organization of a chapter of the Order of

[8] Anne M. Boylan, *The Origins of Women's Activism: New York and Boston, 1797-1840* (Chapel Hill: University of North Carolina Press, 2002), 18.

Eastern Star."[9] The creation of the Mount Desert Chapter provided the women of Somesville and surrounding villages with an opportunity to meet regularly at the Masonic Lodge and to attend to chapter business, as well as a chance to socialize outside of domestic spaces and obligations. The founding of the organization shortly after the construction of a Masonic Lodge in Somesville is likely no accident. The Lodge provided a convenient place to gather, and as an account of the chapter's founding discusses, many social events were held at the new hall, "but the ladies were not quite satisfied," the account notes, "they wished to have a secret organization."[10] The importance of the social aspect of membership to those in the Mount Desert Chapter cannot be overstated; the brief history notes twice that it was a desire for more opportunities for socialization that led to the establishment of the island's first chapter.

Swiss Lettuce Roll Salad – Mrs. Martha Richardson

One-half cup seedless raisins, ½ cup cottage cheese, ½ cup chopped walnuts, ½ cup mayonnaise, salt, pimento, 1 head lettuce. Mix thoroughly raisins, cheese and nuts. Spread the large crisp lettuce leaves thickly with the mixture and roll like a jelly-roll. Bind with strips of pimento. This is a good salad to serve with a large dinner.

Mount Desert Chapter No. 20, Order of the Eastern Star, *Favorite Recipes* (Ellsworth, ME: The American Print, c. 1929).

Appearing under a wide variety of names, female auxiliary organizations like ladies' guilds flourished in nearly all American denominations in the nineteenth and twentieth centuries. They were usually devoted to charity work within the community and beyond or the upkeep and social calendar for the church; these organizations provided church women with a socially-sanctioned activity outside their own homes. Founded in 1772, the Centre Street Congregational Church occupies a building erected in 1836-7.[11] Although less information about the Y.L.G. currently exists, both groups likely produced their cookbooks to support charitable causes related to their missions.

Community cookbooks were a particularly popular and potentially lucrative form of fundraising for women's groups in the late-nineteenth and early-twentieth-century, with more than three thousand published between 1864 and 1922.[12]

---

[9] *A Brief History of Mount Desert Chapter #20, O.E.S., 1894-1920*, 1, Mount Desert Island Historical Society. Somesville is one of several villages located within the town of Mount Desert.

[10] Somesville Clubs Collection, Mount Desert Island Historical Society.

[11] George W. Drisko, *Narrative of the town of Machias, the old and the new, the early and late (*Machias, ME: Press of the Republican, 1904); H.F. Harding, Memorial address on the occasion of the centennial anniversary of the formation of Centre Street Congregational Church at Machias, Me (Machias, ME: Printed by C.O. Furbush, 1884).

[12] Bob and Eleanor Brown, *Culinary Americana: Cookbooks Published in the Cities and Towns of the United States of America During the Years from 1860 through 1960* (New York:

Figure 12.2: Center Street. This c. 1938 postcard shows Center Street, Machias with the Centre Street Congregational Church in the left foreground. Courtesy of Boston Public Library.

Both copies of *Favorite Recipes* are regional examples of an activity practiced by groups of American women nationwide, from the Civil War era to the present. Community cookbooks—collections of recipes contributed by local women and published for sale—were perennial fundraisers for women's organizations. Compiled by groups of women, each recipe was attributed to a donor and often appeared with a few lines describing the merits of the particular recipe or suggesting an appropriate occasion for preparing the recipe. Cookbooks, like women themselves, were no longer relegated to the private sphere.

Creating a community cookbook allowed groups of women to gain experience in public life through collecting and organizing recipes, approaching local businesses to support the cookbook through advertising space, working with a publisher, and, finally, selling the finished product. As historian Anne Boylan identified, by balancing domestic duties and associational work, women operated in "an arena of feminine action that was neither strictly familial nor wholly public; it was 'private' but not 'retired.'"[13] Community cookbooks, by packaging domestic expertise to support organizational causes, are particularly illustrative of this in-between space crafted by organized women in the nineteenth century.

Not only was this essential experience for women outside their homes, but it also created a treasure trove of sources for the historian interested in women's

---

Roving Eye Press, 1961); Eleanor Lowenstein, *Bibliography of American Cookery Books, 1742-1860* (Worcester: American Antiquarian Society, 1972). In their efforts to compile and identify community cookbooks, the Browns and Lowenstein identified about three thousand community cookbooks published between the dates listed, however, due to the lack of an organized effort to collect these texts, they agree there could have been many more published during this period.

[13] Boylan, *The Origins of Women's Activism*, 91.

work and community foodways. Elizabeth Driver notes that "the control women exercised in every stage of the publishing process reinforces the notion that community cookbooks are an authentic expression of local practice."[14] These sources provide a picture of a community unlikely to be included in traditional historical sources: the ingredients available, the dishes enjoyed in homes and at social gatherings, and the role of women in producing community. A focus on food writing suggests consistency between the experiences of rural women in the eastern and western United States. In their articles, Mary Murphy (Murphy, Ch. 4, this volume) and Amy L. McKinney (McKinney, Ch. 6, this volume) reveal insights into life in rural Montana through examination of *The Guild Cookbook* (1910) and the Montana Rural Home that suggest the significant role of food in the lives of women despite regional and period differences.

Women's socializing during this period frequently revolved around food. These activities varied widely from hosting a tea party or luncheon, taking a dainty dish to an invalid friend, preparing cakes or other treats for an associational meeting, or preparing a full dinner for a fundraiser. As Anne L. Bower asserts in *Recipes for Reading: Community Cookbooks, Stories, Histories*, community cookbooks, "quietly or boldly tell of women's lives and beliefs."[15] These are, of course, as Bower reminds us, partial autobiographies. Since they are not intentionally biographical, the researcher must place these texts within the appropriate context to "glean from these texts much about how their women compilers saw themselves and projected their values."[16] In the case of the Downeast editions of *Favorite Recipes*, the context is not frugality or "waste not, want not," as we might easily assume for a relatively isolated and economically depressed region for much of its history. Socialization was the key impetus in the creation and utilization of these cookbooks.

From the collected recipes, a sense of local foodways emerges from the pages. Both special occasion cooking and the simple, hearty staples that composed daily fare are represented here. In the Mount Desert edition of *Favorite Recipes*, homey recipes like Brown Bread, Yankee Bean Soup, Halibut Loaf, and Mustard Pickles provided the foundation for simple family suppers. Both collections overwhelmingly focus on recipes for sweets. The members of the Young Ladies Guild in Machias divided the 189 recipes in their collection into seven sections: bread, cake, cookies, pies, pudding, salads, and supper. With this categorization, it should come as no surprise that nearly three-fourths of the recipes in the collection are for sweets. Recipes for puddings, doughnuts, cookies, cakes, and pies could be produced on Saturday baking days for a sweet ending to family dinners, a treat to tuck into a lunch box, to serve company throughout the coming week, or to share at an associational meeting. Many of these recipes make pervasive use of the staples of

[14] Elizabeth Driver, "Cookbooks as Primary Sources for Writing History," *Food, Culture, and Society* 12, no. 3 (2009), 271.

[15] Anne L. Bower, "Bound Together: Recipes, Lives, Stories, and Readings," in Anne L. Bower, ed., *Recipes for Reading: Community Cookbooks, Stories, Histories* (Amherst, MA: University of Massachusetts Press, 1997), 2.

[16] Anne L. Bower, "Our Sisters Recipes: Exploring 'Community' in a Community Cookbook," *Journal of Popular Culture* 31, no. 3 (1997), 137.

Figure 12.3: Tremont OES Installation. Organizational life afforded women opportunities for socialization. Members of the Mount Desert chapter may have attended the ceremonial induction of officers at the neighboring Tremont chapter, as depicted in this undated photograph. Courtesy of the Southwest Harbor Public Library.

nineteenth-century New England regional baking: raisins, molasses, brown sugar, cinnamon, nutmeg, and vanilla, as well as more exotic ingredients and increasingly available branded products.[17]

Both collections also reflect the emergence of a new type of cookery. Our present assumption, certainly for outsiders, is that Maine food culture revolves around local products: lobster, blueberries, maple syrup, etc. The collected recipes reveal the influence of national commercial brands and food systems (even global food systems) on the rural Downeast diet in the early twentieth century. Both cookbooks are overwhelmingly focused on non-local food sources. In the Mount Desert edition of *Favorite Recipes*, 41% of the recipes directly reference a commercial product or call for an ingredient that could not be sourced locally (canned pineapple or shredded coconut). These name brand products include Pillsbury's Health Bran, Kellogg's All Bran, Dunham's Coconut, Karo Syrup, Dot Chocolate, and Quaker Oats, or ingredients that were made available by technological advances and national and international transportation networks, including various canned products, tropical fruits, marshmallows, puffed rice, and peanut butter. The compilers of the Machias edition of *Favorite Recipes* were less likely to reference a specific name brand product (two products explicitly mentioned are Swansdown Cake Flour and Karo Syrup); however, a number of ingredients could potentially represent nationally advertised products. These include canned pineapple, dates, chocolate, cocoa, gelatin, cornstarch, and various canned vegetables. Like their counterparts in Mount Desert, the home cooks of Machias clearly had access to global food networks with two recipes for bananas included in the collection.

[17] Sandra L. Oliver, *Food in Colonial and Federal America* (Westport, CT: Greenwood Press, 2005); Diane Tye, "A Poor Man's Meal," *Food, Culture & Society* 11, no. 3 (2008): 225-353.

Cocoanut [sic] Dainties

1 scant cup flour, ¼ cup butter, inch of soda, cream together and put on bottom of paper covered pan. Beat 2 eggs, add 1 ¼ cups brown sugar, 1 ½ cups cocoanut, ½ cup walnuts, 2 tbsp. flour, ¼ tsp. baking powder, salt, vanilla. Put on top of other mixture and cook slowly. Let set in pan until cold.

Florence Moan, The Young Ladies Guild of the Congregational Church, *Favorite Recipes* (Machias, ME, 1936).

Conversely, recipes referencing specific local products are relatively rare. Many staple ingredients such as butter, milk, and lard were likely sourced within the community, but the specific notation of local ingredients is rare. In the Mount Desert edition of *Favorite Recipes*, a minimal number of the recipes, just four out of 175, explicitly reference a locally available ingredient (clams, blueberries, maple syrup, and alewives). In the Machias collection, the number of recipes specifically referencing a local ingredient is slightly larger than Mount Desert with recipes utilizing blackberries, dandelion flowers, potatoes, maple syrup, and green corn. Curiously, this cookbook compiled in the home of the Wild Blueberry Festival and at the center of Maine's current wild blueberry production offers not one recipe using blueberries. However, the Mount Desert collection includes several. Recipes for fish are similarly rare with just five.

Blueberry Muffins – Margaret Richardson

One-third cup sugar, ½ cup shortening, 1 egg, 1 cup milk, 2 ¾ cups flour, 4 teaspoons baking powder, ½ teaspoon salt, 1 cup berries, floured.

Blueberry Cake – Mrs. Heath

Three eggs, 1 cup sugar, ½ cup melted butter, 1 cup milk, 4 cups flour, 1 ½ teaspoons cream of tartar, 1 teaspoon soda, 1 pint blueberries.

Mount Desert Chapter No. 20, Order of the Eastern Star, *Favorite Recipes* (Ellsworth, ME: The American Print, c. 1929).

A glance at these data might suggest the early twentieth-century residents of Mount Desert and Machias overwhelmingly ate commercial, processed foods. I would argue for a different interpretation: the ladies of O.E.S. and the Y.L.G. collected recipes utilizing commercial brands or newly available products because that is what they believed their audience wanted. Who could sell a cookbook composed entirely of recipes for baked beans, corned beef hash, fish chowder, or salt fish dinner in Downeast Maine? Undoubtedly, each potential cookbook buyer already possessed tried and true methods for producing these staples. What local women likely were searching for was instruction on how to use new food products, both to produce meals for their families and to support their participation in organizational life.

For both groups, the recipes reflect the types of cooking performed at home (simple family suppers, reliable and inexpensive sweets like molasses cookies to tuck into lunch boxes), but their overall focus is the cooking and baking women did as part of organizational life. For the members of the Young Ladies Guild, hosting Guild Suppers was an essential part of their support for the church. The inclusion of an addendum to their cookbook, providing a guide for planning these events with sample menus and amounts of ingredients speaks to their popularity. Community suppers like those organized by the Guild, sustained both the community and the church, providing a delicious meal and an opportunity for socializing as well as filling the church's coffers. Though rarely acknowledged, fundraising dinners and other events organized by church women's groups were frequently the most successful development activities for ecclesiastical institutions.[18]

In planning to serve a menu of fruit cocktail, creamed chicken with pastry squares, mashed potatoes, buttered peas and carrots, rolls, and dessert, the members of the Guild relied on several conveniences to ease the burden of such a considerable task. These included obtaining a large sponge cake from a baker to be cut into squares for the Peach Shortcake. The greatest time savers, however, were canned fruits and vegetables. The ladies served canned fruit salad supplemented with canned crushed pineapple, grapefruit segments, and cherries. Canned peas and carrots composed the vegetable side dish for the main course, and the sweet finale relied on five large cans of sliced peaches. These products significantly reduced the labor involved to feed seventy-five diners.

Date Bars

2 eggs beaten, 1 cup brown sugar, ¾ cup flour, ½ tsp. baking powder, ½ teas. salt, nuts, dates and 1 teaspoon vanilla. Bake in pan and cut in strips.

Katherine MacLauchlan, The Young Ladies Guild of the Congregational Church, *Favorite Recipes* (Machias, ME, 1936).

The ladies of the Mount Desert Chapter of O.E.S. were also known for their skill in the kitchen and the recipes within their collection suggest the importance of this social function. While there is no lack of substantial family fare, recipes for cakes, cookies, salads, and other delicacies that may have formed the menu for a ladies' luncheon or an afternoon tea are well represented in *Favorite Recipes*. It is quite possible that these recipes provided the foundation for the menus of suppers served at officer appointments and regular chapter meetings. Newspaper accounts of the Mount Desert Chapter's activities frequently note the quality of the spread, such as the comment that "delicious refreshments were served at the close of the chapter" meeting in January of 1932.[19] Snowball Salad, Pineapple Fluff, Date Bars, and a wide range of cake recipes hint at the sort of confections provided at these events.

---

[18] Diane Tye, *Baking as Biography: A Life Story in Recipes* (Montreal & Kingston: McGill-Queen's University Press, 2010), 109-110.

[19] "Somesville," *Bar Harbor Record* (Jan. 27, 1932): 7.

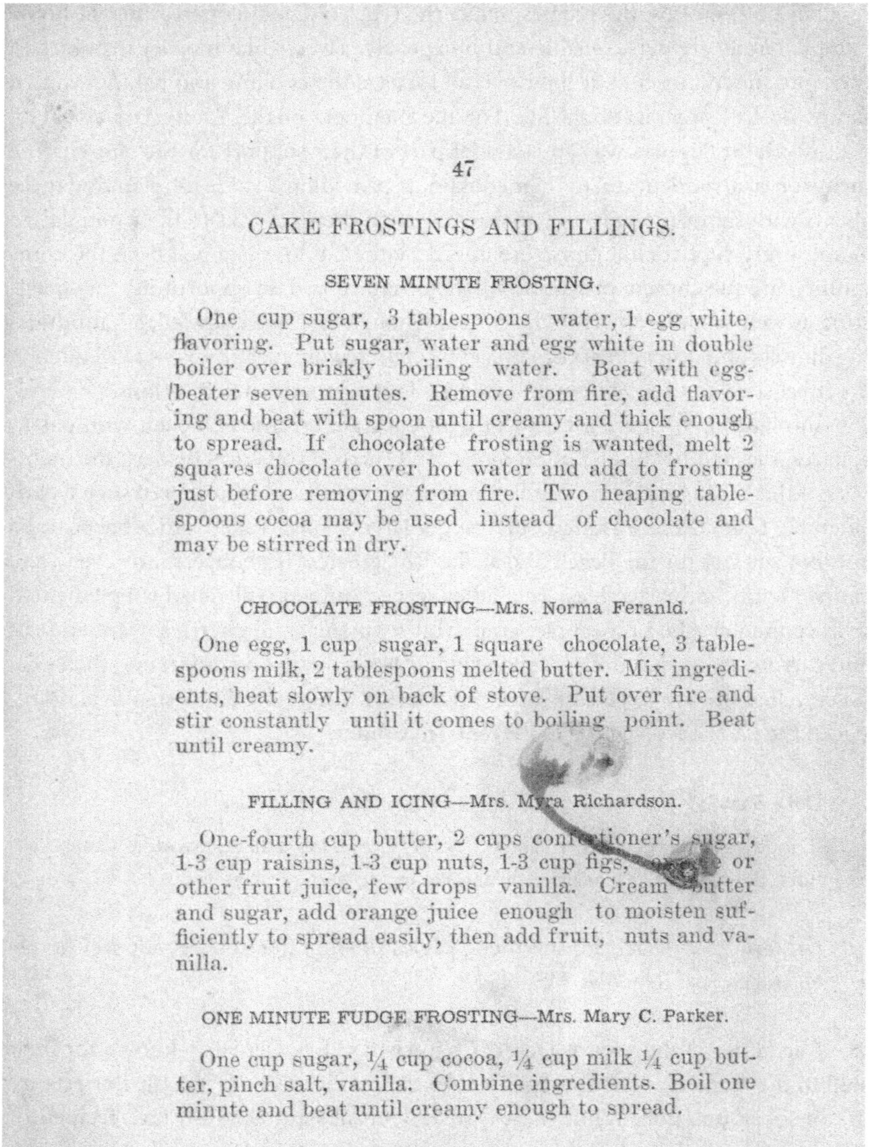

47

CAKE FROSTINGS AND FILLINGS.

SEVEN MINUTE FROSTING.

One cup sugar, 3 tablespoons water, 1 egg white, flavoring. Put sugar, water and egg white in double boiler over briskly boiling water. Beat with egg-beater seven minutes. Remove from fire, add flavoring and beat with spoon until creamy and thick enough to spread. If chocolate frosting is wanted, melt 2 squares chocolate over hot water and add to frosting just before removing from fire. Two heaping tablespoons cocoa may be used instead of chocolate and may be stirred in dry.

CHOCOLATE FROSTING—Mrs. Norma Feranld.

One egg, 1 cup sugar, 1 square chocolate, 3 tablespoons milk, 2 tablespoons melted butter. Mix ingredients, heat slowly on back of stove. Put over fire and stir constantly until it comes to boiling point. Beat until creamy.

FILLING AND ICING—Mrs. Myra Richardson.

One-fourth cup butter, 2 cups confectioner's sugar, 1-3 cup raisins, 1-3 cup nuts, 1-3 cup figs, orange or other fruit juice, few drops vanilla. Cream butter and sugar, add orange juice enough to moisten sufficiently to spread easily, then add fruit, nuts and vanilla.

ONE MINUTE FUDGE FROSTING—Mrs. Mary C. Parker.

One cup sugar, 1/4 cup cocoa, 1/4 cup milk 1/4 cup butter, pinch salt, vanilla. Combine ingredients. Boil one minute and beat until creamy enough to spread.

Figure 12.4: *Favorite Recipes*, page 47. This page of cake frostings and fillings from the Mount Desert edition of *Favorite Recipes* provides a sense of recipes that may have appeared at the close of chapter meetings. Photograph by Jennifer Steen Booher provided courtesy of the Mount Desert Island Historical Society.

Regular association meetings served a critical purpose for the women who organized them. For both the women of O.E.S. and the Y.L.G., their organizations' functions offered, as Diane Tye has argued, "rare opportunities for sociability, personal growth, and even social change. They provided women with culturally approved social outlets and allowed them time away from family responsibilities."[20] For women of the late-nineteenth and early-twentieth centuries, participation in a women's group connected to a church or charitable cause allowed for two indulgences: sweets and time away from their domestic roles. In this sense, as Tye contends, "Banana Bread and Pineapple Squares were subversive in that they helped to carve out precious social time for women."[21] Another layer to the rebellion is the use of early convenience products like cornstarch, gelatin, canned fruits, and more to save labor while producing a dessert worthy of sharing at a social gathering or submitting to a community cookbook.

Pineapple Fluff – Mrs. L.P. Somes

One-fourth pound marshmallows, ½ can pineapple (4 slices), 1 tablespoon lemon juice, ½ pint cream. Cut marshmallows in small pieces and soak in juice of pineapple; there should be ¾ of a cup of juice. If not enough a little orange juice may be added. Add the pineapple, cut into small cubes, and the lemon juice. Set in a cool place until just before serving, then fold in cream stiffly whipped.

Mount Desert Chapter No. 20, Order of the Eastern Star, *Favorite Recipes* (Ellsworth, ME: The American Print, c. 1929).

In this sense, both recipe books are perfectly suited to the women who created them and their increasingly organized network of friends, family, and neighbors. Recipes suitable for quick, hearty, and wholesome family meals and for impressing guests, or fellow attendees of a neighborhood potluck, comingle within the cookbook. The recipes perform the dual function of producing food items simply, quickly, and with easily accessible ingredients – increasingly those produced by national brands and intended to be laborsaving or provide access to previously inaccessible items. The ability to quickly prepare a satisfying meal for the family and a sweet dainty to share with members of the organization were essential factors for allowing women to participate in activities outside the domestic sphere.

Acknowledgements

The Mount Desert Island Historical Society (https://mdihistory.org/) and Special Collections at the University of Maine's Fogler Library supported this research project as did research assistance by University of Maine students Harley Rogers and Caitlin Hillery.

---

[20] Tye, *Baking as Biography*, 161.

[21] Tye, *Baking as Biography*, 162.

—13—

Kitchen Joy

Cherisse Jones-Branch

Mount Horr African Methodist Episcopal Church

Hollywood, South Carolina, USA, 21st Century

This is a sampling of recipes printed in *Kitchen Joy*, a heritage cookbook published in 2017 by the Mount Horr African Methodist Episcopal Church located in Hollywood, South Carolina (Charleston County). Many of the recipes in the cookbook require seafood (shrimp, crab, etc.) which have long been consumed by African Americans descended from the Gullah people of the South Carolina lowcountry. Consisting of Africans from diverse ethnic groups from West Africa, the Gullah created a hybrid or creole language that permitted communication across barriers.[1] Gullah cultural and culinary traditions transcended generations and are still prevalent in the South Carolina lowcountry, Georgia, and Florida where plantations utilizing enslaved labor were prevalent. Some of the recipes presented in *Kitchen Joy*, such as the one for okra soup, are directly derived from the contributors' African ancestors for whom this would have been a staple dish that was usually eaten with rice. All of the recipes below are still to this day, commonly found in and around the surrounding area and in some cases, have become popular dishes served to tourists in local restaurants. They can also be found in other parts of the country as a part of the cultural heritage and foodways black South Carolinians carried with them as they migrated to different parts of the country or passed recipes from one generation to the next.

[1] "Geechee and Gullah Culture," https://www.georgiaencyclopedia.org/articles/arts-culture/geechee-and-gullah-culture and "Gullah History," http://www.beaufortsc.org/guides/gullah-history/. For more information, see also Cornelia Bailey, with Christena Bledsoe, *God, Dr. Buzzard, and the Bolito Man: A Saltwater Geechee Talks about Life on Sapelo Island* (New York: Doubleday, 2000) and Charles Colcock Jones, Jr., *Gullah Folktales from the Georgia Coast*, (Athens: University of Georgia Press, 2000).

Crab Cakes

1 can crab meat
1 egg
1 Tbsp Dijon mustard
½ cup of bread crumbs
½ Tsp baking powder
1 Tbsp. Worcestershire sauce
juice of ½ a lemon
½ onion, chopped
½ bell pepper, chopped

Mix all ingredients together except crabmeat. Then fold crabmeat into mixture and make patties. Place in greased frying pan and sauté on stovetop or bake in oven until done.

Spoon Bread

3 cups of milk
1 cup self-rising corn meal
2 Tbsp of butter or margarine
4 egg yolks, beaten
4 egg whites

Heat milk in large saucepan; stir in butter or margarine until melted. Gradually stir in cornmeal. Cook over medium heat until mixture boils; cook stirring one minute longer. Remove from heat and cool slightly. Stir egg yolk into cornmeal mixture until well blended. Beat egg whites until stiff, but not dry; fold into cornmeal mixture. Pour into greased 2 quart casserole. Bake in preheated over (350 degrees) for 45 to 50 minute, or until deep golden brown. Serve immediately.

Okra Soup

1 large onion, sliced
1 celery stalk, chopped
¼ cup of bell pepper
garlic powder
Adobo seasoning
black pepper
pinch of red pepper
salt to taste
2 to 3 lbs of fresh or frozen cut up okra
2 cups of water
2 lbs smoked neck bones
2 Tbsp. oil

2 lbs pig tails or spare rib tips
onion powder
1 can (14.5 oz) tomato sauce
a pinch of Accent seasoning
2 cans (14.5 oz) stewed tomatoes

Precook the meats. Do not overcook. In a skillet stir fry the okra in hot oil with the onions, green peppers, and celery for 10 minutes until no longer slimy, set aside. In a large pot, put the stewed tomatoes, tomato sauce, water, and a pinch of sugar. Let boil down for about ten minutes. Add the seasonings to taste. Combine the okra mix, tomato mix, and meats and simmer for about 10 to 15 minutes.

Wild Rice Fried Shrimp

2 Tbsp oil
2 lbs frozen shrimp, thawed
2 boxes Uncle Ben's Original Wild Rice (6.25 oz)

Heat oil in skillet over medium heat. Add thawed shrimp, cook until pink. Drain. Cook rice according to package. Add the shrimp.

Frogmore Stew

Corn on the cob, cut into chunks
Shrimp, unpeeled
Smoked sausage, cut into chunks
Butter
Small red potatoes, quartered
Seafood seasoning
Bell pepper, onions and celery, diced

Ingredients are to your taste and preference. Clean and prepare the vegetables and sausage. Boil some water in a large pot that can hold all of your ingredients. Add everything except the shrimp. Cook until nearly done. Add the shrimp, cooking them just until they turn pink. Serve hot.

—14—

"Hospitality was their byword": Food, Tradition, and Creativity in Borderlands Kitchens

Mary Murphy

In 1906 Sarah Roberts, her husband and three of their six children took up a homestead about sixty miles east of Stettler, Alberta. Dr. and Mrs. Roberts were in their fifties. Roberts, a physician, had, because of his own ill health, lost his medical practice and virtually all of the family's resources. Believing that "an active outdoor life" might rescue him and inspired by the success of neighbors who had homesteaded close to Stettler, the family moved from Illinois to Canada. As Sarah wrote, they hoped to acquire "a competence" for their "declining years" and enough money to send their three unmarried sons to college.[1]

One day during the first months on their claim, a young man drove up to their tent, and asked if he could water his stock and have a loaf of bread. Sarah was happy to give him water for they had been fortunate in digging a good well. But she had to tell him that they had scarcely enough bread for their own dinner. Undaunted, the young man asked if she could bake him some biscuit. This request, too, Sarah had to deny, as she had no oven. Finally, he asked if could make "some porritch" on her camp stove. Happily, she said yes, and then gave him some milk and dried applesauce, the latter, as she noted, "quite a luxury."[2]

What were the expectations of hospitality in settler society? Coming into a new country meant entering a world of strangers, riding a seesaw of generosity and suspicion, focusing on one's own survival, and crafting a community. As women made homes on farms, ranches, and in towns and villages, one of their primary responsibilities was feeding their families. But, food also figured as an instrument of binding neighbors and friends together, of establishing relationships of reciprocity, of accruing status and reputation. Food figured not just as fuel, but also as a means of culinary diplomacy.

Sarah Roberts provides several examples of the balancing act that homesteaders managed in their early years. On the journey to their claim, the Roberts' provisions had dwindled to the makings of a few pancakes. One morning when they had lost the trail, they saw a house in the distance and drove up to get directions.

[1] Sarah Ellen Roberts, *Alberta Homestead Chronicle of a Pioneer Family*, ed. Lathrop E. Roberts (Austin: University of Texas Press, 1968).

[2] Roberts, *Alberta Homestead Chronicle*, 35.

Mrs. Carter, the woman of the house, invited Sarah to use her stove to cook their breakfast, but Sarah was both embarrassed by how little she had and fearful that once Mrs. Carter saw her meager food stock, she would feel obliged to contribute something. Sarah did not want to be a burden, and the Robertses drove on. Years later, when Sarah saw Mrs. Carter, she told her why they had not stopped, and Carter laughed because she shared the same experience: before her family had reached their claim, they had nothing but flour and water, and she thought they were going to starve.[3]

Settlers' stories from both sides of the U.S.-Canada border repeatedly tell this tale. Pride is obviously a factor, and in some stories, there is clearly a gendered component to this negotiation. Men did not want to appear unable to provide for their families, and women supported them in their masquerade. It was more the norm than the exception that the first year or so of settling often included times of hunger, but if, as time passed, families still went without adequate food—regardless of the circumstances—men appeared to feel it reflected on their competence, and they went to great lengths to disguise their family's hunger.[4]

Hard Times Pudding

One cup suet chopped fine, one large cup raisins, three teacups sifted flour, one cup sweet milk, one cup molasses, one teaspoon soda, pinch of salt. Put in a greased bowl and steam. Improves with heating.

Mrs. G. M. MGuire, *The Guild Cook Book*, Semans, Sask. 1910

Consideration was also an important component of Sarah Roberts's behavior. Sarah did not want to compromise Mrs. Carter's food supply. When Sarah dipped into her special stores to provide applesauce to the young man who stopped by their tent, she did the exact thing she hoped to spare Mrs. Carter. Sarah could stretch her supply to be generous to one young man; she did not know if Carter could stretch hers to feed five. It was not only that many settlers were poor, but in many homesteading areas, food was difficult to obtain. Once families established gardens and could put up produce, once they had some livestock, they could cushion hard times. But even so, many staples had to be purchased, especially for the winter: stockpiles of coffee, tea, flour, sugar, dried fruit, beans, etc. Such purchases entailed extensive planning and several days of travel by wagon to and from a town.[5] As one woman recalled, "Every bit of food was so precious; it all had to be carted such a distance. There was no margin for failure; and a bad batch of bread was a subject for tears."[6]

---

[3] Roberts, *Alberta Homestead Chronicle*, 18.

[4] For examples, see Sanora Babb, *An Owl on Every Post* (New York: McCall, 1970) and Mary Murphy, *Hope in Hard Times* (Helena: Montana Historical Society Press, 2003).

[5] See, for example, Percy Wollaston, *Homesteading* (New York: The Lyons Press, 1977), 49-50.

[6] Betty G. R. Shaw, "Childhood Memories," *Alberta History* 35, no. 2 (1987): 26.

However, as farmers became more rooted and families had better food supplies, food preparation became a way for women to distinguish themselves. Betty Shaw, whose family homesteaded near Leslieville, Alberta, recalled a "friendly rivalry [arose] amongst the womenfolk to outdo each other, not only in hospitality but in quality of cooking." One became known for her "wonderful pickled carrots"; another was "a wizard at light buns"; Betty's own mother was "famous for her wheat cakes," and no matter what, she always seemed to have a coconut cake ready for company.[7] The cooking skills that homesteading women polished provided physical and emotional sustenance. Carrie Young, the youngest of six children raised on a North Dakota homestead wrote, "My recall of the harshest of these years is mitigated by the goodness of my mother's food and that of her neighbors. These homestead wives, most of them daughters of Scandinavian immigrants, knew how to 'make do,' and they made do very well, indeed. Despair was never so great that it couldn't be pushed back by coffee and *fattigman* fresh from the lard kettle at four o'clock in the afternoon."[8]

Fattigmand No.1

8 yolks of eggs
12 tablespoons heavy whipping cream
4 whole eggs
½ teaspoon cardamom
12 tablespoons sugar
flour to roll

First beat yolks till light and lemon colored. Then add sugar. Beat again. Beat egg whites and add. Then add cream, flavoring, and flour. Roll very thin. Cut with tracing wheel and fry in deep fat to a nice light brown.

George W. Mohn, *Cook Book of Popular Norse Recipes*, 3rd ed., Northfield, Minn., 1924

Pride in cooking took on more elaborate forms for women who lived in cities and villages in the emerging state of Montana and the neighboring provinces of Alberta and Saskatchewan. Close proximity to neighbors and ready access to groceries and water made easier their responsibilities of hospitality. But, town life—even in the smallest villages—also ratcheted up expectations. As Rachel Snell

---

[7] Shaw, "Childhood Memories," 26.

[8] Carrie Young, with Felicia Young, *Prairie Cooks: Glorified Rice, Three-Day Buns, and other Reminiscences* (Iowa City: University of Iowa Press, 1993), ix. Known as a poor man's cookie, fattigman was a deep fat fried Norwegian cookie. It is variously spelled as fattigman, fattigmann, fattigmand. There are 11 different recipes for the cookie in George W. Mohn, *Cook Book of Popular Norse Recipes*, 3rd ed. (Northfield, MN: Mohn Printing Co., 1924), 65-68. The basic ingredients were eggs, sugar, cream, and flour; most were flavored with cardamom.

points out in her essay in this volume, women across the United States and Canada were committed to "an organizational life." Borderlands women organized into all kinds of clubs and auxiliaries in the late nineteenth and early twentieth centuries, clubs organized for self-education and social improvement. One of their tried-and-true fundraisers was the community cookbook, compiled and written by women for women.[9] In addition to telling us something about what western families ate in the late nineteenth and early twentieth centuries, these cookbooks also tell us about the lives of middle and lower middle-class town-dwelling women. As Snell notes, these community cookbooks provide a rich supplement to other sources of social history, allowing us to get rare glimpses of the personalities of otherwise anonymous women, as well the costs and sources of food supplies, the meals women cooked and the dishes they aspired to cook.[10]

Ginger Cordial

4 lbs white sugar, 5 cts worth of burnt sugar, 5 cts worth essence of ginger, 5 cts red pepper, 5 cts worth tartaric acid, one gallon of water. Get the burnt sugar and other stuff at druggists which he mixes in a bottle all but acid which you add to the water yourself, then other stuff and stir. Then put on the stove and let come to a boil, take off and put in bottles.

Mrs. Munro, *Rosetown Presbyterian Ladies Cook Book*, Rosetown, Sask., 1913

The ladies of the Semans, Saskatchewan Presbyterian Guild produced *The Guild Cook Book* in 1910, a considerable achievement considering that Semans, a wheat-growing village north of Regina, on the Grand Trunk Pacific Railway, had only been founded in 1908 and had only 194 residents in 1911. Thirty-one women,

[9] According to Elizabeth Driver, who compiled a comprehensive bibliography of Canadian cookbooks published prior to 1950, Saskatchewan produced a few community cookbooks before it achieved provincial status, and Alberta's first volumes appeared a year or two after the province was created in 1905. In Montana, which became a territory in 1864 and a state in 1889, the first documented cookbook, compiled by the "Ladies of Butte City" appeared in 1881. Elizabeth Driver, *Culinary Landmarks: A Bibliography of Canadian Cookbooks, 1825-1949* (Toronto: University of Toronto Press, 2008).

[10] There are several ways to look at these early cookbooks. Food studies scholars are in agreement that community cookbooks are for the most part trustworthy sources for telling us about the food that people ate and they ways in which they cooked it. The recipes were contributed by members of the community and often included little notes, such as "this is good" or "my mother's favorite" or "this is a nice dessert in hot weather." The titles often include the adjectives "tried" and "tested." In one case, Mrs. Peter A. Spoelstra of Manhattan, Montana contributed a recipe for Deviled Cabbage Wedges with a mustard sauce, and subtitled it, "Children Won't Eat Cabbage? Try This." Dorcas Guild, *Sharing Our Favorites* (Manhattan, MT: Manhattan Christian Reformed Church, n.d.), 154. The fact that many women only contributed one or two recipes and occasionally annotated them suggests that they shared recipes their families enjoyed, although there is, of course, no guarantee of that. It is important to recognize this because commercial cookbooks are often aspirational; in other words, people intend to cook the recipes, or replicate the menus, but often purchase cookbooks without ever using them.

16% of the town's population, contributed 288 recipes.[11] Two, Mrs. J. N. Smith and Mrs. A. E. Olson proffered over thirty recipes each. *The Guild Cook Book* had no out-of-the-ordinary chapters. From soup to beverages, it was full of recipes one could find in any North American cookbook of the time. Like the residents of Semans, most of the recipes were British in origin.

Other authors in this volume have noted the preponderance of commercial products in mid-twentieth century cookbooks and farm publications. Both Rachel Snell in her analysis of Maine community cookbooks from 1929 and 1936 (Snell, Ch. 12, this volume) and Amy McKinney's analysis of the post-World War II *Montana Farmer-Stockman* (McKinney, Ch. 16, this volume) identify the numerous brand-named goods and canned fruits featured in women's recipes. All depended on transportation. In the early twentieth century, which saw the great boom of homesteading in the U.S. and Canadian grasslands, that meant the railroad. In Alberta, Saskatchewan, and Montana, the main and branch lines of the Canadian Pacific, Great Northern, Northern Pacific, and Milwaukee railroads connected metropolitan centers of commercial food production and wholesale grocers to homesteads and hamlets. While early twentieth century community cookbooks do not reference brands as frequently as those from the mid-century, the recipes are still dependent on imported foodstuffs. The lemons, bananas, haddock, oysters, molasses, ginger, almonds, and cocoanut that appeared so often in their favorite and tested recipes were not foods of the prairies and Rocky Mountains. Like the women themselves, they were immigrants to this territory.

Gertrude Smith and Mrs. A. E. Olson (I've been unable to discover her first name) were representative of the women in the Semans Presbyterian Guild. All the contributors to its cookbook were "plain cooks." Mrs. Olson's recipes offered more extensive directions than most, and her savory dishes often called for an attractive garnish. She had a significant advantage over many women of the town. Her husband, "Semans' Pioneer Hardware Merchant," sold stoves. We cannot know for sure, but presumably she did her cooking on the most modern of appliances. Mrs. Olson contributed to virtually every chapter of the Semans cookbook: directions for celery soup, cream codfish, roast turkey, wilted lettuce, baked eggs. She was apparently not much interested in dessert; only "Delicate Cake"—a plain white cake—bears her name. Her recipe for "Raw Oysters on Ice" captured her sense of style as well as one way of serving this very popular delicacy that rail-transport made available across the west.[12]

---

[11] Semans and District Historical Society, *Always a Hometown: Semans and District History* (Semans, Sask: Semans and District Historical Society, 1982) and *The Guild Cook Book* (Semans, Sask.: Gazette Print, 1913).

[12] Paul L. Hedren, "The West Loved Oysters Too! A Look at That Time in America When Those Briny Bivalves Were All the Rage, Even beyond the Missouri River," *Montana Magazine of Western History* 61, no. 4 (Winter 2011): 3-15, 90-91.

Raw Oysters on Ice

Take a block of perfectly clear ice, heat a flat iron, and with it melt out a square cavity, leaving the walls and bottom about one and a half inches thick. Empty all the water out, fill the cavity with fresh blue points. Fold a napkin, place on a large platter; stand the ice on this and garnish with smilax, then here and there among the smilax slices of lemon may be placed.

Mrs. A. E. Olson, *The Guild Cook Book*, Semans, Sask. 1910

Gertrude and J. N. Smith had come to Semans from Ontario; she had studied nursing; her husband claimed a homestead and bought the Massey Harris tractor business in 1908. Both Smiths were active in community organizations: J. N. served on the school board and town council and was a member of the Odd Fellows and Masonic Lodges. Gertrude joined the church choir, Ladies Aid, Sunday School, Eastern Star, and Red Cross. They were community builders. Their daughter, Orma, recalled that her parents got to know other village families by entertaining each other in their homes, and they made an effort "to maintain the refinements to which they were accustomed before coming west."[13] Like Mrs. Olson, Gertrude Smith contributed recipes to all chapters of *The Guild Cook Book*, including several classic English sweet puddings, such as the meringue-topped Queen of Puddings, which no doubt made an impressive finish to these festive meals. In addition to house parties, the Olsons and Smiths attended larger socials at the hotel, where "menus including delicacies" were served.[14]

The Guild Cook Book spoke to these culinary aspirations. Like many community cookbooks, it included a few pages of boilerplate material drawn from other sources. The Presbyterian ladies chose to print a three-page description of Table Service. No matter how much they desired to maintain more metropolitan refinements, it is unlikely that the ladies of Semans actually put this protocol into full practice. The section provided detailed instructions for setting an elaborate table and the order of service for a fourteen-course meal. At least one Semans woman had a sense of humor about table presentation. As an anonymous contributor to *The Guild Cook Book*, she provided a recipe for "An Apple Sea Serpent": a novel, and edible, centerpiece.

An Apple Sea Serpent

Here is rather an amusing dish, but all of which can be eaten. Take a large banana, a large and a small apple, two currants and some strips of candied peel. Make your sea monster's head of the small apple—a nice green one looks most terrifying—and cut his mouth and eyes, putting currants for the pupils and strips of candied peel for the teeth. The body is made by cutting up the other apple in thick slices and then the banana the same way for the tail. Place in a bed of jelly or boiled rice, and you have a sweetmeat which will be quite a curiosity.

The Guild Cook Book, Semans, Sask. 1910

---

[13] Semans and District Historical Society, *Always a Hometown*, 461-63.

[14] Semans and District Historical Society, *Always a Hometown*, 462.

Other community cookbooks also reflect the goal of refinement.[15] In 1911, a Regina cookbook compiled by the Ladies' Aid Society of the Metropolitan Methodist Church included advertisements for silver-plated ware, fine cut glass, pearl-handled cutlery sets, and fine china. The Peart Brothers Hardware store claimed to supply everything women needed to prepare "a dainty meal."[16] Dainty meals were not the meals women cooked every day for their families, but the beautifully presented light meals that women prepared for each other. In that sense, these cookbooks give us a glimpse into the kinds of foods that represented women's "best face."

In most of the cookbooks, like that from Semans, recipes were basic and utilitarian. But, all included dozens of recipes for foods that could be served at ladies' luncheons or teas. Some books had specific sections for tea and luncheon dishes. Recipes included anchovy canapes, pig-in-blankets (bacon-wrapped oysters served on toast), carrot timbales, stuffed baked cucumbers, mock pate de foie-gras (made with calf's liver). [17] The Ladies Aid of Calgary's Knox Church included in its cookbook a chapter on Dainty Dishes and a section on Afternoon Tea Cakes. The "dainty dishes" comprised fruited jellies and puddings and various mousses, many composed in decorative molds—not everyday fare. And unlike some of the other Protestant ladies' groups, the Presbyterians had no objection to spirits. The Ladies Aid recipes called for sherry, whisky, and champagne. Even the more humble Semans cookbook had recipes for molded desserts and tea sandwiches.

Coffee Mousse

Take ½ cup ground coffee, pour 3 gills boiling water on it, cook as you do coffee and strain into bowl; let cool; add the beaten yolks of 4 eggs and a cup of sugar to the coffee, and let cook 3 minutes after the mixture begins to boil; let cool; beat 1 pint of cream until almost butter, pour into mixture, and after beating all thoroughly, turn into tin mould; pack in salt and ice and let stand 4 or 5 hours.

Knox Church Ladies' Aid Cook Book, Calgary, Alberta, 1919

In 1908 ladies "of and near Harrison, Montana," a town of about 200 people in southwest Montana, met to form a club "to promote sociability and help any cause which may seem expedient." They agreed to gather at a member's home every other Thursday from 2 to 5 p.m. and chose "Mystic Circle" as their club name. At their fourth meeting they discussed the question of whether the hostess should serve refreshments and decided to vote on the matter at the next meeting. Orra Marshall hosted that gathering and, as the minutes record, "took the initiative in serving delicious refreshments." The secretary reported a slight kerfuffle when "some sug-

---

[15] Andrea G. Radke, "Refining Rural Spaces: Women and Vernacular Gentility in the Great Plains, 1880-1920," *Great Plains Quarterly* 24, no. 4 (Fall 2004): 227-48; Leslie Holmes, "Westward the Course of Empire Takes Its Way Through Tea," *Past Imperfect* 16 (2010): 66-91.

[16] Ladies' Aid Society of Metropolitan Methodist Church, *Recipes* (Regina, Saskatchewan, 1911), 4, 13, 26.

[17] Ladies Aid, Branch "E" Knox Church, *Cook Book* (Calgary, Alberta, 1919).

gested fining her as we had not yet voted to serve refreshments," and went on to note, "they became very quiet when she said she wouldn't serve them if they were going to fine her."[18]

Marshall's initiative won the day and from that meeting forward "delicious refreshments were daintily served by the hostess." In 1910 the ladies reorganized themselves into a new club. A few things seem to have gone awry. First, they found themselves doing too much work, and second, it appears that they had fallen into a refreshments arms race. Reconstituting themselves the "Daughters of Leisure," the group amended its bylaws to forbid work at club meetings and to limit the hostess to serving only "three things."[19]

Dream Sandwiches

Take one-half cup pecan nut meats, one-half cup stoned raisins, one apple, and add juice of one-half lemon, one dessert spoonful of sugar. Mix well and spread between buttered slices of bread. Dream sandwiches are delicious to serve with lemonade.

Mrs. H. S. Flint, Big Sandy, *The Fort Benton Cook Book*, Fort Benton, Montana, 1916

Food is a basic necessity of life, but memoirs, minutes, and cookbooks demonstrate that it was also a key to hospitality. And hospitality was a key ingredient of settler society. Anthropologist Tom Selwyn writes, "Hospitality converts: strangers into familiars, enemies into friends, friends into better friends, outsiders into insiders, non-kin into kin."[20] In western Canada and the United States, offering food became a means of binding people to each other through webs of reciprocity. It was a source of comfort and a source of anxiety when there was little to be had and the strictures of hospitality could not be met. Food was also a key to social differentiation. Successful production and beautiful presentation accrued status and prestige for housewives who had little other means of gaining recognition.

Many community cookbooks included "metaphorical recipes," the most widely reprinted was "How to Cook a Husband."[21] But the *"Prairie Rose" Cook Book*, compiled by the Prairie Rose Lodge of the Women's Section of the United Farmers of Canada in Craik, Saskatchewan included a recipe for the "The Cook." The compilers gave no attribution, but the "recipe" was drawn partly from a lecture John Ruskin delivered at an English girls' school in the 1860s. It was subsequently extracted and reprinted many times as the frontispiece to cookbooks. In response

---

[18] Mystic Circle, Daughters of Leisure Minute Book, July 23, 1908-June 13, 1910, folder 5, box 3, Harrison Woman's Club Records, 1908-1970, MC 342, Montana Historical Society Archives, Helena, Montana.

[19] Mystic Circle Minute Book.

[20] Tom Selwyn, "An Anthropology of Hospitality," in *In Search of Hospitality: Theoretical Perspectives and Debates*, eds., Conrad Lashley and Alison Morrison (Oxford: Butterworth-Heinemann, 2000), 18.

[21] Gary Draper, "Dishing Dad: 'How to Cook a Husband' and Other Metaphorical Recipes" in *What's to Eat? Entrées in Canadian Food History*, ed., Nathalie Cooke (Montreal & Kingston: McGill-Queen's University Press, 2009), 257-70.

to the question, "What does 'cooking' mean?" Ruskin wrote, "It means the knowledge of all the herbs, and fruits, and balms, and spices; and of all that is healing and sweet in fields and groves, and savoury in meats; it means carefulness, and inventiveness, and watchfulness, and willingness, and readiness of appliance; it means the economy of your great-grandmothers, and the science of modern chemists; it means much tasting, and no wasting; it means English thoroughness and French art and Arabian hospitality. It means . . . that everybody has something nice to eat." Western cooks in the United States and Canada practiced all those skills, but the women of Craik in their recipe also borrowed from an 1893 essay by Haryot Holt Cahoon, an American journalist and suffragist, responding to Ruskin. She noted that if you asked *a woman*, "what does cooking mean?" she might reply, "It means the steaming and the stewing and the baking and the broiling, thrice daily, springs and summers and autumns and winters, year after year, decade following decade. It means perspiration and desperation and resignation."[22]

Female settlers in the North American borderlands blended Ruskin and Cahoon's definitions of cooking every day. Their memoirs and cookbooks testify to the fact that, sometimes desperate, always hard-working, they conjured something nice to eat as often as they could.

[22] Women of Prairie Rose Lodge, *"Prairie Rose" Cook Book* (Craik, Saskatchewan: United Farmers of Canada [Women's Section], n.d.), 84. The recipe for "The Cook" in this book is an amalgam of material from John Ruskin's lecture "Home Virtues" in *The Ethics of the Dust: Ten Lectures to Little Housewives on the Elements of Crystallisation* (London: Smith, Elder, & Co., 1866) and from Haryot Holt Cahoon's essay "Cooking and Servants" in *What One Woman Thinks: Essays of Haryot Holt Cahoon*, ed. Cynthia M. Westover (New York: Tait, Sons & Co., 1893).

—15—

Kent Family Recipes

Sarah Kesterson

Cheyenne, Wyoming, USA, 1870s

T. A. Kent and Amelia Martin were married in December 1870 in London, Ontario, Canada where they were both originally from. Shortly after, the Kents moved to the Wyoming Territory and bought a piece of land in Cheyenne, which was a very rural town at the time. They settled in Cheyenne and began their family. It was stated that, "[Thomas and Amelia's] home ... is a center for hospitality that is as warm and generous as it is gracious, cultured, and refined."[1]

Huckleberry Pudding

1 cup sugar
1 tablespoon butter
1 egg
1 cup of sweet milk
2 teaspoons of cream larder
1 teaspoon soda
A little salt
Coffee cup and a half of berries
Flour enough to make a moderate batter. Boil one hour and a half

Good food and hospitality go hand in hand. In the T. A. Kent Collection at the University of Wyoming American Heritage Center[2] are two mostly handwritten cookbooks compiled by Amelia Kent in the late 1800s, containing all the necessary recipes for rural life in the Wyoming Territory. One cookbook, with the inscription "Amelia Kent – Cheyenne 1871" has several well-thumbed pages of recipes that Amelia undoubtedly used in her daily life in Wyoming.

---

[1] A.W. Bowen and Co., *Progressive Men of the State of Wyoming*, (Chicago, A.W. Bowen and Company, 1903), 452.

[2] *T.A. and Amelia Kent Collection*, collection number 00419, American Heritage Center, University of Wyoming, Laramie, Wyoming.

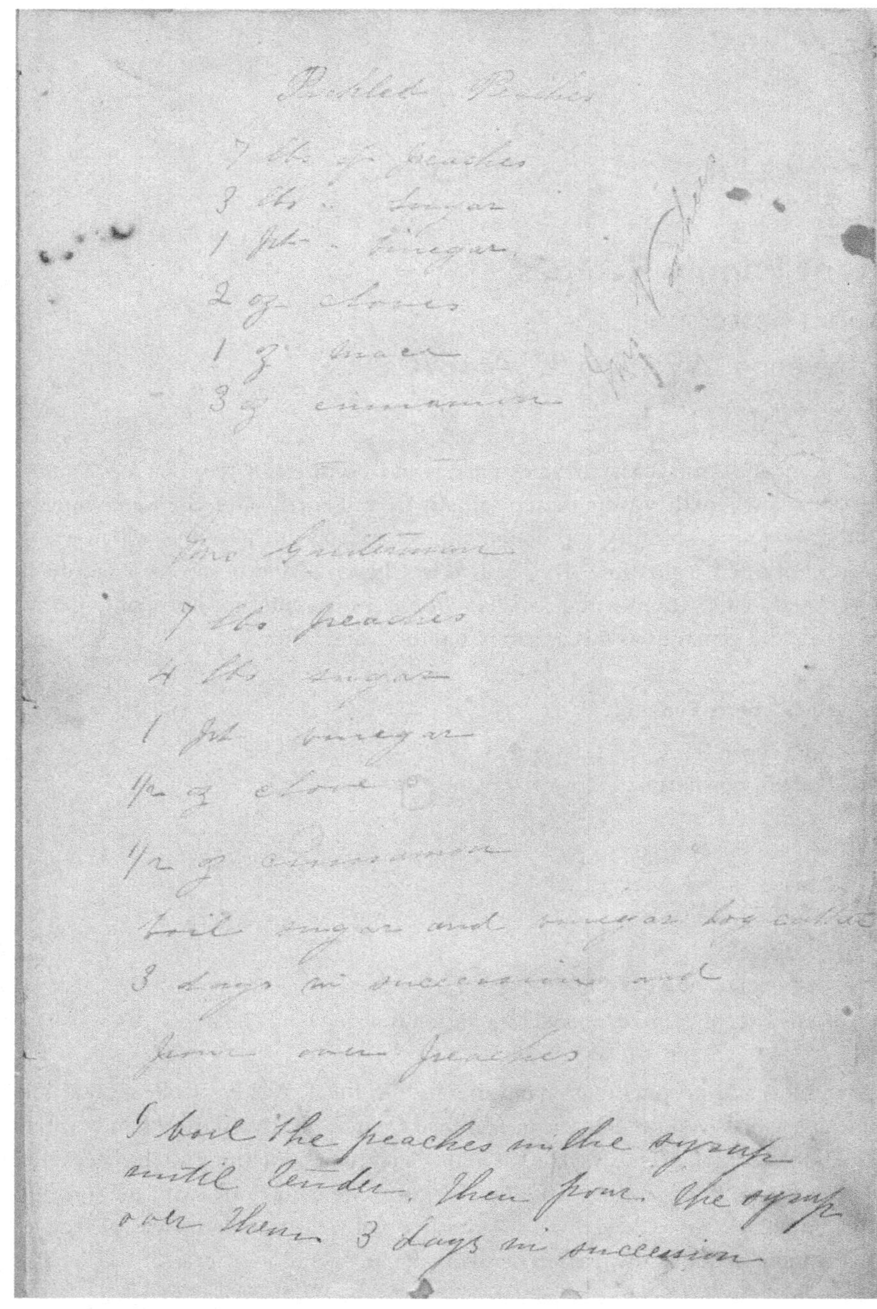
Pickled Peaches

7 lbs of peaches
3 lbs sugar
1 pt vinegar
2 oz cloves
1 oz mace
3 oz cinnamon

Mrs Gutterman

7 lbs peaches
4 lbs sugar
1 pt vinegar
1/2 oz clove
1/2 oz cinnamon
boil sugar and vinegar together
3 days in succession and
pour over peaches

I boil the peaches in the syrup
until tender. Then pour the syrup
over them 3 days in succession

Figure 15.1: Recipe for Pickled Peaches. *T.A. Kent Collection,* Accession No. 00419, American Heritage Center, University of Wyoming.

Pickled Peaches

Mrs. Vorhees
7 lbs of peaches
3 lbs of sugar
1 pint of vinegar
2 oz of cloves
1 oz of mace
3 oz cinnamon

Mrs. Guiterman
7 lbs peaches
4 lbs sugar
1 pint vinegar
½ oz cloves
½ oz cinnamon

Boil sugar and vinegar together 3 days in succession and pour over peaches. I boil the peaches in the syrup until tender. Then pour the syrup over them 3 days in succession.

Among these are recipes for Huckleberry Pudding, Pickled Peaches, Brown Bread, and Mince Meat. All of these recipes provided classic solutions to the problem of keeping food fresh before home refrigeration was introduced in the West. Rural women during this time period needed to be resourceful to create good quality of life for themselves and their families, which is reflected in the creative recipes recorded in Amelia's cookbooks.

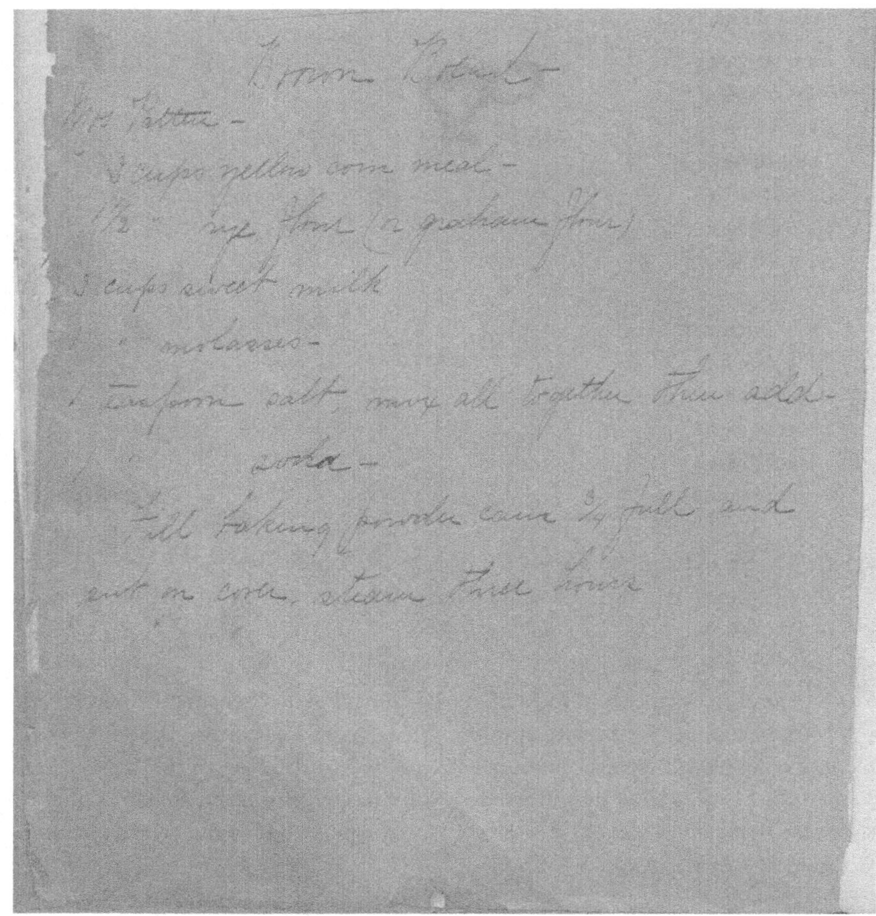

Brown Bread—
Mrs. Patten—
2 cups yellow corn meal—
1½ " rye flour (or graham flour)
2 cups sweet milk
1 " molasses—
1 teaspoon salt, mix all together then add—
1 " soda—
Fill baking powder cans ¾ full and
put in crock, steam three hours

Figure 15.2: Recipe for Brown Bread. *T.A. Kent Collection*, Accession No. 00419, American Heritage Center, University of Wyoming.

Brown Bread

Mrs. Patten –

2 cups yellow corn meal

1 ½ cups rye flour (or graham flour)

2 cups sweet milk

1 cup molasses

1 teaspoon salt, mix all together then add 1 teaspoon soda–

Fill baking powder cans ¾ full and put in crock. Steam three hours.

The Kents eventually sold their Cheyenne property and moved to Denver near the end of the 1800s. Local newspapers from the time show that Amelia primarily handled the sale of their property. Documents from the collection also show that Amelia Kent became a naturalized American citizen through a Denver court in June of 1903.

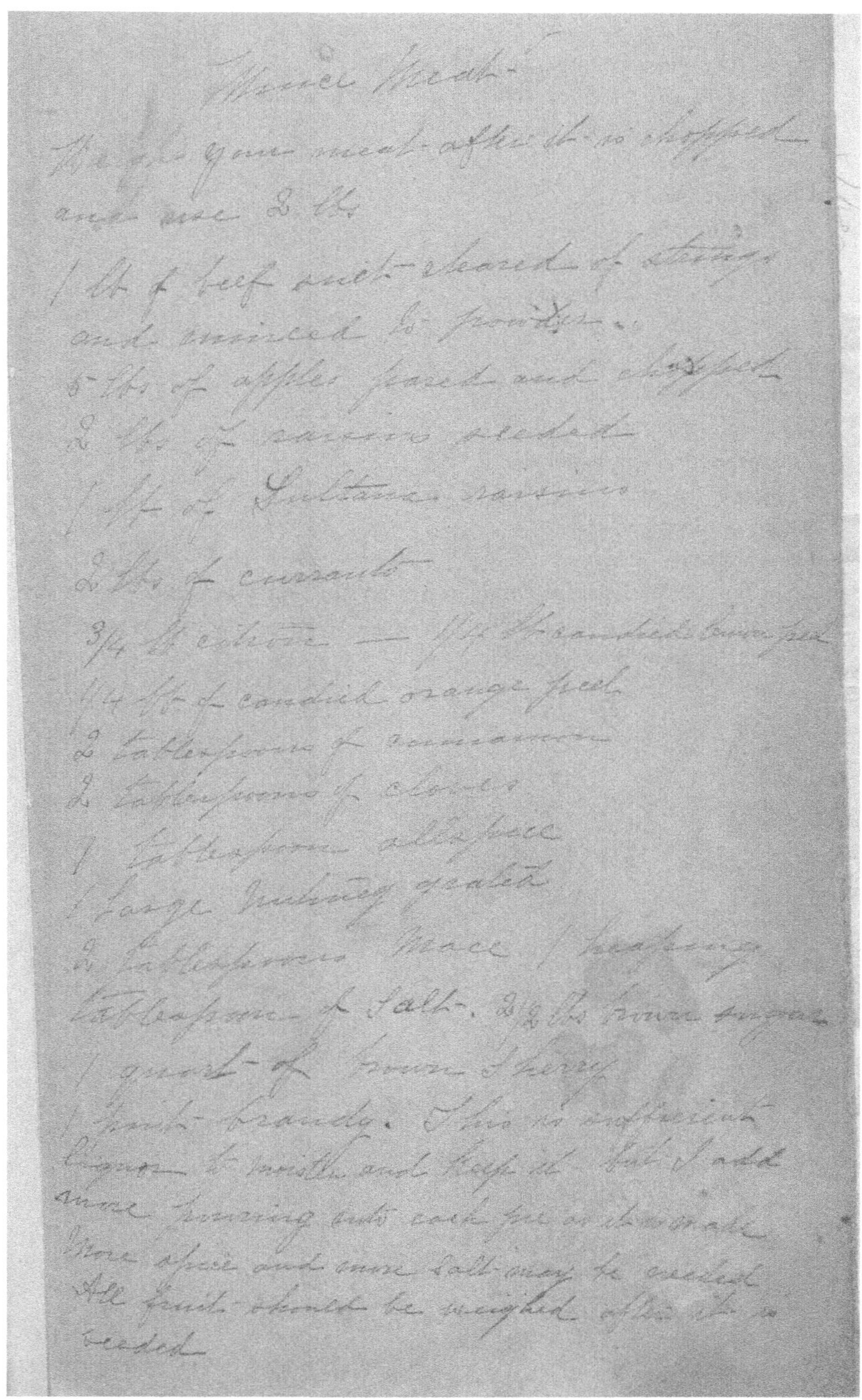

Mince Meat

Weigh your meat after it is chopped and use 2 lbs

1 lb of beef suet cleared of strings and minced to powder.

5 lbs of apples pared and chopped

2 lbs of raisins seeded

1 lb of Sultana raisins

2 lbs of currants

3/4 lb citron — 1/4 lb candied lemon peel

1/4 lb of candied orange peel

2 tablespoons of cinnamon

2 tablespoons of cloves

1 tablespoon allspice

1 large nutmeg grated

2 tablespoons mace 1 heaping tablespoon of salt. 2 1/2 lbs brown sugar

1 quart of brown sherry

1 pint brandy. This is sufficient liquor to moisten and keep it but I add more pouring into each pie as I make. More spice and more salt may be needed. All fruit should be weighed after it is seeded

Figure 15.3: Recipe for Mince Meat. *T.A. Kent Collection*, Accession No. 00419, American Heritage Center, University of Wyoming.

Mince Meat

Weigh your meat after it is chopped and use 2 lbs
1 lb of beef suet cleared of strings and minced to powder
2 lbs of apples pared and chopped
2 lbs of raisins seeded
1 lb of Sultana raisins
2 lbs of currants
¾ lb of citron - ¼ lb candied lemon peel
¼ lb of candied orange peel
2 tablespoons of cinnamon
2 tablespoons of cloves
1 tablespoon of allspice
1 large nutmeg grated
2 tablespoons mace, heaping
1 tablespoon of salt
2 ½ lbs brown sugar
1 quart of brown sherry
1 pint brandy. This is sufficient liquor to moisten and keep it, but I add more, pouring into each pie as it is made. More spice and more salt may be needed. All fruit should be weighed after it is seeded.

—16—

The Montana Rural Home: A Community Cookbook

Amy L. McKinney

"Certain relatively unimportant incidents of our childhood remain vivid in our memories. One such is the green cook book which rested on the high shelf in my mother's pantry off the kitchen where all the baking was done."[1] Amy Martin, the Household Editor of the Montana Rural Home section of the *Montana-Farmer Stockman,* wrote this in her January 1, 1949 editorial titled, "Recipes for New Year." Food preparation and preservation were a central feature of the Montana Rural Home during the post-World War II period, showing the interest and value women placed on food as one of their main domestic responsibilities. Like the family cookbook Martin mentions in her 1949 editorial, the Montana Rural Home provided rural women with a variety of recipes, in essence creating a community cookbook that included recipes from experts and readers who shared family favorites. Every edition of the Montana Rural Home provided Montana women with recipes, and several are included in this article to illustrate the emphasis on home cooking and women's productive labor.

From its inception in 1913, the *Montana Farmer-Stockman* contained a women's section to provide the latest information on domestic work for farm and ranch women.[2] Like other farm journals, the women's pages in the *Montana Farmer-Stockman* focused on domestic issues such as cooking, raising children, decorating the home, and making clothes. Each women's section had feature articles, pictures of dress patterns, needlework ideas, stories and activities for children, as well as reader requests, letters to the household editor, and editorials. Recipes were

---

[1] Amy Martin, "Recipe for New Year," *Montana Farmer-Stockman*, January 1, 1949, p. 27.

[2] At its inception in 1913, the magazine was called the *Montana Farmer* (*MF*) and published by Tribune Publishing in Great Falls, Montana. The title changed to the *Montana Farmer-Stockman* (*MFS*) under the ownership of Montana Farmer Incorporated from 1947 to 1993. The Western Farmer-Stockman Magazines of Spokane, Washington, took over the publishing duties from 1993 to 1996. During this time the name changed back to the *Montana Farmer*. In 1996 it changed hands again, this time to the Farm Progress Company of Carol Stream, Illinois, where it remained until 2002, and again changed its name to the *Montana Farmer-Stockman*. In 2002 Farm Progress consolidated several of its western magazines into the *Western Farmer-Stockman*, which covered Montana, Idaho, Utah, Oregon and Washington. Western Farmer Stockman, www.westernfarmer-stockman.com/. Accessed September 14, 2009.

The Montana Rural Home

Amy Martin
Household Editor

June

Food Conservation and Preservation

By MARY E. LOUGHEAD, Extension Nutritionist, Montana State College

Strawberry Shortcake

Adopting a Child

Information Wanted

Figure 16.1: The Montana Rural Home. Household editor Amy Martin selected topics of interest to Montana's farm and ranch women. Reprinted from the *Montana Farmer-Stockman*, June 1, 1948, p. 23.

included in every edition of the Montana Rural Home either as a feature story, reader request, or in regular columns such as Tested Recipes, Foods Western Style, or Our Family's Favorite Recipes. From 1945 to 1965, over 2,000 recipes were included in the Montana Rural Home.

The women's section of the *Montana Farmer-Stockman* changed its name over the years, from the Montana Home to the Montana Rural Home to the Family and Home, but the focus of its content changed little over the decades.[3] The Montana Rural Home, and in effect Amy Martin and Charleen Schmidt who oversaw its content as Household Editors during the twenty years following World War II, represented *the* authoritative voice in the magazine aimed at rural women in Montana. Amy Martin oversaw the Montana Rural Home section from the early 1930s until her retirement in December 1963. Her selection of articles and topics for editorials focused on women's domestic role in the home. Almost half of her editorials focused on foods and nutrition.

Like the national women's magazines aimed at suburban and urban women, the Montana Rural Home section sought to build a community of women and offered a range of information the editors believed would interest rural women. In 1959, Martin asked readers what they liked or disliked in the Montana Rural Home section. Her readers praised it, and especially specified the recipes as a favorite aspect. Mrs. Allen Chaffin of Missoula County wrote: "As I read the letters from people like me, look at the pictures and study the recipes I feel as though I've made some new acquaintances or spent an hour with a friend."[4] Edna Dunkin of Beaverhead County shared this view, stating she liked "the TIMELY informative articles, inviting recipes, inspiring poems and the interesting letters from farm and ranch women."[5] The emphasis on reader recipes was praised by Mrs. Ethel Lundeen of Lincoln County who stated she liked "the sewing hints and recipes, especially now the 'Our Family's Favorite Recipe' and picture."[6]

Because the written material in the Montana Rural Home was more informed by the Agricultural Extension Service than national women's magazines, its content fits the categories set up by the Cooperative Extension Service in Agriculture and Home Economics, specifically the Home Demonstration agents' annual reports. The section included agricultural production; farm and home buildings; rural organizations and leadership development; public affairs and community development; health (and beauty); social relationships; and farm and home management. Just under 60 percent of the articles from September 1945 to December 1965 and editorials from September 1945 to September 1955 in the Montana

---

[3] For this paper I will use Montana Rural Home because that was the most used title during the time span of this study. For a broader examination of the Montana Rural Home see: "'You Can Live on a Farm and Still Be a Lady': The *Montana Farmer*-Stockman and the Image of the Montana Rural Home" in Amy L. McKinney, "'How I Cook, Keep House, Help Farm, Too': Rural Women in Post-World War II Montana" (PhD Diss, University of Calgary, 2011), chap. 2.

[4] "Home Department—Likes and Dislikes, 'Wanted—Occupation for Teen-agers,'" *MFS,* July 1, 1959, 33.

[5] "Home Department—Likes and Dislikes, 'Suits Me Fine,'" *MFS,* July 1, 1959, 33.

[6] "Home Department—Likes and Dislikes, 'I Like Sewing Hints,'" *MFS,* July 1, 1959, 33.

Home and Farm Management, Number and Proportion of Articles by Category										
	Front Page Feature		Editorial		Feature Article		General Article		Total	
Category	**Total**	**%**	**Total**	**%**	**Total**	**%**	**Total**	**%**	**Total**	**%**
Clothing	22	8	7	7	19	16	80	15	128	13
Family Life	46	17	20	22	21	17	42	8	129	13
Foods & Nutrition	102	39	42	46	37	31	211	40	392	39
Home Management & Family Economics	52	20	22	24	31	26	141	26	246	24
House Furnishings & Equipment	43	16	1	1	12	10	59	11	115	11
TOTAL	265	100%	92	100%	120	100%	533	100%	1,010	100%

Figure 16.2: Home and Farm Management, Number and Proportion of Articles by Category. *Montana Farmer*, September 1945 to December 1946 and *Montana Farmer-Stockman*, January 1947 to December 1965.

Rural Home focused on farm and home management. This largest category was broken into five subcategories: foods and nutrition; clothing; house furnishings and equipment; home management and family economics; and family life. By far the largest number of articles dealt with food, about 40 percent of all the articles, not including the regular series of Tested Recipes and reader requests for recipes found throughout the Montana Rural Home.[7]

Efficiency, conservation, and nutrition were the focal points of the articles that provided meal ideas and used recipes calling for things rural women could make themselves, stressing the importance of women's productive labor. Of the 392 articles dealing with food, 66 articles focused on food preservation and gave women tips, hints, and advice on canning and freezing foods for later use—most of which was food they had produced themselves in their gardens. In a 1954 article Amy Martin explained that, according to surveys and government analyses, about 42 percent of all homemakers nationwide canned. This is a high figure given the national portrayal of women as consumers not producers, but there is no information about how much or how often women canned, what they canned, their reasons for canning, or their location and demographic information. For rural women, that number was much higher, an estimated 80 to 85 percent. Martin cited numerous reasons why women canned including economy, convenience, feeling of security, taste, or "most of all, there is something about a cupboard stacked with cans of fruits and vegetables she has done herself that appeals to the thrifty housewife."[8] Recipe columns emphasized this by telling rural housewives that "Now is

[7] *MF*, September 1, 1946 to December 15, 1946 and *MFS*, January 1, 1947 to December 15, 1965.

[8] Amy Martin, "Home Canning," *MFS*, June 1, 1954, 34.

Figure 16.3: Woman Canning Food. Canning food remained a common task for farm and ranch women who depended on home production of food as part of their home management responsibility. Reprinted from the *Montana Farmer-Stockman*, May 15, 1949, p. 38.

the time to prepare for next winter! By starting right away to make plenty of jams and jellies. You will be surprised at the number of filled jars you will have accumulated by the time the season is over."[9] Every year the late summer editions of the Montana Rural Home offered women various uses for fruits to make jams, jellies, and preserves for their families to use throughout the rest of the year, including the following recipe for strawberry jam.

Strawberry Jam

2 ¼ cups prepared fruit, 3½ cups (1½ pounds) sugar, 4 tablespoons (½ package) powdered fruit pectin. To prepare the fruit: Stem and crush about 1¼ quarts fully ripe strawberries. Measure 2¼ cups prepared fruit into 4-quart saucepan or kettle. To make the jam: Measure sugar into bowl; set aside. Add powdered pectin to fruit in kettle, mix well, and place over high heat. Stir until mixture comes to a hard boil. Add sugar. Bring to full rolling boil and boil hard 1 minute, stirring constantly. Remove from heat. Stir and skim by turns for 5 minutes to cool slightly, to prevent floating fruit. Ladle quickly into glasses. Cover at once with 1/8-inch hot paraffin. Yield: About 5 glasses.

[9] "Tested Recipes: Jams and Jellies," *MFS*, June 1, 1953, 42.

Other recipes utilized foods once they were canned, such as this recipe for cherry pie:

Canned Cherry Pie

(While not new, it is a "must" for a February meal) 2½ cups canned, drained pie cherries, 1 cup cherry juice, 1 cup sugar, 1/8 teaspoon salt, 2 drops almond flavoring, 1 tablespoon quick cooking tapioca, 1 tablespoon melted butter. Pour into nine-inch pie shell. Cover with top crust. Bake in hot oven (450 degrees F.) for 10 minutes. Reduce the heat to 350 degrees. Bake until the crust is a golden brown, about 40 or 50 minutes in all.[10]

Along with jams and preserves, pickle and relish recipes were some of the most requested by readers. These recipes provided rural women with a quick and easy way to "pep up a meal."[11] Using a variety of vegetables and fruits, canned pickled items were a mainstay in rural women's cupboards. Over the twenty-year period of this study, the Montana Rural Home included a variety of recipes for pickled items, far beyond relish and dill pickles. Anything from watermelon (included in the September 15, 1946 edition) to green beans (July 1, 1964 edition) could be pickled and enjoyed throughout the year.

Cousin Mabel's Good Crabapple Pickles

1 cup vinegar, 1 cup granulated sugar, 1 cup tightly packed brown sugar, 3 cups water, 1½ stick cinnamon and 1 whole clove placed in the blossom end of apple. Prepare apples when seeds are turning ripe, wash, peel and add to boiling syrup. Boil apples until clear. Put into hot sterilized jars and seal at once. Green or red coloring may be added to the syrup to make green or red apples for the holiday season.[12]

Canning was a mainstay of food preservation, but most women saw the freezer as essential once electricity and equipment became available. As one woman wrote to the *Farmer-Stockman*, she "just couldn't do without [her] home freezer."[13] For women living in the country, food preservation was an essential part of food and home management, especially during busy times such as threshing or branding when they had to feed extra help. It was the woman's responsibility to ensure that enough food was on hand to feed the family, crew, and guests, a task aided by owning a home freezer. Advertisers understood the appeal of freezing food items for later use, which greatly assisted busy farm and ranch women. In several advertisements, Occident Flour offered a "Bake 'n' Freeze Idea Service" for women, including one with instructions on how to bake and freeze pies for the holidays.[14]

---

[10] "Tested Recipes: Try Some New Recipes," *MFS*, February 15, 1948, 27.

[11] "Tested Recipes: Pickles are Good," *MF*, August 15, 1946, 15.

[12] "Tested Recipes: Pickles," *MFS*, August 1, 1953, 28.

[13] Helen Lee, "I Couldn't Do Without My Home Freezer," *MFS*, June 1, 1954, 34.

[14] *MFS*, November 1, 1953, p. 24.

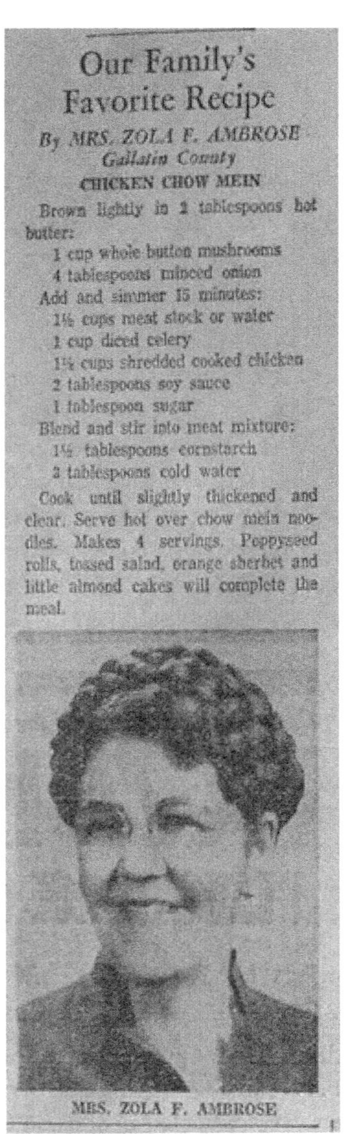

Our Family's Favorite Recipe

By MRS. ZOLA F. AMBROSE
Gallatin County

CHICKEN CHOW MEIN

Brown lightly in 2 tablespoons hot butter:

1 cup whole button mushrooms
4 tablespoons minced onion

Add and simmer 15 minutes:

1½ cups meat stock or water
1 cup diced celery
1½ cups shredded cooked chicken
2 tablespoons soy sauce
1 tablespoon sugar

Blend and stir into meat mixture:

1½ tablespoons cornstarch
3 tablespoons cold water

Cook until slightly thickened and clear. Serve hot over chow mein noodles. Makes 4 servings. Poppyseed rolls, tossed salad, orange sherbet and little almond cakes will complete the meal.

MRS. ZOLA F. AMBROSE

Figure 16.4: Our Family's Favorite Recipe. Mrs. Zola F. Ambrose of Gallatin County submitted her family's Chicken Chow Mein recipe to the Montana Rural Home in 1959. Reprinted from the *Montana Farmer-Stockman*, October 1, 1959, 28.

In "Package Cookies for Your Freezer," the editors of the Montana Rural Home told rural housewives, "[w]hen baking why not make more than one batch and package some for the freezer. If you want to serve a variety at one time you can package them in small quantities or in freezer bags that can be opened and a few of each variety taken out."[15] This Chocolate Pixie recipe was one that readers were told would freeze well, keeping the cookie jar constantly full.

[15] "Tested Recipes: Package Cookies for Your Freezer," *MFS*, April 1, 1959, 32.

Chocolate Pixie

2 cups sifted flour
2 teaspoons baking powder
½ teaspoon salt
¼ cup butter or margarine
4 squares chocolate
4 eggs
2 cups sugar
½ teaspoon vanilla
½ cup chopped walnuts or pecans may be added

Sift flour, measure, then put back into the sifter and sift together flour, salt and baking powder. Melt chocolate and butter or margarine together over very low heat or hot water. Beat eggs until light and gradually add the sugar, beat until well mixed, add vanilla, melted chocolate and shortening. When mixed, stir in dry ingredients and nuts if used. Chill dough over night or hold in freezer until very firm. Form into balls about the size of a small walnut, roll in powdered sugar and place on a cookie sheet about three inches apart. Bake at 300 degrees F for 18 to 20 minutes.

Half the articles on food dealt with food preparation (195 articles), excluding regular recipe columns such as Tested Recipes. This regular feature was in addition to the thousands of recipes printed as a result of reader requests, feature articles, Tested Recipes, advertisements, or another feature that began in the spring of 1959 called Our Family's Favorite Recipe. Martin invited women from around the state to share their favorite recipes with the other readers of the women's section. If their recipes were selected, they would receive two dollars and have their photos printed, as Zola F. Ambrose did for her family's Chicken Chow Mein recipe in October 1959. (Figure 16.4)

The recipes included in Our Family's Favorite Recipes highlighted a variety of tastes and ingredients. From comfort food classics like baked potatoes and beef biscuit pie to sweet treats like no-bake cookies, dream bars, and Missouri Waltz brownies, women from around the state opened their families' cookbooks to share with their extended neighborhood friends.

Pow Wow Buns

½ can lunch meat ground
1 tablespoon onion finely chopped
½ cup grated or finely cubed cheese
1 tablespoon chopped sweet pickles
3 tablespoons melted butter or cream
6 or 8 large buns

Mix all ingredients together, slice the buns in halves and butter very lightly. Fill the buns and wrap each bun in a square of parchment or foil, place on a cookie sheet and bake in preheated oven at 375 degrees for 15 minutes. Serve hot in the wrapping.[16]

Fergus County resident Mrs. Terry Barta's recipe highlighted the ever versatile Jell-O in her family's recipe:

Ribbon Icebox Dessert

Line pan with 9 graham crackers.
Beat together ¼ cup soft butter, 1 cup powdered sugar, 2 tablespoons cream.
Spread over crackers.
Top with 9 more graham crackers.
Dissolve 1 package strawberry jello, 1 cup hot water.
Divide in half. Add to one ½ cup cream. Add to one ½ cup water
Cut jello with cream. Beat fluffy and pour over crackers. Let set.
Let jello with water stand at room temperature. Pour over other jello. Set.
Cut in squares. Serve with whipped cream.[17]

The Montana Rural Home section included recipes from the editors in addition to readers' request for recipes. The recipes often utilized produce that was ripe for that particular time of year and foods that rural women had readily available to them on their farms or ranches. Rhubarb recipes were especially popular and appeared every year in the late spring. Pie recipes were the most common, but the Montana Rural Home offered a variety of uses for rhubarb. As the editors explained, "On almost every Montana farm and ranch is at least one stalk of rhubarb, and there are many ways of preparing that fruit so it is appealing to the eye as well as the taste buds. Combine it with strawberries, pineapple, or other fruits and you've made something new, or just cook a few stalks into a sauce for the breakfast fruit. Rhubarb is tasty, yet very nutritious, containing much vitamin C, which we must include in our diet every day for good health."[18] Knowing it was a common ingredient many women had available to them, the Montana Rural Home sought out different ways to use it, often turning to reader submissions for new ideas.

---

[16] Josephine Bialek, Hill County, "Our Family's Favorite Recipe," *MFS*, July 15, 1959, 26.

[17] Terry Barta, Fergus County, "Our Family's Favorite Recipe," *MFS*, June 1, 1959, 40.

[18] "Tested Recipes: Rhubarb Dishes," *MFS*, July 1, 1960, 24.

Rhubarb Custard Pie

Slice 2 cups rhubarb, cover with boiling water, let stand 5 minutes and drain. Add to rhubarb 1½ cups sugar mixed with the following: 1 heaping tablespoon flour, 3 egg yolks, ½ teaspoon cinnamon, ¼ teaspoon nutmeg, ½ teaspoon lemon juice or extract. After this is all mixed and poured over the rhubarb, put all in an unbaked pie shell and bake 30 minutes. Spread over meringue made with the 3 egg whites, well beaten with 6 tablespoons sugar. Brown in oven.[19]

Rhubarb Marlow

1 cup whipping cream or evaporated milk, 3 cups diced rhubarb, 1 tablespoon water, ¾ cup sugar, ¼ teaspoon salt, ¼ pound marshmallows (16), 2 tablespoons lemon juice, few drops red coloring. Have cream thoroughly chilled. Place rhubarb and water in sauce pan, cover and cook over moderate heat. Watch closely and as soon as juice flows, add sugar and cook until rhubarb is tender but not mushy. Remove from heat. Add salt and marshmallows which have been cut into quarters with a scissors dipped in hot water. Stir to distribute and chill. Place cream in chilled bowl, add lemon juice and whip until very stiff. Fold coloring into rhubarb mixture then fold gently but thoroughly into the whipped cream. Turn at once into chilled freezing tray. Freeze at coldest temperature until firm, about 3 hours. Then return temperature to normal refrigerator temperature and keep in freezing unit until ready to serve.[20]

Wild game was another annual recipe collection the Montana Rural Home provided women, which offered not only recipes, but also instructions on how to prepare the meat prior to cooking. Taking advice from the Extension Service, the 1959 article "Fixing Game Birds," explained that "All game birds are better when they're allowed to hang for a few days. This allows the bird to develop in flavor. … Freshly killed birds should be drawn as soon as possible and the bird should then be hung in a cool place in order to rid them of body heat."[21] Most readers wanted recipes that enhanced the flavor of wild game. The 1946 article "Wild Game" emphasized, "The hunting season is with us again, and many of us do not have enough experience with the cooking of wild game to be sure of the results, so will welcome these recipes prepared by a connoisseur." [22] The following recipes were featured along with the preparation advice.

Baked Pheasant

Clean and cut up for frying. Wipe thoroughly, dip in flour and brown in a frying pan. Place in roaster, sprinkle with salt and pepper. Put enough sour cream in pan to make its depth 1 inch and add 1/8 pound of butter for each bird. Cover and bake at 300 degrees F. from 1½ to 2 hours or until birds are tender. Make a gravy and cover birds before serving.

---

[19] "Tested Recipes: Rhubarb Pies," *MFS,* May 1, 1951, 44.

[20] "Tested Recipes: Rhubarb," *MFS,* May 1, 1954, 36.

[21] "Tested Recipes: Fixing Game Birds," *MFS,* October 15, 1959, 28.

[22] "Tested Recipes: Wild Game," *MF,* November 1, 1946, 22.

Braised Venison

Season with salt and pepper and rub well with flour. Brown in hot fat. Add about one cup of water and cover, then cook very slowly until tender. Cooking time—two to three hours. Turn meat occasionally. (For less tender cuts such as shoulder, neck, breast).

Utilizing every aspect of wild game was also addressed in two groups of recipes both entitled "Variety Meats." As the editors explained the "liver, heart, kidneys and tongue not only offer new interest and flavor in meals, but they are excellent sources of high-quality proteins, essential minerals such as iron, phosphorus, copper and vitamins."[23] The second variety meats included recipes for liver, heart, brains, and sweetbreads.

Boiled Tongue

Thoroughly wash in warm water. Cover fresh tongue with salted water (1 teaspoon salt for each quart of water). Spices and vegetables may be added for seasoning. Cover and cook at simmering temperature (185 degrees F) until tender—3 to 4 hours for large beef tongue. Remove skin, cut away roots. Plunging into cold water after cooking helps to loosen the skin.

Specialty recipes highlighted the diverse cultures and ethnicities throughout Montana and were often submitted by readers. Holidays were often times of the year the Montana Rural Home highlighted family traditions. Sweets usually took center stage as recipes reserved for special occasions were requested and shared, as were these recipes for a "walnut bread, a Croatian or Slovenian sweet bread called Povatea."[24] Several women readers from across the state sent in their version of this recipe, with slight variations in the spelling of the sweet bread and ingredients, reflecting their personal touches and traditions.

Pavatica

Sweet dough

8 cups flour, 1 cup lukewarm milk, 1 ½ cups lukewarm water, 2 or 3 cakes yeast, 1 cup sugar, 4 teaspoons salt, 2 or 3 eggs, ¼ pound melted butter. Mix as any bread or roll dough, adding sifted flour to make a soft dough. Knead and grease the dough well and let rise for 2 ½ to 3 hours, but do not knead down. After it is light turn out on a large table which is covered with cloth and floured. Roll the dough as much as possible, then stretch it to ¼ inch thickness. Trim off the edges which you can use as bread or cut into doughnuts.

---

[23] "Tested Recipes: Variety Meats," *MFS,* January 1, 1947, p. 17; "Tested Recipes: Variety Meats," *MFS,* October 1, 1953, 32.

[24] "Tested Recipes: Povatea," *MFS,* January 1, 1950, 21.

Walnut Filling

1 or 1 ½ pounds walnuts ground or crushed fine, 3 cups milk, 1 cup sugar, ¼ pound butter, ½ to 1 cup honey. Mix all together and bring to a boiling point. Add 3 or 4 beaten eggs and cook until thick. Cool until lukewarm. Spread over dough evenly. Sprinkle with a little cinnamon. Roll as you do for cinnamon roll and twist into oval shape. Put into a well greased pan (roaster is ideal) and let rise in warm place about 1½ hours or until light as bread. Bake in moderate oven two hours. Be careful that oven is not too hot as it can be scorched easily. -Mrs. Claude Fletcher, Musselshell County.

Holiday recipes also provided ideas for entire meals as the Montana Rural Home offered new takes on Thanksgiving, Christmas and Easter meals. Every year also offered menus for Lent that emphasized fish, eggs, vegetables, and cheese recipes. The following recipes reflect the demand for non-meat meals during the Lenten season.[25]

Salmon Casserole with Parsley Biscuits

1 ½ cups medium white sauce, 1 ½ cups canned salmon, 1 cup canned peas, 2 diced hard-cooked eggs. To white sauce add flaked salmon, peas and eggs. Pour into greased 1 ½ -quart casserole. Top with parsley biscuits and bake in hot oven (425 degrees F.) 15 to 20 minutes, or until biscuits are brown. Yield: 6 to 8 servings.

Parsley Biscuits

2 cups sifted enriched flour, 3 teaspoons baking powder, 1 teaspoon salt, 2 to 4 tablespoons shortening, 2 tablespoons finely chopped parsley, ⅔ to ¾ cup milk. Sift together flour, baking powder and salt. Cut or rub in shortening. Add parsley. Add milk to make a soft dough. Turn out on lightly floured board and kneed gently ½ minute. Roll or pat out ½ inch thick. Cut into desired shape. Place on salmon casserole and bake.

Baked Eggs in Macaroni Nests

1 tablespoon salt, 3 quarts boiling water, 6 ounces elbow macaroni, 1 cup grated American cheese, 1 cup milk, 1 teaspoon salt, 1/8 teaspoon pepper, 4 eggs. salt and pepper. Add 1 tablespoon salt to actively boiling water. Gradually add macaroni and continue boiling until macaroni is tender, about 8 minutes. Drain and rinse macaroni. Add cheese. Combine milk, 1 teaspoon salt, and pepper. Arrange macaroni in individual baking dishes. With a spoon, make a hollow in the center of macaroni. Pour ¼ cup milk mixture on each serving of macaroni. Bake in moderate over (350 degrees F.) 15 minutes. Remove from oven and break egg into each hollow. Return to oven and bake 10 minutes. Season with salt and pepper. Yield: 4 servings.

[25] "Tested Recipes: Lenten Foods," *MFS,* March 1, 1948, 29.

Figure 16.5: Occident Flour Advertisement. Several advertisers like Occident Flour included recipes using their products. Reprinted from the *Montana Farmer-Stockman*, October 1, 1950, p. 23.

Fish Pie

1 can tuna or any leftover cooked fish, 2 tablespoons minced onions, 1 pint milk, 2 tablespoons flour, 3 eggs hard cooked, 4 to 8 medium sized potatoes, mashed, 2 tablespoons butter, salt, and pepper. Worcestershire sauce, grated cheese. Break fish into large flakes and arrange on bottom of deep buttered casserole. Saute onion in a little butter until golden brown; then sprinkle over fish. Make a cream sauce: melt butter in saucepan, stir in flour, then gradually add milk, stirring until smooth. Cook gently until slightly thickened. Season to taste and add diced hard cooked eggs. Sprinkle a little Worcestershire sauce over dish; then pour cream sauce over all. Spread mashed potatoes, seasoned to taste, about an inch thick on top of mixture. Sprinkle with grated cheese. Bake at 425 degrees to 450 degrees F until cheese is browned. Serves 4 to 6.

Advertisements from local and national brands also appeared in the women's section. Flour and yeast companies represented the most common food product advertisements. In order to entice women to use their products, their advertisements often included recipes that utilized their products, mainly for breads and desserts, but others shared main dish ideas. Recipes included Prune Brunch Rolls, 30 Minute Rolls, Halloween Doughnuts and Hattie's Garden Crescents from Red Star Yeast.[26] Fleischmann's Yeast featured more main course ideas including Hot Chicken Salad in a Cheese Crust, Pizza Burgers, Shrimp Boats, and Heavenly Hash Supper.[27] Occident Flour provided ideas for tasty desserts including Calico Crumb Cake, Sweetheart Ring, Fruit Refrigerator Cookies, and Butterwhirl Rolls.[28] (Figure 16.5) Baking powerhouse Gold Medal Flour used its increasingly popular marketing tool of Betty Crocker for a series of advertisements featuring recipes such as Stir 'n' Roll Biscuits, Hungarian Coffee Cake, Cinnamon Twists, and Chicken and Dumplings (Prescott, Ch. 39, this volume).[29] Advertisements for Certo, a brand of fruit pectin, offered recipes for making jams and jelly including grape jelly, spiced peach jam, and strawberry jam.[30] Even Nash Coffee advertisements offered recipes for foods that could be served with their coffee including Pineapple Tea Cakes.[31] Despite the growing popularity of canned chicken soup casseroles and assumptions about rural women's fondness for lime green Jell-O molds, no advertisements appeared for canned soups or Jell-O.

Advertisers, cookbook publishers, and homemaking specialists argued that the use of prepackaged mixes was affordable and saved the housewife valuable

---

[26] *MFS* May 1, 1951, p. 46; January 1, 1950, p. 21; October 1, 1950, p. 26; and January 1, 1951, 19.

[27] *MFS* April 1, 1958, 40; November 1, 1958, 23; March 1, 1958, 41; and May 1, 1958, 31.

[28] *MFS,* February 15, 1958; November 1, 1950, 18; December 1, 1950, 14; and October 1, 1950, 23.

[29] *MFS,* December 1, 1950, 16; January 1, 1953, 30; February 1, 1950, 21; and April 1, 1950, 24.

[30] *MFS,* August 15, 1950, 21; July 15, 1950, 25; June 15, 1950, 37.

[31] *MFS,* December 15, 1953, 17.

time. The debate about whether to use prepackaged mixes or convenience foods did not appear in the *Montana Farmer-Stockman* until the mid-1950s when Martin asked "Just how new are mixes?" She asserted that the 200 prepared mixes available on the market were found "from the Montana ranch kitchen to the city apartment kitchenette" and that "mixes have become a part and parcel of baking and meal preparation."[32] Martin emphasized the convenience of mixes; however, only a handful of the thousands of recipes found in the Montana Rural Home section actually used them. Cake mixes were the only advertisements for prepared mixes in the Montana Rural Home. Occident Cake Mix advertisements emphasized the convenience of using their cake mixes in women's baking, stating that the "holiday fruit cake" could be "oven-ready in ½ the time."[33]

The Montana Rural Home section did provide recipes for homemade mixes that "tast[ed] better and cost less than a commercial mix and [would] save time over a home recipe,"[34] suggesting that rural women liked the efficiency and time-saving aspect of mixes, but that commercial mixes lacked the quality or price they wanted. Most recipes in regards to mixes provided rural women with recipes to create their own mixes, as these following recipes emphasize, "Mixes, homemade or grocery kind, save time for the busy homemaker. Here is a homemade mix for delightful jiffy desserts and two other handy homemade mixes."[35]

Brownie Mix

1¼ cups dry milk solids
4 cups sifted flour
4 teaspoons baking powder
2 teaspoons salt
4 cups sugar
1¼ cups cocoa

Sift ingredients together thoroughly. Cover tightly. Keep cool. Makes 10 cups mix.

To Make Brownies
2½ cups Brownie Mix
½ cup chopped nuts
2 beaten eggs
3 tablespoons water
1½ teaspoons vanilla
½ cup melted butter

---

[32] Amy Martin, "Just How New Are Mixes?" *MFS,* June 15, 1954.

[33] *MFS,* November 15, 1950, 29.

[34] "Tested Recipes: Home Made Mix for Chocolate Cake," *MFS,* June 15, 1957, 26.

[35] "Tested Recipes: Handy Mixes," *MFS,* July 15, 1958, 26.

Combine the mix with nuts. Mix separately eggs, water, vanilla and melted butter. Gradually stir this into dry mixture. Blend well. Spread in greased pan (8 by 8 by 2 inches). Bake at 350 degrees F. for 35 to 40 minutes. Cool. Cut into 16 brownies.

Biscuit Mix

7 ½ cups flour
1 cup shortening
3 tablespoons baking powder
3 teaspoons salt
2 cups dry milk solids

Sift the dry ingredients together very thoroughly. Cut in the fat with pastry blender, knives or fingers. Place in a container which can be tightly closed. Store in refrigerator.

When ready to use, measure the amount of mix desired into bowl. Make a shallow well in center of mixture, add the water slowly and stir from the center with a fork, until ingredients are moistened and soft dough is formed. (Use ¼ to ⅓ cup water to 1 cup mixture.) Remove from bowl to lightly floured board. Knead for a few seconds until smooth; then roll out until ½ to ¾ inch thick. Cut into small rounds and bake in hot oven (400 degrees F) for 12 to 15 minutes. Serve at once. Two cups mixture plus ½ to ⅔ cup water make about 14 2-inch biscuits.

Women's home production was favored over mixes they could buy in town. Many rural women had their own milk, cream, butter, and eggs they produced at home, so many prepackaged food items were actually more expensive. A few recipes utilized the ever-popular Jell-O, but even Jell-O was not a common ingredient and was usually found in the context of cooking for a larger crowd.[36]

By the late 1950s and early 1960s, a few features of the recipe section highlighted prepackaged foods, such as "Take a Can of Soup ..."[37] (Ambrose, Ch. 43, this volume)

[36] "Tested Recipes: Food for Fifty," *MFS,* October 15, 1951, 33.

[37] "Take a Can of Soup . . ." *MFS*, August 15, 1961, 29.

Spaghetti Casserole

1 pound ground beef
½ cup chopped onion
¼ cup chopped green pepper
2 tablespoons butter or margarine
1 can (10½ ounces) condensed cream of mushroom soup
1 can (10½ ounces) condensed tomato soup
1 soup can water
1 clove garlic, minced
1 cup shredded sharp process cheese
½ pound spaghetti, cooked and drained

In large skillet, cook beef, onion, and green pepper in butter until meat is lightly browned and vegetables are tender; stir often to separate meat particles. Add soups, water and garlic. [H]eat. Blend with ½ cup cheese and cooked spaghetti in a 3-quart casserole; top with remaining cheese. Bake in moderate oven (350 Degrees F.) about 30 minutes, or until bubbling and hot.

Rosy Red Cookies

1 cup sifted all-purpose flour
1 teaspoon baking powder
½ teaspoon baking soda
½ teaspoon salt
2 teaspoons ground cinnamon
1 teaspoon ground nutmeg
¼ cup butter or margarine
1 cup sugar
2 eggs
1 can (10½ ounces) condensed tomato soup
3 cups uncooked rolled oats
2 cups seedless raisins, chopped
1 cup chopped walnuts

Preheat oven to 350 degrees F. Sift dry ingredients together. In large bowl, thoroughly cream butter and sugar. Add eggs; beat until light and fluffy. Add alternately, dry ingredients and soup. Mix until smooth after each addition. Stir in rolled oats, raisins, and nuts. Drop rounded teaspoonfuls on cookie sheet. Bake in a moderate oven (350 Degrees F) about 20 minutes or until lightly browned.

In the "Reader Response" section readers gave recipes using packaged foods to use when unexpected company arrived or during an especially busy time. The majority of the recipes, however, focused on making items from scratch. Advertisements from the Rural Home section also reflected the focus on homemade items. Although advertisements for Roman Meal porridge, Quaker Oats, Toomey's Flapjack Flour, and Cheerios (all focusing on breakfast meals) were common, advertisements for flour, yeast, seeds for gardens, baking powder, jam and jelly pectin, canning equipment, and cream separators were much more prevalent, constituting over twice as many advertisements in comparison to the convenience foods. Approximately 70 advertisements appeared for convenience foods compared to approximately 140 for yeast and flour.[38]

As the quality and variety of mixes improved and cost decreased by the early 1960s, more discussion centered on the use of mixes when "in a pinch." In April 1961 Martin asked her readers "What do you think of mixes?" She introduced the letters by stating that in general most readers "feel a homemade product is superior in quality, but a mix or commercially-prepared item often fills a need ... primarily of time." To demonstrate the increased use of mixes, Martin quoted a survey of Montana farmers and ranchers which "indicate[d] that over half of them buy cake and pancake mixes, about a third buy biscuit mix, and nearly ¼ buy instant coffee."[39] The responses from the readers indicated an overall acceptance of mixes, except for breads. As Mrs. Oscar Adolph of Musselshell County explained, mixes filled a need when in a hurry: "in short, if most farm wives are like me they enjoy making 'homemade' things, but find convenience foods grand for extra busy times or unexpected company."[40] The letters also expressed concerns or opinions about the use of mixes. Mrs. Louis DePuydt of Phillips County expressed concern for the future generation of homemakers who would become "simply can-opener and ready-mix cooks."[41]

The discussion of convenience foods emphasized the importance of women's productive labor for the farm and ranch economy. The most pointed article in January 1965 by Schmidt emphasized convenience foods but did not frame their use as a way for women to lessen their cooking burden or free up some leisure time. Instead it featured women's economic value on the family farm or ranch. Schmidt argued "It takes far more money per year to hire a farm worker than to pay the little extra cost of the convenience foods which might free you to assume more of the responsibility." She emphasized, "[t]he point is this: Would your time be more valuable to your family if used in facilitating operation of the farm, or ranch or otherwise bringing in outside income—or in being used to prepare all the meals from scratch?"[42] For an urban audience, the assumption was that a woman had

---

[38] *MF*, September 1, 1946 to December 15, 1946 and *MFS*, January 1, 1947 to December 15, 1965.

[39] "Your Letters," *MFS*, April 1, 1961, 31.

[40] "Your Letters: 'Convenience Foods Kept on Hand,'" *MFS*, April 1, 1961, 31.

[41] "Your Letters: 'Home Cooking Has Permanent Niche,'" *MFS*, April 1, 1961, 31.

[42] Charleen Schmidt, "Looking to the Future—Cut Meal Preparation Time With Convenience Foods," *MFS*, January 2, 1965, 36.

to demonstrate she still cared even if she used a mix by adding her own personal touch to food prepared from a can or mix. For rural women, the pitch was in terms of efficiency and cost savings as part of their farm management role. Prepackaged foods, according to Schmidt, freed up more of women's valuable time in order to help with the farm or ranch at a time when family farms were becoming marginalized and increasingly depended on women's wage labor off the farm.[43] Schmidt encouraged women to educate themselves on the latest farm and ranch management methods. If a woman could take over the bookkeeping and record keeping and become an expert on tax, water, and land laws, that would free up her husband to work the land or work with the animals.

The Montana Rural Home provided women with valuable menu ideas and hints and instructions on food preservation. Thrift, nutrition, taste, and ease highlighted the over 2,000 recipes included in the Montana Rural Home in the twenty years following World War II. Household editors explained that they "receive many fine recipes from our readers and we sincerely wish we might publish them all, but space does not permit it." Women submitted recipes in response to requests as well as wanting to spread "neighborly thoughtfulness in passing on something good."[44] The emphasis on reader recipe submissions in addition to recipes by experts helped create a community cookbook for women across the state.

[43] Schmidt, "Looking to the Future," 36.

[44] "From Our Readers," *FS,* July 15, 1946, 15.

—17—

Tamales in the UTSA Mexican Cookbook Collection

Steph Noell

With Recipe Transcriptions and Translations by Carla Burgos

The tamal has been an important part of Mexican heritage since Pre-Hispanic times. The word "tamal" is derived from the Nahuatl word *tamalli*, which means "wrapped food." These tamales were made of a dough, which was typically corn-based, but could also be made of ground beans or rice, and were wrapped in corn husks or banana leaves. Some tamales are thin, the circumference of two or three fingers, while others can fill a dinner plate. Pre-Hispanic tamales were filled with a wide variety of indigenous ingredients, including amaranth, axolotl, fish, frog, fruit, gourds, gopher, honey, rabbit, and turkey eggs. With the arrival of the Spanish, tamales began being filled with old world ingredients like pork and beef. The Pre-Columbian Aztecs made tamales for special occasions like religious festivals and celebrations and their designation as a festive food continues into the present.

At The University of Texas at San Antonio, the Libraries' Special Collections department houses the Mexican Cookbook Collection, the largest library collection of Mexican cookbooks in the United States. The Mexican Cookbook Collection began in 2001 when a local librarian, Laurie Gruenbeck, donated her collection of more than 550 cookbooks collected over thirty years of travels. Today, the collection is composed of more than 2,000 cookbooks, with a special focus on regional cooking, healthy and vegetarian recipes, corporate advertising cookbooks, and manuscript recipe books.

Much of the Mexican Cookbook Collection was created between the 1940s and the present, but the collection does contain a single 18th century handwritten recipe book as well as a few 19th century and early 20th century cookbooks. I focused my attention on our 19th century cookbooks to see how tamales were made before the advent of many modern kitchen appliances like food processors and electric grinders. For centuries, masa has been made by finely grinding wet corn using a *metate y mano* also known as the *piedra de moler* or "millstone." The *metate y mano* is a type of quern or stone hand mill meant for grinding grains and cocoa. Hand-grinding corn for masa is very labor-intensive so it is no wonder that most cooks prefer using modern equipment or buying bags of masa powder from the grocery store.

Some of the 19th century tamal recipes I located come from the state of Puebla, one comes from the state of Durango, and one book's place of origin has not been determined. Tamal recipes do not just vary based on their region of origin, but differ from family to family, so these recipes are certainly not representative of all tamales in their city of origin. The earliest tamal recipe in UTSA's Mexican Cookbook Collection is from one of two 1831 books that shares the title of "earliest cookbook published in Mexico". *El cocinero mexicano, ó, Coleccion de las mejores recetas para guisar al estilo americano: y de las mas selectas segun el metodo de las cocinas española, italiana, francesa e inglesa* was published in Mexico City and it contains one tamal recipe. What is notable about this recipe is that it is made of cacahuazintle, an heirloom variety of corn native to Mexico. Also notable is that the base recipe is for a sweet tamal with options for making it savory mentioned at the end. There were many sweet tamales being made in the 19th century, but most current menus, especially in U.S. restaurants will only list a couple, if any, sweet options.

The other published 19th century cookbook in the Mexican Cookbook Collection containing tamal recipes *Recetas practicas y utiles, sobre cocina, reposteria, pasteleria, etc.* was published in Durango City in 1881. There are four tamal recipes contained in this volume, which also require various levels of sugar. These recipes call for nixtamal, the product of nixtamalization or soaking and partially-cooking corn in an alkaline solution before cleaning and grinding. Nixtamal is used in hominy, tamales, and tortillas. Ground nixtamal is also known as masa. The fillings in these recipes include cheese curds, coconut, mincemeat, and chicken.

Of our twelve earliest handwritten recipe books, only two contain tamal recipes, both of which were written in the 19th century. The earlier of the two was written in 1884 by a woman named Guadalupe Perez in Acatzingo. Most of her tamales are rice-based with only one recipe being corn-based. Perez also includes a recipe for milk filling composed of ground rice, milk, ground almonds, egg yolks, and sugar.

The latest 19th century tamal recipes come from a manuscript cookbook by Manuela Heredia y Cervantes written in 1886. In this book, there is a recipe for a tamal casserole. Much of the ingredients in this recipe aren't unusual, but this is the only one of the 19th century tamal recipes that incorporates hoja santa, which is a pepperleaf, as well as epazote leaves, an herb with gas-relieving properties. This tamal casserole can include layers of mole, hash, or bean paste, depending on the cook's preferences and can be eaten cold.

One of the most noticeable aspects of especially the 19th century manuscript recipes is the knowledge assumed by their authors. If you are reading these recipes, it is assumed that you know how to make dough for tamales, whether it is rice-based or corn-based. It is also assumed that you know how to prepare the leaves or husks for wrapping. These are the lessons handed down from one generation to the next. Some of these tamal recipes specify that it can take multiple days to prepare them as leaves/husks are often soaked overnight as is the corn for masa. What these recipes teach us is that there is not one way to make tamales. What cooks have on hand, what is endemic to their environment, and what is available at the grocery store can create an infinite variety of tamales. It is the flexibility of this food that has ensured a lasting legacy.

El cocinero mexicano, ó, Colección de las mejores recetas para guisar al estilo americano: y de las mas selectas según el método de las cocinas española, italiana, francesa e inglesa. Mexico City: Imprenta de Galvan, a cargo de Mariano Arévalo, Calle de Cadena num. 2, 1831.

Spanish:

Tamales

1. Lavado bien el nixtamál ó nixcómel se enjuga con una servilleta ó paño, se muele y se cierne bien: se le echan luego nueve onzas y media de azúcar, una libra de manteca y la sal correspondiente, agua tibia y anís. Se bate bien todo, y poniendo la masa envuelta en hojas de maíz, quedan formados los tamales.

   En una olla proporcionada se echa una poca de agua, y mas arriba de ella se forma un tapextle ó tabladito, donde se pondrán dichos tamales sin que se mojen para que se cuezan con el vapor del agua, tapándose la olla con un ayate y un plato encima.

   De la misma suerte se hacen los tamales de chile y especia, con sola la diferencia de suprimir el azúcar y el anís.

Otros

2. Se disponen tres libras de maíz cacahunzintle como para atole. Se lava bien, se enjuga con un lienzo y se pone á secar al sol. Después se muele y se cierno por un ayatito, añadiéndosele mas de tres libras de manteca: se le echa luego una poca de agua quebrantada y azúcar molida, batiéndolo hasta que haga como ampollas. Como el azúcar vuelve aguada la masa es necesario tener cuidado que espese bien, y se conoce que está buena, haciendo de ella una bolita, que se echará en agua donde deberá subir ó sobrenadar.

   El relleno se hace de yemas de huevo cocidas, azúcar molida, piñones, acitrón, canela y ajonjolí. Las hojas se ponen á escurrir con anticipación, por ejemplo, en la mañana, si los tamales se han de hacer en la tarde, para que no estén mojadas al tiempo de envolver la masa. Se ponen á cocer los tamales en una olla, en cuyo fondo se habrá echado una poca de agua, y mas arriba se formará una cama ó tapextle con palitos y zacate de modo que no toque al agua. Encima se ponen los tamales, que se conocerá que están cocidos en que suenan como aventados y en que se les despegan las hojas.

   Sin azúcar y con sal pueden rellenarse de chile con jamón; papada ó carne de puerco, todo cocido. También se hacen de especia sin azúcar y con sal.

Otros.

Se toman tres libras de maíz cacahuazintle, media libra de manteca derretida, ocho yemas de huevo, el dulce necesario y una poca de agua caliente. No debe quedar esta mezcla ni aguada ni muy espesa, y se bate hasta que haga espuma.

Se le echa bastante canela, pasas, piñones, almendras, nueces y ajonjolí, y formados los tamales se ponen á cocer como los anteriores, tapándose bien la olla con zacate.

Id. sin cernir

4. Se hacen en iodo como los ya dichos con la diforencia de que será el maíz del común, y no se cierne la masa después de molida.

   Se hacen de dulce mezclando un poco de panecillo para que salgan jaspeados, de chile, de especia y de capulín.

Id. de arroz

5. Se lava el arroz y se pone á secar en una servilleta: cuando lo esté, se pesa una libra, se remuele hasta que se haga polvo, y se echará en un cazo donde se va remojando con leche. Se derrite media libra de mantequilla, y estando casi fria se mezcla con el arroz y se bate con una cuchara de palo hasta que esponje. Aunque es mejor la mantequilla, puede usarse en su lugar de manteca. Se conoce que está de punto la masa haciendo de ella una bolita, que echada en una tasa de agua sube ó sobrenada. Entonces se le añade media libra de azúcar en polvo sin batirla mucho. Se hacen los tamales, que se rellenarán con postre de bienmesabe y se cocerán como se ha esplicado en los artículos anteriores, con la precaución de acomodarlos parados para que no se vacíen.

English:
Tamales

1. Wash the nixtamál or nixcómel thoroughly, rinse it with a napkin or cloth, grind it and close it well: mix nine and a half ounces of sugar, one pound of butter and the corresponding salt, warm water, and anise. Mix everything well and wrap the dough in corn husks to form tamales.

   A little water is poured into a pot provided, and above it a tapextle or tabladito is formed, where these tamales will be put without getting wet so that they cook with the steam of the water, covering the pot with a washcloth and a plate on top

   Chili-and-spice tamales are made in the same way, with the only difference in eliminating sugar and anise.

Others

2. Three pounds of cacahunzintle corn available for atole. Wash and rinse well, then place it on a piece of cloth to dry in the sun. Next grind it, and pass it through a sieve, adding more than three pounds of butter. Add a little bit of water and powdered sugar, beating it until it bubbles. As the sugar moistens

the dough, it is necessary to be careful that it thickens well, and it is known that it is good to make it into a ball, which will be thrown in water, where it should rise or float.

The filling is made from cooked egg yolks, powdered sugar, pine nuts, acitrón, cinnamon, and sesame seeds. The leaves are drained in advance, for example, in the morning, if the tamales are to be made in the afternoon, so that they are not wet at the time of wrapping the dough. The tamales are cooked in a pot, at the bottom of which a little water will have been poured, and above a bed or tapextle with sticks and grass so they do not touch the water. The tamales are put on top. It will be known to be cooked in that they sound solid and in which the leaves are detached.

Without sugar and with salt they can be filled with chili with ham; fatty meat or pork, all cooked. They are also made with spice—without sugar and with salt.

Others

Three pounds of cacahuazintle corn, half a pound of melted butter, eight egg yolks, the necessary sweet and a little hot water are taken. This mixture should not be watery or very thick, and beaten until it lathers. You add enough cinnamon, raisins, pine nuts, almonds, nuts, and sesame seeds, and, when the tamales are formed, they cook like the previous ones, covering the pot with grass.

Id. without sifting

4. They are made in iodine like the aforementioned, with the difference that it will be common corn, and the masa does not close after grinding.

They are made sweet by mixing a bit of sweet bread roll in order to bring out the marbling of chili, spice, and chokecherry.

Id. Rice

5. The rice is washed and dried on a napkin: when it is, a pound is weighed, removed until it becomes dusty, and it will be thrown into a saucepan where it is soaked with milk. Melt half a pound of butter, and being almost cold mix with the rice and beat with a wooden spoon until it absorbs. Although butter is better, oil can be used instead of butter. Note that the dough is coalescing into a ball, which is thrown into water and rises or floats. Then you add half a pound of powdered sugar without beating it much. Tamales are made, which will be filled with bienmesabe dessert (dessert prepared with honey, egg yolk, and ground almonds) and cooked as explained in the previous articles, with the precaution of accommodating them standing so they do not empty.

Recetas practicas y utiles, sobre cocina, reposteria, pasteleria, etc. Segunda edición. Durango City: Tip. Mercantil, 1881.

Spanish:

Tamales

Tamales de cuajada

A una libra de nixtamal, tres de cuajada, doce onzas de azúcar, diez huevos batidos como para marquesote, una de mantequilla fría; se revuelven bien, se hacen los tamales y se cuecen en el horno.

Tamales de coco

Se pone un cuarterón de nixtamal, se refriega, se despica, se pone á secar y se muele; se le revuelve un coco rallado y molida, se baten dos libras de Manteca como para los tamales de azúcar y cuando ya esté de punto se revuelve con la masa y dos libras de azúcar en polvo, se bate la masa mucho hasta que se eche una bolita en el agua y no se suma, entonces se hacen los tamales adornándolos con pasas, almendras y pedacitos de dulces cubiertos.

Tamales de picadillo

Despicado y bien refregado el nixtamal, se muele con una rajita de canela y un poquito de clavo, se le añade Manteca fría, sal, y un polvito de azúcar, se bate la masa rociándola de cuando en cuando con agua fría para que no se reseque demasiado; ya que la masa estáde punto se van untando las hojas bien lavadas y secas, poniéndoles en medio el picadillo, adornado con pasas, almendras y aceitunas: luego se cuecen.

Tamales de gallina

Preparada la masa en las hojas como en los anteriores, se prepara la gallina cocida y cortada en pedacitos chicos, seguisa en mole ó en la salsa que se quiera, procurando quede con poco caldo para que pueda server de relleno, y se cuecen como todos los tamales.

English:

Tamales

Curd Tamales

A pound of nixtamal, three of curd, twelve ounces of sugar, ten beaten eggs as for marquesote, one of cold butter; stir together well, make the tamales and bake in the oven.

Coconut Tamales

A quarter of nixtamal frayed, disheveled, dried and ground; it is mixed with a grated and ground coconut. Beat two pounds of lard for the sugar tamales and when it is ready it is stirred with the dough and two pounds of powdered sugar, the dough is beaten a lot until it is a ball in the water and does not sink, then make the tamales by decorating them with raisins, almonds and pieces of covered candy.

Minced Tamales

Once the nixtamal is well rubbed, it is ground with a cinnamon stick and a little clove, cold shortening, salt, and a little sugar powder all mixed together, the dough is beaten by spraying it occasionally with cold water so that it does not dry out too much; when the dough is well kneaded, the leaves are well washed and dried, putting in the middle the mincemeat, garnished with raisins, almonds and olives: then they are cooked.

Chicken Tamales

Prepare the dough in the leaves as in the previous ones, then cook the chicken and cut into small pieces, cook in mole or in the sauce that is desired, trying to keep it with little broth so that it can serve as a filling, and they are cooked as all the tamales.

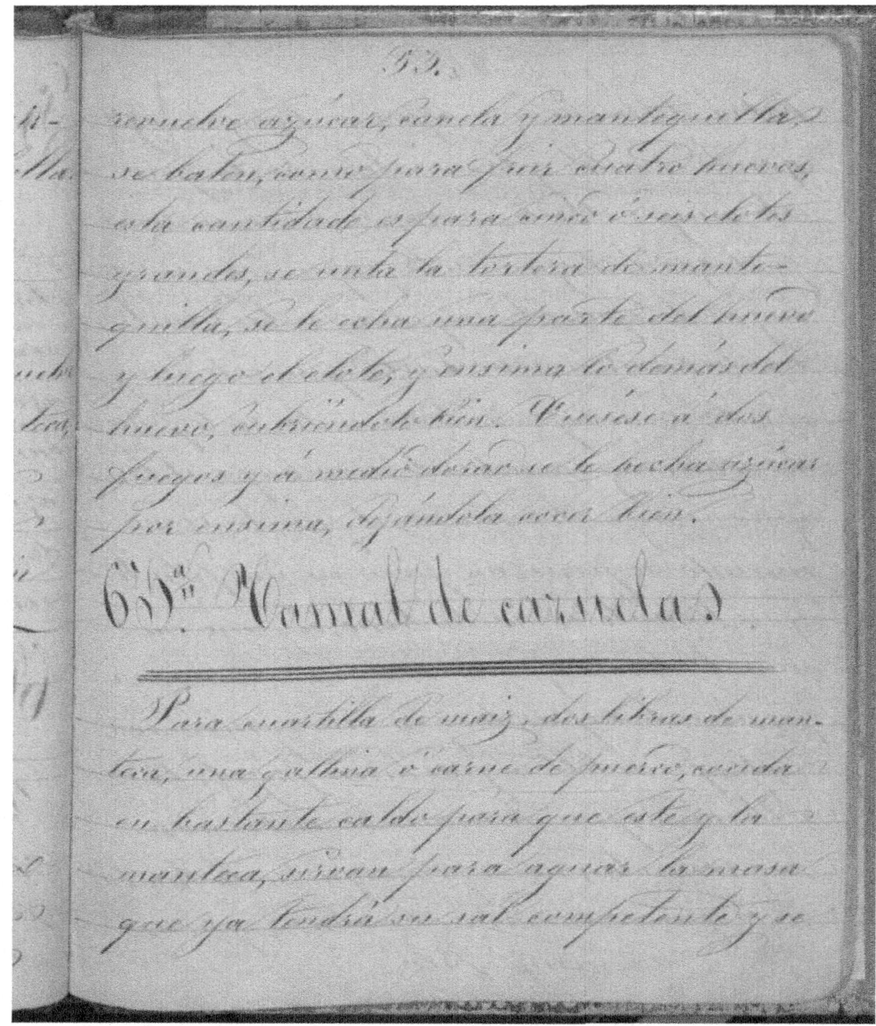

Figure 17.1: Mexican Cooking Notebook pg 57. Manuela Heredia y Cervantes, "[Mexican cooking notebook]: manuscript", 1886. Retrieved from https://digital.utsa.edu/digital/collection/p15125coll10/id/12214/rec/1

Heredia y Cervantes, Manuela. "[Mexican cooking notebook]: manuscript", 1886.

Spanish:

#63 Tamal de cazuelas

Para cuartilla de maíz, dos libras de manteca, una gallina ó carne de puerco, cocida en bastante caldo para que este y la manteca, sirvan para aguar la masa que ya tendrá su sal competente y se habrá deshecho con agua se le sigue agregando el caldo y la manteca, hasta que esté muy suelta la masa, se le echan unos pedazos de hoja santa pequeños y unas hojas de epasote se pone en la lumbre, ha de hervir mucho hasta que esté muy cocido si se espesa demaciado se le puede echar agua caliente sino hay caldo, y no se deja de menear, el punto se ve cuando se pone un poco en un plato y se levante como la leche, se pone en una tortera, hoja santa, sobre esta se van poniendo capas, las que uno quiere, con mole, picadillo ó pasta de frijol, la última capa de masa se cubre con hoja santa; no se pone ya en la lumbre, solo que se coma á otro día, ó que esté muy frio.

English:

Tamal Casserole

For corn pastry, two pounds of butter, a chicken or pork meat, cooked in enough broth so that it and the butter serve to dilute the dough that will already have its needed salt and have been dissolved with water keep adding broth and butter until the dough is very loose, a few pieces of small pepperleaf are added and some epasote leaves are put on the fire, it must boil until it is well cooked if it is too thick you can add in hot water if there is no broth available, and it does not stop moving around until it is ready when it is put a small amount on a plate and rises like milk, it is put in a pan, a piece of pepperleaf, and on top of it add layers, as much one wants, with mole, hash, or bean paste, until the last layer of dough is covered with a pepperleaf; it is no longer put on the fire, only that it is eaten another day, or when it is very cold.

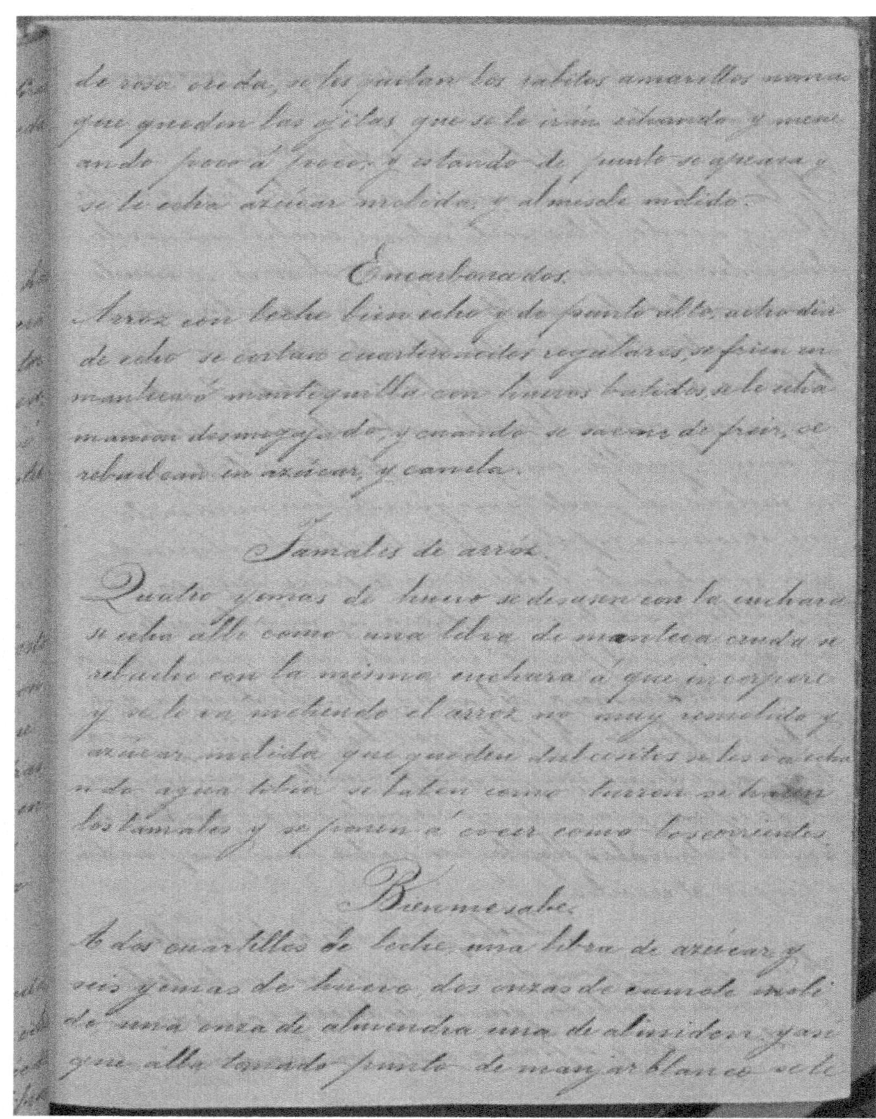

de rosa oreada, se les pulan los rabitos amarillos para
que queden las ojitas que se le irán echando y mene
ando poco á fuego, y estando de punto se apeara y
se le echa azúcar molida, y almiscle molido.

Encarbonados.

Arroz con leche bien echo y de punto alto, a otro dia
de echo se cortan cuarterones regulares, se frien en
manteca ó mantequilla con huevos batidos, se le echa
mamon desmoronado, y cuando se acaba de freir, se
rebosan en azúcar, y canela.

Tamales de arroz.

Quatro yemas de huevo se desasen con la cuchara
se echa allí como una libra de manteca cruda se
rebuelve con la misma cuchara á que incorpore
y se le va echando el arroz no muy remolido y
azúcar molida que queden dulcesitos se les va echa
ndo agua tibia se baten como turron se hacen
los tamales y se ponen á cocer como los corrientes.

Bienmesabe.

A dos cuartillos de leche una libra de azúcar y
seis yemas de huevo, dos onzas de camote moli
do una onza de almendra una de almidon y ase
que alla tomado punto de manjar blanco se le

Figure 17.2: Libro de recetas de cocina. Guadalupe Perez, "Libro de recetas de cocina", 1884. Retrieved from https://digital.utsa.edu/digital/collection/p15125coll10/id/11440

Perez, Guadalupe. “Libro de recetas de cocina”, 1884.

Spanish:

Tamales de arróz

Quatro yemas de huevo se desasen con la cuchara se echa allí como una libra de manteca cruda se rebuelve con la misma cuchara á que incorpore y se le vá metiendo el arróz no muy remolido y azúcar molida que queden dulcesitos se les va echando agua tibia se laten como turrón se hacen los tamales y se ponen á cocer como los corrientes.

Tamales de arróz

Se lava el arróz se escure y se muele bien y á cada libra y á cada libra se le echan cuatro onzan de almendra molida con agua fría al arroz se muele en seco se bate la manteca un poco con la mano que es media libra a cada libra de arróz y in mabaten se va amasando suabemente todo hasta que se aga una masa blanda se le echa un pedaso de mantequilla una poca de sal molida y azúcar molida al gusto y así que esté bien amasada que se conosca esponjada se le echa la almendra y se va echando leche poco á poco que sea un cuartillo y se bate con cuchara en una tasa de agua se toma el punto echando una poca de masa sé se sube ensima del agua lla está buena y sí se baja al fondo le falta que batér, en una poca de agua se desase un poco de franesillo ó carmín que quede espeso y en cada oja se meta un poquito y se hasen los tamales flojitos por arriba para que puedan esponjar al coserlos canela, y una oja de naranja, se le da punto alto para que fría se puedan cortar pedasitos para llenar los tamales: se ase la vís pera.

Leche para llenar los tamales.

Se muele un poco de arroz, se desase en la leche y almendra molida, yemas de huevo, y azúcar al gusto, se cuela y se pone á cocer con una raja de canela, y una oja de naranja; se le da punto alto para que fria se puedan cortar pedasitos para llenar los tamales: se ase la víspera.

Tamales Corrientes.

A una maquila de maíz, dos libras de manteca azúcar al gusto; y tantita sal.

English:

Rice Tamales (Version 1)

Break four egg yolks with a spoon. Add a pound of shortening, mixing together with the same spoon until it is blended. Gently add in the semi-ground rice and powdered sugar until it is sweetened. Add warm water and beat until it is like the texture of nougat, the tamales are made and cook as usual.

Rice Tamales (Version 2)

The rice is washed, and drained and ground well. Add four ounces of ground almonds for each pound of rice with cold water. Beat the shortening by hand using a half a pound for each pound of rice. Continue kneading until a soft, spongy dough is formed. Add the almonds and milk little by little up to a quarter of a cup and continue beating with a spoon until it is ready. Use a cup of water to figure out if the dough is ready. Get a cup of water and put a little bit of dough in. If the dough floats it is ready. If it sinks to the bottom, it needs to be beaten again. Add a little franesillo or carmine to a little bit of water to thicken it, adding a little bit to each leaf so they can get spongy as you cook them. The tamales are done loose. To cook the tamales, add cinnamon and orange peel. Cook to high boiling point so that you can cut it into small pieces when it is cooled down to fill the tamales: they will be prepared on the day before you need them.

Milk to Fill the Tamales

Grind a little rice, dissolve into milk and ground almonds, egg yolks, and sugar to taste, strain and cook with a cinnamon stick and an orange leaf; boil so that when it is cold it can be cut into pieces to fill the tamales: it is prepared the day before.

Common Tamales

Two pounds of butter sugar to taste; and a bit of salt to 6.6 pounds of corn.

—18—

Brains, Skill, and Butter: Sample a Feast of History in Century-Old Cookbooks

Katie Mayer

Peruse the cookbooks of yore in the Oregon Historical Society Research Library (OHS), and you'll encounter recipes that inspire reactions from curiosity to cringes: ham boiled with hay, creamed spaghetti on toast, pigeons in casserole, twenty gallons of "sour krout," and pork cake (with raisins and frosting, lest you think this means meatloaf—a recipe attempted by my colleague Sarah Stroman (https://www.ohs.org/blog/pork-cake.cfm).

And those aren't the only intrigues and oddities. The cookbooks are rife with eggs and butter. Measurements include not only the familiar cups and teaspoons, but also decidedly non-standard quantities such as a "teacupful" or "butter the size of a walnut." Oven temperatures, described with terms such as slow and quick, moderate and hot, leave much to the imagination. And, speaking of the imagination, a great deal of it is required for a current-day cook, as the recipes often consist of little more than a list of ingredients.

These observations come from my perusal of several cookbooks published in Oregon during the late 1800s and early 1900s, including: *The Web-Foot Cook Book* (1885), published in Portland; *A Portland Girl at the Chafing Dish* (1897), by Alice H. Sansbury; the *Alpha Club Cook Book* (1904), compiled by the women of Baker City; the *Cherry City Cook Book* (circa 1911), published by the Ladies' Auxiliary of Unity Church in Salem; and the *Practical Cook Book* (1912), compiled by the Woman's Auxiliary to Pacific College in Newberg. In addition to the published dishes, some of the books contain recipes handwritten on blank pages by previous owners.

Along with soups and cakes and brains on toast, historic cookbooks yield juicy hints about the cooks who provided and used the recipes, the equipment available to them, and the abundance or scarcity of various foods. But, more than 100 years later, it's not always easy to read between the lines. An invaluable guide to interpreting the cookbooks is *The Way We Ate*, by Jacqueline B. Williams[1], who describes the evolution of cookery among emigrants to the Northwest. Williams's descriptions are a vivid reminder of how different kitchens then were from those

---

[1] Jacqueline B. Williams, *The Way We Ate: Pacific Northwest Cooking, 1843-1900*. (Pullman, WA: Washington State University Press, 1996).

today. During the era when these cookbooks were written, cookstoves were made of cast iron or steel and burned fuel such as wood, coal, or kerosene. Cooks regulated temperature with complex sets of dampers that took practice to master. Rotary egg beaters began to appear in the 1870s, providing mechanical alternatives to whisk-type tools, but they were no match for the power of a modern mixer. Though standardized measuring cups and spoons entered use during the mid-1880s, Williams notes that "impressionistic measurements," such as butter the size of an egg, appeared in cookbooks well into the twentieth century. Both types of measurement appear throughout the cookbooks I consulted, sometimes in the same recipe.

As for the lack of instruction in recipes, brevity was a mark of the cooks' expertise, whether they were readers or writers. "The women of yesteryear learned the art of cookery at an early age and did not require standardized recipes," Williams writes—they might not write down a recipe at all unless someone requested it. Without the unwritten knowledge behind the recipes, to cook from a historic book today requires a spirit of experimentation and an openness to experiencing spectacular failure.

Obviously, I couldn't resist a go at it.

I decided to attempt Julia Miller's Never-Fail Sponge Cake from the *Alpha Club Cook Book*, reasoning that even if the cake were a disaster, the irony would be delicious. The recipe is as follows:

Never-Fail Sponge Cake

Four eggs, beat whites stiff enough to remain in bowl when inverted. Add ½ cup granulated sugar. Beat yolks well and add ½ cup sugar. Beat for 5 minutes. This being important as the delicate texture of the cake depends upon it. Add to the yolks the juice and rind of 1 lemon. Beat together altogether thoroughly. At this stage beating is the order. Add 1 cup of flour. The flour is to be stirred in with light turn of spoon. The mixture should now look like a puff ball. Bake in moderate oven 25 minutes. Just before putting in the oven, sprinkle 1 tablespoon granulated sugar on top. This gives the cake the crackled appearance so much desired.

Miller's recipe includes more instructions than most, but even so, I had a list of questions far longer than the recipe itself, including: How long to beat the egg whites after adding sugar; when to add the beaten whites to the batter; what temperature a "moderate oven" would be; what size and type of pan to use; whether to grease the pan; and how to tell when the cake is done. To answer them, I did what any modern cook would do, which was to scour the Internet for sponge-cake recipes that would help me fill in the gaps.

Here's what I learned: Miller's recipe is an example of a fatless sponge cake, which relies on the air beaten into the batter to rise, rather than a leavener such as baking powder or soda. The cake is baked in an ungreased tube pan, so the batter can cling to the sides as the cake rises. Once removed from the oven, the pan is immediately turned upside down and left that way until the cake cools completely, so it won't collapse.

THE NEVER-FAIL SPONGE CAKE.

Four eggs, beat whites stiff enough to remain in bowl when inverted. Add ½ cup granulated sugar. Beat yolks well and add ½ cup sugar. Beat for 5 minutes. This being important as the delicate texture of the cake depends upon it. Add to the yolks the juice and rind of 1 lemon. Beat altogether thoroughly. At this stage beating is the order. Add 1 cup of flour. The flour is to be stirred in with light turn of spoon. The mixture should now look like a puff ball. Bake in moderate oven 25 minutes. Just before putting in the oven sprinkle 1 tablespoon granulated sugar on top. This gives the cake the crackled appearance so much desired. MRS. JULIA MILLER.

Figure 18.1: Mrs. Julia Miller's recipe for a Never-Fail Sponge Cake appears on page 94 of the Alpha Club Cook Book, which was compiled by the women of Baker City, Oregon, and published in 1904. Photo credit: Robert Warren, Oregon Historical Society.

Once equipped with enough information to pretend I knew what I was doing, I rolled up my sleeves and, in a nod to historical accuracy, attempted to beat the egg whites with an old rotary beater. I cannot recommend this approach (nor, I imagine, would the women of yesteryear). It went well enough for the first five minutes, but then futility set in: after adding the sugar and trying unsuccessfully to whip the whites into stiff peaks for a period of time that felt like eternity but was actually 20 minutes, I sighed loudly, wrote "EGGS FOREVER" in my notes, and moved on.

"Moving on" meant beating egg yolks, which I continued to do with the rotary beater because I was committed. This went better than the eternal beating of the whites, although it was a true arm workout after the mixture stiffened. I added the flour, then the egg whites, and then probably overmixed the batter. I poured the batter into my tube pan, slid the pan into a 350-degree oven, set the timer for 25 minutes as the recipe suggested, and only then realized I had forgotten to sprinkle the top with sugar as directed. I decided that I frankly did not care and proceeded to sit anxiously in front of the oven like a contestant on the *Great British Baking Show*.

While 25 minutes in a moderate oven may have been sufficient for Julia Miller, it was not sufficient for me, as the cake was still raw. Around 55 minutes, it had stopped rising, was browned on top, and sprang back when I poked it, so I deemed it done. And, while it was not a perfect sponge cake, it was not a failure. It was drier and denser than it should have been, and probably overbaked, but still light, sharply lemony, and willingly eaten by brave OHS library and museum staff.

Emboldened by the knowledge gained during my first attempt, I tried the cake again, this time rejecting the rotary egg beater in favor of my trusty electric hand mixer. I slightly reduced the lemon and added a teaspoon of vanilla to suit my own taste. This time, I remembered to sprinkle the top with sugar, and I reduced the baking time to about 45 minutes. Sponge Cake No. 2 was a clear improvement: it rose higher, had a more delicate and slightly richer flavor, and was, as Julia Miller promised, pleasantly crackly on the top. I'll never know how my version (or my arm strength) compares to Miller's, but I think she'd be happy to know that her recipe truly stood the test of time.

Selected recipes

These are some of the dishes that particularly caught my attention in the cookbooks I consulted. Some, such as pork cake or brains on toast, stood out because they were odd or surprising to my particular food-related sensibilities. Others are representative in some way, such as commonality of the dish, ingredients, or technique. For instance, variations on the devil cake appear in more than one book, and the white mountain cake and scrambled eggs reflect the copious quantities of eggs and dairy called for throughout the books. Variations on the macaroni and cheese recipe were also common, but they, too, are surprising to the modern eye, because they call for long pasta broken into short pieces, rather than the short pastas one would typically find in macaroni and cheese recipes today.

Sweet

In *The Way We Ate: Pacific Northwest Cooking, 1843-1909,* Jacqueline B. Williams notes that pork cakes were a method of preserving cooked meat. Though the name of the cake conjures visions of meatloaf, this recipe produces a baked good similar to fruitcake.

Pork Cake (Original)

Contributed by Fannie L. Baker to the *Practical Cook Book*, compiled by the Woman's Auxiliary to Pacific College in Newberg, Oregon, 1912

One and one-half cups brown sugar, two-thirds cup finely chopped pork, 2 eggs well beaten, 1 cup rich buttermilk, 1 cup raisins dusted with flour, 1 cup nut meats, ½ teaspoon of cinnamon, nutmeg and allspice, ¼ spoon of cloves, 1 spoon of soda sifted in sufficient flour to make stiff batter. Bake in loaf in moderate oven and frost when cool.

Scripture cakes required the cook to know (or look up) Bible verses to determine what ingredients to use.

Scripture Cake

Contributed by Mrs. O. E. Moran to the *Alpha Club Cook Book*, compiled by ladies of Baker City, Oregon, 1904.

Four cups 1 Kings 4:22; 2-3 cups Judges 5:25 (last clause); 2 cups Jermiah [sic] 6:20; 2 cups First Samuel 30:12; 1 cup Numbers 17:8; 2 cups Nahum 3:12; 2 tablespoons 1 Sam. 14:25. Season to taste. 2 Chronicles 9:9; 6 tablespoons Jermiah [sic] 17:11; a pinch of Leviticus 2:13; 1 cup Genesis 49:12 (last clause); 2 teaspoons Amos 4:5 (baking powder), Follow Solomon's prescription for making a good boy. Proverbs 23:14, and you will have a good cake.

Devil Cake

Contributed by Mrs. E. H. Woodward to the to the *Practical Cook Book*, compiled by the Woman's Auxiliary to Pacific College in Newberg, Oregon, 1912.

Three-fourths cup brown sugar, ¼ cup white sugar, ½ cup butter, ½ cup sour milk, 2 cups flour, 2 eggs beaten light, 1 teaspoon soda.
Dark part—One cup chocolate ground, ½ cup brown sugar, ½ cup sweet milk, yolk of 1 egg, 1 teaspoon vanilla. Let boil, when cool stir into cake and bake in two layers.

White Mountain Cake

Contributed by Mrs. Proffitt to the *Alpha Club Cook Book*, compiled by ladies of Baker City, Oregon, 1904.

Whites of 11 eggs, a large cup of sugar, 1 teaspoon cream of tartar in little more than 1 cup of flour, 1 teaspoon almond extract. Bake in 3 layers. Take whites of 4 eggs for icing. Grate a whole cocoanut on icing between layers. Sprinkle well with cocoanut on top and sides.

Bran Gems

Handwritten on blank pages at the back of the *Alpha Club Cook Book*, compiled by ladies of Baker City, Oregon, 1904.

2 eggs – 3 tablespoonful of Molasses
1 qt of sweet Milk – 2½ cups of flour – Salt
2½ cups of Cooking Bran – Baking Powder

Savory

In *Portland: A Food Biography*,[2] Heather Arndt Anderson writes that the *Web-Foot Cook Book* was the first cookbook published in the Pacific Northwest.

Brains on Toast

Contributed by Mrs. J. D. Holman to the *Web-Foot Cook Book*, Portland, Oregon, 1885.

Let the brains lay in cold salt water for half an hour, then pour boiling hot water over them. After standing a few minutes pour off the water, skin them, put into a frying pan with three spoonsful of hot butter, stir them well, adding an egg or two while doing so, a little salt and pepper. Lay nicely browned toast on a hot platter, put a good spoonful of brains on each piece. Serve hot.

---

[2] Arndt Anderson, Heather. *Portland: A Food Biography*. Big City Food Biographies Series. Lanham: Rowman & Littlefield, 2015.

Macaroni and Cheese

Contributed by Ida N. Lachner to the *Alpha Club Cook Book*, compiled by ladies of Baker City, Oregon, 1904.

Break macaroni into inch lengths and drop into boiling salted water. Boil 15 minutes and drain. Butter a baking dish and put in a layer of macaroni, bits of butter and plenty of grated cheese, and a little salt and pepper. Then add another layer of macaroni until dish is full, adding enough milk to almost cover. Bake in hot oven from 20 to 30 minutes. Macaroni served with tomato sauce is also very nice.

Corn mustard

Cherry City Cook Book, compiled by the Ladies' Auxiliary of Unity Church in Salem, Oregon, circa 1911.

Slit lengthwise with a sharp knife, six ears of fresh corn, scrape kernels out of shells and off of cob into basin. Add four eggs, one-half cup of sweet cream, a lump of butter half the size of an egg, salt to taste. Yolks and whites of eggs may be beaten separately and whites added just before baking. Bake a golden brown.

Mayanoise [sic]

Handwritten on blank pages at the back of the *Alpha Club Cook Book*, compiled by ladies of Baker City, Oregon, 1904.

2 yolks of Eggs Olive Oil to thicken
½ teaspoonful of Salt ½ mustard 1 dash of Pepereka [sic] dash of Pepper, Lemon

Pigeons in Casserole

Contributed by Mrs. R. Cartwright to the *Cherry City Cook Book*, compiled by the Ladies' Auxiliary of Unity Church in Salem, Oregon, circa 1911.

Allow one pigeon for each person, lard the breast of each with a slice of pickled pork, slit the skin and insert a small piece of truffle, then stuff with the following dressing: Two cups of stale bread crumbs, one tablespoon of minced onion browned in butter, one-half small can of minced mushrooms, one minced truffle, a sprinkle of paprika, and Buckeye mace. Put a slice of butter in casserole, dredge birds lightly with flour, turn them in the melted butter, add one cup of water and bake in medium oven for one hour. Then add the juice and remaining mushrooms, salt and thicken with browned flour. Serve with cress and orange salad with French dressing.

Peanut Sandwiches

Cherry City Cook Book, compiled by the Ladies' Auxiliary of Unity Church in Salem, Oregon, circa 1911.

Spread slices of white bread with any preferred brand of peanut butter, and sprinkle with chopped celery.

Beef Steak Balls

Contributed by Mrs. Chas. T. Kirkhart to the to the *Practical Cook Book*, compiled by the Woman's Auxiliary to Pacific College in Newberg, Oregon, 1912.

Use round steak, slice thin, cut in pieces about 3 inches square. Chop together 1 medium-sized onion and 3 slices of bacon, a few bread crumbs; season with salt and pepper. Put a small portion of mixture in pieces of beef steak and pin it well with tooth-picks. Boil until tender. Make gravy and serve hot.

Scrambled Eggs

Contributed by Bertha K. Terrell to the to the *Practical Cook Book*, compiled by the Woman's Auxiliary to Pacific College in Newberg, Oregon, 1912

Butter the size of walnut in skillet, add ½ cup cream. When hot break in 6 eggs and stir till slightly cooked.

PART III

Nostalgia and Foodways

—19—

Introduction

Cynthia C. Prescott
with contributions by Maureen S. Thompson

A good meal feeds both body and soul. It also can be a powerful conduit of memory. My mother once took her friend Karin to lunch at Charm Family Restaurant in Ohio's Amish country. It was Karin's first visit to an Amish restaurant. Ignoring my mother's recommendation of the broasted chicken (breaded and then fried in a pressure cooker to produce a crispier coating), her friend opted for the pan-fried version. At the first bite she burst into tears. She never thought she would taste her grandmother's fried chicken again—a beloved recipe her family believed to have died with her grandmother. In fact, it—or a very similar recipe—lived on among distant Amish and Mennonite relations, and was being served daily to "English" (non-Amish) tourists in the charming village of Charm. That one bite of pan-fried chicken could cause a suburban librarian to cry openly in public speaks volumes about how familiar tastes live on in our individual memory. Uniting many individual memories of flavors and family togetherness paints a portrait of nostalgia's connection to cultural values and community identity.

The first two sections of this Rural Women's Studies Association community cookbook focused on what we can learn from cookbooks as publications. In parts IV and V we will explore political uses of food and the impact of globalization on US foodways. Sandwiched between those research-heavy sections, Part III provides a sweet and comforting filling. These stories and flavors take us back to seemingly simpler times, celebrating the culinary skills of beloved home cooks. Yet that does not mean that we are abandoning a scholar's critical eye as we invite you to share these nostalgic contributions.

In this section, we drill down to the level of individual recipes and the lore often associated with those recipes. We juxtapose a few unusual recipes against the tried-and-true tastes that are central to individual and family memories from different subcultures throughout North America. In the process, we uncover the value of women's domestic work, their place within their community, and connections to the wider world.

For centuries, labor performed in and around the home formed the basis of countries' economies. Every member of the family worked and contributed to household production. Only after the advent of wage labor did many family members work outside of the home, which introduced Victorian middle-class notions of men working outside the home while wives tended to the domestic sphere. For rural women, there was little distinction between paid and unpaid labor as they performed whatever chores were necessary for their families to prosper. Gendered labor was ubiquitous throughout history with women undertaking most duties associated with food preparation.

Social mores dictated that ladies be composed and modest, but rural women who produced the tastiest dish at a community potluck were publicly recognized for their culinary skills. Contests at county and state fairs prompted women to compete with one another for prizes including dishware, trophies, and later, cash. When men won contests, they also earned bragging rights; conversely, women bestowed honor upon their households. Some women shared prize-winning recipes in community cookbooks compiled to raise funds for church or community projects (perhaps omitting some essential ingredient from their secret recipe). Throughout the twentieth century, cooking contests increased in popularity, often in conjunction with media publications or brand-name products. Recipes that were passed down through generations of cooks often had backstories. Examples of such are discussed throughout this section.

Ironically for a cookbook—and for historians normally obsessed with documentation—several of these essays praise recipes that were *not* recorded for posterity. As Katie Mayer points out (Mayer, Ch. 18, this volume), nineteenth- and early-twentieth-century women learned to cook at an early age. They relied on experience and observation, rather than standardized recipes, to produce tasty food. Several prided themselves on cooking from memory. Much of their expertise they passed on orally (Cates, Ch. 24, this volume), only writing it down when someone outside their household requested it. Cooking delicious food without relying on a written recipe demonstrated their expertise and ensured that they, like Tracey Hanshew's Maw-maw, would not have to divulge their kitchen secrets (Hanshew, Ch. 27, this volume). Some were highly inventive—such as the award-winning creations of the Bradley women of the Delmarva Peninsula (Morris, Ch. 20, this volume). Others perfected classics such as the fried chicken that my mother's friend feared had died with her grandmother.

There are striking similarities among the heritage recipes shared in this section. Contributors emphasize their mothers' and grandmothers' role in "making do" with scarce resources on the farm, in contrast to the social class aspirations on display with many of the community cookbooks in Part II. The heirloom entrée recipes shared in this volume reflect efforts to stretch scarce resources to feed families hungry from physical labor on the farm. Many of the favorite recipes shared in this section are for hearty dishes featuring stewed meat with noodles or dumplings.

Despite these parallels, comparing the recipes in this volume highlights important cultural differences. Cooks in the central United State relied heavily on chicken and wheat-based pastas (Cates, Ch. 24, this volume; Riney-Kehrberg, Ch. 25, this volume). German heritage clung to potato-based dumplings and vinegar both as a beef brine and for pickling cabbage (Speyer, Ch. 26, this volume). Those on the East coast incorporated shellfish, particularly crab (Morris, Ch. 22, this volume), but also shrimp in South Carolina (Jones-Branch, Ch. 13, this volume). The rice-producing South Carolina Lowcountry not surprisingly incorporated more rice than did the wheat- and corn-producing Great Plains. While less well represented within this volume, North American corn (maize) was a staple throughout much of the Midwest and South, and later became a primary additive to processed food in the form of the sweetener high-fructose corn syrup. Okra was common throughout the South, indicating enslaved Africans' influence on the foodways of not only their descendants but those of the Euro-Americans whom their descendants served as cooks both before and after emancipation (Jones-Branch, Ch. 13, this volume).

Anthropologists and immigration historians find that foodways often persist through generations who are otherwise culturally assimilated. Yet as nations of immigrants, both the US and Canada reveal the way that cultural influences spread far and wide. Not only did tamales become popular north of Mexico (Noell, Ch. 17, this volume), but Latin American influences can be found in rural French Canada. That Myrtle Dougall called her Meso-American-inspired buns "Spanish" suggests her social class aspirations, and that rural Canadians joined white Californians in whitewashing Mexican ethnic heritage by labeling it "Spanish" in the early twentieth century (Wilson, Ch. 30, this volume).[1] The prevalence of Indian-inspired curry in Canada (Wilson, Ch. 7, this volume) suggests the lasting impact of British colonialism throughout the British Empire as well as the prevalence of immigrants from throughout the globe in Canada. That Anglo-Americans persisted in viewing curries as exotic throughout the twentieth century suggests its divorce from that empire, and the lasting dominance of blander white American foodways centered on red meat, potatoes, and breads and sweets made from bleached wheat flour and pure white sugar.

The recipes shared here and elsewhere in this volume emphasize baked goods such as rolls, pies, or cakes that were much-sought-after at church dinners and other community events (McKenzie, Ch. 29, this volume). That so many contributors were eager to share these baked goods suggests the important role that comforting starches and sweets serve not only in filling hungry bellies and fueling farm labor, but in nurturing emotional comfort. It also emphasizes the skill these recipes for raised breads, light cakes, and flaky pie crusts require, particularly for rural women cooking over a coal stove or open hearth—skills many have lost in a shift toward manufactured foods since World War II. As women embraced paid labor outside the home, they were no longer around the kitchen to tend to rising dough. It simply made practical sense to rely on commercial bakeries. But sliced sandwich loaves and packaged desserts are packed with processed ingredients and preservatives (if no longer the trans fats that once promised to keep these products shelf-stable for many weeks). Refined carbohydrates such as bleached white flour and added sweeteners produce smooth textures and consistently pleasant flavors, but can contribute to obesity and type 2 diabetes. While a carb-heavy diet offered energy to fuel physically demanding field labor, it is at odds with the nutritional needs of today's increasingly sedentary population. That so many contributors—

[1] William Deverell, *Whitewashed Adobe: The Rise of Los Angeles and the Remaking of Its Mexican Past* (Berkeley: University of California Press, 2004).

themselves mostly academics increasingly confined to desks and computer screens for whom consuming such foods likely will contribute to increasing waistlines and potentially poorer health—chose to share treasured recipes for baked goods, and that so many people throughout North America suddenly embraced similar home baking during the 2020 pandemic (Prescott, Ch. 48, this volume) suggests that they mourn the move away from homemade bread and treats.

Moreover, baked goods play a central role in socializing. Whether offering refined teatime treats (Murphy, Ch. 14, this volume) or a family gathering over coffee (Jellison, Ch. 23, this volume), baked goods offer a chance to gather and to share labor or leisure. When the creators of this volume gathered over pastries at a French bistro during an academic conference in the heart of Washington, DC, they shared a comradery not so unlike that celebrated in these reminiscences.

If the kitchen is the hub of the home, Part III is the heart of this volume. It celebrates the ways that families and communities come together around the kitchen table—the "Kitchen Joy" that inspired the title of the cookbook published by the Mount Horr African Methodist Episcopal Church in Hollywood, South Carolina (Jones-Branch, Ch. 13, this volume). The women's stories held within this section highlight the ways that women poured their soul into the meals that they prepared for their family and friends. Within this section we step away from the critical scholarly eye present in many of the essays in this volume. Setting aside dispassionate analysis, contributors to Part III embrace warm memories and celebrate the accomplishments of less learned ladies whose lives revolved around nurturing their families and communities.

On the surface there might appear to be an anti-feminist bent within the reminiscences in this section. After all, the first generation of RWSA members were scholars who innovated ways to identify and document the work that rural women did (Jensen et al., Ch. 2). They asked—as Virginia Scharff (Scharff, Ch. 53, this volume) does near the end of this volume—who did the heavy lifting? In contrast, the stories in Part III tend to portray women's cooking as a labor of love. For example, Elsie Swafford Riney demonstrated her love for her family by stretching the household budget with homemade chicken and noodles (Riney-Kehrberg, Ch. 25, this volume). After her husband's death, she decided that cheap manufactured ramen noodles "made a fine substitute"—but her granddaughter disagreed, remaining loyal to Riney's mother's recipe.

Joseph Cates's essay "Grandmama's Cooking Traditions" (Cates, Ch. 24, this volume) is particularly instructive in this regard. Where Rebecca Sharpless's (Sharpless, Ch. 3, this volume) and Kathryn Harvey's (Harvey, Ch. 5, this volume) essays in Part I highlight the ways that recipes became standardized, Cates' essay in this section reveals how recipes were passed down within his and many other families: as oral traditions, with quantities of ingredients measured by sight and feel rather than precise instruments. While Cates reports various family members loving particular dishes, his essay makes clear that what made that food most precious was not his Grandmama's expertise in preparing admittedly simple dishes, but that it was "lovingly cooked." In contrast to Tracey Hanshew's Mam-maw (Hanshew, Ch. 27, this volume), Cates does not remember his Grandmama as having secret recipes. Instead, she had exacting standards, and even chased her sister-in-law out of the house for failing to follow her methods precisely. Yet Cates suspects that his renditions of her recipes never taste as good not only because he relies on store-bought vegetables rather than those he grew and canned himself, but because his Grandmama included touches to which he was not privy.

Applying scholarly analysis to Cates' reminiscence is even more revealing, allowing us to discover who was doing that heavy lifting. He begins by telling us that his paternal grandmother "quit work to take care of my older sister and me while our parents worked" (Cates, Ch. 24, this volume). Yet what follows is a recounting of her daily "chores"—in other words, all of the domestic and farm labor that she completed *while* caring for her two grandchildren "along with a few other neighborhood kids." In the morning she cooked breakfast, cleaned up, and helped with field work, then prepared a simple midday meal. During the heat of the day she enjoyed apparent leisure time with her "stories" (television soap operas). Yet even during this downtime she crocheted and continued to care for several young children, and began preparing meat, two vegetables, and homemade biscuits or cornbread for supper. Somewhere in there she also found time to can the many vegetables that she picked. In what sense, then, had Joseph's grandmother quit working? She had ceased doing paid off-farm work in order to focus on unpaid domestic and field labor, the same labor that women had done for centuries before her.

It is also telling that Cates recounts most of his grandmother's recipes in passive voice in a manner that erases the actor: dumpling dough "would be floured and rolled out," "deboned chicken was added back to the broth." Only when Cates' grandmother chose to deviate from tradition, such as leaving boiled eggs out of the chicken and dumplings, or substituted jelly for icing on a white layer cake, does Grandmama appear in Cates' retelling of her recipes. In each case, Grandmama regains agency because these choices represent a labor of love: she leaves out the boiled eggs (to her son's consternation) or replaces jelly for frosting, because that is how Joseph preferred to eat those dishes. As this example makes clear, all too often memory disguises or even devalues the realities of domestic labor. Yet what remains crystal clear to the rememberer is the love that motivated these highly repetitive tasks. While the individual tasks involved in these labor-intensive recipes might go unappreciated, the skill and affection with which they did so lives on in family lore and personal remembrances.

Some of these essays and recipes are tinged with a golden haze of nostalgia, but if read carefully, they nonetheless reveal much about women's work and ways of knowing. In this section, we drill down to the level of individual recipes, and the lore often associated with those recipes. We juxtapose a few unusual recipes against the tried-and-true tastes that are central to individual and family memories. In the process, we uncover the value of women's domestic work, their place within their community, and connections to the wider world.

—20—

The Bradley Women and *The Delmarva Farmer* "Cook of the Month" Contest

Sara E. Morris

My grandmother remains the best home cook I have ever known. Yes, I know you are thinking that sentimentality has tainted my taste buds, but that is not the case. I have been blessed to grow up in a family of good cooks. My mother, a trained home economist, often comments that her mother, grandmother, and mother-in-law were all good cooks, and sometimes she lumps herself into that list. While my memories of my great-grandmother are limited, I honestly didn't know I was so dietarily lucky until I got older. I thought everyone ate like we did. But as good as they all were, my maternal grandmother, Mary Ellen Bradley Hastings Wix or Mom-Mom Wix, remains the best cook I have ever known. My brother and I still lament that she started watching her cholesterol in the mid-1980s, and her fried chicken became a baked "fried" chicken and applesauce replaced oil in baked goods. We were both thankful that towards the end of her life she threw caution to the wind and cooked like she did during the early 1980s again. In 1978 my mother, Elizabeth Hastings Morris, and great-grandmother, Myra Walker Bradley, won *The Delmarva Farmer's* "Cook of the Month" contest in consecutive months. Ironically, despite her best efforts and frequently entering, the family's best cook could not win the contest and as I remember it, winning became a life goal.

My family hails from the Delmarva Peninsula. Delmarva takes its name from Delaware, Maryland, and Virginia. My maternal Great-Grandparent's farmstead straddled the Mason-Dixon Line with some of the buildings in each state, between Delmar, Maryland/Delaware, and the corner where the line turns north to create Delaware's western boundary. They grew truck crops like cantaloupes, strawberries, and cucumbers on the sandy and well-draining soil of the lower Peninsula. These were typical crops found on the region's farms before the poultry industry took off in the latter half of the twentieth century. My grandmother, like many of her generation, married a man who did not farm and moved to the edge of a town about half an hour away. There she had a garden and raised chickens. After being widowed she eventually married again and moved to a larger patch of land near Harrington, Delaware. There my grandparents tended a huge garden and were so obsessed with their bounty that my mother joked they checked their lima beans for ripeness every eight hours. My mother grew up spending summers picking truck crops on her grandparent's farm and became the first member of her family to go to college. She majored in home economics and landed a job in Chestertown, Maryland as a Cooperative Extension 4-H Agent. She married a local dairy farmer and became a farmwife, using her college education to provide for and take care of her family and community. All three generations of Bradley women were active in their community, kept clean houses, grew, froze, and canned most of their food, and sewed and mended the family's clothing. The patterns of their lives were typical of their contemporary rural and farm women.

Growing up there were two things I knew about the "Cook of the Month" contest. My mother and her grandmother, whom I called Mom-Mom Bradley, both won the contest. Mom won first in July of 1978, the second month of the contest with her "Company Beef Steak." Mom-Mom Bradley's "Squash Casserole" won the next month. Laminated copies of the articles announcing their triumph hung on the inside of one of our pantry doors. I read them often and I always got a kick out of my mother stating, "I don't buy these convenience foods ... so I can never use those recipes that call for a box of this or a can of that."[1] By the time I could read she had long given this up. I remember one time she quizzed me on what was wrong with her story's photo. I couldn't figure out that she was pretending to pour paraffin into already sealed canning jars. The story of Mom-Mom Bradley's win, in August opened with "The ability to cook prize-winning recipes is obviously inherited."[2] Given that they did not share names, *The Delmarva Farmer* declared they did not know the connection until they'd reach out to Mom-Mom Bradley. The article, written just after my great grandmother's left eye had been removed due to a tumor, stated that both winners admitted that the best cook in the family was the one who had not yet won.[3] Mom-Mom Bradley died four years later when I was seven—the article's photo is how I remember her. The other thing I knew about the contest was that Mom-Mom Wix had not yet been declared "Cook of the Month."

The women in my family took pride in their ability to create and tweak recipes, and they regularly demonstrated these skills with others through both recipe and cooking contests. They were not alone. Women's magazines and the women's section of farm publications ran articles on how to enter competitions and how to increase the likelihood of winning during the 1960s through the 1980s.[4] The Delmarva Chicken Cooking Contest, which began at the Delmarva Poultry Festival in 1949, grew into the National Chicken Cooking Contest. Amy Sutherland in *Cookoff: Recipe Fever in America* explained that among those on the competition cooking circuit only the Pillsbury Bake-Off eclipsed this contest in prestige.[5] Myra Bradley entered this local competition numerous times and won in initial rounds. Among her prizes was a miniature version of the "World's Largest Frypan" which

---

[1] Sharon Denny, "Contest Novice is 'Cook of the Month,'" *The Delmarva Farmer* (July 18, 1978): 10.

[2] Jim Schmit, "Grandma is 'Cook of Month,'" *The Delmarva Farmer* (August 15, 1978): 12.

[3] Schmit, "Grandma is 'Cook of Month,'" 12.

[4] For select examples see: Irma Kaufman, "How to be a Winner in Cooking Contests," *Farm Journal 93,* (July 1969): 38; Patrice G. Adcroft, "How to Win a Cooking Contest," *Good Housekeeping* 188, no. 4 (April 1979): 262.

[5] Southerland, Amy, *Cookoff: Recipe Fever in America* (New York: Penguin, 2004), 14-15.

is the logo of the festival and where they cooked batches of Maryland Fried Chicken for consumption by attendees. While a high school student in Seaford, Delaware my mother altered one of her mother's recipes and submitted it to the festival. Mom made it to the final round and traveled to Denton, Maryland (the contest moved around through the lower Peninsula) to cook for the judges. Although she did not win, she enjoyed the experience. According to my mother, Mom-Mom Wix frequently submitted recipes to all types of contests. She had many winning recipes with the Delaware chapter of the American Heart Association contests. I am glad someone enjoyed her obsession with cholesterol—it wasn't me. And of course, she also sent them to *The Delmarva Farmer.*[6]

Despite the cultural, social, and agricultural uniqueness of Delmarva, the region went without a dedicated agricultural/rural publication until the 1970s. Larger and more well-known papers such as the *Progressive Farmer* and the *Lancaster Farmer* occasionally covered the Peninsula, but not consistently. Chesapeake Publishing, the publisher of several papers on Maryland's Eastern Shore, recognized this void in the mid-1970s. Their initial solution, *The Central Shore Farmer*, was a monthly supplement included in those papers began in 1976. When ad sales demonstrated that the area could support a dedicated agricultural news source, they launched *The Delmarva Farmer*, "The agribusiness newspaper of Maryland, Delaware and Virginia" in May 1978.[7] Perhaps due to its birth during a time of transition for rural and farm women or a lack of resources, the paper did not have a "Women's Section." While it covered some activities of the Extension Homemaker's Clubs, the "Country Cooking" section which once a month included the "Cook of the Month" remained the only regular content focused on women readers. All the households in my family got *The Delmarva Farmer*, even my grandmother who lived on about ten acres a couple of miles from town. Both she and her husband had grown up on farms and although they had both sought careers that took them off the farm, her first as a sales clerk and then as a seamstress and him as brakeman, they still felt connected to farming and rural culture enough to take a paper with the word farmer in the title.

The "Country Cooking" portion of the paper took off. I am sure the success had much to do with the second and third winners of the contest. The staff at the paper prepared submitted recipes and had taste offs at work to declare the winner. At other times they enlisted the help of the local Homemaker Clubs. By 1983, just five years after the paper started, they published a collection of recipes. In the introduction to *The Delmarva Farmer Country Cooking Cookbook*, editor Bruce W. Hotchkiss declared this section of the paper among the most read and that only twice in 312 publications had they not run a "Country Cooking" column.[8]

[6] Elizabeth H. Morris, interviewed by Sara E. Morris, March 2, 2020, in possession of the author.

[7] Carol Kinsley, "40 Years of 'The Farmer,'" *The Delmarva Farmer* (March 24, 2014): n.p.; Bruce Hotchkiss, "The Farmer's Birth," in possession of the author.

[8] *The Delmarva Farmer Country Cooking Cookbook: A Treasury of Keepsake Recipes Reprinted from The Delmarva Farmer* (Shawnee Mission, Kansas: Circulation Service, 1983).

The cookbook, which included recipes submitted to the paper and not necessarily winners, included recipes from all three Bradley women. Proof Mom-Mom Wix was still trying.[9]

My mother and grandmother talked on the phone every Sunday morning at 9:00. The tradition started years before I was born, when the cost of long-distance calls necessitated planning and this mother and daughter pair lived about sixty minutes apart. I only heard one side of these conversations, but I do remember them talking about recipe contests and what Mom-Mom should enter in *The Delmarva Farmer.* They talked about this too when they saw each other and they always shared recipes. There were always recently acquired newspaper and magazine clippings with recipes or index cards of something one of them tasted at a recent covered dish dinner. They talked about and analyzed every recipe—if they'd made it they talked about how to change something. Eventually *The Delmarva Farmer* abandoned the enter whatever type of dish you wanted method and picked themes/ingredients for each month. This did not deter my Grandmother. She was going to win this thing and she kept sending them her creations.

Finally in 1995—seventeen years after her family members—she won. *The Delmarva Farmer* wanted recipes with raisins. As I remember it, some local children or youth organization had been gifted a huge amount of raisins and needed to figure out what to do with them. This is not based on proof, but my memory—*The Delmarva Farmer* is not on microfilm. The theme of raisins was perfect for Mom-Mom Wix. My mother remembers that she had an affinity for them. She sent in her "Pop-Pop's Raisin Cookies" and it earned her the coveted title "Cook of the Month." Looking back this might have been the perfect win. The cookies were originally made by her Grandmother, Alpha Beatrice Hastings Bradley for Mom-Mom to eat as an after-school snack. This grandmother had been one of the people to teach my grandmother to cook and the name of the cookies honored Mom-Mom's father, Albert. It was a legacy recipe and this added to the significance of the win. Mom-Mom also mentioned in the interview that she sometimes substituted the raisin filling with a homemade mincemeat to appeal to my grandfather. (At Christmas she'd mark the cookies filled with mincemeat with an M made from fork pricks—I only made the mistake of grabbing an M cookie once.) It was a recipe and a win with family legacy, and this probably made the victory sweeter.[10]

Not surprisingly the article focused on the fact that it had taken Mom-Mom Wix so many years to win. I remember how happy she was when she won and the photo announcing her triumph shows her in her kitchen looking so very happy. I was in college when she won and I remember my mother and grandmother saying that the torch had been passed and it was my turn to win. I think for a few months we waited for a theme to match something I could enter, but that summer

[9] The recipes in the cookbook by the Bradley women were: Elizabeth Morris, "Economy Pizza,"44-45, "Oatmeal Pie,"81-82; Myra Bradley," Cheesy Squash Casserole," 49, Mary Ellen Wix, "Dieter's Dream Chicken," 37.

[10] Sharon Morgan, "Winning Tradition," *The Delmarva Famer* (February 4, 1995): 24.

the contest stopped. The paper was going through editorial changes and the roles of women in agriculture had evolved beyond their kitchens. I'd never make it a four-generation achievement.

Like many rural and farm families, food, either through growing, preparation, or sharing is the way my family, on both sides, demonstrated love. This makes total sense because besides sleep and church, meals were the one time the never-ending work of farm life stopped. Whether it was eating on a Wednesday or Christmas dinner, in my family it meant sitting together and taking a break. My father never ate meals around at the barn or in the fields. He stopped what he was doing (or eating was delayed), washed up, and came inside. The hour-long trips to my mom's parents were fitted or squeezed between milking or on a coveted "weekend off" when we had hired help and could be away during a milking. My mother's family, although they were not dairy farmers, understood and accepted these rhythms of farm life. Their devotion to cooking reflected these family and rural values. Winning *The Delmarva Farmer* contest might have validated Mom-Mom's aptitude as a cook to herself and her larger community, but I hope all of those meals around her table and ours demonstrated to her that we already considered her a champion of country cooking.

Squash Casserole

By Myra Bradley Delmarva, Maryland, 1970s

2 lbs yellow squash, sliced
1 small onion, chopped
½ green pepper, chopped
⅓ c butter or margarine
2 eggs, beaten lightly
½ c milk
½ cup sharp cheddar cheese, shredded
1 t sugar
6 or 8 crackers, crumbled
Additional cheese and crackers crumbs for the top

Cook the squash in boiling salted water to cover, until just tender. Drain and set aside. Meanwhile, sauté onion and green pepper in butter until tender. Add cooked squash with eggs, milk, cheese, cracker crumbs, and sugar.

Season with salt and pepper, spoon into greased casserole, top with additional cracker crumbs and cheese. Bake at 350° degrees for one hour. Serves 6. Will freeze

Company Beef Steak

By Elizabeth H. Morris Delmarva, Maryland, 1970s

1 to 3 lb. blade chuck roast (about 2 inches thick)
Marinade
2 T vegetable oil
1 T Soy Sauce
½ tsp rosemary
½ tsp ground pepper
¼ tsp dry mustard
⅓ c wine vinegar
2 garlic cloves, minced

Place beef in plastic bag in baking dish. Combine the marinade, pour in bag and seal. Refrigerate 24 hours, turning the bag several times. (Beef should lay flat in the pan.)

Remove beef from marinade—pour marinade in 2 cup or larger measuring cup. (Modern practice would advise against this) Sprinkle commercial meat tenderizer on beef—let stand 20 minutes.

Add to marinade and mix well, 2 T ketchup, 1 T Worcestershire sauce, 1 T Steak Sauce.

Put beef in broiler pan, pour half of sauce over beef. Broil 20-30 minutes. Turn and brush with remaining sauce; broil 15-20 minutes or till desired doneness. (Has a charred appearance.) Can be cooked on an outdoor grill (serves 6)

Pop-Pop's Raisin Cookies

By Mary Ellen Wix, Delmarva, Delaware, 1930s

Filling
1 ¾ c raisins
2 T flour
¾ c sugar
1 ¼ c boiling water
Boil until thick and let cool

Dough
1 c butter or margarine, softened
1 ½ c sugar
¾ c sour milk
½ t baking powder
1 t baking soda
About 4 c flour

Cream butter or margarine and sugar together. Add milk, baking soda, baking powder and enough flour to handle. Roll dough 1/8 inch thick and cut with a 3 inch biscuit cutter. Place on a lightly greased cookie sheet. Spoon 1 tablespoon of the raisin mixture on each cookie. Cover with another cookie and seal edges with finger or fork. Bake at 350 degrees for 20 minutes or until lightly brown.

Makes approximately 5 dozen cookies.

This recipe has been made with butter flavored Crisco and works great. You can also use homemade mincemeat instead of the raisin mixture.

—21—

Lady Baltimore Cake

Sara E. Morris

Demarva Peninsular (Delaware-Maryland Border Region), USA, 20th Century.

No matter the occasion, my father's family always celebrated with the same cake, a dry white almond cake covered with delicious caramel icing. At the kids table my cousins and I let our ice cream melt into the cake to make it palatable. My grandmother, Elizabeth W. Morris, obtained the recipe from a can of Spry shortening and it became her go to cake for any special occasion. The Morris family called this a Lady Baltimore Cake. If you know anything about cakes, you know that there is a Lady Baltimore Cake, but it is a white layer cake filled with fruit and nuts. It is nothing close to my Grandmother's.

How or why my grandmother began calling this a Lady Baltimore remains a mystery. My mother and I have made many attempts to determine how this happened. All we have found is a transcription of pages from the 1935 Spry cookbook, *What Should I Cook Today?*, on a website with the recipe for a Tri-Layer White Cake. This cake has all the same ingredients minus the almond flavoring. Perhaps this is where Grammy got her inspiration. When she was alive, she would only say it was from a Spry container.[1]

Today for me the cake is nostalgic. I want it on my birthday because of memories. When my dad was little, he always wanted a cake made solely of icing—one year when the baking went wrong he got a bunt pan full of icing. After a few slices of icing his adult self admitted, that is was not a great idea. After that my mother just made a white cake mix and added almond flavoring. This is how we make the cake now, it tastes much better, and we still call her a Lady Baltimore.

---

[1]Recipe Curio, "Cakes, What Shall I Cook Today?," https://recipecurio.com/cakes-what-shall-i-cook-today/, accessed 3/25/2020.

Figure 21.1: Elizabeth W. Morris, surrounded by her grandchildren (L to R—Paul T. Qualey, Sara E. Morris, Bradley M. Morris, and Marjorie E. Qualey) in her kitchen with a Lady Baltimore baked by her daughter, Anne Qualey. Morris family collection.

Lady Baltimore Cake

By Elizabeth W. Morris

¾ cup Spry
1 tsp. almond extract
½ tsp vanilla
¾ tsp salt
2 cups sugar
3 tsp baking powder
3 ¼ cups sifted flour
½ cup milk
½ cup water
6 egg whites (¾ cup)

Combine Spry, extracts and salt. Add sugar gradually and cream until light and fluffy. Add baking powder to flour and sift 3 times. Add small amount of flour mixture to creamed mixture alternately with combined milk and water. Mix after each addition until smooth. **(In separate bowl)** Beat egg whites until stiff but not dry and fold into mixture until well blended. Pour into greased and floured tube pan. Bake at 350° oven for 1 hour or a bit longer.

Quick Caramel Frosting

By Elizabeth W. Morris

½ cup butter or margarine
1 cup brown sugar
¼ cup milk
1 ¾ cup sifted confectioner's sugar

Melt butter in saucepan; add brown sugar; boil over low heat 2 minutes, stirring constantly. Add milk; continue stirring until mixture comes to a boil; remove from heat and cool.

Add confectioner's sugar, beating well after each addition until of spreading consistency.

Notes on Frosting
Make 1 ½ quantities and use light and dark brown sugar- and usually use butter. Have on occasion used ⅓ margarine and didn't detect a difference in taste.

If you make a boxed cake double this recipe because the cake is smaller and you can build it up with icing. There is also leftovers—eat on anything, even a spoon.

—22—

Morris Family Recipes

Elizabeth H. Morris

Delmarva Peninsula (Delaware-Maryland border region), USA

Easy Apple Cake

4 c diced apples, unpeeled (save any liquid from apples)
1 ½ c granulated sugar
½ c packed brown sugar
2 eggs
1 c vegetable oil
1 t vanilla
1 c chopped nuts
¼ t water
3 c flour
2 t baking soda
1 tsp salt
1 ½ t cinnamon
1 t nutmeg
¼ t ground gloves

Combine apples, granulated sugar, and brown sugar. Let sit for one hour. Beat eggs, add vegetable oil. Mix well. Add vanilla and any liquid from apples. Mix well. Sift together flour, soda, salt, cinnamon, nutmeg, and cloves. Add egg mixture.

Mix well. Add apple mix and chopped nuts. Use ¼ cup water to rinse any sugar-syrup from apple bowl; add to batter. Mix well. Pour into greased and floured 10-inch tube pan. Bake at 350 for 1 hour. Cool 10 minutes. Remove from pan.

Easy Crab Soup

Elizabeth H. Morris, Delmarva Peninsula

4 slices bacon, chopped
2 qt. water or stock
3 lbs. crushed tomatoes
2-10 oz. pkg. frozen mixed vegetables
2 c. diced potatoes
1 ¾ cups shredded cabbage
3 medium stalks celery, chopped
1 medium onion, diced
2 Tbsp. seafood seasoning (Old Bay)
1 tsp. salt
¼ tsp. pepper
1 lb. Maryland crab meat

Put bacon and water in 8 qt. pot. Simmer 30 minutes. Add remaining ingredients except crab meat. Cook 30 minutes at simmer until vegetables are tender. Add crab meat to soup and heat gently. Makes 6 quarts. Make for a crowd or the freezer.

Harvestore Bars

Elizabeth W. Morris, Delmarva Peninsula (1980s)

4 cups quick oats
1 stick oleo, melted
1-cup brown sugar
½-cup light Karo syrup
12 oz. chocolate chips
2 cups peanut butter

Preheat oven to 350. Combine oats, oleo, brown sugar, and Karo syrup in a large bowl with a spoon. Pour into a greased 13 X 9 inch pan. Bake for 10 to 12 minutes. Let cool 45 minutes to 1 hour. Melt 12 oz. of chocolate chips and 2 cups peanut butter in the microwave—4-5 minutes at 50%. The chocolate chips do not melt until they are stirred, so stir half way through. Spread. Cool before cutting.

Granny's Lemon Snowflake Sugar Cookies

Elizabeth H. Morris, Delmarva Peninsula, 1990s

1 c. softened butter
1 c. powdered sugar
1 c. granulated sugar
1 c. vegetable oil
2 eggs
1-teaspoon lemon extract
4 c. flour
1-teaspoon baking soda
1-teaspoon cream of tartar
1-teaspoon salt

Preheat the oven to 375. Cream the first four ingredients together. Add the eggs and lemon extract. In a separate bowl, mix the flour baking soda, cream of tartar and salt and add to the other mixture.

Form dough balls the size of a quarter. Roll in granulated sugar. Place them on a cookie sheet and flatten with a glass bottom dipped in sugar. Bake for 8 to 10 minutes. Do not let the edges brown. Cool on a rack. Makes 80 cookies

Applesauce Deluxe

Four generations of the Morris family, Delmarva Peninsula, 1970s

1 package (3 oz) Jell-O (Red works best—do not use lime or lemon)
1-cup boiling water
1 ½ cups applesauce
1-teaspoon lemon juice

Dissolve Jell-O in boiling water. Blend in applesauce and lemon juice. Pour into individual molds or a serving dish. Chill until firm.

—23—

Bischoff Family Coffee Cake

Katherine Jellison

Recipe of Ella Bischoff Winkelmann

Western Nebraska, USA, 1930s

Editor's Note: In contrast to the expertise demonstrated by the women in Sara Morris's family (Morris, Ch. 20, this volume), Katherine Jellison points to the one recipe that her mother-in-law—"a terrible cook"—was able to produce successfully.

My mother-in-law, Ella Bischoff Winkelmann, was born on a farm in western Nebraska in 1909. Her parents were immigrants from Germany (lower Saxony), and she inherited this recipe from her mother, so my husband and his siblings assume it originated in Germany. My mother-in-law married in 1930 and gave birth to four children between 1931 and 1955. According to all four children, she was a terrible cook who ruined practically every recipe she ever tried. The exception was her mother's coffee cake recipe. All of her children, her children's spouses, and her grandchildren loved Ella's coffee cake. She continued to bake it until well into her 90s. She passed away in 2006.

The recipe my husband and I inherited is typed on a yellowed recipe card, and I reproduce it verbatim below. Keep in mind, however, that my mother-in-law lived her entire life on the dry high plains of western Nebraska. The recipe might need adjustment for locations of lower elevation and higher humidity. The recipe also omits some key pieces of information and instruction. For example, the butter, sugar, and cinnamon mixture noted at the bottom of the recipe is to be spread over the top of each cake before baking. The cakes should be baked on cookie sheets, and each one will be about the size of a twelve- to fifteen-inch pizza. The recipe lists no baking time, but the cakes are done when the crusts are brown and the butter, sugar, and cinnamon have formed into a nice glaze.

Bischoff Family Coffee Cakes

Makes three cakes.
1 package yeast. There are three pieces in a package. (Use one piece.)
1 teaspoon sugar.
¼ cup water.
Mix together in mixing bowl or small bowl. Let raise a little.

Scald one cup milk. Let cool. When lukewarm add 1 cup of sugar and ½ teaspoon salt. Mix this and the yeast mix. Beat this with a fork. Add 2 cups flour and beat well. Add about another cup of flour and knead well. Set in a warm place. I turn my oven on for a few minutes at 150 degrees then turn it off. Set the dough in the oven. When double in size divide in three or four sections and roll out. Melt a little butter, 1 cup sugar and ½ teaspoon cinnamon. Bake at 375 degrees.

—24—

Grandmama's Cooking Traditions

Joseph E. Cates

I was born in rural Alabama in the late 1970s. My paternal Grandmama, Exa Pritchett Cates, quit work to take care of my older sister and me while our parents worked. Before I started school, I spent every weekday with her while my parents worked, and, once I started school, I spent every weekday there during the summer returning home to my parents at night. I grew up watching Grandmama's routine every day. She was always a multitasker; she looked after her grandkids along with a few other neighborhood kids while simultaneously doing all her daily chores. She got up early each morning, cooked breakfast for my Granddaddy, usually biscuits and sausage, maybe some grits, and always oatmeal for herself. After breakfast, she would clean up, and if it was harvest time, she'd go into the field that sat on the hill behind my grandparents' house to pick peas or butter beans before the day got too hot. We would go up to the fields with her to help with the harvest. During late summer, I picked and shelled bushels of peas, shucked many ears of corn, and cut okra off the plants. I still remember the sting of the okra plant. We were never far from her sight. As the heat of the day arrived, she would head inside and begin cooking dinner. (This would be considered lunch for those outside the South.) Sometimes, she would have us go outside to play keeping an eye on us through the window, and knowing her dog, Hobo, would keep us herded in the backyard. We were forbidden to venture into the front yard.

Dinner for my Grandmama was never an elaborate affair; it was a simple dish. She always preferred a tomato sandwich with mayonnaise and black pepper or a banana sandwich with mayonnaise. Sometimes, she would fry up some tripe or bologna or something similar. Biscuits were usually involved. After this meal, she would finally sit for a short while and watch her TV stories: *Days of Our Lives*, *Another World*, and *General Hospital*—though the latter eventually changed to *Santa Barbara*. *Days of Our Lives* and *Another World* received most of her attention as she simultaneously crocheted. The last of her stories never received as much attention, because she had to start cooking supper.

Supper was *the* meal of the day. It almost always consisted of meat, two vegetables, and either fried cornbread or biscuits. If she was angry with my Granddaddy, she'd make a casserole, because he hated those "damn one pot meals" as he called them. The meat was usually some type of chicken though beef and pork would occasionally make an appearance. Her most memorable chicken dishes were Smothered Chicken (fried chicken cooked in gravy), Coca-Cola Chicken,

Chicken and Rice, and Chicken and Dumplings. For vegetables, it was usually what came out of the garden: pink-eye purple hull peas, corn (often creamed or on the cob), butter beans, fried okra or fried squash, collards, turnips, mustard greens, snap beans, potatoes of various kinds or whatever else they had planted that year. Along with the meal, there was generally a plate of freshly sliced cucumbers, tomatoes, and radishes. The meal always ended with a dessert: blackberry pie, pound cake, four-layer jelly cake, butter or chocolate rolls, and sometimes, freshly made chocolate or banana pudding. Written-down recipes were never used. She had a recipe box that sat on top of the refrigerator, but I never remember her taking it down to use any of the recipes contained within. When I was older and she taught me her recipes, she mostly showed me how the recipes were made, demonstrating each step, but sometimes she just related the recipe to me without making it. Her recipes were always an oral tradition as I am sure that's how they were passed down to her. The kitchen was her domain, and as long as she could physically continue to cook, she usually did not let anyone help; she was specific on how things were to be done. I remember one time when Granddaddy's sister-in-law, my Aunt Bonnie, stirred the eggs into the hushpuppy batter before it was time to drop them into the oil, and Grandmama got so angry, she didn't just chase her out of the kitchen—she literally chased her out of the house until it was time to eat. I don't remember Grandmama's recipe for hushpuppies, but I do remember the dry ingredients were mixed in a bowl; the eggs were cracked and sat in a well in the dry mixture waiting for the buttermilk to be added just before they were spooned into the hot oil. When her health deteriorated, she began to refuse to eat much, and I would go cook for her knowing if I cooked it, she would eat it—if for no other reason than to be polite. Since she was the person who mostly taught me how to cook (Mama taught me a few recipes), she was usually satisfied with how I cooked her food, and she would eat everything I put on her plate.

My favorite was her Chicken and Dumplings, which was an all-day affair. She started in the morning by boiling the chicken with just black pepper and salt. After it had cooled for at least an hour, the bones could be removed, and the freshly made broth preserved for later. The dumplings consisted of flour, oil/lard, and water. Some people used milk in place of the water. Once this mixture was ready, the dough would be floured and rolled out to a one-eighth inch or a one-quarter inch thickness, cut into one and one-half inch strips, and then two-inch long rectangles. These would need to dry for several hours. Once the dumplings were dry, the deboned chicken was added back to the broth with more pepper and salt and brought to a boil. At this point, sliced boiled eggs could be added, but since I did not like boiled eggs, she would often skip this step, much to my father's dismay. While the chicken broth was boiling, the dumplings would be added. There was a technique to adding the dumplings. A large spoon would be used to push the chicken and eventually the dumplings out of the way so one dumpling at a time could be added to the pot. This was to prevent the dumplings from sticking together. Once all the dumplings had been added, and had puffed up just a bit, and the broth had thickened, the dish was ready.

Vegetable soup was a close second favorite dish that was easier to make. Any leftover vegetables from supper would be frozen in Ziploc bags. Once enough had been gathered from various meals, the vegetables would be taken out and put in a pot with Grandmama's homemade tomato juice and diced pieces of meat. The meat was whatever was on hand. While it often was beef chunks, it occasionally could be ground beef or from a pork roast. This dish was simply cooked until ready. The freshness of homegrown vegetables and homemade tomato juice could not be beat. Throughout my life, I have loved her vegetable soup. When I would come home from graduate school in Mississippi, I was often sent back with butter tubs full of Chicken and Dumplings and/or Vegetable Soup.

Grandmama was a simple cook, but one of the best I've ever known. Her Smothered Chicken was another favorite. I have never been able to fry chicken correctly; it's either burned or underdone. This recipe makes it a little easier. The chicken pieces were salted and peppered and soaked in buttermilk before being dredged in flour. The chicken was fried in a large skillet then taken out to drain off some of the grease. Most of the grease (usually Crisco or lard) was poured out of the pan. The chicken was then added back in and water was added, just enough to almost cover the chicken. A top was placed on the skillet and the chicken continued to cook and make its own gravy. The result was chicken so tender it would fall off the bone. This was usually served with mashed potatoes.

Her Coca-Cola Chicken was another simple recipe. Salted and peppered chicken pieces were added to the same frying pan used to fry chicken, but this time a cup of cola (RC or Coke) and a cup of ketchup were added in with a few dashes of hot sauce. The chicken was cooked over medium heat until it showed doneness by slightly separating from the bone. The taste was like barbecue chicken though the sauce was much thinner than barbecue sauce.

Grandmama's Chicken and Rice was probably her simplest dish. It consisted of boiling a salted and peppered cut up chicken-on-the-bone in a skillet. Once the chicken was done, rice would be added and cooked with a top on the skillet until the rice was cooked. This was often a dinner dish and not a supper dish because of its simplicity and the fact that she rarely served vegetables with it.

Grandmama's recipes were hard to write down in traditional recipe form. Except for the Coca-Cola Chicken, measurements were eyeballed, not exact. They came from decades of cooking experience. When I began school, my Grandmama hated not seeing us daily, so she cooked for the family every Wednesday night. My parents, sister, and I would be there on those Wednesday nights and leave afterwards, plus my sister and I stayed overnight on Fridays. Incidentally, those Wednesday night meals were the reason our small rural church did not have Wednesday night services like a lot of Southern churches. My family made up half the congregation, and it would have been useless to have a service without us. The Wednesday night meals were some of my happiest food memories. I will always remember that my Grandmama got it into her head that I liked meatloaf. I did not, but I could never tell her. She would make meatloaf especially for me. I also remember that each year for my mother's birthday, Grandmama would make a jelly cake. It was a regular white layer cake but instead of icing, she used her homemade plum jelly as filling between the layers and on top. It was sweet and tart and delicious.

Whereas many of Grandmama's recipes were simple, her desserts often were not. She still didn't use recipes, but instead baked and made desserts by instinct and years of experience. Of course, with baking, things need to be a bit more precise, so exact measurements were used, but she knew all the ingredients and measurements by heart. One recipe I never mastered, mainly because it was not a favorite of mine, was her chocolate pie. It was one of the few things she taught my aunt how to make. She was a demanding teacher when it came to desserts. In her later years, she had chronic obstructive pulmonary disease (COPD) from many years of smoking, and was not able to stand over the stove and cook like she used to because of her oxygen tank. However, her chocolate pie was in demand at family gatherings, so she supervised my aunt cooking it. Everything had to be done exactly to her specifications. I have watched the process and seen how angry she could get if my aunt did not follow the recipe exactly.

Other recipes I did learn to make. Her blackberry pie was one of them. Four cups of freshly picked blackberries or dewberries (I never could tell the difference) would be combined with one-half cup sugar and a cup of water. This mixture would be brought to a boil and cooked for 10 minutes. She would then strain out the seeds and place this strained mixture in a flat bowl and a pie crust would be placed over the top. Grandmama was not the kind of cook to make her own pie crusts; she simply bought the frozen kind. The blackberry pie was then cooked at 350 degrees (Grandmama baked all things at 350) until the crust was golden brown. Granddaddy loved this pie and would often pour sweetened condensed milk over it or occasionally have it with ice cream.

A variation on this was her fruit cobbler. The above recipe for the fruit filling could be used with any fruit: peaches, plums, or blackberries; it could basically be any fruit you wished. The difference was that with a cobbler, the fruit mixture was not strained after cooking. Again, the oven would be heated to 350 degrees. A three-quart baking dish with one stick of butter would be melted in the dish while the oven was preheating. Then she would combine one cup sugar, one and a half cups self-rising flour, one and a half cups milk, and usually a few dashes of cinnamon for peaches or I like ground ginger for plums; nothing else was needed for the blackberries. These ingredients were then slowly mixed to prevent clumping. The batter was poured over the melted butter. It was important not to stir the butter and batter together. The fruit was then spooned on top, gently pouring in the syrup. The batter would rise to the top during baking. It usually took about 30 to 45 minutes baking time. She knew it was done when it was golden brown on top.

As far as I know, another dessert my grandmother made only for the immediate family was butter rolls. This recipe was the one exception to the 350-degree rule, because it was a version using her biscuit recipe. The oven would be heated to 475 or 500 degrees. She would begin with approximately four cups of flour. This was always approximate as it was added to her biscuit bowl, which was a large flat wooden bowl in which flour was always kept and flour was added to the bowl as needed. I remember that her biscuit bowl sat in the cabinet in a plastic bag to keep the flour fresh. She added to it only when making biscuits. She would combine roughly three tablespoons of shortening or occasionally leftover bacon grease and enough buttermilk to the flour. I estimate about one and a half to two cups of buttermilk were used to create the correct consistency. The dough should be wet. She then worked and kneaded the dough in the biscuit bowl. Once the dough was to her satisfaction, she would pinch off a ball and work it pulling out the sides and pinching the bottom together until the top was smooth. Then she placed it in a greased cast iron skillet. She would repeat this process until biscuits filled the skillet. If she was making just biscuits, they would be cooked hot and fast in the oven usually 5-10 minutes. If she was making her butter rolls, a deep thumbprint was made in the top center of the biscuit. A pat of butter was placed in the center and a spoonful of sugar was added on top of the butter. If she was making chocolate rolls, then a teaspoon of chocolate powder was added on top of the sugar. The rolls were placed in the oven and cooked for 5-10 minutes just like her biscuits. As the rolls baked, the butter would bubble and melt the sugar and/or chocolate spilling over the sides of the biscuit dough.

Exa Cates, my much beloved Grandmama, passed away in 2012 at the age of 89. She is missed by her family and friends every day. I do my best to keep her culinary traditions alive. I love making her recipes, because they give me a sense that she is still with me. Some of her recipes like her vegetable soup are impossible for me to recreate without a lot of time and a garden full of vegetables. I can buy all the ingredients at the grocery store, but it will never be the same as what came out of her garden: vegetables she picked with her own hands and lovingly cooked. There is just something special about a grandmother's cooking, and no matter how hard we try, it can never be truly replicated. She had her own special touches that I probably was never privy to, but I can come close. And I can share this food with others and spread the love she always shared with my family and me.

—25—

Chicken and Noodles

Pamela Riney-Kehrberg

Adapted from the Recipes of Elsie Swafford Riney and Jennie King Swafford

Western Kansas, USA, 1910s

This is my great-grandmother Jennie King Swafford's recipe for chicken and noodles. She received it from her mother-in-law. I learned to love it in the kitchen of my grandmother, Elsie Swafford Riney. The onion and carrots are my additions to the recipe. I also discovered that the noodles needn't be dried, but can be used right after cutting. My grandmother always dried her noodles.

This was a recipe born of hard times. My great grandparents raised six children on a wind-swept western Kansas farm. They were tenants and poor. There was never enough money. But they did raise chickens, and a little bit of chicken with lots of broth and noodles would stretch a long way.

I learned to love this recipe in my grandmother's kitchen. She and my grandfather didn't have a lot of money, either, but my grandmother loved to cook, and was a wizard with chicken and noodles. She made this recipe with whole canned chicken, the Swanson brand, which can be hard to find these days. (Canned chicken also doesn't taste as good to 21st century tongues.) Fifty years into their marriage, my grandfather died, and Grandma never made this recipe again. She discovered ramen noodles, and told me that they made a fine substitute. I disagreed, but I didn't tell her. She had loved cooking because she did it for my grandfather. After he died, she didn't care to cook any more.

I continue her tradition. This is one of my favorite meals. It is comforting and filling. It reminds me of generations of women in my family who cooked hot meals to show their love to their families.

Chicken and Noodles

Boil one stewing hen (3-5 pounds). Retain and de-fat broth. Bone the chicken, and set aside the meat.

Noodles

One cup flour
One egg
Half an eggshell of water
½ teaspoon salt

Mix all ingredients together, thoroughly. Flour the rolling surface. Roll dough to ⅛ inch thickness. Using a sharp knife, cut noodles as thickly as desired. Lay on a kitchen towel, and allow to dry. Or, if you want to use them immediately, they can be used without drying.

When you are ready to make your chicken and noodles, sauté an onion and two medium carrots in a small amount of cooking oil. When they are slightly browned, add 6 cups chicken broth (supplement water from cooking chicken with canned or boxed broth if necessary). Bring to a low boil. Add chicken and noodles, cook until noodles are soft. This should not take more than 10-15 minutes.

—26—

Sauerbraten mit Oscar, Gerhardt, Fredrich und Freunde

Joan M. Speyer
Hampden, Maine, USA, 20th Century

In the early 1960s when I was in high school, my mother, as a celebration of my father's March birthday, first produced a traditional German meal her mother had made: *sauerbraten, kartoffelkloesse, und kothol* (pot roast, potato dumplings, and red cabbage). This celebration became a tradition that traveled with my parents, Chic (Doris) and Walter Speyer, when they moved from their 1940s suburban home in Huntington, New York to their early 1800s home in rural Winterport, Maine.

I played a small role in the grand preparation, that of *küchenhilfe* (kitchen helper); my father and brother were simply to stay out of the way. With coordinated efficiency, Chic had already marinated a roast for three days in a red wine vinegar brine, which later would be converted to gravy. Filling the house with anticipatory smells, she had browned the roast and set it to simmer in the brine on the day of the meal for three to four hours, had shredded red cabbage in readiness for it to steam for about an hour, and had cooked, cooled, peeled, and riced potatoes. The ricing process involved forcing the potatoes through a metal basket with long handles, producing rice-like squiggles that dried from early morning to late afternoon. The Winterport wood stove still operating in March aided the drying process, crafting a potato dumpling that was more apt to hold together and rise during boiling. About an hour and a half before the meal, Chic would call me to her side to dust her hands with flour as she formed the riced potatoes into dumplings. In the middle of each dumpling, Chic hid a crouton from bread cubes she had fried in butter earlier that day.

Cooking the dumplings in a large pot of boiling water was the last step, one that invariably made Chic anxious. Were the dumplings sufficiently dry and floured to hold together and rise? One year in Huntington, Walter, enlivened by vodka martinis, entered the kitchen to oversee the process (generally he was in the kitchen only to eat). We dissolved in tears of laughter as he addressed the dumplings: "Oscar, come on, you can do it! Gerhardt, don't dally! Heinrich, get out of Oscar's way! Congratulations, Fredrich, you've made it!" Once he added this guidance to the preparations (although there never seemed to be a correlation between the naming and the "hanging together" of the dumplings), we routinely called him to the kitchen thereafter for the Naming of the Kartoffelkloesse. We never knew the names of the dumplings until Walter christened them, nor likely did Walter.

For a number of years, I have given favorite recipes to my nephew Erik and my two step-granddaughters, Caitlin and Fiona, as ongoing Christmas presents. This traditional meal will live through those gifts, and, perhaps, some March—post-2020 coronavirus—we will gather at Auntie J/Grandma's home in Maine for "Walter's sauerbraten meal."

Sauerbraten mit Kartoffelkloesse und Rotkohl

(German Pot Roast with Potato Dumplings and Red Cabbage)

A Wagenbauer/Speyer Recipe That Passed from Grandmother to Mother to Daughter and Traveled from New York to Maine

Submitted by Joan M. Speyer of Hampden, Maine in memory of her mother, Chic (Doris) Speyer and her grandmother, Mae (Mary Anna) Wagenbauer

Sauerbraten (pot roast):
Marinate 4 lb. roast (bottom or top round) for three days, turning once per day (brine marinade below). On cooking day, remove roast from marinade and brown all sides on top of stove in a fair amount of oil in large pot; reserve marinade. Browning will take about 20-30 minutes on medium heat. Add marinade with all seasonings. Cover, bring to boil, and simmer for 3 hours. (This can be done on the stove top or in a 325 degree oven.) Remove meat and thicken marinade to make gravy if desired. (To thicken, whisk together a slurry of flour and water, add in a bit of the hot marinade to temper, then whisk the slurry into the marinade.)

Brine Marinade:
1 cup red wine vinegar to 1 cup water—until meat is covered
2 tbsp. sugar
1 tbsp. lemon juice
sprinkle of pepper
12 whole cloves
6 bay leaves
2 medium onions, sliced

Kartoffelkloesse (Potato Dumplings)

Use 5 lbs. russet potatoes. The day before the meal, cook potatoes in jackets in boiling water until cooked through but still firm. Early on the day of the meal, peel and rice with potato ricer. Put on cloth towels to air dry (will dry best on non-humid day or near a wood stove). Allow at least six hours for drying.

Make croutons: cube bread and brown in margarine.

Close to cooking time, combine potatoes with some flour, 2 eggs, and dash of nutmeg. Add just enough flour to form firm potato dumplings. (Making the dumplings will be easier if you have a helper to keep flouring your hands.) Form each potato dumpling with a crouton in center. Set dumplings on plate and hold until ready to cook.

Boil large pot of water. Add dumplings to gently boiling water and cook until they rise to top of water and then for approximately another 3 minutes. Scoop out with slotted spoon and keep warm in oven until all dumplings are cooked.

Rotkohl (Red Cabbage)

Cut one fat head of red cabbage. Slice one peeled apple and one onion. Put all in a large pot with ½ cup vinegar (red wine or apple cider), 2 tbsp. sugar, and a little water. Cook on low heat for approximately 1 hour.

—27—

At Mam-Maw's Table

Tracey Hanshew

> "Lord we cleared this land, we plowed it, sowed it, and harvested. We cooked the harvest, it wouldn't be here, we wouldn't be eatin' it if we hadn't done it all ourselves. We worked dog-bone hard for every crumb and morsel, but we thank you just the same anyway Lord for this food we're about to eat. Amen."—Jimmy Stewart as Charlie Anderson in *Shenandoah*, 1965.[1]

Every meal at Mam-maw's table began with grace. Everyone held hands, and we often took turns, so that at each meal a different family member was responsible for praying aloud at the table ... grateful for the food, for the hands that prepared it, and for the good Lord who helped us get through the day to day. It seems every family has a person who is their glue, the anchor that grounds the family. Mozell Hanshew provided that for her family. She was relatively quiet, working almost non-stop as many women do, especially those trying to farm in remote drought-prone areas. She saw her family through thick and thin, never boasting about the "plenty" and always finding blessings among the "lean." She often used her talent in the kitchen to make "a little something to eat" that provided physical nourishment but more importantly, a central location to gather that reaffirmed no one was alone, that together the family would be okay, and serving as a reminder that it was the unity found in that exercise of sitting at a common table, holding hands in prayer, that shaped individual character. Today's modern table may not be completely identical to Mozell's, but the function of her table was not exactly as those previous to hers either. The historical continuity that extends beyond the usage of the table itself is in the metaphor of the gathering at the table as the center of family activity. For centuries and in various cultures, the hearth was the nucleus for people in homes, villages, and communities. In twentieth century, rural America, the transition from hearth to kitchen table carried over the practices and traditions of gathering in a location central to food preparation and consumption. An epicenter for families, the table then became a place to discuss life and to work through its challenges. By extension, the kitchen table in rural communities also became a symbol for the space where people gathered to support each other, relax, and enjoy conversation, food, philosophy, politics, and concerns. This essay ex-

---

[1] James Lee Barrett, *Shenandoah*, directed by Andrew McLaglen (Universal City, CA: Universal Pictures, 1965).

plores through a case study in rural Bosque County, Texas how the kitchen table of a phenomenal cook, who created recipes and cooking methods passed down to the sometimes three or four generations seated at the table, became a way to preserve heritage. Her reputation for cooking and conceiving the best dishes, particularly in hard times, and being creative when having little to work with were lessons humbly shared through her actions in the home as well as the community. This kitchen table reveals how this central location became a place that grounded a family who farmed together, worshipped together, and contemplated challenges of rural life building on a centuries old custom of gathering around a hearth.

Communing around a fire and taking sustenance there has for centuries been a tradition in most societies. The term "hearth," first used before the 12th century, represents the area in close proximity around a fire, or later in history the ledge or seating near a fireplace. But the role of the hearth as the gathering place around the fire has also come to mean "home" as in longing for the comforts of home.[2] In American history the fire and earthen ovens used by Native Americans functioned as an essential site to discuss tribal matters. In Iroquoia hearths between two family apartments within the greater communal longhouse organized physical space and reinforced clan values. The hearth "embodied an ethic of sharing and reciprocity between kin groups who, although separated, 'boile in one kettle, eat out of one dish, and with one spoon, and so be one.'"[3] When longhouses were replaced by European style single-family cabins in the 18th century, the Iroquois style maintained an open hearth and smoke hole rather than incorporating the fireplace and chimney used by European colonists. European colonists brought a style that consisted of large open hearths that in early New England burned "three-fifths to three-quarters of an acre of timber per year" again drawing family close for warmth as well as for survival.[4] Spreading to the frontier building on new land like that in the Cumberland area the "home was the center of the pioneer's world ... the family hearth, source of warmth, sometimes light, and always food."[5] As time and agriculture advanced, families worked lands together. Newly arrived immigrants like Mozell's family who reached the United States in the 1800s brought old customs with them (see Figure 27.1). In rural areas of Germany and Russia similar to many countries across Europe, the norm was larger family farms: "the 'big family' commonly comprised between twenty-five and thirty people [where] ... sons and their families, unmarried daughters, and various relatives and friends of the family" worked together. [6] Technological advances in agriculture as well as social and cultural changes resulted in increasingly more children moving away

[2] *Merriam-Webster.com Dictionary*, s.v. "hearth," accessed March 29, 2020, https://www.merriam-webster.com/dictionary/hearth.

[3] Daniel K. Richter. *The Ordeal of the Longhouse: The Peoples of the Iroquois League in the Era of European Colonization*. (Raleigh, NC: The University of North Carolina Press, 1992), 19.

[4] David B. Danbom, *Born in the Country: A History of Rural America*, 2nd ed. (Baltimore: The Johns Hopkins University Press, 2006), 35.

[5] Harriette Simpson Arnow, *Seedtime on the Cumberland* (East Lansing: Michigan State University Press, 2013), 305.

[6] Hélèn Yvert-Jalu, "Hearth, Home and Rural Community," *The Unesco Courier*, (1989), 12.

Figure 27.1: Ed and Margaret Koonsman's children back row left to right: Herman, Luther (Luke), Juanita; front row: Evelyn, Mozell, Neva. Hanshew family private collection.

IREDELL, TEXAS EST. 1870

Figure 27.2: Iredell, Texas, est. 1870. Hanshew family private collection.

from their "family home and set up their own 'hearth'" resulting in fewer people around it.[7] Because the frontier environment increased space between families in areas where more land was needed to adequately feed livestock, or to grow crops, the burden of single-family farming led to rural communities often socially functioning similar to extended families working farms together.

Mozell grew up in Bosque County, Texas on a farm between Iredell and Meridian. She met and married into the Hanshew family who lived north of Iredell, where she and husband Ivis remained the rest of their lives. Similar to rural ranching areas across the American West, and due to the "economic and ecological spheres necessary for daily survival," Bosque county farmers and ranchers developed a somewhat "fused" familism where hegemonic norms originated and defined within primary-kin-oriented activities often originating in the home, combined with extended-kin-oriented familism.[8] In rural areas where multigenerational families lived, sometimes in the same house, and worked together on the same property, familism developed in more of a closed system. But in the case of the Hanshews where they lived with adjoining properties or in very close proximity to each other, nuclear and expanded identities developed. Leaving Iredell and driving northbound on FM 216, the former property of J.C. Hanshew (Ivis' grandfather) is about two miles out of town. Continuing a few more miles is Ivis and Mozell's place, part of which adjoins Ivis' brother Lloyd's property, and continuing northbound near the Erath county line is Ivis and Lloyd's childhood place where their father W.K. Hanshew lived. The individual properties primarily farmed by near "kin" kept families close and tied to land that could be challenging in the Texas climate.

Helping my Papa (pronounced Paw-Paw), Ivis, dig a waterline once, and having to use pickaxes to do part of it by hand, I asked him how he ever got anything to grow around that area, he said "yeah, it makes you wonder why anybody would buy this ol' rock doesn't it?" That seemed fitting to me at the time. But Bosque County was at one point known as good farmland. Located in Central Texas, Bosque County is approximately eighty miles southwest of Dallas-Fort Worth and sixty miles north of Waco. The Hanshews lived in north Bosque county about six miles outside of the town of Iredell.

The area near modern day Iredell was first settled in 1849 by Dixon (Manse) Walker who was a Lieutenant in Command of the Bosque County Rangers, and the Bearcroft family.[9] That same year the State of Texas made a land grant for what was to become the "city of Iredell" in the amount of "... 17 ⅔ labors of land ... on the main prong of the Bosque River, about ½ mile below the mouth of Duf-

---

[7] Yvert-Jalu, "Hearth, Home and Rural Community," 12.

[8] Peter L. Heller, Gustavo M. Quesada, David L. Harvey, and Lyle G. Warner, "Rural Familism: Interregional Analysis" in *The Family in Rural Society*, Westview Special Studies in Contemporary Social Issues. ed. Raymond T. Coward and William M. Smith, Jr. (Boulder, CO: Westview Press, 1981), 76.

[9] Bosque County History Book Committee, *Bosque County: Land and People (A History of Bosque County, Texas)*, (Dallas, Texas, 1985), 50. (https://texashistory.unt.edu/ark:/67531/metapth91038/: accessed April 27, 2020), University of North Texas Libraries, The Portal to Texas History, https://texashistory.unt.edu; crediting Denton Public Library.

Figure 27.3: Iredell Hotel. Hanshew family private collection.

fau Creek."[10] The first permanent residence in Iredell was built by Ward Keeler. A native of New York, and surveyor of Bosque County, Keeler purchased land there and built a log cabin near the present site of Iredell. There he founded the town in 1870 on a "50 acre tract ... bordering the south side of the Bosque River" and named the town "after his son, Ira, and attached the 'dell' because the new town lay in a valley."[11]

The Texas Central Railroad came to Iredell in 1880 and the population grew as did business. According to an Austin paper, the *Texas Siftings*, an article published April 29, 1882 reported that Iredell had "350 inhabitants, a half dozen general merchandise houses, one drug store, one blacksmith shop, one livery stable, two hotels, twin steam cotton gins, one of the best mills, and decidedly the best school in Bosque County ... also an abundance of ... female beauty and fleas ... [and] a brass band."[12]

The community established along the river was a farm and ranch population and remains so to some extent today. Like countless similar communities across the United States, Iredell endured fire, flood, and drought. Although the town grew up along the Bosque River, much of the farmland out of town was away from the river and out of reach of irrigation for many even after that technology

---

[10] Bosque County History Book Committee. *Bosque County,* 50-51. A labor of land is a Spanish land unit equal to 1 million square *varas*, or 177 acres. *Handbook of Texas Online*, "LABOR [LAND UNIT]," accessed April 27, 2020, http://www.tshaonline.org/handbook/online/articles/pfl01. Uploaded on June 15, 2010. Published by the Texas State Historical Association.

[11] Bosque County History Book Committee, *Bosque County,* 51.

[12] Bosque County History Book Committee, *Bosque County,* 52.

became available. Dry dirt farming gives added weight and purpose to a kitchen table in that it requires frequent prayer and special attention to weather bulletins. My grandparents, Ivis and Mozell, married in 1933 and began farming just as the county saw a decline in agriculture due to an economic depression followed by a succession of dry years. "The total number of farms [in Bosque county] dropped from 2,229 in 1930 to 1,558 in 1950, ... agricultural production and some livestock production decreased [but] manufacturing picked up the slack. Manufacturing establishments steadily increased in number and value every census year after 1947."[13] One of those manufacturing establishments was the garment factory in Iredell where my grandmother took a job in town as a seamstress. Even when she worked full-time in town, she continued to "keep" her kitchen in the same manner she always had with the table the center of family activities.

In the center of the house, the kitchen and dining area—large but combined and open—placed the table itself as the center of the household. Meals were served in a certain order, and at a young age knowing the proper way to place the silverware on either side of the plate was as important as knowing to fill the tea glasses with ice last in the process due to the Texas heat. Most of the time stoneware was set or situated at each place setting which had a placemat, though not all of them matched. Food was served or "dished up" in bowls or on platters, never in the pans in which it was cooked. After being cleared and cleaned, the table often became a tool for various other needs. An adequate height for a sewing worktable, my grandmother used it to cut out patterns to sew new clothes, quilt tops, or other things like hot-pads or sausage sacks. She sewed many things from dresses, blouses, aprons, garden bonnets, and even our blue jeans—most often doing so without a store-bought pattern. She could look at a dress and cut her own pattern from newspapers to make it similar or better than the store bought one. When she got a new sewing machine, smaller than her "old" Singer powered by a large foot-press, the electric machine in a portable case could be used in various locations. The kitchen table sometimes became the sewing table. As a young girl I was taught to sew sausage sacks from material similar to a cheese cloth and did so without a pattern as she taught me to keep the seams straight and ensure the outcome was the right size to keep the packages uniform at one to one and a half pound sacks. Scraps of material were salvaged for other purposes. Quilt tops fashioned from the remainders of old dresses formed colorful patterns that recorded our family history. Most quilts that she made utilized the centers of each block to record the names, birthdays, and anniversaries of family members. These were then passed down through the family, a hand-made heirloom begun at the same table where we gathered so that no matter where it would later be used, it functioned to stave off cold but also provided warmth from home.

Theirs was a working farm, having a large garden and crops to feed the livestock. They raised cattle, chickens, sheep, and hogs, and for a while had a milk cow. Horses were used to work the cattle, and everything had a purpose. When it came

[13] *Handbook of Texas Online*, Kristi Strickland, "BOSQUE COUNTY," accessed April 27, 2020, http://www.tshaonline.org/handbook/online/articles/hcb10. Uploaded on June 12, 2010. Modified on April 9, 2018. Published by the Texas State Historical Association.

BAPTIST CHURCH
FIRST BAPTIST CHURCH ADJACENT TO RIVERSIDE CEMETERY 1884

Figure 27.4: First Baptist Church, Iredell. Hanshew family private collection.

time to process food, again the table became a center of production. Whether sorting vegetables from the garden or packaging meat, a small assembly line formed around the table. Someone drawing the short straw might be stuffing the sausage sacks, while the lucky one at the end of the line just taped the butcher paper and had to remember the correct spelling of "sausage" and what year it was.

This table was also a minor first aid station where plenty of bumps and lumps were assessed, splinters removed, and scrapes cleaned and patched up … an occasion that sometimes included a cookie to make it all better.

Food and eating as a family at the table then is important. And invoking that tradition of communing around the hearth, the table experience ties families and traditions together. "Grandmothers' and mothers' cooking is not so much about the tastes of the food as the feelings of security and safety represented by it."[14] Because the Hanshews lived close together north of Iredell and the town itself was the central location for the extended rural area, it was similar to other small farming towns that came together for various occasions often at the school or at church. Community gatherings, unless a specific work event on someone's farm, often occurred in-town. Small farms like those in Bosque county were often interdependent. When people came from areas around Iredell, they were often identified by geographical features, like Spring Creek, or Flag Branch, areas that at one point had also been an organized community with a church or school at the turn of the twentieth century. One did not necessarily have to farm to be accepted into the community as farmers went to town for church and school after they were con-

---

[14] Michael Owen Jones and Lucy M. Long, eds. *Comfort Food: Meanings and Memories.* (Oxford, MS: University Press of Mississippi, 2017), 7.

solidated, and community members sometimes helped with barn raisings or other occasions because they knew each other from church. Opal Bateman, who grew up in Spring Creek, described what community meant to her as being "the church and school. Because there was [sic] some who didn't have any children in school off and on, you know. I remember one family that didn't have any children, but they was [*sic*] very much a part of the community because they came to church."[15] Church in rural communities like Iredell were plentiful. With an average population of 300 and three churches one could still be selective.

The Baptist church had the largest congregation, followed by the Methodist, and the smallest was the Church of Christ. Church and school provided reasons to get together but really instilled a sense of belonging, regardless of which denomination one was. Often when one church hosted a special event, like a revival, members from other churches visited and were welcomed in. Opal Bateman told of "all-day singings and weeklong revivals at church. School plays and Christmas pageants provided another opportunity to congregate as did ice cream socials hosted by neighbors."[16] Popular with the Baptist were church dinners, often called dinner on the ground, left from days when the church services were held in open tabernacles or later in buildings without air conditioning. Dinner on the grounds after Sunday morning service moved outside to eat in the shade in hopes of finding a breeze to help in the sweltering Texas heat. At church dinners, one always knew to get in line early and search out familiar plates and cookware to identify the best tasting dishes ... anything my grandmother cooked, Opal Bateman's fresh rolls, or another church member—Ida Lee's pies. A child or newcomer did not take long to identify the best, and recipes were guarded secrets to keep the popularity of these dishes and reputations secure. Mam-maw cooked a variety of things well, her specialties were fried chicken, pinto beans, cornbread, and desserts. She made her own pie crusts and crusts for fresh blackberry cobbler, sprinkling any scraps of dough with cinnamon and sugar to serve hot out of the oven to the grandkids. She baked desserts at least once a week, sometimes more, because Papa liked to have them at every meal, and often would grab cookies or tea cakes in between meals. She rarely if ever used a cookbook and even created her own cake that just became known as Mam-maw's cake. Some ladies at church would occasionally try to replicate Mam-maw's dishes, but they never succeeded, and having no recipe to share, she did not have to divulge her secrets.

Food was an important way of reinforcing belonging and acceptance in the community and through relationships akin to extended family. Once a church member, Bob Hughes broke his leg and my dad, Papa, and a farmer whose property was between ours and the Hughes's, finished getting his hay in while Mozell made extra food to take over to ease the workload of Bob's wife Josie. Working

---

[15] Opal Bateman, interviewed by Sharon Siske-Crunk, March 12, 1993 in Iredell, Texas, quoted in *Southern Farmers and Their Stories: Memory and Meaning in Oral History* by Melissa Walker. (Lexington, KY: University Press of Kentucky, 2006), 197-198.

[16] Opal Bateman, interviewed by Sharon Siske-Crunk, March 12, 1993 in Iredell, Texas, quoted in *Southern Farmers and Their Stories: Memory and Meaning in Oral History* by Melissa Walker. (Lexington, KY: University Press of Kentucky, 2006), 203.

together for events like barn raisings, to help those in need, raising funds for a new building, centered around the need, but also food. Laura Bateman remembered the thresher coming to their place near Iredell when she was a kid as a time when "... we always had to cook for them [the threshers], you know. It was quite a big day when we'd have to cook. ... And the ladies would get together and cook that dinner. They'd swap out. If it was at my house today, they help me. If it was over at their house tomorrow, I helped them. That's the way we did the work, swapped out."[17] Any illness, hospitalization, birth of a child, or just as an act of kindness required food, home made from scratch to be delivered. Similarly, any pie plate or casserole dish received from a neighbor was always returned replenished.

From helping a family in need to raising money for school or the volunteer fire department, helping the community included farmers from around Iredell and sometimes neighboring towns throughout Bosque county as well. Fundraising for example consisted of a plate dinner where tickets were sold at a set price for "all-you-can-eat," contributions ranged from donating meat for a main dish like fried catfish or BBQ brisket to side dishes brought in a pot-luck style. For school fundraisers cake walks were popular. For 50 cents a chance, one could take a turn walking around a masking tape circle on the gym floor with numbered squares. Similar to musical chairs, you walked around the circle until the music stopped. A number was drawn by a student in the class raising money and if stopped on the specific number called, you could win a cake. This was always popular early in the carnival because one had to ensure to get the best cake and would often ask "who made this" before selecting.

Sowing and harvesting food even after mechanization often remains generational. Families raised on the land recognize that this is also by the land and do so in a way that keeps them tied to it and in a way that people outside of rural areas do not understand. For many in the West their connection to the land remains in the name of specific locations, not unlike towns named after founders, but when identifying the Hanshew place, one knows it was farmed by one or more generations. Farms and ranches throughout rural America have earned those names like badges of honor from caretakers who lived from that land. Modernity has created a world "... in which industrialization and capitalist economic philosophy have created a very real physical as well as emotional distance between our work and the things we use. We rarely see an entire process of creating something from start to finish ... while the mobility associated with the freedom to explore new paths and new selves oftentimes cuts us off from our roots and dilutes a sense of continuity with places or people."[18] The table was a family foundation at the Hanshew's, one that extended into Iredell and other areas of Bosque county. My grandmother cooked what we had, and we ate what was on the plate. Every meal was eaten at the table ... no exceptions other than the days my Papa was working in the field to finish before the weather changed, then she would take lunch to him and they'd

---

[17] Laura Bateman, interviewed by Sharon Siske-Crunk, January 20, 1994 in Meridian, Texas, quoted in Melissa Walker, *Southern Farmers and Their Stories: Memory and Meaning in Oral History* (Lexington, KY: University Press of Kentucky, 2006), 205.

[18] Jones and Long, *Comfort Food*, 6.

share cold fried chicken, bread, or some tea cakes on the tractor. At that table lessons were taught about hard work, perseverance, being a good person and about fun, where layers of relationships were revealed as grandparents who had played the dominoes game called "42" together for years would then oppose each other to "teach" the grandkids to play. To a child watching the knowing looks exchanged like a foreign language proved that years of living and working together transcended communication methods most couples relied on as silent exchanges revealed volumes. Acting on those lessons by staying dedicated to the town community, consistently sharing the food prepared in the kitchen providing an example of the importance of reliability when neighbors and church members needed it, Mozell's reputation and how good she cooked, was almost always a comment made about her. Mam-maw's legacy was preserving the kinships built between the people in town and the rural farmers around Iredell where the value of kindness was revealed by sharing food.

Figure 27.5: Lonnie, Mozell, and Glenda Hanshew. Hanshew family private collection.

Figure 28.1: Ivis and Mozell Hanshew, October 28, 1933 wedding photo, paternal grandparents of contributor Tracey Hanshew. Hanshew family private collection.

—28—

Hanshew Family Recipes

Tracey Hanshew

Bosque County, Texas, USA, 20th Century

Chess Cake

Margaret Graves Davis

1 package/box yellow cake mix
1 egg
1 stick butter melted
Combine the above 3 ingredients and press into a 13 x 9" pan

1 box powdered sugar 16 oz. or about 3 ½ cups
1 cream cheese block softened 8 oz.
1 teaspoon vanilla

Mix powdered sugar, cream cheese, and vanilla together then pour on top of crust and bake for 40 minutes in a 350° oven.

This modern recipe comes with a telling story that the family reminisces about each time we eat this cake. The recipe comes from a family friend, Margaret. Margaret lived up the road from my grandparents near the Bosque – Erath county line, about 60 miles north of Waco, Texas. She and her husband Tyn had a beautiful property with a garden near the house and a big red barn with the pastures behind which bordered property leased by my grandfather.

When my grandparents, Ivis and Mozell, were "courting" they sometimes went out with Margaret and Tyn, who were also courting at that same time. In the fall of 1933, both couples decided to marry. Margaret was not yet eighteen years old, so she and Tyn decided to elope. They asked my grandparents to go with them, almost talking them into eloping with them! But my grandmother did not want to face her parents with news of an elopement, and they waited until their planned date to marry. Although the delay was only one day, Margaret and Tyn eloped on the 27th and my grandparents married on the 28th it always made for a great "remember the time…" story with my grandfather teasing my grandmother about her making him wait to marry.

The Weathers Brothers

October, 1941 WW II

Figure 28.2. The Weathers Brothers left to right: Glen, Cleo, Wayne, Edward, Charles. Wayne Weathers is the maternal grandfather of contributor Tracey Hanshew. Hanshew family private collection.

Mam-maw Weathers' Buttermilk Pie

Nancy Weathers Hanshew

2 eggs
2 Tablespoons lemon extract
4 Tablespoons cornstarch
2 cups sugar
½ cup butter
1-pint buttermilk
2 unbaked pie shells

Beat first five ingredients together until smooth. Add 1 pint of buttermilk. Pour into 2 unbaked pie shells.

Bake 10 minutes at 425o then change the temperature to 350o and continue baking for 40-45 minutes.

This recipe comes from my great-grandmother on my mother's side. Mam-maw Weathers had five sons and three daughters, so this low-cost dessert was a favorite that ensured everyone had a piece. From rural northwestern Arkansas, the Weathers sent all five boys to war during World War II, four to Europe and one to the Pacific. Miraculously they all made it home safely. This pie is still a favorite at family reunions. Note: this is like a chess pie, but this recipe uses lemon extract instead of vanilla.

Tea Cakes

Mozell Hanshew

2 cups sugar
½ cup sweet milk
1 teaspoon vanilla extract
3 eggs
1 tablespoon baking powder
1 teaspoon baking soda
½ cup butter or shortening
3 cups of flour (more if needed)

Mix sugar, eggs, butter, milk, and vanilla. Sift baking soda and flour, then stir into liquid ingredients and mix until thick. Pat out the dough on a well-floured dough board, adding flour as needed to work with the dough, to about ½ inch thick. Cut out with a cookie cutter or snuff glass. Bake 15 minutes at 350°.

This recipe is one passed down from my grandmother, and I expect has been in the family for generations. I am certain it is the oldest recipe I have. These tea cakes are a combination cookie and cake but not as dry as a scone or a biscuit. They were admittedly not our favorite as kids because they are not overly sweet. But my grandfather (Papa) liked them, so my grandmother made them often. My Papa appreciated that they were "good to take on the go." Memories of him grabbing two tea cakes on his way out to the barn, or a few more to go on the tractor for hours of plowing, only hint at his mastery of snacking and fondness for sweets. The simple ingredients would have been available during most any time since the mid-1800s and in remote areas. When I was a kid my grandparents raised chickens and had a milk cow, so we had fresh eggs, milk, and butter. Note the distinction of sweet milk as many of her recipes also used buttermilk. Most of the time my grandmother used a tin cookie cutter, standard size, but sometimes she cut the dough with a snuff glass. The snuff glass was a clear beveled glass similar in size to modern tumbler, having a wide rim that made the tea cake/cookies larger, and I know she sometimes used this to save time.

Figure 28.3: Tracey Hanshew's Lemon Meringue Pie. Photo by Tracey Hanshew.

Lemon Meringue Pie

Tracey Hanshew

45 minutes preparation, 1-hour chilling, 12-15 minutes baking. Makes 10 servings.
9-inch prebaked pie crust

Filling
4 large egg yolks
3 large eggs
1 cup granulated sugar
¾ cup fresh lemon juice
2 tablespoons cornstarch
½ cup (1 stick) chilled butter, cut into small pieces

Meringue
4 large egg whites
¼ teaspoon cornstarch
¼ teaspoon cream of tartar
½ cup superfine sugar
1 teaspoon vanilla extract

1. Preheat oven to 350° F. To prepare filling, in top of a double boiler, whisk together egg yolks, eggs, sugar, lemon juice, and cornstarch. Place over simmering water. Cook over medium heat, stirring constantly, until thick enough to coat the back of a spoon. Do not let mixture boil. Remove mixture from over water. Stir in butter. Pour into crust.
2. To prepare meringue, beat egg whites at medium speed until foamy. Beat in cornstarch and cream of tartar until soft peaks form. Gradually beat in sugar and vanilla at high speed until stiff, but not dry, peaks form.
3. Spoon meringue over filling to edge of crust. Use the back of a spoon to raise soft peaks. Bake pie until meringue is golden, 12 to 15 minutes. TIP: Make sure the meringue reaches the edge of the crust to prevent the filling from seeping out.

This pie is my mother's favorite and I have been making it for about 15 years now. The original recipe called for the meringue to be piped on, but I do not have a bag or decorative tips, and my grandmother Mozell taught me to just use the back of the spoon to make soft peaks on the meringue (see the picture on the recipe) so that is how I still make it. She made the hot pad beneath it as well. She was a talented seamstress, and could see a dress, cut a pattern with old newspaper, and make it look as good or better than the original. She never wasted anything, even scraps of cloth were recycled into square hot pads for taking things out of the oven. The yarn hot pad in the photo is one she made as a gift. We often got them included in our Christmas or birthday presents. My grandfather cut a wood frame in an octagon shape, and nails placed 1" apart which held the yarn. My grandmother used a bobby pin to guide the thread that tied the centers where the yarn crossed. She made many of these, experimenting with assorted colors, keeping the ones that "didn't turn out" for herself and giving away the other beautiful sets she made over the years.

Figure 28.4: My grandparents Ivis, Mozell, and daughter Doloris. Mam-maw sewed the sun bonnets, good for shading from the hot Texas sun. Hanshew family private collection.

Peanut Patties

Pat Fitzgerald

2 cups sugar
2 cups peanuts
1 cup powdered sugar
½ cup Karo syrup
½ cup milk
1 teaspoon vanilla
¼ cup water
¼ teaspoon salt
½ teaspoon red food color

Boil sugar, Karo syrup, water, milk, and salt until a candy thermometer reaches 235 degrees F or 113 degrees C. Test by dropping a small amount of candy mixture into cold water which should produce a soft-ball consistency. Then add 2 cups peanuts parched slightly. Remove from heat. Add 1 teaspoon of vanilla, ½ teaspoon red food coloring, 1 cup powdered sugar (be sure to add powdered sugar last). Stir then pour into muffin tins or drop onto wax paper to let candy dry.

DeLeon, Texas is peanut country. Having plenty of peanuts and pecans (the state tree of Texas) was helpful for making a variety of pies, cakes, and candy. Candy was a special treat reserved for the holidays.

Peanut candies such as peanut brittle were popular with soldiers during the American Civil War because they did not melt. Peanut candies became popular around DeLeon, Texas, in the early twentieth century because Spanish peanuts became the dominant crop there in the 1910s. Peanut patties like these made with confectioner's sugar are credited to Anthony George who started the Tyler Candy Company in Tyler, Texas in 1941.[1]

[1] Mary O. Parker, "Sweet on Pink Peanut Patties," *Texas Highways: The Travel Magazine of Texas* (December 2012), 16-19.

Figure 29.1: Audrey Williams (nee Syme) 1926-2019 Circa 1944. McKenzie personal collection.

—29—

Sour Cream Pie and Nana's Buns

Diane McKenzie
Recipe of Audrey Williams
Alston, Alberta, Canada, 1960s

My Mom's pie making skills were famous. One particular type of pie she made with great care, was legendary as well. Amongst our rural community, our immediate family, and extended families she was known for her wonderful pies of all stripes but most notably for her "Sour Cream Pie." Coveted at community potlucks, family picnics, or seasonal gatherings with either sides of my extended family, Mom's Sour Cream Pie would draw much regard.

Watching the "grown-ups" strategically plan how they would manage to be one of the large crowd to secure a piece of my Mom's delicious pie was entertaining for me as a young person. Necks strained to see if her pie was at the end of the table in the "dessert section" at the potluck gatherings. Eyes darted, scanning the crowd to estimate the odds of being lucky enough to find a piece remaining when the long line of food lovers had filed by the pie pans taking their selections.

My mother's much preferred brand of lard for the crust was Tenderflake©. The center was a creamy cooked mix of currants and sour cream. The meringue, atop the spectacular currant loveliness, was always a challenge. Achieving enough height from the egg whites and just the right beautiful brownness—I can still see the strain on her face, peeking in ever so carefully, holding open a slim crack of the oven door. It was the final challenge of the pie trifecta: crust, filling, and topping.

These are memories from a nearly bygone era of domesticity when community and families gathered regularly at tables filled with homemade food; those tables acting as the center of their social world. I hope my Mom enjoyed the cooking and baking and the acclaim of sorts. I think of her always when I am in my own kitchen; celebrating the successes of her teachings and I think knowing, to some extent, her frustrations as a creation fails and hits the trash can. I think of how her generation spent so much of their lives preparing food for others.

In a generational shift Mom, now a Nana, became renowned for her dinner buns, aptly dubbed "Nana's Buns." I don't remember which grandchild personalized her delectable sweet buns with her namesake but we all remember the smell of them baking and the sound of the pan coming out of the oven and being placed on the counter.

Our Mom and Nana recently passed away. One of her granddaughters talked about how much love Nana had shown her family and community through her cooking. She showed love and patience teaching her children and grandchildren to cook, and after becoming a grandmother she compiled a recipe book of favorite foods and each of her children received a beautiful hand-written copy "lovingly dedicated by Nana."

French Cream Pie (Sour Cream Pie)

From Audrey Williams

1 cup currants
⅓ cup sugar
1 cup sour cream
2 eggs (keep whites for meringue)
½ tsp. cinnamon
Pinch of salt
1 tsp. baking soda (added last)

Bake a good, rich pie shell. Cook the filling in a good sized pan as it rises as it cooks. When thick put in shell and top with meringue. Lightly brown.

Nana's Buns

2 pkgs. or 2 T. Fleischmann's Traditional Active Dry yeast (dissolved in 1 cup lukewarm water and 2 tsp. sugar)

Set aside and mix the following:
½ cup sugar
2 eggs
1 cup milk
1 cup boiling water
1 tsp. salt

Have your mixing bowl ready with approximately 7 cups flour. Add yeast to above mixture and pour over flour, mixing with a heavy wooden spoon.

Have ¼ cup Crisco melted (but not hot) and with fingers work into the dough. Set to rise once (about 1 hour) knead, form buns and put in 12 ½" X 17" greased pan and set to rise again (about 1 hour each time). Bake 450 degrees F. 10-12 mins. Remove and butter tops.

Cinnamon Rolls

From Audrey Williams

Make smaller buns and then spread left-over dough in a smaller greased pan. On surface of dough, spread butter, sprinkle flour, brown sugar and cinnamon.

Roll, cut in bun size pieces and place in same pan.

Bake same as buns but watch closely to prevent burning.

—30—

Spanish Buns

Catharine Wilson
Recipe of Myrtle Dougall
Merrickville, Ontario, Canada, 1930s

Throughout the Great Depression, my grandmother Myrtle Dougall made lots of main courses featuring beans and eggs, and she stretched out her meat supply with dishes such as Shepherd's Pie. I know these details because she kept a diary for fifty-one years, starting in 1930. She lived in the village of Merrickville, Ontario, Canada. Grandpa ran the local sawmill, and even though times were hard in the 1930s, the Dougalls were more fortunate than many. He always had work because villagers needed a steady supply of firewood for cooking and heating their homes. My grandparent's home was a popular spot for "transients" who left a symbol in chalk or coal by their front door as an indication to other travelling men that it was a good place to get a meal. Grandma fed these men in her back-kitchen. As a treat for the family, Grandma and Grandpa and their only daughter, my mother, occasionally drove to Smiths Falls to see a Shirley Temple movie. For a sweet treat to eat, Grandma made Spanish Buns. According to historian William Woys Weaver, this recipe is called "Spanish" because it is like a cake made in Latin America. My grandmother got it from her friend, Jessie Newell, who lived in a rural community in Gatineau, Quebec. Clearly it was a family favorite as she frequently made it and on one occasion, she served it to the Women's Missionary Society as it is great with hot tea or coffee. Curious to know what these Spanish Buns were like, my daughter and I made them.

Fortunately, we also have Grandma's collection of handwritten recipes which she started in 1914, before she was married. She clearly had a sweet tooth as most are dessert recipes, but she also recorded recipes for hand lotion, cleaning silver, and cures for whooping cough and pimples. We have added some additional details below to her original recipe in italics for Spanish Buns. They are delicious! They are a light-textured, spicy-sweet cake with a chewy-gooey, crusted topping.

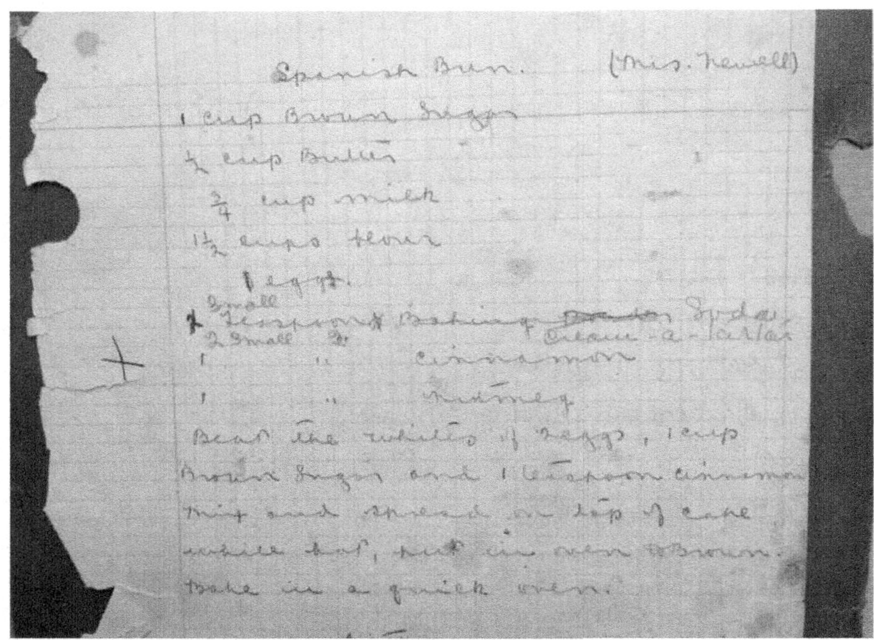

Spanish Bun. (Mrs. Newell)

1 cup Brown Sugar

½ cup Butter

¾ cup milk

1½ cups flour

1 egg

Small
1 teaspoon Baking Soda,
2 Small " Cream-a-tartar

1 " cinnamon

1 " nutmeg

Beat the whites of 2 eggs, 1 cup Brown Sugar and 1 teaspoon cinnamon mix and spread on top of cake while hot, put in oven to Brown. Bake in a quick oven.

Figure 30.1: Handwritten Recipe for Spanish Buns

Figure 30.2: Spanish Bun on a plate.

Spanish Buns

I cup brown sugar
1 ½ cups flour
1 teaspoon baking soda
2 teaspoons cream-a-tartar
1 teaspoon cinnamon
1 teaspoon nutmeg (You might want to halve this, if you are not keen on nutmeg.)
½ cup butter (melted)
¾ cup milk
1 egg

Bake in a quick oven. A "quick" oven is a term that denotes temperature and is from the era of wood-burning stoves without a temperature gage. Today it means 375-400°F. Combine the dry ingredients. Then add the wet ingredients. Stir the mixture vigorously with a wooden spoon. Pour it in a greased 8x8 inch glass dish and bake for 35 minutes at 375° or until a clean knife inserted into the batter comes out clean.

Topping:
Beat 2 egg whites, 1 cup of brown sugar, and 1 teaspoon of cinnamon. Mix and spread on top of cake while hot. Put in oven to brown. Browning took 10-15 minutes. Remove and cool. Cut into squares.

—31—

Zucchini Bread

Cynthia C. Prescott

Ohio and Oregon, USA, 1980s

Growing up in suburban Ohio in the 1980s, my family grew a vegetable garden every summer. My father tended our grassy lawn, dumping the grass clippings into our compost pile. While our neighbors didn't appreciate the compost pile's appearance, they joined us in benefiting from its work. Over time, that compost—combined with manure provided by a family friend who kept horses on his property on the outskirts of the city—served to replace topsoil that had been stripped by developers who mass-produced modest three-bedroom split-level houses in our neighborhood in 1959.

That garden produced a variety of vegetables, including the hundreds of tomatoes that my mother loved eating but hated to can, and an over-abundance of zucchini squash. Zucchini vines always seemed to threaten to take over the rest of the roughly 20x10-foot garden, if not the entire yard. In zucchini season, it was hard to pick and eat them quickly enough, before they grew to the size of baseball bats. We considered those behemoths inedible, so my mom would leave them out by the road on trash day. Usually a refuse worker or other passerby would claim them, probably to make zucchini bread.

A standard joke told both in suburban central Ohio and in rural southern Oregon—and likely throughout the United States—warns people to be sure and lock their car doors during zucchini season. Otherwise, you're likely to return to your vehicle to discover that someone has dumped their surplus zucchini in your car.

When my husband and I bought our own Midwestern 3-bedroom house on a quarter-acre lot, I felt guilty for not planting a garden of my own. But as a dual-career couple living in an age of agribusiness and convenience foods, growing a garden doesn't feel like the best way to spend our time and energy. And the growing season in North Dakota is just too short to grow all the produce my parents produced in abundance in Ohio. So I stock up at my local farmer's market during our short growing season, and otherwise rely on squash likely shipped 2,000 miles from Mexico.

I never really liked zucchini growing up. We regularly ate a side dish of sautéed zucchini with tomatoes, onions, and topped with cheddar cheese. I relied on lots of melty cheese to make it palatable. Now as an adult I actually enjoy including the mild-flavored squash in a variety of recipes. I have yet to embrace my mother-in-law's habit of slicing raw zucchini onto lettuce salads, however. And without an overabundance growing in my own yard, I don't feel a need to hide surplus zucchini in chocolate cake or other recipes, as many gardeners do. But my favorite way to consume zucchini will probably always be in zucchini bread. My younger daughter, who adores it as much as I do, often pleads with me to bake my mother's zucchini bread.

Zucchini bread recipes are common among gardeners. Recipes vary widely, but tend to be quick breads containing ample quantities of cinnamon and other warm spices. My friend Robin Hayes grew up on a dairy farm in southern Oregon. She swears by her family's recipe, which is dense and studded with dried fruit, similar to a fruit cake. The origins of that recipe are unknown, but Robin suspects it came from a magazine such as *Good Housekeeping* in the 1980s or 1990s. But in my family, zucchini bread should be light, moist, and cinnamon-y, following the recipe my mother received from a friend while she and my father were in graduate school in Seattle, Washington, in about 1969.

Culver Family Zucchini Bread

Submitted by Cynthia Prescott

3 cups flour
2 cups sugar
1 tsp. baking soda
1 tsp. salt
¼ tsp. baking powder
3 tsp. cinnamon
3 eggs
1 cup salad oil (I use canola.)
3 tsp. vanilla extract
2 cups grated, peeled zucchini

Preheat oven to 350° F.

Beat eggs until light. (An electric mixer really helps. My mom and I use Kitchenaid stand mixers for this step. Before I got my Kitchenaid, though, I would do this by hand with a wire whisk.)

Add vanilla and oil slowly, beating all the time.

Add zucchini and stir well.

In a separate medium-sized bowl, combine the dry ingredients. Then add gradually to the wet mixture, and mix well.

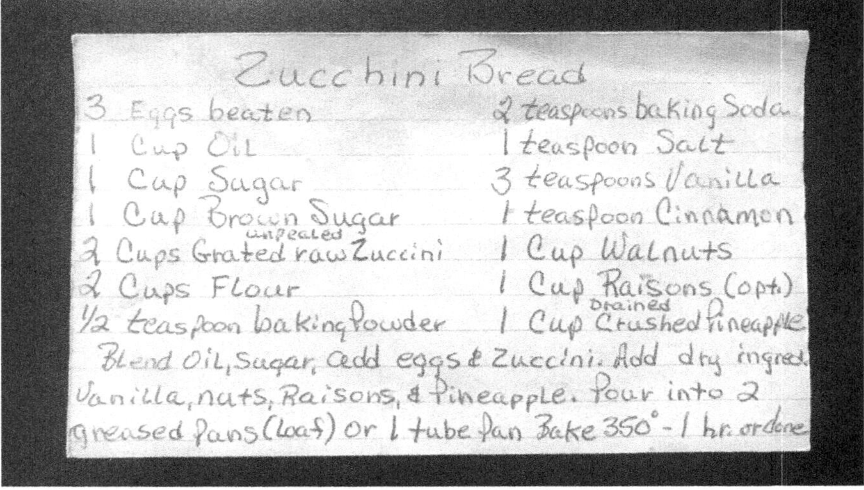
Zucchini Bread

3 Eggs beaten
1 Cup Oil
1 Cup Sugar
1 Cup Brown Sugar
2 Cups Grated unpealed raw Zuccini
2 Cups Flour
1/2 teaspoon baking Powder
2 teaspoons baking Soda
1 teaspoon Salt
3 teaspoons Vanilla
1 teaspoon Cinnamon
1 Cup Walnuts
1 Cup Raisons (opt.)
1 Cup Drained Crushed Pineapple

Blend Oil, Sugar, add eggs & Zuccini. Add dry ingred. Vanilla, nuts, Raisons, & Pineapple. Pour into 2 greased Pans (loaf) or 1 tube Pan Bake 350° - 1 hr. or done

Figure 31.1: Hayes Family Zucchini Bread recipe. Photo by Robin Hayes.

Grease 2 or 3 medium-sized loaf pans well with cooking spray. (My mom uses 2 loaf pans. I prefer to use 3, so that I can get it cooked through while keeping the outer crust tender.)

Divide batter evenly among the pans. Bake 45-55 minutes, or until cooked through.

Hayes Family Zucchini Bread

Submitted by Robin Hayes

3 Eggs beaten
1 Cup Oil
1 Cup Sugar
1 Cup Brown Sugar
2 Cups Unpeeled Grated raw Zucchini
2 Cups Flour
½ teaspoon baking Powder
2 teaspoons baking Soda
1 teaspoon Salt
3 teaspoons Vanilla
1 teaspoon Cinnamon
1 Cup Walnuts
1 Cup Raisins (opt.)
1 Cup Drained Crushed Pineapple

Blend Oil, Sugar, add eggs & zucchini. Add dry ingred. Vanilla, nuts, Raisins, & Pineapple. Pour into 2 greased Pans (loaf) or 1 tube Pan. Bake 350°–1 hr. or done.

—32—

Blackberry and Apple Jelly

Margaret Thomas-Evans

Vivid childhood memories of jelly dripping from a homemade jelly bag suspended from an improvised stand (the upturned bathroom stool) bring back the smell and taste of my mother's homemade blackberry and apple jelly made from fruit gathered from the apple trees and blackberry canes in our garden. This ritual occurred every fall, much to my fascination. As a country woman and lifetime member of the Women's Institute, which is famous for "Jam and Jerusalem," my mother carried on a tradition of jam and jelly making from my grandmother.

As girls, my sister and I learned to wash, peel, and chop fruit. Gradually, we were allowed to stir the jam as it was simmering on the stove and wash the jars in preparation for them to be filled with delicious jelly. Dad was summoned to securely attach the bag to the dripping stand using knots learned in Boy Scouts. When he was sure it was ready, the contents of the heavy pan were ladled into the bag. Severe admonishments were issued to stay away from the dripping bag with a large basin below to catch the flow which slowed gradually to drips overnight. The next day the liquid was boiled again. Mother always took the task of filling the jars after first testing a sample on a saucer to make sure it had reached setting point. Then came the agony of waiting for it to cool sufficiently to be eaten. I always cleaned up the test saucer, licking every remnant of jelly from it (when no-one was watching), but I wanted more. To this day, this is my favorite preserve best served with warm scones fresh out of the oven and a cup of tea.

Blackberry and Apple Jelly

Ingredients

3 lbs. of blackberries (washed and any stalks or bugs removed)

2 large apples (We used Bramley apples but others can substitute—washed, cored, and diced.)

1 pint water

1 lemon (juiced)

1 lb. sugar (approximately—varies on quantity of juice)

Steps

1. Gather the ingredients and utensils needed.
2. Make sure to have a clean tea towel or jelly bag (washed in boiling water to remove any taint of food or detergent). We had a cloth specifically used for jelly making, stained deep purple over the years. The bag or cloth needs to be suspended from a stand or upturned stool and firmly attached—it can be tied on with string.
3. Place the prepared blackberries, apples, water, and lemon juice in a large heavy-based saucepan. It needs to hold the fruit mixture and sugar.

4. Bring the fruit to a boil and simmer gently for 20 minutes or until all the fruit is soft.
5. Gently place the fruit and juice into the jelly bag or tea towel which has been securely attached to a stand. Leave to drip overnight. Do NOT squeeze the bag as this will make the jelly cloudy.
6. Measure the juice. For every 20 ounces of juice use one pound of sugar.
7. Place the juice and sugar into a large saucepan and stir until all the sugar has dissolved. Bring to a boil and simmer for 10 to 15 minutes or until the setting point is reached (test by spooning a small amount on to a chilled saucer, place it in the refrigerator for 5 minutes. Take out the saucer and test to see if it is starting to set. Push at the jelly which should wrinkle when touched). Remove the scum from the surface from time to time while simmering.
8. Carefully fill the clean, sterilized jars with the hot liquid, then cover, seal, and store in a cool, dark place.

—33—

Harvest Photographs

Pamela Riney-Kehrberg

Figure 33.1: Found fruit, by Pamela Riney-Kehrberg

Figure 33.2: A bountiful harvest of pears, by Pamela Riney-Kehrberg

–34–

Mom's Rhubarb Relish

Marie Kenny

Susan Jane (Misener) Gunn was married on December 14, 1938 to Sheldon Gunn. She was a farm wife, with a very busy life inside the home and outside helping her husband on the land. Rural farm life is challenging at any time but it was even more so during those pioneering days of no running water or electricity. She began a family of ten children with her first a miscarriage in 1939. I am the second youngest of the children. I can honestly say I never heard my Mother complain, she was resilient, creative and dedicated. Life had a way of just moving forward as family members young and older all worked and played together. I am very proud of my heritage; I will always be a country gal at heart! This relish was a traditional treat at our home.

This is a very flavorful addition to any meal as a side condiment. It is also delicious on burgers! My family also love it on a sandwich or with a salad! It's easy, it's fresh and it›s loaded with flavor!

Mom's Rhubarb Relish

Susan Jane (Misener) Gunn
West Saint Peter's, Prince Edward Island, Canada, 1940s
Submitted in her memory by Marie Kenny

8 cups of diced fresh or frozen rhubarb
6 large onions diced
4 cups white sugar
1 tsp. Salt
4 tsp. Cinnamon
2 tsp. Allspice
2 tsp. Cloves
¾ cup of vinegar

Put all ingredients in a large pot
Bring to a boil, turn heat back to medium and cook!
Stir often to prevent burning, the consistency will be like a jam spread!
Enjoy!

—35—

November Mincemeat

Pamela Snow Sweetser
Maine, USA, 1950s

Janet Riley was only seventeen when she married Ansel Snow in 1948.[1] They built a home on the Snow family's 250-acre farm three miles from the village of Masardis, Maine, population 523. Ansel went to work for the Bangor and Aroostook Railroad. Janet became a homemaker and a culinary artist who created dishes by look, feel, smell, and taste as much as by measurements. She excelled at shaping a recipe to make it distinctly hers. She learned how to make mincemeat from her mother-in-law, and then created her own version of it. She supplemented her kitchen resources by raising vegetables in her large garden, foraging for wild fiddleheads, berries and hazelnuts, and picking apples in the orchard, then drying, pickling and preserving her harvests. November was the time to make venison mincemeat, her final canning task before winter.

In October, my mother stocked up on suet, cider, spices, and both dried and candied fruits; bought the rum and brandy with money she had squirreled away; and waited for the last ingredient. In those days, deer hunting season opened on October 21 and ended November 30. Ansel was a skilled hunter and a crack shot, guaranteeing that before Thanksgiving his wife would have venison for her mincemeat.[2] After he killed a deer, Dad dressed and cured the carcass, then butchered and wrapped the meat for Mom to preserve.

Expensive and labor intensive, each year's mincemeat was an opportunity to create subtly different flavors with spices and fruits. Mom experimented freely with her recipe that "you could put in any damn thing you wanted." Except for the liquor—only brandy and rum would do. Weeks of gathering and preparing culminated in two days of fierce cooking and canning. The result: dozens of gleaming quarts of crimson brown mincemeat triumphantly lining her cellar storage shelves. During our long winters, mincemeat cookies, cakes, and pies were desserts that often doubled as part of a meal's main course.

---

[1] Janet Riley and Ansel Snow are the author's parents. This essay comes from the author's personal memories and oral interviews with 89 year old Janet Riley Snow January-February 2020, Presque Isle, Maine.

[2] Maine Department of Inland Fisheries and Game, "Maine Hunting and Trapping Laws, 1949-1950" (1949). Inland Fisheries and Wildlife Law Books. 174. https://digitalmaine.com/ifw_law_books/174.

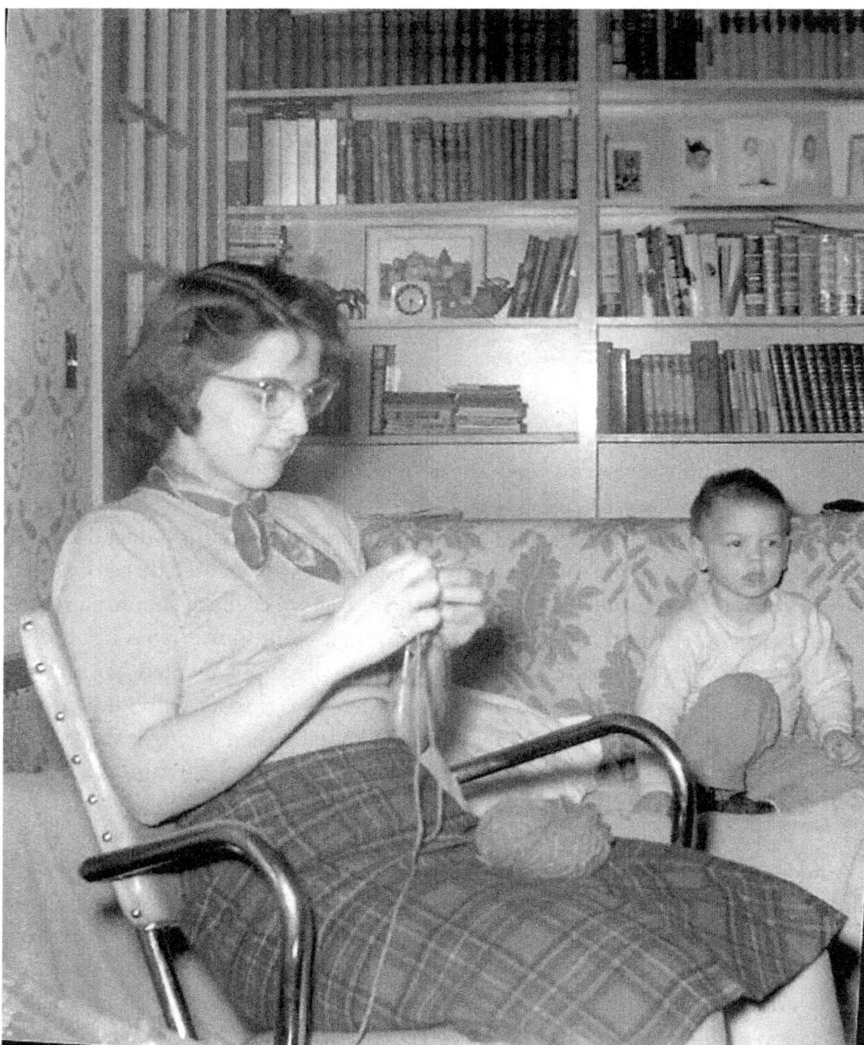

Figure 35.1: Janet knitting while 2-year-old son, Geoffrey, watches cartoons. Courtesy Snow Family Collections, 1958.

With very little money to buy Christmas presents, my mother instead used her time and talents to craft gifts from our family. She was a fiber artist who could knit just about anything and a baker who made delectable breads and delicate holiday sugar cookies.[3] More prized than mittens or socks were the eatables. Only the most special recipients, like her parents, received beribboned jars of mincemeat and large mincemeat pies in their boxes. She also donated mincemeat pies and cookies to holiday bake sales where they were reliable money makers for her clubs and church.

---

[3] Despite the hours and years Janet spent in her kitchen, the Snow family collections have no extant photographs of her cooking.

My parents were active members of their small but thriving community in northeastern Aroostook County, Potato Empire of the World. Janet was part of a strong women's circle involved with Ladies Home Extension, Women's Club, and, principally, the Congregational Church where she taught Sunday School. This web empowered women, connecting them with each other and folks in other towns around the region. One particular activity that galvanized women was the Congregational Church Supper. Occurring several times a year, suppers were enormously popular events that supported the church and provided a social venue not only for Masardis, but also for other towns in the area. The women organized and executed each one, cooking for hundreds of diners who purchased tickets in advance and ate in shifts. Many women had their own specialty dishes or baked goods. While my mother was most famous for her Parker House rolls, her venison mincemeat desserts were a close second, always in high demand, always disappearing with the first wave of diners.

Church suppers provided women an opportunity to share recipes which were seldom written down, but instead preserved by oral tradition. For a woman with plenty of prior cooking knowledge, any new dish had a basic formula that could be readily catalogued in the recipe file in her head. Recipe exchanges invoked the culinary muse in my mother, inspiring mouth-watering possibilities for a new dish or dessert to present at home or the next church or Grange supper. Cooking had the potential to bring women status and agency that went beyond the kitchen table.

For Janet, cooking was more than feeding her family nutritious, tasty meals on a slender budget. It was a medium for her creativity. It lent purpose and motivation to her household work. It required culinary skills, imagination, and a measure of daring to transform ordinary meat, potatoes and vegetables into mouth-watering casseroles and soups unlike dishes served at other mothers' tables. Her November mincemeat was autumn's reassurance of savory and versatile winter fare. To me it symbolizes the lifeway my parents shared and the world where I grew up in northern Maine.

November Mincemeat

Janet Riley Snow, Circa 1949

Preparation Time
2 days; total cooking time: 5-6 hours; makes 20-25 quarts

Ingredients (may vary by availability or cook's preference)
10 lbs venison: use neck meat, lesser cuts, and meaty bones
4 lbs. beef suet

4 ½ lbs. raisins
4 ½ lbs. currants
1 lb. golden raisins
1-2 lbs. hazelnuts
3 ½ oz. candied lemon peel
3 ½ oz. candied orange peel
8 oz. citron

5 lemons—zest & juice
5 oranges—zest & juice
4 lbs. apples
10 qts. apple cider

2 TBLs salt
4 ½ TBLs cinnamon
2 TBLs nutmeg
2 ½ tsp. cloves
2 ½ tsp. allspice
2 ½ tsp. mace
2 ½ tsp. ginger
2 ½ tsp. coriander

1 fifth (750 ml) brandy
1 fifth (750 ml) dark rum

Instructions
In addition to measuring cups and spoons, you will need extra-large bowls, enamel or stainless steel kettles, a strainer (no aluminum), ladles, and long handled spoons (preferably wooden); canning utensils, along with sturdy knives, a meat cleaver, a meat grinder, a set of scales, a canner or pressure cooker, 20-25 quart size glass canning jars with covers and jar rubbers or lids and bands.

Day One

1. Put 2-3 quarts of water to boil in your large pot, then assemble tools and utensils. Set up the meat grinder. Check jars and lids (if using old fashioned style) for nicks; wash and rinse; set aside and cover with clean cloth.
2. Submerge meat and bones in boiling water; if necessary, add more to keep meat covered. Return to boil, then reduce to simmer and cook until tender, about 2 hours.
3. While the meat is cooking, grind up the suet.
4. When the meat is done, strain through a fine sieve. Do not use the broth or bone marrow. Discard or feed to your dogs and cats.
5. Allow meat to cool completely, then pick meat off the bones, cut up larger hunks and run it all through the grinder. Combine ground meat and suet, cover and refrigerate.

Day Two

1. Measure out dry and candied fruits and combine with the apple cider in a very large kettle; add the meat and suet. Bring up to a simmer, but do not boil; stir often to prevent scorching.
2. While meat mixture is simmering, peel and cut up apples. Set aside. Measure salt and all spices into a bowl, stir to blend and add with the apples to the meat. Simmer two hours, stirring often. Add more cider if necessary to maintain the simmer. Prepare canning jars while meat is cooking.
3. When the mixture is fully cooked it should be very thick. Remove from heat. Spoon a little out, cool, then taste to make sure flavors have blended satisfactorily. Adjust seasonings if necessary.
4. Stir in brandy and rum until you get consistency for a pie filling. If you prefer to cook out the alcohol in the rum and brandy, add them during cooking. However, the presence of the spirits will be diminished.
5. Pack immediately into hot jars, leaving a half inch head space. Process jars according to your chosen method.
6. As the mincemeat cools, some of the suet will rise to the top of the jars forming a thick layer that works as a preservative helping seal out bacteria. Later when you open the jars this can be spooned off to use in other dishes that call for fat. Stored correctly, suet keeps for a long time.
7. Serve prepared mincemeat as a side dish or bake into pies, cookies or cakes.[4]

---

[4] As a young wife, Janet owned two cookbooks: Meta Given's *Modern Encyclopedia of Cooking,* (Chicago: J. G. Ferguson & Associates,1949), and *Better Homes and Gardens Cookbook,* (Des Moines: Meredith Publishing Co., 1951). No written copy of her venison mincemeat recipe has survived. For the RWSA cookbook project, she resurrected it from memory and had a few consults with those two old cookbooks she still owns.

—36—

Two Cakes and Three Generations

Sara Egge, Sharon Egge, and Harriet Namminga
Southeastern South Dakota, USA, 20th Century

When my grandparents, Jacob and Harriet Namminga, moved into an assisted living facility in southeastern South Dakota, my mom received my grandma Harriet's recipe box. In it were dozens of handwritten recipes for casseroles, pies, jams, breads, and other dishes. At Thanksgiving that year, when all my aunts, uncles, and cousins gathered for the annual meal, my mom brought out the box. Perhaps I'm exaggerating, but I think I heard a collective gasp in delight as family members crowded around the table, reading through the recipes.

Some took photos of my grandma's cherished recipe for rhubarb jam. Others wrote down the recipe for her hands-down-best-ever pecan pie. I remember how careful we all were when handling the recipe cards. Some were brown, brittle, and flaking at the edges. Others had splotches of spilled sauce or grease, making them soft and prone to tearing.

The recipes themselves—their lists of ingredients and step-by-step directions—were precious, but what I remember most were the stories shared around the table. My grandparents raised four girls on a farm, and my mom and her sisters spent their childhoods milking cows, raising hogs, and feeding chickens, among so many other things. Farming and family, along with their Dutch Reformed faith, ordered their lives. Sometimes a recipe prompted memories of something ordinary, like weekly visits to relatives' houses after Sunday church. Other recipes recalled milestones, like moving away from home or getting married.

The conversation flowed across generations, with many voices weaving the stories together. These are the stories I love most—stories that start with one person and finish with another; stories that blend years so that time feels held in suspension; stories pieced together from a kaleidoscope of perspectives.

I am contributing two recipes to the RWSA cookbook, and I have asked my grandma, Harriet—who turned 90 in 2020—and my mom, Sharon, to share their perspectives about these recipes. I have included mine as well.

Harriet: Sour cream cake (or spice cake) came from my mother (Nancy Dyk). We made it every week as we had plenty of sour cream. When I made it, I usually put brown sugar frosting on it. It went to many funerals and seldom did a piece come back in the pan. Family loved it too. Always good comments.

Applesauce cake came from Grandma Namminga (Rena Bruinsma). And the brown sugar frosting. Everyone loved it except those who did not like raisins.

Sharon: Two favorite cake recipes come to mind during my growing-up years and my own housekeeping years. Applesauce raisin cake was Grandma Namminga's (Rena Bruinsma's) recipe. Sour cream chocolate cake was Grandma Dyk's (Nancy Dyk's) recipe.

Every Saturday we baked a cake for Sunday and the week. We always had applesauce on hand as we had apple trees on the farm where I grew up from age 7 years on. Mom canned upwards of 100 quarts in the fall. And we always had fresh sour cream since we milked cows—anywhere from 18 to 24 cows milked twice a day.

By the time we were 10 years old, we were able to bake a cake with a little help. So, every 4th Saturday you baked the cake (4 girls). Every Sunday afternoon we met at an aunt/uncle house. Kids played and the grownups visited. The men sat in the living room and the women sat in the dining room. Some days there were lots of laughs—sometimes sad stories. At 3:00 pm, the hostess made trays for the men—coffee or tea, always cake and cookies. The kids had lunch in the kitchen or, in summer, outside. The women sat at the dining room table. The favorite frosting for the cake was brown sugar boiled frosting.

We carried our lunch in a tin lunch pail. It rode in the bike basket or we carried it to school. Cake wrapped in waxed paper was usually included for noon lunch.

Cake was also included in the Karo syrup pail lunch we carried in the spring/summer/fall to the field for Dad as he planted, cultivated, or harvested. Hot coffee with cream and sugar was carried in a quart jar. Sandwiches were usually the main course. This lunch was eaten at 10:00 am and again at 3:00 pm.

Sara: I remember eating sour cream chocolate cake in the summer, with homemade vanilla ice cream we churned all day. Each cousin had to take a turn cranking the metal handle on the old wooden churn. We counted each rotation to make sure no one shirked their responsibility. At "tea time," the afternoon meal at 3:00 pm, my aunts served the cake and ice cream. I can still see the ice cream, melting and swirling into the delicious chocolate cake.

For as long as I can remember, my mom has made applesauce cake for special occasions. It was my birthday cake for many years. My mom often made it when I returned home to visit during college and graduate school. While I have few specific memories of these moments, I remember how we always seemed to have the same conversation. We all chattered in anticipation about how good the cake was while someone cut and served it. We teased my dad because he is the only member of our family who does not like raisins, which for us was unbelievable. As we received our pieces, the room gradually fell silent, except for some "mmm" sounds or short in-between-bites comments like "so good" or "delicious." As soon as we finished, we began to rationalize another piece. It never took long before we were dishing up seconds.

My mom made applesauce cake as a surprise for lunch on the day of my wedding. This is the one cake I remember. The delightful frenzy of the day stopped as she brought out the pan. We did not say much, at least not that I can remember. But I recall every detail of how good that cake tasted and how much it meant to me.

Applesauce Cake

2 cups sugar
¾ cup shortening
2 eggs
2 ½ cups flour
1 tsp. salt
1 tsp. cinnamon
½ tsp. allspice
½ tsp. cloves
2 tsp. baking soda
1 tsp. baking powder
2 cups applesauce, warmed
1 ½ cups raisins
½ cup nuts (optional)

Cream sugar, shortening, and eggs together. Sift flour, salt, cinnamon, allspice, cloves, baking soda, and baking powder. Add to creamed ingredients alternately with warm applesauce. Stir in 1 ½ cups raisins. Bake for 30 minutes in a 9 x 13 inch cake pan at 350 degrees or until a toothpick comes out clean. Frost with brown sugar frosting when cake is cool.

Brown Sugar Frosting

¼ cup margarine or butter
¾ cup brown sugar
5 tbsp. milk or cream
2 cups powdered sugar, plus or minus
½ tsp. vanilla

In a saucepan, combine margarine, brown sugar, and milk. Heat and stir until boiling. Boil 1 minute. Remove from heat and beat in 2 cups powdered sugar. Add vanilla. Spread on cake.

Sour Cream Scratch Cake

2 cups sour cream
4 eggs
1 tsp. vanilla
2 cups flour
1 ½ cups sugar
½ tsp. salt
2 tsp. baking soda
3 tbsp. cocoa (heaping)

Beat sour cream, eggs, and vanilla. Sift flour, sugar, salt, baking soda, and cocoa. Add the dry ingredients to the wet ingredients. Bake at 350 degrees for 30 minutes or until a toothpick comes out clean.

Written on the back: "We made this recipe every week. Sometimes left out cocoa and added spices. Cinnamon, nutmeg, cloves, ½ tsp. of each."

—37—

Grammie Botsford's Molasses Cookies

Rachel Snell

Poultney, Vermont, USA, Probably Late 19th Century

My maternal great-grandmother, Elisabeth Botsford, lived on a dairy farm in Poultney, VT. My mother has fond memories of visiting her every summer in the 1960s and always finding these cookies in one of the cookie jars in her pantry. My treasured childhood memories include making these cookies with my Mom and siblings growing up, carefully rolling the dough in sugar and—the most coveted task—gently pressing the sugared balls with a crystal tumbler inherited from Grammie Botsford.

Grammie Botsford's Molasses Cookies

1 cup butter (softened)
1 cup sugar (plus more for rolling)
1 cup molasses
1 tablespoon ginger
1 egg
½ teaspoon kosher salt (reduce to ¼ teaspoon if using salted butter)
1 tablespoon baking soda
¼ cup boiling water
5 cups flour

Original recipe (from Sue Snell's manuscript recipe collection, dictated by Elisabeth Botsford):

Bake 350 10-12 mins.

1 T baking soda into cup you use for molasses.

¼ cup boiling water stir into baking soda. Add ¼ C more water. Mix into butter, sugar & molasses. Add ginger, egg & flour. Chill dough.

Roll into balls. Put on cookie sheet press with bottom of glass that has been coated with Crisco.

My Adaptation:

In a large bowl, cream together the butter, sugar, and molasses. Add the egg, ginger, and salt. Mix well.

In the cup used to measure the molasses, combine the baking soda with the boiling water plus an additional ¼ cup water and add to the mixture.

Add flour. Chill the dough until firm.

Preheat oven to 350 degrees.

Roll about two tablespoons of dough into balls and coat with sugar. Place on a greased cookie sheet and press with a glass coated in cooking spray.

Bake 10-12 minutes.

—38—

Chocolate Pudding

Eli Bosler

Ohio, USA, 1940s

This is a recipe for chocolate pudding from my grandma that she brought with her when she moved to Ohio from Rhode Island. (She moved to Ohio with my grandpa after they met in the Civilian Public Service (CPS) camp at the Rhode Island State Hospital, during World War II. She was a lab technician and he was a conscientious objector, working as an orderly.) According to her, this recipe dates back to at least her grandmother. Grandma Bosler turned 100 in December of 2019.

Chocolate Pudding

Ingredients

1 quart of milk (4 cups)

1 cup of sugar

2 packages of unsweetened chocolate. (Today that translates to eight squares (2oz) of unsweetened Bakers chocolate.)

A pinch of salt

4 mounded TBLS of corn starch (per grandma mounded NOT heaping)

1 TSB Vanilla

Preparation

Assemble double boiler with water just to the bottom of the second pan

Cooking

Put almost all the milk (3.5 cups) into the double boiler over medium low heat.

Add the sugar, salt, and chocolate (per recipe cut the top off chocolate envelope and roll into the milk. However, with Baker's chocolate you do not have to cut or roll the package into the milk).

With the leftover milk add the corn starch and mix until smooth, add the milk and corn starch mixture to the rest of the milk stirring constantly over medium heat until thickened. About 10 minutes.

Remove from heat.

Add vanilla and mix in.

PART IV

Politics and Authority

—39—

Introduction

Cynthia C. Prescott

Whether passed orally from mother to child (or grandmother to grandson (Cates, Ch. 24, this volume)), or passed on an increasingly battered index card (Prescott, Ch. 31, this volume), reproduced in the home section of the local newspaper (McKinney, Ch. 16, this volume), or printed in the pages of a cookbook (Prescott, Ch. 11, this volume), cooking skills have always been shared within families and communities. Children learned by watching and helping their mothers cook. Rural folk produced much of their food and purchased staples such as sugar and flour in bulk at general stores while urbanites relied on grocers, and later, supermarkets, for foodstuffs. But that knowledge transfer became more formalized at the turn of the twentieth century. The academic field of home economics developed, calling for more standardized recipes, detailed instructions, and an increasing emphasis on food science (Sharpless, Ch. 3, this volume). American food processing companies manufactured female "experts" to distribute expertise and market their products. The fictional Aunt Jemima—played by a series of African-American women—manipulated racialized mythology of the Old South to market pancake mix (a phenomenon we unpack more thoroughly in this volume's Conclusion (Prescott, Conclusion, this volume). Meanwhile, teams of white female home economists employed by other processed food brands communicated with consumers under the guise of Mary Blake (representing Carnation), Ann Pillsbury (Pillsbury), and many others. After World War II, it became common to print recipes directly on packaging of name brand products, particularly processed foods such as Campbell's condensed soup (Ambrose, Ch. 43, this volume). As more women entered the paid workforce, convenience items were produced by large-scale industries such as canned fruits and vegetables, cake mix, and frozen foods, including Swanson "T.V. dinners," introduced in 1954, made for consumers partaking of America's favorite pastime.

By far the most prominent of manufacturers' fictional food authorities was General Mills' Betty Crocker. Beginning in the 1920s, home economist Marjorie Child Husted reached millions of North American homemakers through print and radio under the guise of the Betty Crocker character. At Gold Medal Flour headquarters, a small army of home economists responded to letters from homemakers under the Crocker name, offering suggestions and recipes. Perhaps more importantly, they offered confidential advice to cooks who increasingly lived in cities far from the familial networks and oral traditions of previous generations.

Betty Crocker recipes offered step-by-step instructions for producing traditional American recipes using newly-introduced electric stoves and labor-saving devices. Company home economists identified irregularly-shaped pans as a primary culprit in baking failures, crusading for national standardization in pan sizes. In response to scarcity during the Great Depression and rationing during World War II, Betty Crocker advised homemakers on ways to stretch scarce resources to feed their families. Increasingly she offered foolproof recipes verified in the General Mills test kitchen and by a select group of homemakers. Eventually General Mills packaged her expertise into a highly successful cookbook, which remains the go-to reference for beginning cooks and bakers in the United States to this day. Over time, as women increasingly entered the paid labor force, leaving less time for cooking and baking, her recipes gradually yielded market share to cake mixes and other processed foods—all marketed under the Betty Crocker brand.[1]

Meanwhile, government agencies offered educational programs grounded in domestic science. Like Betty Crocker and the publishers of Montana Rural Home (McKinney, Ch. 6, this volume), extension agents from the United States Department of Agriculture provided valuable information to homemakers. They taught women ways to safely and effectively produce and preserve food to feed their families. Agents tutored rural women on food safety, nutrition and health. But like Betty Crocker and Aunt Jemima, those government employees also sought to indoctrinate their rural audiences in particular uses of and attitudes toward food.

In this section we examine the roles of food experts in shaping foodways in North America and track the spread of new goods and tastes through two world wars and beyond. The three longer essays in this section center on different angles of food politics and knowledge transfer over the past century in Iowa, USA. Sara Egge explores the way that Iowa suffragists politicized food production and consumption in the early twentieth century (Egge, Ch 40, this volume). She also points to government food conservation efforts during World War I. Jenny Barker Devine (Barker Devine, Ch. 44, this volume) examines extension agents' efforts to persuade Iowa farmwomen to diet after World War II—efforts that floundered because they did not align with rural women's shared identity at a time of agricultural crisis. Pamela Riney-Kehrberg (Riney-Kehrberg, Ch. 45, this volume) then outlines her strategies for educating twenty-first-century Iowa university students on rural women's work and agricultural history by focusing on food production and consumption. In her essay and accompanying sample of primary source materials (Riney-Kehrberg and Prescott, Ch. 46, this volume) she offers guidance to readers on constructing their own food history course.

Shorter contributions interspersed through this section likewise highlight the influence of home economics training and government policies related to food production and consumption. During the Great Depression, home economics programs promoted simple recipes such as "Domecon Cake" (Benson, Ch. 41, this

---

[1] Susan Marks, *Finding Betty Crocker: The Secret Life of America's First Lady of Food* (University of Minnesota Press, 2007); Laura Shapiro, "'I Guarantee':: Betty Crocker and the Woman in the Kitchen," in *From Betty Crocker to Feminist Food Studies*, ed. Arlene Voski Avakian and Barbara Haber, Critical Perspectives on Women and Food (University of Massachusetts Press, 2005), 29–40, http://www.jstor.org/stable/j.ctt5vk2tn.6.

Figure 39.1: Arthur Rothstein, photographer, Mrs. H.H. Poland, wife of rehabilitation client, with preserved food. Mesa County, Colorado, October, 1939. Library of Congress, Prints & Photographs Division, Farm Security Administration/Office of War Information Black-and-White Negatives. Public domain.

volume) that nonetheless was likely out of reach for many struggling to feed their families. Extension agents urged farm women to preserve garden produce and meat through extensive canning (see Figure 39.1). Government investigators uncovered persistent hunger during the depression (Prescott, Ch. 42, this volume). They also documented the experiences of formerly enslaved African Americans (Riney-Kehrberg and Prescott, Ch. 46, this volume). Hunger remained a concern as World War II lifted the United States out of the Great Depression. Government propaganda then praised and encouraged agricultural production in wartime (Prescott, Ch. 42, this volume).

Sometimes regarded as drudgery, cooking has made a comeback. Daytime talk shows on the major television networks and shows on cable networks such as the Food Network and Cooking Channel feature contemporary female food experts such as Molly Yeh (Prescott, Ch. 49, this volume) and Ree Drummond (Prescott, Conclusion, this volume)) who update the cooking instruction delivered a century ago by fictional food experts in print and on radio. Popular primetime (evening) programming focus more on competitions featuring a growing pantheon of celebrity chefs. Yet those vying to become the next Food Network Star must demonstrate their ability to not only produce impressive food, but to share tips that can be readily adopted by home cooks.

Another trend in food television is catering to US citizens' expanding palates. In the cooking show *Chopped*, professional chefs compete to transform unusual ingredients into a gourmet meal. Other shows offer a virtual culinary vacation by highlighting unusual cuisines, whether that be exotic ethnic specialties or local dives. As long-distance travel became easier with the advent of commercial jet air service, many North Americans ventured to foreign countries. While some looked for familiar foods by seeking out the McDonalds restaurants that were spreading around the globe or reluctantly experienced unusual dishes, as Cynthia Prescott presents in her piece titled "Pavlova," (Prescott, Ch. 47, this volume) others embraced opportunities to sample local cuisine. Even Betty Crocker's growing line of cookbooks to supplement the beloved *Big Red* eventually embraced global flavors. As we explore more in Part V, food is an important component of immigrant culture (Chen, Ch. 52, this volume), and throughout the last century many new culinary delights were introduced to the American mainstream. Most major cities feature Mexican, Asian Indian, Thai, Vietnamese, Japanese, and Chinese restaurants. A growing number include Ethiopian and Middle Eastern cuisine or reflect regional influences. For example, Cuban restaurants are prevalent throughout South Florida. We have even learned to cook some exotic dishes at home, and due to the pandemic, homemade meals were essential during the country's initial shutdown (Riney-Kehrberg, Ch. 55, this volume).

Over the past two decades, there has been a rise in food history and food studies that incorporate a range of disciplines, a topic Pamela Riney-Kehberg addresses in her article, "Teaching Food History" (Riney-Kehrberg, Ch. 45, this volume) Because we consume food on a daily basis, it occupies our thoughts and controls some of our actions. Food can be used for political purposes, as Sara Egge explains in her essay (Egge, Ch. 40, this volume). What we eat or reject eating can also signify our values, such as eating a vegan diet to reduce our carbon footprint or refusing to eat meat to spare animal lives. Because food is required for healthy living, acquiring and preparing it occupies a substantial portion of our lives. That became even more true when a pandemic hit as we prepared the essays and recipes in this volume—a topic that we will explore in greater depth in Part V (Prescott, Ch. 48, this volume). Here in Part IV, we focus on the ways that food preparation, preservation, and consumption have been shaped through knowledge transmission, and the ways in which that knowledge exchange can be politically charged and at times shaped by power relationships. Throughout this section, we highlight tensions between urban and rural, teacher and student, and efforts to bridge those divides.

—40—

Cake and Politics

Sara Egge

"Attention, Housekeepers of Iowa!" declared the 1916 headline, written in all-caps and outlined by a decorative border. Below it was a photograph of Anne May Easton Mills (Annie May, or May), a suffragist from Des Moines, Iowa. She stood beside a table with a sifter suspended in her left hand over a large, white mixing bowl. Her right hand held a spoon or spatula, which she pointed downward into the bowl. On the table was another white bowl and a few ingredients for baking. The text of the article explained that Mills had created a recipe for an "eggless, butterless, milkless cake ... [which] promises to become widely known as the Suffrage Cake."[1] Not only was the "new delicacy" delicious, but it also promised to "play an important part in the suffrage campaign." For only a ten-cent donation to the "suffrage treasury," Iowans could receive the secret recipe.[2]

While the Suffrage Cake campaign was noteworthy, as it appeared in a number of newspapers across Iowa, it was one of a number of fundraisers spearheaded by suffragists in which food was the appealing feature.[3] What is striking about it is the way its author framed it to appeal to home cooks, both urban and rural. "Easier times are predicted for the cook as a result of the active part an enterprising Iowa suffragist is taking in financing the suffrage campaign."[4] This opening line recalled a common refrain from the time that women, especially but not only in rural contexts, were laboring drudges overwhelmed by work.[5] In addition, the recipe was neither pretentious nor fancy, and it came "highly recommended" for its "economical features."[6] Finally, the absence of eggs, butter, and milk was striking as they served as essential ingredients featured in some combination in nearly all of the cakes baked by urban and rural women at the time. Mills targeted patterns of

---

[1] "Attention, Housekeepers of Iowa!" *Boone County Democrat,* April 17, 1916.

[2] "Attention, Housekeepers of Iowa!"

[3] The propaganda appeared in local newspapers across Iowa, including *The Bayard News* of Bayard, *The Marble Rock Journal* of Marble Rock, and *The Courier* of Waterloo.

[4] "Attention, Housekeepers of Iowa!"

[5] Nancy Grey Osterud, *Bonds of Community: The Lives of Farm Women in Nineteenth-Century New York* (Ithaca: Cornell University Press, 1991), 145-47; Deborah Fink, *Agrarian Women: Wives and Mothers in Rural Nebraska, 1880-1940* (Chapel Hill: University of North Carolina Press, 1992), 62-67.

[6] "Attention, Housekeepers of Iowa!"

food consumption directly by offering alternatives to these staples. The emphasis in the article mattered; the value of the ten-cent donation was the recipe itself, not necessarily its financial support of woman suffrage.

The state leaders of the Iowa Equal Suffrage Association (IESA), the organization that created this propaganda, configured it to match what they understood to be the expectations of early-twentieth-century Iowans. They hoped to convince voters to support an amendment granting women in the state the right to vote. It was on the primary election ballot, scheduled for June 5, 1916, so the April recipe campaign was timely. But most voters considered woman suffrage controversial, so fundraising that emphasized food was a way to deradicalize the cause. They presented a cake recipe without eggs, milk, and butter as attractive, tapping into issues of productivity and accessibility that marked Iowa's foodways. Most rural women practiced home production, raising the foodstuffs, especially poultry and dairy products, that comprised the recipes they prepared. Since daily access to a grocery or general store was a luxury, they purchased in bulk those few things they could not grow themselves. Rural women also sold or traded excess goods, especially eggs and dairy items, at groceries and local markets, feeding the demand for such commodities to an increasingly urban population. These urban consumers enjoyed easier access to grocery stores and their wider selection of goods, which created both shared and distinct food cultures between urban and rural peoples.[7]

Cake recipes, used weekly in many Iowa households, had an expected list of ingredients shaped heavily by rural home production and the urban markets connected to it. Most relied extensively on basics like wheat flour, sugar, eggs, and dairy items like milk and butter. The absence of three of these essential components in the Suffrage Cake recipe, and the IESA's emphasis on that absence, was curious. Perhaps Mills offered the recipe because she understood how disease or drought could create shortages. Maybe she considered how preservation techniques or refrigeration practices could falter, spoiling goods as a result. But she also probably knew how patterns of informal neighborhood exchange could counteract threats of scarcity.[8] The date of its appearance is telling, for by 1916, domestic scientists, inspired by the rise of industrial and technological invention, had worked for nearly four decades to apply science to improve the American diet as they understood it.[9] In this light, the appeal of Mills's offer of "easier times" for the home cook with an "economical" Suffrage Cake, without its eggs, milk, and butter, was in its scientific innovation. While Mills hoped intrigue from both urban and rural audiences would produce ten-cent donations, she also was tapping into domestic science and its appeal across Iowa's shared, yet distinct food cultures.

---

[7] Deborah Fink, *Open Country, Iowa: Rural Women, Tradition, and Change* (Albany: State University of New York Press, 1986), 32, 46-51. For example, it was not until the 1920s that commercially-produced butter was available.

[8] Mary Neth, *Preserving the Family Farm: Women, Community, and the Foundations of Agribusiness in the Midwest, 1900-1940* (Baltimore: Johns Hpokins University Press, 1998), 40-62.

[9] Laura Shapiro, *Perfection Salad: Women and Cooking at the Turn of the Century* (Berkeley: University of California Press, 2009).

For city dwellers, with access to groceries and a growing number of store-bought items, she believed scientific cookery was inspirational. For rural cooks, with limited access to these kinds of items, she assumed the recipe was aspirational.

May Easton Mills was a prominent civic leader in Des Moines, where she lived with her husband, Pleasant, a businessman who had founded the White Lane Transfer & Storage Company, which became a major hauling and carrier business.[10] Born in Dallas County, Iowa to John Easton, a lumber dealer, she had attended Grinnell College before marrying Pleasant in 1883.[11] By 1916, she was a seasoned advocate for woman suffrage. She was a founder of the IESA when it organized in the early 1900s, and she continued to serve on its board. In 1913, she served as the chair of an extensive "River to River" automobile and lecture tour. Her aim was to explicitly engage with rural people, and she arranged for stops only in small towns. She also provided her own vehicle at no cost to the IESA for a caravan that crossed the state twice, starting in Des Moines before moving west.[12] When planning for the amendment campaign began in the fall of 1915, she became its publicity chair. Not only did she work behind-the-scenes; she was also a vocal supporter. Her 1916 New Years' resolution "to put Iowa on the suffrage map in June" appeared in newspapers across Iowa.[13]

On paper, then, Mills was not a rural woman. She was an elite living in Iowa's largest city, with more time, money, education, and financial resources to devote to woman suffrage than most rural women had. Pitching the Suffrage Cake recipe to include rural Iowans perhaps involved a number of assumptions on her part. But she also believed that just because rural people were less inclined to engage with the cause did not make them automatically opposed. In fact, suffragists like Mills recognized that rural and urban Iowans often had more in common than they realized. In particular, domestic expectations, especially around the work of food production, processing, and preparation, created common experiences among all women, and sharing recipes often bridged distinctions marked by locality, as well as class, religion, and ethnicity. In this way, food was an effective political tool, one that could create coalitions, many times in unexpected ways. Mills advertised her Suffrage Cake recipe to attract rural women, a group often less involved with but not necessarily less interested in suffrage, which demonstrates the power she placed on food to forge new and important political alliances.

---

[10] "Civic Leader Dies," *Council Bluffs Nonpareil,* May 22, 1953; United States Interstate Commerce Commission, *Interstate Commerce Commission Reports: Motor Carrier Cases, Volume 5, Decisions of the Interstate Commerce Commission of the United States (Finance Reports)* (Washington, DC: Government Printing Office, 1939), 451-53.

[11] Anna Easton, Dallas Center, Dallas, Iowa, *Tenth Census of the United States, 1880,* page 247A, Roll 335, Microfilm, Bureau of the Census (Provo: Ancestry.com, 2012); Frank Moody Mills, *Something About the Mills Family and Its Collateral Branches with Autobiographical Reminiscences* (Sioux Falls, S. D.: n. p., 1911), 207-11; "Iowa College Yearbook 1880," page 12, *U. S. School Catalogues, 1765-1935* (Provo: Ancestry.com, 2012).

[12] "Suffragists on Hawkeye Tour," *The Courier* (Waterloo, Iowa), Sept. 1, 1913; "Suffrage Women to Stump State," *Quad-City Times* (Davenport, Iowa), Sept. 2, 1913; "Progress of the Suffrage Cause," *Creston Plain Deal,* Sept. 9, 1913.

[13] "Push Suffrage Fight in Iowa," *Quad-City Times* (Davenport, Iowa), Dec. 31, 1915.

Suffragists in Iowa had planned successful campaigns around food production for at least two decades. In 1900, Eleanor Stockman, a prominent suffrage leader from Cerro Gordo County who was married to George Stockman, a physician in Mason City, responded to a national fundraising effort spearheaded by the National American Woman Suffrage Association (NAWSA).[14] NAWSA asked each state association to contribute something to represent the state, and Iowa's organization appointed Stockman the chair of their entry.[15] Stockman suggested that Iowa do its part by sending hogs, a foodstuff many Americans associated with the state. While NAWSA leaders endorsed Stockman's plan, they encouraged her to sell the pigs at market and send the money instead. Stockman eventually secured donations of ninety-five hogs, along with ten loads of corn, raising four-hundred-sixty dollars in the process. Stockman's "pig money" was no laughing matter; her contribution made Cerro Gordo County the second-highest donor of all the counties in the United States.[16]

Food production and fundraising continued to prove an essential combination during the 1916 amendment campaign, but success was not a guarantee. Before Mills advertised her secret recipe, the IESA organized a fall fundraiser with the slogan "Iowa Corn for Iowa Women."[17] The group solicited Iowa farmers, both men and women, to donate either a bushel of corn or the price of a bushel of corn. This special "Votes for Women Corn" promised to "pour streams of golden coins in to the suffrage coffers," with "quality and excellence guaranteed."[18] The IESA also planned to have a booth at the Iowa State Fair at which farmers could register their donated bushels. While state suffrage leaders anticipated a large turnout, it is difficult to assess the outcome of the corn campaign because they left few detailed records of it. The IESA relied heavily on NAWSA to fund the 1916 campaign—and continued to fundraise into the spring—which indicates that "golden coins" from "golden corn" did not flood their coffers.[19]

Donations of hogs or corn offered an important fundraising opportunity for suffragists in that they explicitly targeted farmers as producers of foodstuffs. In doing so, the IESA attempted to deradicalize woman suffrage and engage with rural people who might not do so on their own. Mills widened the IESA's scope by shifting to food consumption, tapping into broader conversations about domestic

---

[14] Eleanor Stockman, Mason City, Cerro Gordo County, Iowa, *Thirteenth Census of the United States,* page 3B, Roll T624_396, Microfilm, Records of the Bureau of the Census (Provo: Ancestry.com, 2006).

[15] "Iowa Women and Hogs," *Cedar Rapids Republican,* [1900], Eleanor Stockman Scrapbook, folder 1, box 22, Iowa Woman Suffrage Collection, State Historical Society of Iowa, Des Moines, Iowa; "For the Suffrage Bazaar," *Sioux City Journal,* Dec. 2, 1900.

[16] "Iowa Women and Hogs," Eleanor Stockman Scrapbook, folder 1, box 22, Iowa Woman Suffrage Collection, State Historical Society of Iowa, Des Moines, Iowa; "Dear Iowa Friends," Eleanor Stockman Scrapbook, folder 1, box 22, Iowa Woman Suffrage Collection, State Historical Society of Iowa, Des Moines, Iowa.

[17] "Equal Suffrage Column," *Spencer News,* Aug. 17, 1915.

[18] "Equal Suffrage Column."

[19] Louise Noun, *Strong-Minded Women: The Emergence of the Woman-Suffrage Movement in Iowa* (Ames: Iowa State University Press, 1969), 253.

economy and public concerns about health, safety, sanitation, nutrition, and disease that began in the late-nineteenth century and continued into the twentieth.[20] In the case of food, groups of reformers, mostly located in northeastern states, created schools to investigate a scientific approach to cooking. In the process, they modernized the American diet by emphasizing precision, standardization, and meal planning over taste. While they had an incomplete understanding of nutrition, they prescribed certain ratios of protein, carbohydrate, and fat in their recipes, promoting these measures in cookbooks they began to publish in the 1880s and 1890s.[21] In this way, cookbooks produced in the late nineteenth and early twentieth centuries were increasingly prominent with a national audience.

Other types of cookbooks came out of nineteenth-century efforts by women to organize collectively into clubs devoted to shared interests or goals. Compiling community cookbooks became public affairs built out of recipes donated by members of a particular group. Temperance unions, suffrage organizations, social clubs, church societies, and other women's groups created cookbooks, often designating them as fundraisers. But scholars point out that cookbooks accomplished much more than just securing funds. They serve as fantastic historical documents that reveal how women from rural and urban backgrounds cultivated a shared political identity. When they contributed a recipe—anything from a cherished once-a-year holiday meal to an ordinary staple—they made their affiliations visible to public scrutiny. Cookbooks validated their stances on political matters and challenged the ways domesticity attempted to confine or limit women. Situated within the wealth of literary practices nineteenth-century women undertook, from signing petitions to publishing literature to writing songs, poetry, and newspaper articles, cookbooks and the recipes within them showcase how women leveraged political power out of sometimes limited resources.[22]

[20] For a look at the ways obesity became a twentieth-century concern born out of these conversations about nutrition and health, see Jenny Barker-Devine's article in this volume (Barker-Devine, Ch. 43, this volume).

[21] Shapiro, *Perfection Salad*.

[22] Anne Bower, "Our Sisters' Recipes: Exploring 'Community' in a Community Cookbook," *Journal of Popular Culture* 31 (Winter 1997): 137-51; Anne Bower, "Cooking Up Stories: Narrative Elements in Community Cookbooks," *Recipes for Reading: Community Cookbooks, Stories, Histories* (Amherst: University of Massachusetts Press, 1997), 29-50; Mary Anna DuSablon, *America's Collectible Cookbooks: The History, the Politics, the Recipes* (Athens, Ohio: Ohio University Press, 1994); Barbara Epstein, *The Politics of Domesticity* (Middletown, Conn.: Wesleyan University Press, 1986); Laurel Foster, "Liberating the Recipe: A Study of Food and Feminism in the early 1970s," *The Recipe Reader: Narratives, Contexts, Traditions* (Burlington, Vermont: Ashgate, 2003), 147-68; Lynne Ireland, "The Compiled Cookbook as Foodways Autobiography," *The Taste of American Place,* edited by Barbara Shortridge and James Shortridge (New York: Rowman and Littlefield, 1998), 111-17; Jessica Derleth, "'Kneading Politics': Cookery and the American Woman Suffrage Movement," *The Journal of the Gilded Age and Progressive Era* 17 (July 2018): 450-74; Kennan Ferguson, "intensifying Taste, Intensifying Identity: Collectivity through Community Cookbooks," *Signs: Journal of Women in Culture and Society* 27 (2012): 695-717.

Suffrage associations published about a half dozen cookbooks between 1886 and 1920.[23] These books offered a range of recipes, including soups, roasts, pies, and other dishes.[24] Scholars point out that while producing cookbooks might seem odd for women agitating for equal rights, they were relying on what they knew best. Shared domestic experiences not only bound women across rural and urban contexts; for some it was the only way they could offer support for the cause. Moreover, cookbooks shielded women from attacks on their character. Critics often snidely said that neglectful mothers would allow their children to starve while they went to the polls, so cookbooks provided evidence to the contrary. Like Mills's Suffrage Cake recipe, cookbooks often appeared during campaigns, designed by suffragists to raise funds and reach wider audiences. Scholars also add that publishing allowed women to gain skills as editors, advertisers, and salespeople. They also built networks by securing endorsements from famous people and politicians.[25]

The range of recipes in suffrage cookbooks makes it difficult to compare Mills's recipe for Suffrage Cake. Some were basic while others were complicated, with ingredients only the wealthy or well-connected could acquire. Of all the cookbooks suffragists created, one appeared a year before Mills produced her recipe. *The Suffrage Cook Book,* published in Pittsburgh, contained recipes from a number of notable suffragists. With a bold blue cover that featured Uncle Sam, the book also contained images and jokes. Governors from eight states with woman suffrage legislation provided endorsements. The cookbook served not only to disseminate tried-and-true recipes; it was also an effective political weapon. A recipe titled "Pie for a Suffragist's Doubting Husband" called for "1 qt. milk human kindness" followed by "8 reasons: War, White Slavery, Child Labor, 8,000,000 Working Women, Bad Roads, Poisonous Water, [and] Impure Food."[26] Another called "Anti's Favorite Hash" listed ingredients of "1 lb. truth thoroughly mangled, 1 generous handful of injustice...[and] 1 tumbler acetic acid (well shaken)."[27] In the "Cakes, Cookies, Tarts, Etc." section, there was no recipe touted as eggless, butterless, or

[23] A list of suffrage cookbooks includes *The Woman Suffrage Cook Book* (1886 and 1890), *The Holiday Gift Cook Book* (Rockford, Ill.: 1891), *Wimodaughsis Cook-Book* (Washington, DC: 1892), *Washington Women's Cook Book* (Washington State: 1909), *The Suffrage Cook Book* (Pittsburgh, 1915), *Suffrage Cook Book: A Collection of Recipes* (Detroit, Mich.: 1916), and *Choice Recipes Compiled for the Busy Housewife 1916* (Clinton, NY: 1916).

[24] The Janice Bluestein Longone Culinary Archive at the University of Michigan Library has a number of suffrage cookbooks. See, Janice Bluestein Longone Culinary Archive, Special Collection Research Center, Hatcher Graduate Library, University of Michigan Library, Ann Arbor, Michigan, https://www.lib.umich.edu/janice-bluestein-longone-culinary-archive-0.

[25] Jan Longone, "'The Old Girl Network': Charity Cookbooks and the Empowerment of Women," Lecture, William Clements Library, University of Michigan, Ann Arbor, Michigan, http://lecb.physics.lsa.umich.edu/CWIS/browser.php?ResourceId=1179; Derleth, "'Kneading Politics,'" 450-65; Megan Elias, *Stir It Up: Home Economics in American Culture* (Philadelphia: University of Pennsylvania Press, 2008), 6-7, 20-22, 30-40.

[26] L. O. Kleber, *The Suffrage Cook Book* (Pittsburgh: The Equal Franchise Federation of Western Pennsylvania, 1915), 56, 147.

[27] Kleber, *The Suffrage Cook Book*, 56.

milkless. In fact, all of the cakes had at least one—but usually all three—of these ingredients. Only one recipe, an entry entitled "One Egg Cake," designated a limit. While it indeed listed only one egg, it also contained one cup of butter and another cup of "sweet milk," as well as specific amounts of sugar, flour, baking powder, and raisins.[28]

In a twist of fate, about two years after the IESA published propaganda about the Suffrage Cake, recipes promoting the absence of eggs, milk, and butter began to appear widely, created not only by urban domestic scientists but also rural home cooks. In April 1917, when the United States joined the fighting in World War I, Iowa-born Herbert Hoover took charge of the Food Administration. Its conservation program encouraged Americans to ration food, especially meat and wheat, as a patriotic act. It advocated substitutions for these commodities, sharing recipes with alternatives to certain staple ingredients.[29] Despite its efforts at rationing, consumption of meat and wheat actually increased during the war because European demand propelled agricultural production.[30] But, as scholars note, the Food Administration succeeded when it imposed some substitution rules, like requiring corn meal, barley, rye, or oatmeal in a one-to-four ratio with wheat for bread.[31]

The Food Administration directed its wartime recipes at both rural and urban women, believing their domestic roles put them on the front lines of food conservation. Rural newspapers, farm journals, and extension service publications all catered to farmers while women living in cities responded to propaganda in newspapers. Elite women often acted as cheerleaders, publicly endorsing Food Administration recommendations through temperance societies, federated women's clubs, and other collective associations.[32] As the government channeled eggs, milk, and butter to troops, home economists with connections to the Food Administration developed "culinary innovations" for cakes and breads that lacked these staple ingredients.[33] Recipes now called for Crisco, oil, or vinegar and water.[34] Cookbooks published during the war by reputable domestic scientists contained recipes that they had tailored to reflect these substitutions. Other government publications featured recipes with straightforward titles, like "War Cake."

[28] Kleber, *The Suffrage Cook Book*, 133.

[29] William Mullendore, *History of the Food Administration* (Stanford: Stanford University Press, 1941), 84; Harvey Levenstein, *Revolution at the Table: The Transformation of the American Diet* (New York: Oxford University Press, 1988), 144-46.

[30] Levenstein, *Revolution at the Table,* 144, Wilfred Eldred, "The Wheat and Flour Trade Under Food Administration Control: 1917-1918," *The Quarterly Journal of Economics* 33 (Nov. 1918): 67-68.

[31] Neil Buschman, "The United States Food Administration During World War I: The Rise of Activist Government Through Food Control During Mobilization for Total War," (Master's Thesis: Auburn University, 2013), 67; Eldred, "The Wheat and Flour Trade Under Food Administration Control," 68.

[32] Tanfer Emin Tunc, "Less Sugar, More Warships: Food as American Propaganda in the First World War, *War in History* 19 (April 2012): 210-12.

[33] Tunc, "Less Sugar, More Warships," 209-10.

[34] Tunc, "Less Sugar, More Warships."

War Cake

1 cup molasses
1 cup corn syrup
1 ½ cups water
1 package raisins
2 tablespoons fat
1 teaspoon salt
1 teaspoon cinnamon
½ teaspoon cloves
½ teaspoon nutmeg
3 cups rye flour
½ teaspoon soda
2 teaspoons baking powder

Boil together for 5 minutes the first nine ingredients. Cool, add the sifted dry ingredients and bake in two loaves for 45 minutes in a moderate oven. This cake should be kept several days before using. It makes about 20 to 25 servings. If desired 1 cup of oatmeal may be used in place of 7/8 cup of flour.[35]

Many rural women responded enthusiastically to recipe alternatives, believing their sacrifice a patriotic duty. In this way, food conservation offered women an opportunity to make a public, political stand in support of the war. It also politicized women and their domestic roles as home cooks in the same way community cookbooks and suffrage recipes did. Rural women created alliances of like-minded individuals, intent to contribute in the way they knew best. During the war, women not only saved "every morsel of food," as one local community history put it, but they also gardened, canned, preserved, and bought foodstuffs according to the ratios mandated by the government.[36] Many experimented with new recipes themselves, sending the final results into local newspapers. Prized above all were recipes for cakes without eggs, milk, and butter because extreme shortages of these three staples had made their prices skyrocket. Whereas molasses, honey, sorghum, or other sweeteners could serve as substitutes for sugar, rural people initially struggled to bake their cakes in the absence of eggs, milk, or butter.[37]

May Mills developed her Suffrage Cake almost two years before most of the "-less" recipes appeared in cookbooks, newspapers, and other publications. Wartime shortages of eggs, milk, and butter, therefore, did not influence the way in which she advertised the secret recipe. Instead, Mills offered a scientific innova-

[35] United States Food Administration, *War Economy in Food, With Suggestions and Recipes for Substitutions in the Planning of Meals* (Washington, D.C.: Government Printing Office, 1918), 27-28.

[36] *Pingree, 1880-1980,* page 72, North Dakota County and Town Histories, North Dakota State Library, Bismarck, North Dakota, http://www.digitalhorizonsonline.org/digital/collection/ndsl-books/id/43784/.

[37] Tunc, "Less Sugar, More Warships," 209-12.

tion that sidestepped the basic staples of rural home production. Unfortunately, Mills's secret recipe remains a secret—no publication, archival collection, or other document related to woman suffrage in Iowa contains a copy. Considering the substitutions advocated by home economists, the Food Administration, and other home cooks only two years later, it is likely that Mills created something similar to those recipes that appeared during wartime. Perhaps some vinegar and water, Crisco, or oil made her "new delicacy" so delicious.

Food offered significant opportunities for rural and urban women to engage in politics. Purchasing a secret cake recipe could foster engagement with a controversial cause without causing concern. Contributing to a community cookbook could stake political stances publicly. Publicizing a cake recipe without eggs, milk, or butter during wartime—whether in a cookbook with a national audience or in a local newspaper—signaled patriotic sacrifice. Women built coalitions, many that transcended rural and urban contexts. In this way, Mills framed her recipe as labor-saving and economical, building intrigue and speaking to domestic expectations both urban and rural women shared, even as scientific cookery was reshaping expectations about the American diet. These efforts blurred boundaries between country and city, raising questions about the categories themselves and challenging any sense that rural and urban were rigid constructs. But, to be sure, while shared domestic labor created opportunities to bridge differences, inequalities remained. Using food in political campaigns did not erase disparities of class, ethnicity, religion, race, locality, and other factors. In the case of the Suffrage Cake, while it could inspire urban cooks, for rural ones, it was more likely a recipe to which they aspired. Nevertheless, the Suffrage Cake deradicalized a controversial cause, politicizing in the process any women, rural or urban, willing to purchase a copy.

—41—

Domecon Cake

Lynne Byall Benson
Farmington, Maine, USA, 1930s

This was a popular recipe for a simple chocolate cake that was found in many home economics cooking curricula and cookbooks of this era. It was called "Domecon" Cake, which was short for "domestic economy," to which home economics was sometimes referred.

Domecon Cake[1]

2 oz. grated chocolate
¼ c. fat
½ c. boiling water
1 c. flour
¼ tsp. soda mixed with ¼ c. sour milk
1 egg
1 c. sugar

Mix ingredients in order given. Bake in 2 layer tins in moderate oven. Put together with a chocolate cream filling and cover with white mountain frosting.

[1] Farmington State Normal School and University of Maine at Farmington, "Recipes 1935" (1935). *Home Economics*. 2. https://scholarworks.umf.maine.edu/home_economics/2.

White Mountain Frosting for Domecon Cake (7-Minute Frosting)[2]

Ingredients

1 cup sugar

¼ teaspoon salt

½ teaspoon cream of tartar

2 egg whites

3 tablespoons water

1 teaspoon vanilla

Instructions

Combine all ingredients except vanilla in a stainless steel heavy bottomed saucepan. Place over medium low heat and beat with an electric hand mixer constantly for 5-7 minutes, or until icing is fluffy and stiff peaks form when beaters are removed. Remove from heat and stir in vanilla. Ice cake. It takes two recipes of this to ice a layer cake.

Notes

You'll need two recipes of this icing to ice a layer cake. This recipe doubles beautifully, no need to make two separate batches, just double it and make it all at once.

[2] "Grandmama's Failproof 7 Minute Frosting" https://www.southernplate.com/failproof-7-minute-frosting/ accessed 4/17/20.

—42—

Photographic Essay: Hunger During the Great Depression and World War II

Cynthia C. Prescott

Hunger was widespread in North America during the Great Depression. Farmers on the Great Plains saw their lands devastated by drought and massive dust storms that destroyed crops and carried away topsoil. Farmers in less hard-hit regions struggled to find markets for their crops and shifted away from production for market toward earlier models of self-sufficiency. Meanwhile, growing numbers of urban dwellers struggled to find food. In the United States, a variety of federal New Deal programs provided desperately needed aid to urban and rural populations. The Resettlement Administration (later the Farm Security Administration, or FSA) hired photographers to document their struggles. The most famous of the resulting photographs is Dorothea Lange's portrait of the Migrant Mother (Figure 42.1).

Originally captioned by Lange "Destitute pea pickers in California. Mother of seven children. Age thirty-two. Nipomo, California," it is an iconic image that captured the American imagination. Its greatest power came from the way that it evoked Christian symbolism of the Madonna and child. At the time of its creation, it also echoed popular recent monuments that celebrated white settler women in the form of an iconic Pioneer Mother carrying "civilization" to supposedly savage lands and peoples.[1] In popular memory, Lange's photo came to symbolize the plight of Dust Bowl migrants pushed off of tenant farms by drought and mechanization—a story best known today through the fictional Joad family in John Steinbeck's *The Grapes of Wrath*. A quarter-century after she took that famous photo, Lange recalled:

> I saw and approached the hungry and desperate mother, as if drawn by a magnet. I do not remember how I explained my presence or my camera to her, but I do remember she asked me no questions. I made five exposures, working closer and closer from the same direction. I did not ask her name or her history. She told me her age, that she was thirty-two. She said that they had been living on frozen vegetables from the surrounding fields, and birds

[1] Cynthia Culver Prescott, *Pioneer Mother Monuments: Constructing Cultural Memory* (Norman, OK: University of Oklahoma Press, 2019), chap. 2.

Figure 42.1: Dorothea Lange, photographer, Destitute pea pickers in California. Mother of seven children. Age thirty-two. Nipomo, California. Nipomo, San Luis Obispo County, California, March 1936. https://www.loc.gov/item/2017762891/. Library of Congress, Prints & Photographs Division, Farm Security Administration/Office of War Information Black-and-White Negatives. Public domain.

that the children killed. She had just sold the tires from her car to buy food. There she sat in that lean-to tent with her children huddled around her, and seemed to know that my pictures might help her, and so she helped me. There was a sort of equality about it.[2]

But Lange's memory of her anonymous subject was inaccurate. While Lange, like other FSA photographers, normally took detailed notes to accompany their images, Lange was in a hurry the day that she took this photo. Researchers later uncovered the identity of Lange's "Migrant Mother": Florence Owens Thompson. Photography curator Sarah Hermanson Meister suggests that this image might not have captured the American imagination as powerfully had its viewers known that the Migrant Mother was Cherokee.[3] While Resettlement Administration/ FSA photographers worked hard to document the struggles of Americans of diverse ethnicities, their choices of which scenes to photograph often were dictated by cultural stereotypes. For example, Russell Lee produced a series of images of "Spanish-American" (Hispanic, or Latinx) women plastering an adobe house in New Mexico,[4] and of African-American women doing field labor (Figure 42.2). In contrast, Amish and Mennonite farmers were viewed as being frozen in time and embodying older communitarian values.[5] Moreover, it was images of whites—or individuals that many viewers assumed to be Euro-American—that garnered the most sympathy at the time and in the decades since. The hunger of white farmers and urbanites captured public attention, but many expected Native Americans and African Americans to be poor, and their plight elicited less public attention. Most FSA photographs of African Americans depicted them hoeing or chopping cotton. These presumably were sharecroppers who struggled to produce enough of that cash crop to feed their families.

While many rural families who managed to stay on their farms were able to supplement their diets by expanding their gardens and raising livestock, migrant farm workers and urban residents were more dependent on commercial food production. They had few other options to feed themselves (Figure 42.3). But only wartime demands finally lifted the nation out of the depression. Attention soon turned toward feeding hungry people both home and abroad.

The slogan "Food for Freedom" originated in Great Britain during the early years of World War II. It was adopted by the US in the early 1940s to promote

[2] Dorothea Lange, "Lange's "The Assignment I'll Never Forget: Migrant Mother," *Popular Photography*, Feb. 1960, quoted in Hanna Soltys, "Research Guides: Dorothea Lange's 'Migrant Mother' Photographs in the Farm Security Administration Collection: Introduction," research guide, accessed December 22, 2020, https://guides.loc.gov/migrant-mother/introduction.

[3] Sarah Hermanson Meister and Dorothea Lange, *Dorothea Lange: Migrant Mother* (New York: The Museum of Modern Art, 2019).

[4] See, for example: Russell Lee, "Spanish-American Women Plastering an Adobe House, Chamisal, New Mexico" (image), accessed December 22, 2020, https://www.loc.gov/item/2017742746/.

[5] Stephen D. Reschly and Katherine Jellison, "Shifting Images of Lancaster County Amish in the 1930s and 1940s," *Mennonite Quarterly Review* 82(3): 469-483.

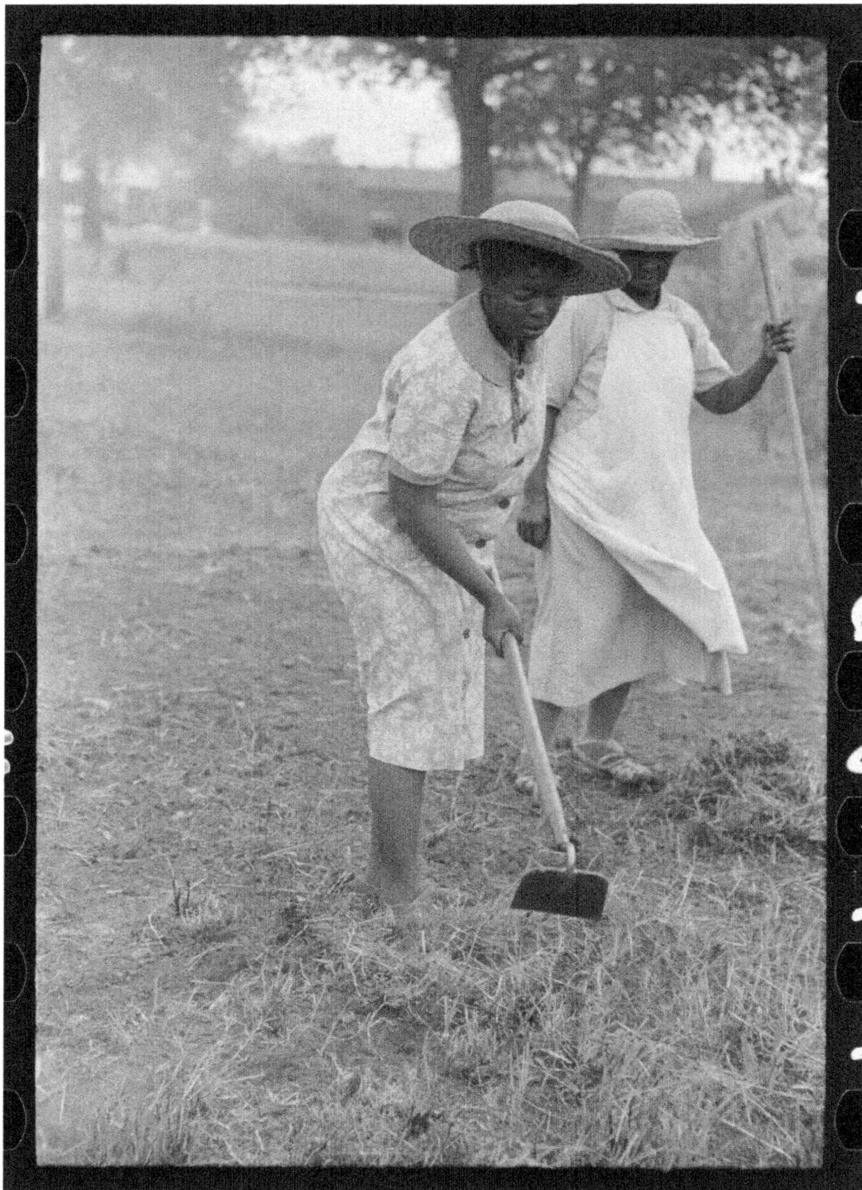

Figure 42.2: Russell Lee, photographer. Negro women hoeing, Picayune, Mississippi. United States Picayune Mississippi Picayune, October 1938. https://www.loc.gov/item/2017738462/. Library of Congress, Prints & Photographs Division, Farm Security Administration/Office of War Information Black-and-White Negatives. Public domain.

Figure 42.3:. Vachon, John, photographer. Foraging for food in the city dump, Dubuque, Iowa. United States Iowa Dubuque. Dubuque, 1940. Apr. Photograph. https://www.loc.gov/item/2017719383/. Library of Congress, Prints & Photographs Division, Farm Security Administration/Office of War Information Black-and-White Negatives. Public domain.

efforts to increase production and conserve scarce resources, to feed both British people and Americans (Figure 4). These efforts escalated after the US entered the war in December 1941.[6] This propaganda campaign echoed one of the "Four Freedoms" that President Franklin D. Roosevelt laid out in his January 1941 state of the union address. In it, he called for an end to US isolationist policies. Instead, he argued that the nation should seek a world founded on four essential freedoms: freedom of speech, freedom of worship, freedom from want, and freedom from fear.[7]

But World War II threatened a return to want that in some ways echoed the hardships of the Great Depression of the 1930s. Restrictions on food imports and the diversion of foodstuffs to troops overseas produced shortages of essential items. Through propaganda films and posters, the US federal government advocated conservation of agricultural lands and increased production both on farms and through household victory gardens. It also rationed food, gasoline, and other scarce resources to ensure equitable distribution among all Americans.

---

[6] "Wartime 4-H Support - World War II," accessed December 20, 2020, https://4-hhistorypreservation.com/History/WW-II_Support/#TOC-08.

[7] "Our Documents - President Franklin Roosevelt's Annual Message (Four Freedoms) to Congress (1941)," accessed December 20, 2020, https://www.ourdocuments.gov/doc.php?-flash=false&doc=70#.

Wartime propaganda sought to encourage farmers to remain on the soil, portraying agricultural labor as essential to the war effort and white male farmers as soldiers of the soil.[8] Note the gender roles encouraged in this Farm Security Administration exhibit image. It casts men as producers, generating vast quantities of eggs, fruit, vegetables, meat, and dairy products. Women, in contrast, are responsible for preserving that agricultural wealth through canning and for tending to the children.

[8] Katherine Jellison, "Get Your Farm in the Fight: Farm Masculinity in World War II," *Agricultural History* 92, no. 1 (2018): 5, https://doi.org/10.3098/ah.2018.092.1.005.

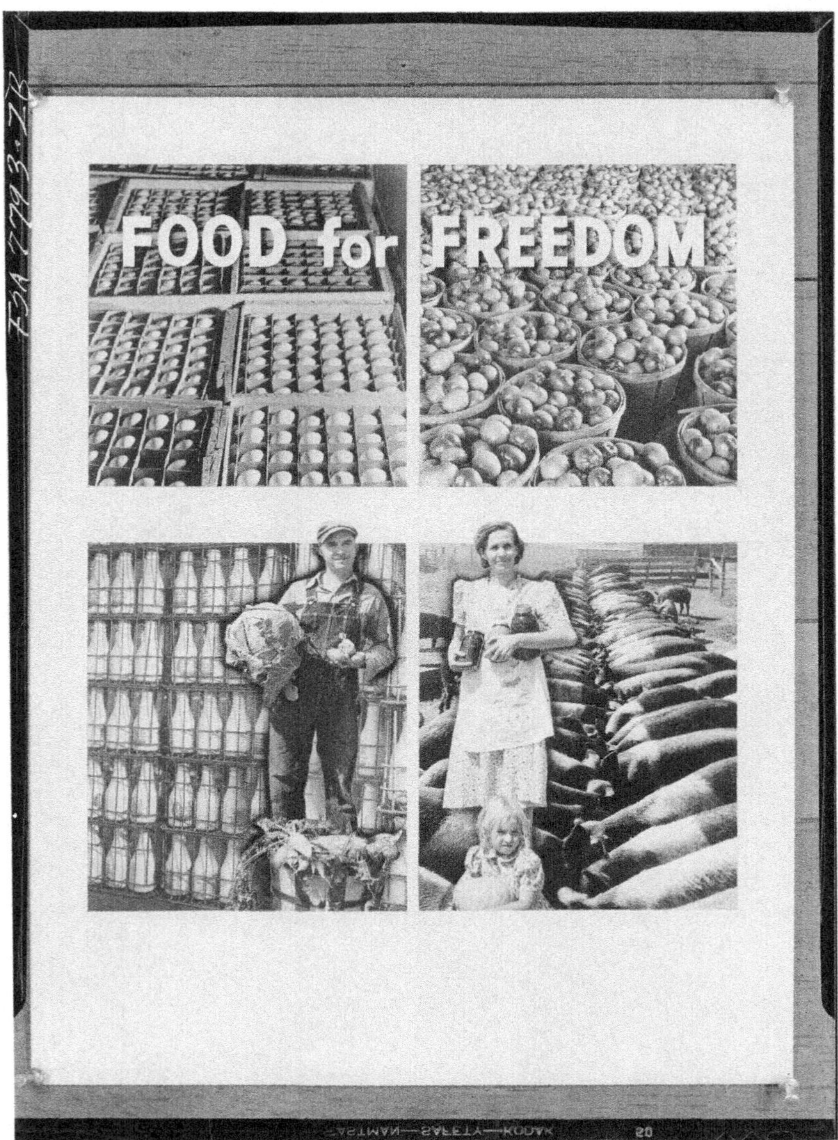

Figure 42.4: Farm Security Administration exhibit Food for Freedom. United States United States, 1941. Photograph. https://www.loc.gov/item/2017762110/. Library of Congress, Prints & Photographs Division, Farm Security Administration/Office of War Information Black-and-White Negatives. Public domain.

—43—

Soup for Dessert? My Mother's "Secret" Cake Recipe

Linda M. Ambrose

Southern Ontario, Canada, 1950s

When my Mom was raising six kids on a busy farm, she never knew who might drop in, but she did know that she would likely be expected to serve them a meal, including dessert, or at least a "treat" with a cup of tea. Yet even farm kitchens sometimes run low on eggs, butter, and milk, and therefore, the options for a classic cake recipe can be very limited. And in my mother's kitchen, even if the refrigerator was in need of restocking, the baking bin quite likely had a few essentials. In situations like that, the recipe my Mom most often turned to did not require the fresh ingredients that typically ran scarce on a seasonal basis. When she needed a fast, easy, flavorful dessert that she could whip up in one bowl, her go-to recipe was usually none other than "Tomato Soup Cake."

Tomato soup and cake sounds like a very unlikely combination. And maybe that's why in our household, it came to be called simply "spice cake," to keep the secret ingredient secret, and to maintain the appeal. Tomato soup surely doesn't sound like an appetizing dessert ingredient, but in fact, this now classic recipe results in a moist and tasty spice cake that only improves after a day or two—that is, if there are any leftovers! The main ingredients (shortening or lard, white sugar, flour, baking soda, cinnamon, cloves, and raisins) were staples in every rural kitchen. And canned tomato soup, the secret ingredient, was something that thrifty rural homemakers learned to stock up on, whenever it went on sale, sometimes as cheaply as three, or even four, cans for a dollar.

With the rise of cheap, shelf-stable canned goods in the postwar years, rural homemakers often relied on the convenience and economy of canned food for their busy lives.[1] My mother Doreen McGuire (1923-2019), who was a homemaker in rural Grey County in Southern Ontario for more than sixty years beginning in 1946, knew a lot about hard work and long days on the farm. Having come of age during the Depression years, she also knew a great deal about thrift and how

[1] For more on how different consumer patterns shaped family foodways, see Diane Tye, *Baking As Biography: A Life Story in Recipes,* (Montreal: McGill-Queen's University Press, 2010).

to "make do."[2] Even on those rare occasions when she had a bit of extra cash from the sale of cream to the local co-operative creamery, it was still a five-mile drive to get to the store in town. Midweek trips to town were usually only emergency runs for a part at the equipment dealer's or the hardware store when a piece of farm equipment broke down. Otherwise, those excursions were reserved for Saturday night grocery shopping at the general store. And because my mother never did get her driver's license, she learned to keep ingredients on hand for little emergencies.

According to the commercial website for Campbell's Soup, the recipe for this unlikely treat was in circulation as early as the 1920s or 30s, but the soup company's official records of the cake only date from October 1940. Then, the infamous soup got its big break when, in 1949 "the cake recipe appeared in the *New York Times*, and in 1960 it became the first recipe to appear on a soup label."[3] As the Campbell's website reveals, the popularity of the recipe continues because "While the recipe may not be listed on the label anymore, Campbell's Kitchen still sees many consumers looking for the recipe for this long-time favorite, with nearly 65,000 views a year to various versions of the recipe on CampbellsKitchen.com."[4]

Many variations of the recipe exist, with or without eggs, more or less water, and combined with a commercial cake mix or not. But the version my mother whipped up from the staples in her kitchen resembled the recipe that was featured on the soup can label, beginning in 1960: no eggs, no milk, no butter, no cake mix, required. The recipe found wide circulation among friends and family members, and it was frequently republished in community cookbooks produced by churches and women's groups. Indeed, the print copy I refer to in my kitchen appeared in one of those ubiquitous community cookbooks and it was offered for inclusion by my Aunt Eileen McGuire, my mother's sister-in-law. Her version simply listed the ingredients and, assuming the baker had some kitchen skill and experience, offered only these instructions: "Dissolve soda in soup. Mix as usual and bake until done." When I first asked my Mom for clarification on what was "usual," she reminded me that I knew what to do when baking a cake: cream the fat and the sugar, then add the wet and dry ingredients alternately and pour the batter into a prepared pan. And she added, "just bake it until it's done." Of course. How simple!

Aunt Eileen's published version is the same one my Mom always made, and the one I served to my kids in the 1990s and now to my grandkids. This tried and true recipe is the plain and simple one from the back of the can, that first circulated sixty years ago. Here's what you need for the cake, according to my Aunt's recipe, baked in an 8" x 8" pan at 350° F:

---

[2] I have written more of my reflections on my rural family's foodways in Linda M. Ambrose and Joan M. Jensen, eds., *Women in Agriculture: Professionalizing Rural Life in North America and Europe, 1880-1965,* (Iowa City: University of Iowa Press, 2017). See especially "Preface," x-xi.

[3] Campbell Soup Company, "A Spicy History of Campbell's Tomato Soup Cake," January 5, 2015. https://www.campbellsoupcompany.com/newsroom/news/2015/01/05/a-spicy-history-of-campbells-tomato-soup-spice-cake/ (Accessed March 2, 2020).

[4] Campbell Soup Company, "A Spicy History of Campbell's Tomato Soup Cake."

Figure 43.1: Tomato Soup Cake, from the author's kitchen.

Tomato Soup Cake

1 c. white sugar
1 ½ c. flour
⅓ c. Crisco or shortening
1 tsp. cinnamon
1 can condensed tomato soup
½ tsp. cloves
1 tsp. baking soda
1 c. raisins

Dissolve soda in soup. Mix as usual and bake until done. [approximately 1 hour]

If you want the cake to be a bit fancier, add a simple butter icing. But it's delicious as it is, served in big generous squares right from the pan!

—44—

3,000 Tons to Lose: Farm Women and Weight Control

Jenny Barker Devine[1]

For four decades, from 1914 until 1954, nutrition education programs provided through the Iowa State Cooperative Extension Service emphasized home-based food production and preservation practices. Nutritional guidelines reflected the physical demands of farm labor. A well-nourished body was a healthy body. Then abruptly, in 1955, home economists like Ora B. Moser in Lyon County, Iowa inaugurated year-long programs to teach farm women "a sound basis of weight control." Moser focused on weight reduction, noting "half of Iowa women are overweight and… Lyon County has her share of overweight women." With 175 Lyon County farm women participating, Moser began with a January weigh-in and estimated her group should aim to lose a combined 1,660 pounds. Over the course of the year the group shed 960 pounds, and Moser celebrated the altered bodies of farm women who had reconsidered their conceptions of health, as well as time-honored practices and foodways. She tied food choices and body weight to larger moral questions when she optimistically reported that the women had become "more weight conscious," and aware of "their responsibility in helping to develop the very best food patterns within their own families."[2]

County-level weight control programs of the mid-1950s are curious because of their sudden appearance and intimate nature. Home economists kept meticulous activity records but usually steered clear of vital health statistics. They focused on agricultural and food products produced: quarts of vegetables canned, kitchens made more efficient, or fireless cookers employed. Historians have long used these records to debate the reciprocal nature of extension programming and, at first glance, the abrupt shift in nutrition education suggests an imposition of urban, gendered beauty ideals on unwitting farm women. Yet tracking weight marks such an unusual departure that it provides a unique opportunity to explore the complex tangle of stakeholders behind extension programming. Federal and state agencies, corporate entities, the medical establishment, land-grant colleges, agribusinesses, and farm families amid economic crisis were all invested in what Iowa farm wom-

[1] The author would like to thank Lauren Hemmerle and Barb Fernandes for their research assistance.

[2] Ora B. Moser, "Lyon County," *Annual Narrative Report* (Ames: Iowa State Cooperative Extension Service, 1955), 10-11. Hereafter cited as *ANR*.

en ate, and how much they weighed, in 1955. In designing the extension programs, researchers at the Iowa Agricultural Experiment Research Station (IAERS) and Iowa State College (ISC) had to balance popular demand for quick results with long-term needs for data collection and careful research. Farm women were not always enthusiastic because, as Sara Egge noted in her essay, for rural women from diverse backgrounds and traditions sharing food went hand-in-hand with forming new bonds related to education and politics. Food fostered common experiences, and extension programs offered opportunities for adult education, as well as comradery and support. The individualized nature of weight control simply did not align with the identity-driven mission of homemakers' clubs.

The seeds of Iowa's extension weight control program were sown in the late 1940s when, with the advent of modern sanitation, vaccines, and antibiotics, heart disease and other chronic illnesses became leading causes of death in the United States. In 1948, Congress established the National Heart Institute (NHI) within the National Institutes of Health (NIH), to support cardiac research, provide training for physicians, guide the construction of diagnostic and treatment facilities, and to oversee the "development of community programs for control of these diseases." The NHI's priority was amassing data and fostering consensus on the exact pathology of heart disease. Physicians understood the mechanics of the heart, but not the environmental or hereditary conditions that led to disease. Research was critical because, according to historian Nicholas Rasmussen, "national authorities routinely monitored their population's births and deaths, but not their illnesses or the characteristics and activities of the people most like to suffer them."[3]

The only longitudinal data showing correlations between body weight and lifespan came from the life insurance industry. In the 1930s, actuarial scientists determined that people who maintained a consistent weight tended to live longer, bolstering assumptions that excess weight caused chronic conditions and early death. Insurance companies used this data to develop tables listing statistically ideal weights for adults over the age of 30, with "overweight" defined as anyone weighing just 10 percent above the ideal, and obesity as anyone weighing 20 percent above. They encouraged policy holders to see correlations as causation, and reinforced such misconceptions by providing physicians with branded weight tables. Public health researchers, cardiologists, and research scientists, on the other hand, understood that statistical correlations among predominantly wealthy, white insurance policy holders barely scratched the surface. They needed data on the actual prevalence of heart disease, diabetes, and other chronic illnesses, as well as methods for measuring the relationships between disease, nutrition, genetics, environment, and physical make-up.[4]

Nationwide research projects required collaboration between federal and state agencies. In partnership with the NIH, the USDA asked state agricultural experiment stations to find out more about what Americans ate and, over the course of six months in 1948, researchers at the IAERS interviewed 1,072 Iowa women

[3] Nicholas Rasmussen, *Fat in the Fifties: America's First Obesity Crisis* (Baltimore: Johns Hopkins University Press, 2019), 1, 56-57.

[4] Rasmussen, *Fat in the Fifties*, 2, 61-62.

about their eating habits. Under the direction of Dr. Pearl Swanson, the assistant director of the IAERS and the head of home economics extension, the project determined caloric intakes and the nutritional values of women's diets over the life course. Those interviewed ranged in age from 30 to over 70 years old, and they lived in urban, rural, and open country, or predominantly agricultural, areas. The majority identified as housewives, most lived on moderate incomes, and most had an eighth-grade education or less. Approximately 43 percent of the women qualified as overweight or obese when evaluated using ideal weight tables. Yet women consumed far fewer calories and less nutritious food than recommended by the National Research Council, leading Swanson to question the utility of ideal weights. She recommended researchers focus on discerning how nutrition affected overall health, as opposed to weight alone.[5]

Broad, federally-funded studies were critical to advancing medical research, but they did little to win over a citizenry seeking straightforward solutions. In the public imagination, the insurance industry had conclusively identified the dangers of obesity and diet was the only known treatment. In 1949, NIH scientist Edward Stieglitz embraced this reality when he declared obesity a leading health issue "ranking with tuberculosis in importance." Public support was critical because researchers hoped that President Harry Truman's proposed universal national health insurance program would generate an avalanche of data from mass health screenings. By 1953, however, congressional support dwindled and medicine remained in private hands. Fiscally conservative policy makers found it cost-effective to posit obesity as a behavioral problem, compelling public health authorities to use weight control programs to gather information. No clinical services, prescriptions, or medical interventions were required, and emphasizing individual behavior removed conversations linking nutrition with environment, class, race, ethnicity, and social justice. Furthermore, the life insurance industry was ready to supply branded informational materials for use in public health initiatives.[6]

In 1953, the state of Iowa launched a multi-faceted effort to address heart disease by establishing diagnostic centers at urban hospitals, supporting research at the University Hospital in Iowa City, training health care professionals, and studying mortality statistics to determine the prevalence of hypertension, arteriosclerosis, and congenital heart disease. The Department of Public Health (DPH) also partnered with the Iowa Tuberculosis and Health Association, the Iowa Heart Association, and the YWCA to conduct mass screenings and host weight-loss courses. The DPH provided printed materials, while local organizations provided qualified leaders: nurses, dieticians, and home economics teachers who obtained the approval of the county medical society. By the end of 1954, the program was limited to just a dozen cities and towns. In Cedar Rapids, for example, the YWCA

---

[5] Pearl Swanson, Elisabeth Willis, Emil Jebe, Janice M. Smith, Margaret A. Ohlson, "Food Intakes of 2,189 Women in Five North Central States," *Research Bulletin* 33, no. 468 (Ames: Iowa Agriculture and Home Economics Experiment Station), 476-499. Available through the Iowa State University Digital Depository, http://lib.dr.iastate.edu/researchbulletin/vol33/iss468/1.

[6] Jonathan Engel, *Fat Nation: A History of Obesity in America* (New York: Rowman and Littlefield, 2018), 2, 56-57; Rasmussen, *Fat in the Fifties*, 46-47, 77, 82, 118-121.

coordinated with a dietician from the hospital to form Calories Anonymous. The "diversified homemakers and working gals," bonded over their shared interest in losing weight and motivated one another with a "penny-a-pound" penalty for gaining weight. Within a few years, the urban programs floundered due to competition from commercial groups promising better results, such as TOPS (Taking Off the Pounds Sensibly), incorporated in Wisconsin in 1952.[7]

Programs for rural Iowans were slower in coming because those charged with their development wanted scientifically-based dietary recommendations that encouraged long-term behavioral change. Throughout the early 1950s, Pearl Swanson prioritized home economics extension programs that helped rural families transition to electrical appliances and the modern marketplace. In her research, however, Swanson built on her 1948 study of women's eating habits with more surveys, and with laboratory research on how rodent and human bodies metabolized various nutrients, proteins, fats, and carbohydrates. At the same time, Dr. Ercel Eppright, chair of the Food and Nutrition department at ISC, conducted research on the diets of Iowa's children. For Swanson and Eppright, it was one thing to know what Iowans ate, but it took time to develop recommendations for how to maximize nutrition. Both Eppright and Swanson wrote scientific publications, made conference presentations, collaborated with USDA scientists, and from time to time spoke at state-level homemakers conventions and issued brief press releases. But in 1954, their work was only in the early stages of reaching the public by way of extension programming.[8]

Local newspapers frequently reprinted syndicated stories about dieting and weight loss, while the farm press published very little. Rural audiences were hungry for more information. The most reputable options came from commodity organizations, which readily stepped in with promises for both weight control options and opportunities to promote agricultural products. The National Dairy Council disparaged the absence of dairy products from reducing diets and began marketing "lite" options such as ice milk, cottage cheese, and skim milk. They also commissioned research at land grant colleges and sponsored well-publicized weight loss contests. In April 1954, the Iowa Ice Cream Manufacturers and Iowa Milk Dealers Association held their annual meeting in Des Moines, where twelve members weighed-in and claimed to have shed a combined 229 pounds over eight to twelve weeks. Their secret was a dairy-rich diet developed by researchers at Michigan State University. That June, in conjunction with National Dairy Month, the Buchannan County Dairy Council sponsored their own contest featuring a

---

[7] Engel, *Fat Nation*, 89; US Public Health Service, Bureau of State Services, *State Heart Disease Control Programs as planned for 1954 and 1955* (May 1954), 19; "Calories Anonymous Picnic," *The Gazette* (4 July 1954).

[8] "New Markets for Milk Output in Iowa Developed" *The Muscatine Journal* (16 June 1949); "The University of Minnesota to Honor Dr. Pearl Swanson," *Ames Daily Tribune* (14 May 1951); "Housewives to Hear Value of Research," *Des Moines Register* (12 February 1950); In May and June 1951, one press release discussing the importance fats and carbohydrates in a well-rounded reducing diet was published in several small-town newspapers, including the *Monroe County News* (14 May 1951), *The Britt News Tribune* (24 May 1951), *The Alton Democrat* (24 May 1951), and the *Postville Herald* (6 June 1951).

diet of "basic foods such as meat, cheese, butter, fish, poultry, ice cream, fruits, and vegetables." The *Iowa Bureau Farmer*, the official publication of the Iowa Farm Bureau Federation, reported on the contest not as a story of farm families pursuing better health, but farmers marketing dairy products. In just four weeks, Mervin Hall, a thirty-five-year-old farmer, lost twenty-eight pounds, won the top prize of a weekend getaway to Chicago, and demonstrated that his products offered an effective means to lose weight.[9]

The promotion worked. The following week, the *Iowa Farm Bureau Spokesman* received numerous letters from Iowans, primarily women, who wanted to know more about both the diet and how to capitalize on this new marketing strategy. Mrs. Willard E. Light of Lisbon, Iowa, was eager to "advertise America's Dairyland." The *Spokesman* editor, Dan Murphy, recommended that readers contact their county home economist for more information. The problem for public health authorities and researchers like Swanson was that commodity-based programs promised quick results, not long-term solutions. They also generated data on production, profit, and consumer habits, not health, which further complicated efforts to understand the correlations between weight and chronic illness.[10]

As the residents of Buchannan County raced to take off pounds, the IAERS prepared the scientifically-grounded weight control curriculum that home economists like Ora B. Moser in Lyon County administered in 1955. Murphy's suggestion that Iowa Farm Bureau members interested in weight loss appeal to county home economists likely assured Swanson that extension programs were in demand, but she wanted to teach good nutrition habits producing results in months not weeks. Furthermore, her insistence that the programs be labeled as weight control, as opposed to weight loss, allowed her to frame the discussion in terms of overall health and include those women who needed to gain or maintain weight. Swanson and Eppright emphasized this goal when they rolled out the extension programs with a national Weight Control Colloquium at ISC from 18-20 January 1955. Just as the women of Lyon County weighed in for the first time, the colloquium brought together a "galaxy of speakers." Established scholars presented on all facets of nutrition, weight control, genetics, sociology, psychology, internal medicine, physiology, and education. The message was clear: extension programming was based on science and endorsed by leading experts.[11]

Purported to be the "first nation-wide meeting of its kind," the colloquium was open to the public and registrants came from thirty-five states. At its conclusion, the proceedings were immediately published in a cohesive volume available to the public at the respectable but accessible price of $2.50. The keynote speaker,

---

[9] Advertisement, *Sioux City Journal* (8 November 1955); *Weight Reduction Through Diet*, National Dairy Council (East Lansing: Michigan State College, 1951), YouTube, https://www.youtube.com/watch?v=9fxji5xkXOA, accessed 18 January 2020; Lillian McLaughlin, "In Dairy Diet Test, Twelve Lose Weight," *Des Moines Tribune* (14 April 1954), 21; Cone Magie, "Iowans Prove You Can Reduce on Diet of Dairy Products," *Iowa Farm Bureau Spokesman* (17 July 1954), 8.

[10] "Letters to the Editor," *Iowa Farm Bureau Spokesman* (31 July 1954), 3.

[11] "Nation-wide Experts to Gather for Weight Control Meeting," *Ames Daily Tribune* (15 January 1955).

Dr. James M. Hundley from the NIH, stated that the goal of the colloquium was to raise public awareness, develop interdisciplinary connections, and initiate collaborative public health studies. He said, "The unfortunate cosmetic and physical effects of obesity are matters of common knowledge through personal observation. Undesirable as mere fatness may be, one could scarcely justify a public health program on these considerations. The case against obesity rests on much more serious grounds." He dismissed the efficacy of the insurance tables and went on to frame obesity as a social justice issue, noting higher rates of obesity and chronic illness among African Americans. Newspapers across Iowa reported on the event with great excitement, summarizing presentations and providing running commentary. The *Des Moines Register* captured Swanson and Eppright's message perfectly when it hailed the colloquium as a "benchmark" for changing public attitudes toward weight control. The author editorialized that "the latest scientific findings upset many of the earlier ones (as well as stacks and stacks of popular 'common sense' notions on the subject). More than that, they reveal how much is still to be learned before there is a really solid body of proved facts on all phases of the question."[12]

Presenters at the colloquium agreed on three general assertions: that body weight, as it related to general health, was a critical public health issue; that research into effective weight control was still in its early phases; and there were still more questions than answers as they moved beyond ubiquitous actuarial data. In their presentation titled "Food Intake and Body Weight of Older Women," Swanson and her research team reiterated the colloquium themes as they implicitly laid out a full justification for extension weight control programs. First, they used insurance tables and the 1948 study as the basis for state-wide estimates, speculating that "Iowa women over the age of 30 were carrying around 3,000 tons of body weight that possibly they might be better off without." Open country women carried most of that weight; 53 percent of those in open country areas were moderately or excessively overweight, compared to 36 percent in rural communities and 41 percent in urban areas. Still, body weight was not a behavioral or moral issue for the authors. Women needed education, not will power, to change their eating habits.[13]

Swanson and her collaborators surmised that the prevalence of excess weight could be attributed to labor saving technologies, sedentary lifestyles, or inappropriate applications of weight tables. They urged the audience to consider how age, height, body build, and body composition complicated what constituted a "normal weight," for adult women. Emphasizing numbers on a scale overshadowed the more critical need for women to maintain a nutritious diet. Swanson and her

---

[12] "Don't Let People Fool You – Exercise Does Help You Reduce," *Ames Daily Tribune* (21 January 1955); "Finding Out More About Overweight," *Des Moines Register* (20 January 1955); James M. Hundley, MD, Laboratory of Biochemistry and Nutrition, National Institute of Health, "Need for Weight Control Programs," in *Weight Control: A Collection of Papers Presented at the Weight Control Colloquium*, Ercel S. Eppright, Pearl Swanson, and Carrold A. Iverson, eds. (Ames, Iowa: The Iowa State College Press, 1955), 9. Hereafter cited as *Weight Control.*

[13] Pearl Swanson, Harriet Roberts, Elisabeth Willis, Isabel Pesek, and Pauline Mairs, "Food Intake and Body Weight of Older Women," in *Weight Control*, 81-82.

collaborators hesitated to directly link body weight to chronic illness, but they found strong correlations between body weight and the likelihood that women self-reported physical discomforts such as disordered circulation and digestion, bone and joint pain, fatigue, and headaches. Nevertheless, a diet with a simple reduction in calories, that did not take energy values and nutrition into account, did not resolve these discomforts.[14]

They justified the need for education by sharing accounts of women undertaking diets based on popular advice. One woman reported she cut out all dairy products to reduce dietary fat, but continued eating excessive amounts of doughnuts and candy. Other women subsisted on breadstuffs and coffee. Even medically supervised diets lacked basic nutrients, leaving women lethargic and hungry. The researchers found that Iowa women wanted detailed meal plans that did not drastically alter their traditional foodways, with measured portions and foods that the whole family could eat. The researchers expressed confidence that the IAERS could meet this demand. Their plans laid out well-balanced menus that minimized but did not eliminate non-nutritive starches, fried foods, and desserts. They concluded, "People obviously need constructive and personal help in reduction programs … With some help and direction, however, failure may turn into success."[15]

Swanson's message was well-received by the scientific community and in June 1955 she won the prestigious Borden Award from the American Institute of Nutrition for her research. It would seem that with her leadership, the Iowa extension service, with well-established hierarchies and home demonstration clubs, provided an ideal mechanism for delivery and data collection. The USDA agreed. In February 1955, nutritionist Evelyn Blanchard of the Federal Extension Service issued a memo recommending how information from the colloquium should be presented as extension programming. County home economists could help women lose weight if the women "want to," but they should "not expect too much," and they should make nutrition education their goal, not actual weight loss. Home economists should readily admit that knowledge about weight control was still limited and, most importantly, programs should "do no harm. Overweight should not be made a moral issue. It is not a sin to be fat."[16]

Blanchard followed the lead of Dr. Ruth Leverton, dean of Home Economics at Oklahoma A&M, who gave a presentation at the colloquium on the dangers of "weight control propaganda." Leverton stated programs should "adopt the positive approach and emphasize good food habits." Iowa extension personnel put this into practice when, rather than attempt to discredit the dairy diet, they collaborated

[14] Swanson et al, "Food Intake and Body Weight in Older Women," 85-86.

[15] Swanson et al, "Food Intake and Body Weight in Older Women," 94-95.

[16] Evelyn Blanchard, "Let's Talk Extension Nutrition: Impressions from Weight Control Colloquium As They Have Bearing on the Extension Program," (Washington, D.C.: USDA, 18 February 1955), 3.

with the Buchannan County Dairy Council for its second annual four-week reducing contest in 1955. The county extension service joined as a co-sponsor and agents offered their services.[17]

Extension programs provided further opportunities to study the power of group weight control activities, a relatively new concept. In his colloquium presentation, William D. Simmons from the Berkley Department of Public Health defined weight loss support groups as an "undefined procedure." It was not psychotherapy, but it went beyond nutrition education by bringing together individuals interested in reducing their weight. He then called for further research into group "preventative programs" to change broader community attitudes about food and nutrition. Women participating in home demonstration clubs provided a receptive audience, having heard lessons on nutrition for decades. And because they were not entirely devoted to weight control, clubs presented an opportunity to determine whether education served as a preventative measure.[18]

In practice, no matter the good intentions of state and national leaders, several factors complicated message delivery and data collection in Iowa. First, homemakers clubs received distilled versions of the research from the IAERS through a training school system, initially developed in the 1910s. Most women who joined extension homemakers clubs did so at the township level, where monthly programs were administered by members who attended county-level training schools. County home economists provided instructions and materials at the training schools, and then once or twice a year dropped in on each club to conduct a unique lesson and assess the women's activities. Overall, training schools proved effective, but because of its departure from standard extension programming, and its basis in personal, medicalized information, some messaging was lost in translation as it filtered through to the township levels.[19]

Those filters varied with the leadership and the level of interest in a county. County home economists, in collaboration with advisory committees made up of local club women, enjoyed autonomy in selecting annual programs. In some counties, weight control programs were highly developed and enlisted the help of medical professionals. Hancock County kicked off a year-long weight control program with a January training school for township leaders featuring talks by a public health nurse and four local physicians, including "The Boobytraps of Weight Control," by Dr. Buckover. In contrast, the home economist in Iowa County, Alverda James, simply gave the same presentation to several township clubs on weight control throughout January and February, with a demonstration on how to prepare a low-calorie hamburger casserole. This is not to imply that James was an

[17] Ruth Leverton, "Weight Control Propaganda," in *Weight Control*, 166-169; "62 Enter Diet Contest; Scales Get a Workout," *The Bulletin-Journal* (Independence, Iowa), 27 May 1955.

[18] William D. Simmons, "Group Methods on Weight Reduction," in *Weight Control*, 219-230.

[19] Jenny Barker-Devine, "Quite a Ripple But No Revolution": The Changing Roles of Women in the Iowa Farm Bureau Federation," *Annals of Iowa* 64, no.1 (Winter 2005), 1-36.

ineffective agent. She led a delegation of 4-H members to a state conference and ran a robust home economics program focused on home improvements and state politics. She simply did not prioritize weight control.[20]

Members of home demonstration clubs did not embrace weight control programs because the issue was private and peripheral to their shared identity as farm women. Homemakers clubs emphasized comradery, but weigh-ins could be embarrassing and divisive. In Lyon County, Moser's report reveals an empathetic but judgmental assessment of those women unable to shed pounds. She was careful to echo Swanson's directives when she emphasized how women changed their eating habits and those of their families, but following succinct comments about women who gained and maintained weight she composed a full paragraph describing four overweight women, "the most sensitive" of the group, who needed to "strive harder for normal weight." She hoped that peer pressure would eventually compel them to change their behavior.[21]

Comments about physical appearance may have been especially difficult for farm women to process. Weight control programs were imbued with sexism, as they assumed women's total responsibility for food preparation and family health. Furthermore, Blanchard urged extension leaders to "do no harm," but the entire concept was premised in shame. Historian Colin R. Johnson observed that by the early twentieth century, the "hard women" of rural America struggled to meet consumer-based feminine ideals for beauty, fashion, and behavior. Their bodies were both shaped by and clothed in the demands of physical labor. Calloused hands, sun-hardened skin, and muddy boots were at odds with the fragile, diminutive bodies esteemed in popular culture. Johnson concluded, "to be a rural woman in the United States was to be a woman steeped in shame—shame about one's body, shame about one's clothing, shame about one's myriad failings as a wife and mother, shame about pretty much everything."[22]

Swanson justified extension programming by citing her 1948 study showing how open country women tended to be heavier than their urban counterparts, but her publications never grappled with the unique situations of farm women's food environments and nutritional needs. As urban women increasingly enjoyed supermarkets that afforded access to broad food choices, farm women still oversaw food production and preservation at home. What they could not grow, such as flour and sugar, they bought in bulk. They tended to eat seasonally, with food choices affected by meteorological events, disease, pests, and the homemaker's ability to effectively preserve food. And for urban women, Swanson mentioned sedentary lifestyles as a cause for weight gain, but she never posed the question of how manual labor and physical strength shaped farm women's bodies. Such data was beyond her purview. When Dr. Jean Mayer, from the Harvard School of

[20] *The Britt-News Tribune* (5 January 1955); Elsie Van Wert, "Hancock County Hash," *The Britt-News Tribune* (25 January 1955); *Williamsburg Journal-Tribune* (13, 10, and 27 January 1955, and 10 February 1955).

[21] Moser, "Lyon County," *ANR*, 1955.

[22] Colin R. Johnson, *Just Queer Folks: Gender and Sexuality in Rural America* (Philadelphia: Temple University Press, 2013), 177.

Public Health, presented on "The Role of Exercise in Weight Control" at the 1955 colloquium, he summarized contemporary understandings of physical activity when he said there were only "uncertain" correlations between physical activity and body weight. In fact, most physicians recommended that those seeking to lose weight avoid exercise because strenuous physical activity could exacerbate heart conditions. Researchers understood the high caloric needs of laborers, soldiers, and athletes, but they did not have enough data to develop exercise programs for weight loss.[23]

In subsequent years, county home economists reported minimal interest in weight control. In 1959, Granda B. Holleywell, the Lee County home economist, conducted a training school for seventeen township leaders about low-calorie refreshments. After presenting the training school lesson to 145 women across the county, township leaders' evaluations revealed that artificial sweeteners were expensive, impractical, and only for people "on very strict diets." Club members appreciated having the information, however, and enjoyed learning about how to meet nutritional needs while reducing calories. Few women expressed interest in follow-up meetings on weight control because "people could diet at home."[24]

This is not to say that farm women were not interested in health, heart disease, diabetes, and nutrition. They simply did not conflate weight control with these larger issues. In 1955, Greta W. Bowers, the Marshall County home economist, noted that even though "very little is done during the women's meetings about health," women's clubs raised funds for research in polio, cancer, and heart disease, while increasing numbers of women in the county sought health insurance and regular medical exams. They were also eager to learn about freezing garden produce and Bowers concluded that frozen foods permitted a wider use of healthy fruits and vegetables. That same year, the Iowa Farm Bureau Federation Women's Committee initiated collaborations with the Rural Health Committee of the State Medical Society to secure doctors for rural areas, encourage farm families to receive vaccines, and to develop health education programs. But their activities had limits. In 1961, Alice Walters, the Greene County home economist, reported that except for one township club, weight control "didn't really get off the ground too well." Nevertheless, township clubs coordinated a mass testing program for diabetes. Walters was both proud of the effort required to test nearly 900 Greene County residents and frustrated by the fact that "there is no accurate method of evaluating accomplishments as we cannot ask [people] to report back the results of further examinations with their own doctor."[25]

Finally, weight control programs floundered because in 1955, agriculture was in crisis. Commodity prices crashed as a result of overproduction and withdrawn

---

[23] Jean Mayer, PhD, D.Sc., "The Role of Exercise in Weight Control," in *Weight Control*, 199-210.

[24] Greta Bowers, "Marshall County," *ANR* (1955), 16-17; Granda B. Holleywell, "Lee County," *ANR* (1959), 11-12.

[25] Christine Inman, "Medical Society Interested in Farmers' Problems," *Iowa Bureau Farmer* (27 August 1955), 14; Mrs. H.L. Witmer, "Rural Health Meeting Step Toward Solutions," *Iowa Bureau Farmer* (23 March 1957) 28; Alice Walters, "Greene County," *ANR* (1961), 7-8.

federal price supports. Many women directed their energies toward sustaining their family operations. Bowers reported that in Marshall County, women were interested in learning how to keep the farm accounts, finding work outside the home for supplemental income, or performing farm labor to save on the cost of hired help. With so many families struggling financially, weight control and adapting one's diet was seen as a luxury. On the other hand, a few enterprising farm women joined commodity organizations, such as the Iowa State Dairy Association and the Iowa Swine Producers Association, to promote their products and stimulate consumer demand. They may have used lessons on weight control to hone their messaging to urban consumers. By the late 1950s and early 1960s, women began holding promotional events with retailers. In January 1956, for example, exactly one year after the extension service rolled out weight control program, the *Farm Journal & Country Gentleman* reported that farmers across the state of Iowa addressed low prices with promotional events, making "a bigger dent in the surplus than Government buying." While some county farm bureaus and commodity groups hosted "pork lifts," or giveaways, others like Linn County planned a series of events under the guise of Pork Promotion Week. In late January, the women of Linn County set up displays in grocery stores and spoke with shoppers about the nutritive benefits, lean qualities, and low cost of pork.[26]

Like the Dairy Association, the Iowa Swine Producers Association was eager to tap into consumer demands for weight loss products. They promoted pork as a high-protein, nutrient-dense food and invested in research on the development of lean meat. Articles on how to lose weight were rare in the farm press, but articles on how to advise consumers about nutrition became increasingly common. In October 1956, the *Iowa Farm Bureau Spokesman* reported on growing consumer demand for high protein diets that included meat, dairy, and eggs. Those promoting commodities should "reassure people it is perfectly safe to eat all the protein they want and enjoy… stress that protein is non-fattening." The following year, in September 1957, the women's pages of the *Iowa Farm Bureau Spokesman* covered a meeting of the National Livestock and Meat Board, with a detailed table levels of fat, protein, and calories in lamb, beef, and pork. And in March 1960, an article in the *Farm Journal* touted the importance of the "hog's new silhouette," when it noted that consumers were willing to pay premium prices for lean cuts. "Tell your city friends how much better pork is now," the author concluded. Given the similarities in tone, it stands to reason that Extension weight control programs played a role in the ways that farm women talked to consumers. Like the extension programs, the farm press encouraged farmers to ground conversations in scientific research.[27]

As Pamela Riney-Kehrberg mentions in her essay (Riney-Kehrberg, Ch. 45, this volume), the history of food teaches us about the broader interactions of gen-

[26] Greta Bowers, "Marshall County," *ANR* (1955), 16-17; "Farmers 'Lift' Tons of Pork," *Farm Journal & Country Gentleman* (January 1956), 24; "Promote Pork Week Planned, January 26-February 24," *The Gazette* (Cedar Rapids, Iowa) (4 January 1956).

[27] J.L. Anderson, "Lard to Lean: Making the Meat-Type Hog in Post-World War II America," in Warren Belasco and Roger Horowitz, eds., *Food Chains: From Farmyard to Shopping Cart* (Philadelphia: University of Pennsylvania Press, 2009), 29-46; "Low-Protein Diets Are Still Appearing," *Iowa Farm Bureau Spokesman* (17 October 1956), 4; "New

der, race, culture, and class in the United States. The story of extension and weight control provides insight into the many forces that shaped the development, dissemination, and reception of home economics programs, as well as the debates that shaped Americans' contemporary understandings of nutrition, the body, and health as individual, rather than collective concerns. In the mid-1950s, Iowa's open country was in the midst of unsettling change. New technologies, depopulation, and other social, political, and economic realignments, altered women's roles and transformed how people ate. Younger women were less likely to grow gardens or preserve produce. If they preserved homegrown foods, they favored labor-saving freezing methods. They were less likely to bake, and more likely to use packaged foods and eat at restaurants. Women wanted more information about overall health, but did not see weight control as central to improving conditions for their family. Finally, Iowa's farm women thought more critically about broader food systems, working with commodity organizations to identify new markets for overproduced goods. They demanded for better healthcare while public health researchers scrambled to pursue research hampered by decentralized healthcare systems.[28]

It was within this context that the extension service introduced weight control programs that struggled to take root and then slowly faded by folding back into more generalized nutrition lessons. Swanson and researchers at the IAERS were committed to nutrition education, not imposing ideal weights on farm women. Their willingness to pull back the programs rolled out in 1955 demonstrates both their hesitation in conflating nutrition programs with weight control, as well as the power that women's clubs held when deciding on annual programming. It also matches the trajectory of national trends tracked by historian Nicholas Rasmussen, who found that public discussions of a "deadly obesity epidemic" receded by the mid-1960s. By then, researchers no longer relied on ideal weights tabulated by insurance companies, and they understood better the myriad genetic, environmental, behavioral, and physiological factors leading to heart disease, diabetes, and chronic illness. The development of medications for hypertension, high cholesterol, and other risk factors changed conversations between physicians and patients, while Swanson's insistence on a balanced diet had become standard advice with new caveats about sodium intake and balancing specific types of fats. In the end, Iowa's scientifically grounded weight control programs provided farm women with good information, but did not succeed in yielding much data or long-term transformations of women's diets and bodies.[29]

Studies Show Meat Has More Protein But Less Far and Calories," *Iowa Farm Bureau Spokesman* (28 September 1957)16; John A. Rohlf, "The Hog's New Silhouette," *Farm Journal* (March 1960), 135.

[28] "When You Eat Away From Home," *Wallace's Farmer* (1 January 1955), 30; "How Much Do You Bake?" *Wallace's Farmer* (15 October 1955), 30; "It's Good to Eat Away from Home," *Wallace's Farmer* (18 April 1959), 56; "What's Happened to the Farm Garden," *Wallace's Farmer* (8 October 1966), 41.

[29] Rasmussen, *Fat in the Fifties*, 3, 118-121.

—45—

Teaching Food History

Pamela Riney-Kehrberg

My food history course, America Eats, grew out of a conundrum. I enjoy my agricultural and rural history offerings, and think they have enormous value for students, but selling those courses to undergraduates was becoming increasingly difficult. Given students' resistance to taking classes that seemed too serious, too dull, and too detached from their lives, I needed to find a way to make what I wanted to teach more appealing. I also needed to find a way to draw non-history majors into the history program with an accessible, mid-level class that might in some way pique their curiosity. Food history seemed like the logical answer. What could be more relevant than food? We all must eat, and we are all deeply attached to the foods that we love. Food is at the very center of our beings.

Out of this realization came America Eats (a course name borrowed from Joe Anderson, at Mt. Royal University in Calgary). What I have found over a number of semesters is that food brings students in, and keeps them interested. This course is a mixture of many different approaches to food. Students learn about basic agricultural history. They also learn about the connections between food and gender, family, immigration, policy, economic, diplomatic, and military history. There is no aspect of American history that is excluded from discussion. It is a course that makes use of a wide variety of primary sources, from WPA interviews with individuals who had been enslaved, to cookbooks, to farmer memoirs. Students also have the opportunity to experiment with historical aspects of cooking, as they attempt to make a Great Depression meal, using three potatoes, two carrots, and an onion. We end the semester by considering the question of who raises our food, and whether or not it matters if that food is grown on a small farm or a large one, by family farmers or a corporation. Although I teach the course broadly, the topic allows the instructor to teach as broadly, or as narrowly, as they choose.

Topics

There are numerous approaches to this kind of a course, but mine is tailored to the needs of an audience that is made up of non-majors who may have taken their last survey of U.S. history in high school. On the first day of instruction, the class completes an exercise (suggested by Minoa Uffelman at Austin Peay University) that helps them to examine their preconceived notions about food and the labor involved in its preparation.[1] I ask them to tell me how, had they lived 200 years ago, they would have gone about making a bowl of mashed potatoes. These are students who can, of course, go to the store and purchase mashed potatoes ready-made, with a side of gravy. They don't even have to pop a container in the microwave if they go to the grocery store deli. Figuring out the whole process involves a good deal of discussion. We proceed from the planting of potatoes, through the long and arduous process of growing and harvesting, only to realize that there are many other ingredients and processes required that are equally tedious and involved. Most, for instance, want butter for their potatoes, which requires an additional discussion of the making of that ingredient. From that beginning, students are prepared to think about food in new and more complex ways than students may have previously.

I take a chronological approach, moving from Native American peoples in various locations throughout the North American continent to (more or less) the present day. I want to give the students a number of different topics to chew on, so we talk about growing food, preparing food, distributing food, and regulating food. Each historical era has its own tales to tell. In the colonial era, we discuss differences between Native American and European foodways. Early American history lends itself to a discussion of massive changes in the technology of agriculture, as well as the technology of food preparation. The Civil War is dense with food history, involving opportunities to talk about the diets of both soldiers and civilians, north and south. We spend a fair amount of time on the life-and-death logistics of feeding people in wartime. There is far more technology to discuss in the post-war period, with an emphasis, too, on a new governmental interest in growing food, with the creation of the United States Department of Agriculture. The Progressive Era finds the class exploring more governmental approaches to food reform, changes in American kitchens, and a growing interest in home economics. The World Wars changed attitudes toward food and government involvement in food and nutrition, here and abroad, while the Great Depression taught many sad lessons about hunger throughout the U.S. The period since World War II has been filled with discussions about the relationship of food to diplomacy, the proper federal role in food and nutrition policy, and numerous arguments about what kind of food really is best for the American public. We savor the irony that while fewer and fewer Americans are serious cooks, the kitchens they want in their homes are increasingly elaborate and expensive. These are kitchens that my students' great great grandmothers would have appreciated, with their big families and constant cooking, but that they could only dream of, given the size of most homes, the relative poverty of many families, and the limited technology of the day. The COVID-19 pandemic of 2020 will provide new opportunities to discuss American foodways, in a time when restaurants were closed to sit-down customers, and people, many of whom had limited cooking skills, had to figure out how to feed their families. The pandemic also put strains on food distribution, as panic buying set in throughout the country.

---

[1] Minoa Uffelman, "Teaching Rural History in an Urban Age," in Pamela Riney-Kehrberg, ed., *Routledge History of Rural America* (New York: Routledge, 2016), 368.

This is only one way to organize a food history course. Others organize their classes according to topic, treating growing, distributing, and preparing food, as well as food policy, as separate units. It is also possible to take a commodities approach, focusing in on the various food products about which historians now have a considerable body of literature – for example, pumpkins, tomatoes, soy, dairy, and swine. My approach is tailored to students who may have a minimal background in U.S. history, and therefore need a chronological structure as scaffolding. No matter how the course is taught, however, it provides a useful framework to discuss the interactions of gender, race, culture, and class in the United States. This course also takes into account numerous approaches to American history: agricultural, technological, political, military, diplomatic, economic, gender, cultural, and social.

Readings

Course readings combine a wide variety of materials, both primary and secondary. Currently, I assign four books, plus a number of shorter articles and primary sources. The books are William Cronon, *Changes in the Land: Indians, Colonists, and the Ecology of New England*, Laura Ingalls Wilder, *Farmer Boy*, Rebecca Sharpless, *Cooking in Other Women's Kitchens: Domestic Workers in the South, 1865-1960*, and David Masumoto, *Epitaph for a Peach*.[2] Cronon helps students to understand the differences between the ways Native Americans and English settlers approached both the land and food. Wilder's narrative provides minute descriptions of many different tasks related to mid-nineteenth century food acquisition and preparation, and is a testament to the joy of food, written by someone who grew up hungry. With *Cooking in Other Women's Kitchens*, Sharpless introduces my Midwestern students to something they probably have never thought of before, which was the presence of servants cooking in family homes, and the racism African American cooks experienced as part of their work. Finally, Masumoto, from the point of view of a farmer, teaches students about the calculations involved in bringing a peach to the American table.

I assign some shorter primary sources, as well, for weekly discussion. These include a selection of WPA interviews of formerly enslaved individuals (Riney-Kehrberg and Prescott, Ch. 46, this volume). The narratives on the Library of Congress American Memory site are searchable by topic, making it easy to track down those with information about foodways. I also use government propaganda posters from World War I and World War II, and settler accounts, such as selections from Rebecca Burlend's autobiographical guide to frontier Illinois, *A True Picture of Emigration*. Guidebooks for people going to the gold fields would work equally well. I have found a number of articles to be useful, all available through JSTOR, such as Richard Steckel, "A Peculiar Population: The Nutrition, Health,

[2] William Cronon, *Changes in the Land: Indians, Colonists, and the Ecology of New England* (New York: Hill and Wang, 2003); Laura Ingalls Wilder, *Farmer Boy* (New York: HarperCollins, 2008); Rebecca Sharpless, *Cooking in Other Women's Kitchens: Domestic Workers in the South, 1865-1960* (Chapel Hill: University of North Carolina Press, 2010); David Masumoto, *Epitaph for a Peach: Four Seasons on My Family Farm* (New York: HarperOne, 1996).

and Mortality of American Slaves from Childhood to Maturity," Knut Oyangen, "The Gastrodynamics of Displacement: Place-Making and Gustatory Identity in the Immigrants' Midwest," Greta de Jong, "Staying in Place: Black Migration, the Civil Rights Movement, and the War on Poverty in the Rural South," and Scarlett Lindeman, "Trash Eaters."[3] These smaller pieces help the class to focus on a particular issue of interest without requiring as much sustained energy.

The readings provide students with exposure to a wide variety of historical methods and approaches, and can be adjusted to the educational programs of students in the course. A class heavy on history majors might have a different mix of materials than a course heavy on students studying dietetics, elementary education, or agriculture. One semester, I assigned Michael J. Eula, "Failure of American Food Reformers Among Italian Immigrants in New York City, 1891-1897," which intrigued my dietetics students.[4] They had never considered the way in which culture worked against those who were attempting to change the dietary habits of new arrivals from Italy in the late 19th century. Convincing these immigrants to "reform" their diets meant asking them to abandon key elements of their ethnic identity, and food reformers ran into a wall of resistance. Hopefully, as those dieticians move forward in their careers, this bit of historical information will stick with them, and help them to more carefully examine the needs of clients from diverse racial and ethnic backgrounds.

Writing Assignments

I have used a number of different writing assignments with this class, and there are many other possibilities that may be used in the future. My current assignment involves students cooking, and then reflecting on the experience and its historical implications. Students are required to make a Great Depression dinner for five people, using three potatoes, two carrots, and an onion. If they are so inclined, they can also use up to five slices of bacon. These are easy-to-find, inexpensive items that would have been common fare for many in the 1930s. If they wish, they may also use $1.00 (the equivalent of .05 in 1933) to purchase additional items for their meal, but those foods must be period-appropriate. For instance, students cannot purchase a cheap pizza, and call it dinner, since frozen pizza had not been invented. They are also forbidden from purchasing Kraft Macaroni and Cheese, since it was quite expensive in the 1930s, and was marketed as a luxury item. They

[3] Richard Steckel, "A Peculiar Population: The Nutrition, Health, and Mortality of American Slaves from Childhood to Maturity," *Journal of Economic History* 46, 3 (September 1986): 721-741; Knut Oyangen, "The Gastrodynamics of Displacement: Place-Making and Gustatory Identity in the Immigrants' Midwest," *Journal of Interdisciplinary History* XXXIX, 3 (Winter 2009): 323-348; Greta de Jong, "Staying in Place: Black Migration, the Civil Rights Movement, and the War on Poverty in the Rural South," *The Journal of African American History* 90, 4 (Autumn 2005): 387-409; Scarlett Lindeman, "Trash Eaters." *Gastronomica: The Journal of Food and Culture,* 12, 1 (Spring 2012): 75-82.

[4] Michael J. Eula, "Failure of American Food Reformers Among Italian Immigrants in New York City, 1891-1897," *Italian Americana* 18, 1 (Winter 2000): 86-99.

can purchase a can of milk, some pasta, canned or fresh vegetables, or ingredients for meal-stretchers such as biscuits (pro-rating more expensive items such as a sack of flour to fit the size of the servings).

Once they have made and eaten their meal, they write about the experience. Their three to four-page reflection needs to address the following issues: How much did their ingredients cost? What did they cook with the ingredients? Did they purchase any additional items? What? Did they get any help from a parent, grandparent, or other experienced cook? (This was both allowable and suggested, since getting by in hard times often required people to ask for help.) How many people did their meal feed? How far could they stretch their ingredients if they needed to feed large numbers of people with very limited funds? I provide a USDA pamphlet about nutrition on a budget: did the government's advice go far enough in addressing the concerns of very poor people, who relied on a diet of foods such as potatoes, carrots and onions? If this was what a family ate on a regular basis during the depression, what did this tell the writer about what daily life was like for the poor?[5]

The assignment works well, in the sense that it pushes students to develop historical imagination, and to walk for just a little while in the shoes of families who lived in severely constrained circumstances. The students seem to enjoy the assignment, and many of them share the experience with their parents while home on holiday or over a weekend. Many also use the assignment to talk for the first time with parents and grandparents about cooking and diets in the past. The prospect of making something edible from these ingredients can be intimidating for students with little cooking experience, but I strongly encourage them to work with a friend or family member who can help them with the assignment, and they often come away from the project with new skills and a new appreciation of what it takes to feed a family. Their culinary decision making often surprises me. I had not realized until assigning this project how few students are acquainted with home made soup, the choice I would automatically make when confronted with this particular array of ingredients. They seem more inclined to variations on mashes and hashes.[6]

There are a couple of other assignments I have also used. One involves students writing a three-generation family history of food and eating. Students must interview a parent and a grandparent, preferably but not necessarily, from the same side of the family about food habits over time. They have to think about how their family acquired food (grown or purchased), in what forms it came (fresh, frozen, pre-prepared), who cooked the food, and how it was eaten (together, at the table, or in front of the t.v., perhaps). They also need to think about how often they consumed meals outside the family home. The assignment requires students to link these changes over time to broader changes in American life, such as the

[5] Rowena Schmidt Carpenter and Hazel K. Stiebeling, *Diets to Fit the Family Income*, U.S. Department of Agriculture, Farmer's Bulletin No. 1757 (Washington, D.C.: U.S. Government Printing Office, 1936).

[6] For a full description of the project and its results, see Pamela Riney-Kehrberg, "Building Historical Imagination with Three Potatoes, a Carrot and an Onion," *Teaching History*, 35, 1 (Spring 2010): 12-22.

transition from farm to town, larger numbers of women going out to work, and changes in the proportion of the family income devoted to the purchase of food. Another food assignment involves role playing. Students are required to imagine themselves the parent of a family of five in March of 1933. They are on relief (welfare), and have $2.50 to purchase food for a week. They must use the ads in a historical newspaper collection to devise a grocery list, and period appropriate cookbooks to come up with a menu. I give them a set of hints, for example, "Feel free to use family resources and family recipes—you might want to talk to your grandmother, great aunt, or mother! Keep in mind, poor people would have eaten very little meat, and a whole lot of vegetables, such as potatoes, carrots, cabbage, and onions." Like the students cooking with three potatoes, two carrots, and an onion, they must write a three or four page reflection on their experience.[7] I allow students to complete this project in pairs, if they prefer, and have had students experience difficult moments of reckoning with partners, as they discovered the complexities of working within a budget.

There are many other intriguing possibilities. I have considered offering students an array of historical cookbooks, and asking them to analyze one as a primary source. Given the number of cookbooks available in my university's collection (Iowa State is a land-grant school with an old and venerable program in home economics and food science), this would be logistically relatively easy. Students could also be asked to analyze food advertising, historical kitchens, and government advice about food and nutrition (Children's Bureau and USDA pamphlets would be a great resource), and wartime food propaganda. Perhaps they could write the history of a particular food product, or food-oriented holiday. Megan Birk at the University of Texas Rio Grande Valley assigns a different sort of paper: "Instead of a midterm, you will write a short paper (5-8 pages) about a meal that best represents you, or your family. Discuss the cultural significance of the meal and the traditions surrounding it; what is served, how is it served, why is the meal important to you? Give some consideration to where that food came from and how it came to be traditional to your family." (https://static1.squarespace.com/static/5d3878547ea6120001bb0da8/t/5d41e7827fcfcd000123becc/1564600195503/Birk+food+2010+BIRK.pdf) This assignment, in many ways, is a shorter version of a multi-generation family food history. I have shaped my choice of assignments to the fairly large size of the class (48 students), with a wide variety of majors, most outside the history program. A formal research-based paper might be more appropriate to advanced students with experience analyzing primary sources.

Conclusions

For most students, food is an intrinsically interesting topic. Food history taps into this interest, and demands that students think more analytically about the meals that they consume on a daily basis. Even when my students and I are discussing the ways in which people ate one and two hundred years ago, those stu-

[7] For a full description of this project, see Pamela Riney-Kehrberg, "Feeding a Family of Five: Role Playing the Great Depression," *Teaching History: A Journal of Methods* 22, 2 (Fall 1997): 59-63.

dents are thinking about the differences between historical eating experiences and their own. They are wondering, could I eat that? How would I prepare that? What would my life be like, if I had to grow, harvest, or perhaps kill, the vast majority of the food that I ate? What would it be like to be forced to work for every bite? These are important questions to contemplate, and precursors to those with which we end the course: does it matter who raises our food? Should we be concerned whether that food is grown on a small farm or a large one, by family farmers or a corporation? Is there a morality, an ethic, of food, and if so, what is it? How does the way in which we eat affect the way in which we live our lives, and the way in which others live their lives? If we want our students to think seriously about the importance of food, beyond a daily filling of their bellies, a food history course is a good place to begin.

—46—

Federal Writers' Project Slave Narratives

Pamela Riney-Kehrberg and Cynthia Prescott

Pamela Riney-Kehrberg incorporates a wide range of primary source materials into her food history course, America Eats (Riney-Kehrberg, Ch. 45, this volume). Here we share excerpts from one type of primary document that she guides students to analyze.

The Federal Writer's Project sent its employees across the country during the 1930s to collect oral histories from individuals who had been enslaved prior to emancipation. The interviewers gathered people's memories of slavery, recording information about a number of topics. Most of the individuals interviewed were quite elderly, and had been children during slavery. Their stories were collected during the Great Depression, the most serious economic downturn in American history. Their accounts of slavery likely were influenced by all of these factors, as well as by power differentials between the former slaves and their more privileged interviewers.

Foodways were not a primary focus of these interviews, but references to food and food preparation do appear in several of them. These recollections emphasize the limited food supplies allowed to enslaved people and the plainness of their fare. Yet some cooks managed to make tasty food despite the limitations they faced. Notice the ways that access to certain foods marked both racial boundaries between masters and enslaved persons, and also social hierarchies within enslaved populations.

Please note: Some of the language used in the interviews would not be considered acceptable today. WPA interviewers also attempted to capture speakers' dialects in ways that oral historians would not use today. The text reproduced here is true to the interview, and reproduced as recorded by the interviewer from the WPA.

Ellen Cragin, Little Rock, Arkansas, Age Around 80 or more[1]

Plenty to Eat

My father would kill a hog and keep the meat in a pit under the house. I know what it is now. I didn't know then. He would clean the hog and everything before he would bring him to the house. You had to come outside the house and go into the pit when you wanted to get meat to eat. If my father didn't have a hog, he would steal one from his master's pen and cut its throat and bring it to the pit.

My folks liked hog guts. We didn't try to keep them long. We'd jus' clean 'em and scrape 'em and throw 'em in the pot. I didn't like to clean 'em but I sure loved to eat 'em. Father had a great big pot they called the wash pot and we would cook the chit'lins in it. You could smell 'em all over the country. I didn't have no sense. Whenever we had a big hog killin', I would say to the other kids, 'We got plenty of meat at our house.'

They would say back, "Where you got it?"
I would tell 'em and they would say, "Give us some."
And I would say to them, "No, that's for us."
So they called us "big niggers."

Annie Huff, Ex-slave, of near Macon Georgia[2]

All food was raised on the plantation and cooked in the family kitchen. Every one had the same kind of food and the game caught or killed by the elder sons was a delicacy relished by all. When the family meal was served, a mischievous collection of black children would sometimes crawl under the table and meddle with each person seated there. Instead of being scolded, they would receive luscious morsels from the hands of the diners. Mrs. Huff often laughingly stated that she knew not which was more annoying—"the children or the chickens, as neither was disciplined.'

Jane Johnson. Ex-Slave 90 Years Old[3]

Yes sir, us had plenty of rations to eat; no fancy vittles, just plain corn bread, meat and vegetables. Dere was no flour bread or any kind of sweet stuff for de slaves to eat. Master say sweet things 'fected de stomach and teeth in a bad way. He wanted us to stay well and healthy so us could work hard.

---

[1] Works Progress Administration, *Slave Narratives: A Folk History of Slavery in the United States From Interviews with Former Slaves*, Volume II: Arkansas Narrative, Part 2, accessed May 22, 2020, http://lcweb2.loc.gov/mss/mesn/PDFs/022.pdf.

[2] Works Progress Administration, *Slave Narratives: A Folk History of Slavery in the United States From Interviews with Former Slaves*, Georgia Narratives, Part 2, accessed May 22, 2020, https://archive.org/details/slavenarrativesa22166gut.

[3] Work Projects Administration, *Slave Narratives: A Folk History of Slavery in the United States From Interviews with Former Slaves* Volume XIV, South Carolina Narratives, Part 3, accessed May 22, 2020, http://www.gutenberg.org/files/36022/36022-h/36022-h.html.

Tines Kendricks, Trenton, Arkansas, Age 104[4]

… All de cookin' in dem days was done in pots hangin' on de pot racks. Dey never had no stoves endurin' de times what I is tellin' you 'bout. At times dey would give us enough to eat. At times dey wouldn't—just 'cordin' to how dey feelin' when dey dishin' out de grub. De biggest what dey would give de field hands to eat would be de truck what us had on de place like greens, turnips, peas, side meat, an' dey sure would cut de side meat awful thin too, Boss. Us allus had a heap of corn-meal dumplin's an' hoecakes. Old mis', her an' Mars Sam, dey real stingy. You better not leave no grub on your plate for to throw away. You sure better eat it all iffen you like it or no ….

Charlie Richardson, Webb City, Missouri. Interviewed by Bernard Hinkle.[5]

[**Interviewer:**] How did most of you cook—in the cabins or in the "big house"?
[**Richardson:**] Most of the negroes cooked in the cabins but my Mammy was a house girl and lots of times fetched my breakfast from the masters house. Most of the negroes, though, cooked in or near the cabins. They mostly used dog irons and skillets, but when they went to bile [boil] anything, they used tin buckets.
[**Interviewer:**] What food did you like best Charlie. I mean, what was your favorite dish?
[**Richardson:**] It warn't no dish. It ware jest plain hoe cake mostly. No dishes or dish like we has nowadays, No Sah! This here hoe cake was plain old white corn meal battered with salt and water. No grease. Not much grease, jest 'nough to keep it from stickin'. This here hoe cake was fried just like flap-jacks, only it were not …. When we didn't have hoe cake we had ask cake. Same as hoe cake only it was biled. Made of corn meal, salt and water and a whole shuck, with the end tied with a string.

We never had no flap-jacks in the cabins. No Sah! Flap-jacks was something [special] for only Marster Mat Warren and the Missis ….

[4] *Slave Narratives* Volume XIV.

[5] Works Progress Administration, *Slave Narratives: A Folk History of the United States From Interviews with Former Slaves.* Volume X: Missouri Narratives, accessed May 22, 2020, https://memory.loc.gov/mss/mesn/100/100.pdf.

Pavlova

Cynthia C. Prescott

Australia and USA, 1980s

I grew up in Columbus, Ohio, USA. The year that I turned nine, my father took a research sabbatical in Australia. My mother, 12-year-old brother, and I traveled with him. After a few weeks of sightseeing in Hawaii and at the Great Barrier Reef on Australia's northeastern coast, we landed in our temporary home of Adelaide, South Australia. We were still getting settled on my ninth birthday, so not only would I not have a birthday party with my friends, but it wasn't even possible for my mom to bake my usual choice of birthday cakes: a Texas sheet cake topped with fudgy chocolate frosting. Attempting to make my birthday feel as normal as possible under the circumstances, my father visited a local bakery in search of a birthday cake. But the closest thing they had available on such short notice was pavlova. He purchased an individual-sized pavlova for me to sample, asking whether it would be an acceptable substitute. Picky eater that I was, I was appalled and offended that he was offering this fruit-and cream-topped marshmallowy meringue as a substitute for my beloved brownie-like chocolate cake.

We soon discovered that pavlova is a much-loved dessert in both Australia and New Zealand—so much so that Australians and New Zealanders each insist that their country invented the dish. They agree that the dessert was named in honor of famed ballerina Anna Pavlova, who toured both nations in 1926. Researchers Dr. Andrew Paul Wood and Annabelle Utrecht recently announced that they had identified more than 150 meringue-based cake recipes that resemble pavlova that were published prior to Anna Pavlova's 1926 tour. Most were produced in Germany or in the United States by German immigrants. Meringue recipes were extremely popular among American housewives in the late nineteenth century as hand-crank egg beaters became widely available. (See Katie Mayer's adventures producing a fatless sponge cake with this nearly 150-year-old technology in this volume. (Mayer, Ch. 18, this volume) Wood and Utrecht theorize that pavlova-like recipes reached Australia and New Zealand on the back of cornstarch boxes. It is the addition of cornstarch and vinegar to beaten egg whites that produces pav-

Figure 47.1: Pavlovas at Narrandera Christmas Party, Narrandera, New South Wales, Australia, December 1984. Culver family private collection.

lova's signature crunchy exterior and marshmallowy interior, a combination that sets it apart from crunchier French meringue cookies and silkier Swiss and Italian meringues typically used as frostings or toppings.[1]

While our home base that year was the relatively large city of Adelaide, we spent three months that year in Narrandera, a town of about 3,000 in central New South Wales, while my father was doing research at a fish hatchery. While in Narrandera, we attended a community Christmas party where the local women had prepared enormous pavlovas that filled full-sized baking sheets (see Figure 47.1). Most were topped, naturally enough, with the classic combination of whipped cream and sliced strawberries and kiwi fruit, thus celebrating in-season summer fruits while maintaining the traditional Christmas color scheme imported from Europe. As I recall, I carefully picked out the fruit to eat separately, and then scooped out the marshmallowy filling, leaving the crunchy shell and whipped cream behind.

I read somewhere that you must taste a new flavor seven times before you will develop a taste for it. I certainly tasted pavlova more than seven times over the course of our year in Australia. And, over time—as much as I despised my mother's assurances that I would "learn to like" new foods—I developed a taste for pavlova. So much so, in fact, that a decade after that initial birthday fiasco, I actually requested a strawberry-topped pavlova instead of a chocolate cake on my 19th birthday [see Figure 47.2].

[1] "The Dessert Australians and New Zealanders Are Squabbling Over," Food52, May 5, 2016, https://food52.com/blog/16810-the-dessert-australians-and-new-zealanders-are-squabbling-over.

Figure 47.2: My 19th birthday pavlova, on my mother's special pavlova plate, Columbus, Ohio, USA, August 1994. Author's private collection.

My mother enjoyed eating pavlova from that first taste shortly after our arrival in Australia. Throughout our year in Australia and upon our return to the United States, my mother practiced to produce a proper pavlova. She eventually settled on a recipe that she adapted from an Australian cookbook and the recipe printed on a special ceramic pavlova plate (see Figure 2) that someone gave her after we returned to the US, combined with tips acquired from Aussie friends. Advice on how to make a good pavlova varies widely, but most Aussies feel strongly about their own methods. While some advocate using very fresh and cold eggs, most recommend using older eggs that sat out at room temperature for a full hour prior to beating. And be sure that your mixing bowl is clean and free from residual fats, which can prevent the egg whites from forming a stable foam.

Upon returning to the United States, my mom and I faced several challenges reproducing Australian pavlovas. Our first challenge was fairly easy to overcome: translating our favorite recipe from Australian to US baking terminology. "Castor sugar" (or "caster sugar," in the American spelling) is more commonly labeled "superfine" or "baker's" sugar in the US. Australian "cornflour" is equivalent to US "cornstarch"—and is quite distinct from American "corn flour," another name for the much rougher ground cornmeal used in making cornbread. We also needed to translate from metric into imperial measurements. The recipe as I have included it here is our translation and adaptation to ingredients readily available in the United States.

The second challenge was far tougher: producing a crispy outer shell that did not crack and collapse or grow chewy in Ohio's far more humid summers. Installing central air conditioning in our house made this somewhat easier. Now that I live in much drier North Dakota, I have far more ideal weather conditions under which to bake this delightful summer dessert, but I still have a ways to go to convince my children to eat it with me.

Pavlova

6 egg whites at room temperature
1.5 cups caster [superfine] sugar
3 tsp. cornstarch, sifted
1.5 tsp vinegar

Preheat oven to 350° F.

Beat the egg whites until stiff. Add ½ cup caster sugar and beat until dissolved (about 5 minutes).

Add the remaining sugar, 1 or 2 Tbsp at a time, beating well after each addition.

Add the sifted cornstarch and the vinegar, folding in lightly but thoroughly.

Cover a large oven tray with aluminum foil and turn the mixture onto the foil. Spread into a thick 9-inch circle.

Reduce the oven temperature to 300° F and bake for 75 minutes. Turn off the heat and leave the pavlova to cool in the oven with the door ajar.

Just before serving, spread with sweetened whipped cream and top with fresh fruit.

Chocolate Sheath Cake (Texas Sheet Cake)

½ cup margarine
½ cup vegetable shortening
¼ cup cocoa
1 cup water
2 cups sugar
2 cups flour
1 tsp. baking soda
½ cup buttermilk or soured milk
2 eggs, slightly beaten
1 tsp. vanilla

Combine margarine, shortening, cocoa and water in saucepan; bring to a boil. Stir until blended. Sift sugar and flour together in a large bowl. Dissolve soda in buttermilk. Add cocoa mixture, buttermilk mixture, eggs, and vanilla to flour mixture; beat or mix well. Pour into greased jelly roll pan. Bake at 400° for 20 mins. Cool, then frost with Chocolate Frosting.

Chocolate Frosting

½ cup margarine
5 Tbsp. milk
¼ cup cocoa
1 lb. confectioner's sugar
1 tsp. vanilla

Combine margarine, milk, and cocoa in saucepan; bring to a boil. Add sugar and vanilla. Mix or beat with a mixer. Frost cake immediately.

PART V

Twenty-First-Century Foodways

—48—

Introduction

Cynthia C. Prescott

Reporter Marilyn Hagerty's review of her town's new chain restaurant went viral in 2012, transforming this earnest octogenarian into a media darling known as the Olive Garden Lady (see Prescott, Ch. 49, this volume). Less than a decade later, her very rural state of North Dakota was an epicenter of a pandemic that killed more than 2.5 million worldwide, sickened 100 million, closed borders, and disrupted global trade.[1]

Global connections shape North American foodways in the twenty-first century. Hagerty, a descendant of Danish immigrants to the Great Plains, reports on not only Italian chain restaurants but also local Japanese, Mexican, and Somali cuisine. Marshall Islanders displaced by global climate change enjoy traditional breadfruit stew in their new homes in Springdale, Arkansas (Chen, Ch. 52, this volume). Global trade networks bring breadfruit to Springdale and both fresh and canned pineapple to North Dakota in the dead of winter. North Dakota wheat and sugar beets, in turn, appear in a surprising number of products worldwide. A growing percentage of the foods North Americans of all ethnicities consume are highly processed and made with white flour and added sugar or corn syrup. Many of the foods that we eat are produced and marketed by a small number of multinational corporations. Supermarkets and big-box supercenters sell meat raised on factory farms and slaughtered by poorly paid immigrants in towns like Springdale. As the essays and recipes in this section highlight, even rural places are experiencing and embracing these global connections.

The impact of these processes was not experienced equally, however. Backlash against globalization and its impact on both the environment and human health grew at the turn of the twenty-first century among North Americans with sufficient means to pursue other options. Demand for "organic" foods—under US Department of Agriculture guidelines, foods produced without the use of synthetic fertilizers, pesticides, and herbicides and without genetic engineering—grew. The "farm to table" (or "farm to fork") movement seeks direct connections between farmers and restaurants or home kitchens without being handled by a distributor or marketer. Farmers' markets became an increasingly popular way for small farmers, ranchers, and artisans to sell their products directly to urban consum-

[1] "Coronavirus Death Toll and Trends - Worldometer," accessed March 13, 2021, https://www.worldometers.info/coronavirus/coronavirus-death-toll/.

ers. The "clean food" movement, meanwhile, calls for eating whole, unprocessed foods (Garceau, Ch. 61, this volume). Various fad diets focused on avoiding certain foods, such as wheat gluten, grains, and dairy aligned themselves with these claims for clean eating. Though the specifics varied, each of these seeks a return to supposedly purer—or at least less processed—foodways of previous generations. For example, Catharine Wilson offers a twenty-first century healthier update to a classic 1950s-style casserole (Wilson, Ch. 50, this volume). Like the "back to the land" movement of the 1970s (Scharff, Ch. 53, this volume), it also promises a return to older relationships between producer and consumer. While organic foods grew in market share among wealthier consumers, the working poor in both urban and rural settings increasingly relied on cheap, processed foods produced by agribusiness conglomerates. Those goods were often sold by big-box stores operated by multinational corporations on the outskirts of cities where cheap land met cheap labor. Local grocery stores closed in both small towns and central cities, generating "food deserts" bypassed by trade networks stretching across the nation and beyond, exacerbating hunger in the midst of plenty.

Global trade networks carry goods and ideas, but they also carry diseases. On March 11, 2020, as we were preparing this volume for publication, the World Health Organization declared COVID-19 to be a pandemic. Seemingly overnight, our lives changed dramatically, shaped by so-called "social distancing." Shelter-in-place orders required people to remain inside their homes except to provide or receive essential services. Demand for sanitizing wipes (needed to clean frequently touched surfaces) and toilet paper (not actually an immediate need for this respiratory illness) left store shelves bare. Schools and houses of worship closed indefinitely. The spread of the scourge taught many living in urban places just how connected we are to one another, and how divorced they had become from rural life.

COVID-19 also changed many people's eating habits. Restaurants closed their dining rooms. The Olive Garden Lady reluctantly stopped eating in restaurants and instead reported on her take-home shrimp scampi.[2] For those with sufficient resources, stress-baking and stress-eating grew increasingly commonplace. Others faced growing hardships. School cafeterias closed, and many searched for ways to continue feeding hungry children who previously relied on school nutrition programs for most of their meals. Food pantries struggled to meet increased demand as unemployment rates skyrocketed.

As communities and nations around the world instituted restrictions to slow the spread of Severe Acute Respiratory Syndrome Coronavirus 2 (SARS-CoV-2), the virus causing COVID-19, we posted a call via social media asking people to document their experiences during the outbreak. We close this volume with their research, reflections, and recipes. Several contributors comment on the challenges of acquiring food and household goods as the contagion disrupted just-in-time supply chains. Some embraced a trend toward elaborate home baking (Berg Burin, Ch. 59, this volume), gardening, and preservation, while others struggled to simply get meals onto the table with paid and unpaid work piling up and children under-

---

[2] Marilyn Hagerty, "Takeout Meals Popular in Grand Forks," *Grand Forks Herald*, December 5, 2020, sec. A.

Figure 48.1: Empty stores at SuperTarget store, Grand Forks, North Dakota, USA, April 8, 2020. Photo by author.

foot (Egge, Ch. 56, this volume). Rebecca Stoil (Stoil, Ch. 58, this volume) touches on all of these themes as she shares her exploits attempting to maintain Jewish holiday traditions in her new home in the American South. Virginia Scharff (Scharff, Ch. 53, this volume) challenges us to contemplate who is doing the heavy lifting in the midst of the pandemic. Samantha Ammons and Krista Lynn Minnotte seek to answer Scharff's question with their research on the pandemic's impact on work-family conflict (Ammons and Minnotte, Ch. 62, this volume). Through both scholarly research and informal reflections, presented throughout this volume, we seek to tell the stories and reveal the meanings of home production and consumption—whether the labor performed at the kitchen table engages mind or stomach, in isolation or within community.

—49—

Putting the Little Town on the Prairie on Culinary Maps

Cynthia C. Prescott

This is a tale of two food writers. Each woman followed her husband to the same small college town in northeastern North Dakota where I have lived since 2007. Once there, each gained acceptance by the local community through her spouse. Each built a career around food journalism. And each found fame by playing on personal connections to the New York City food scene to sell her take on North Dakota cuisine. Together, they have put Grand Forks, North Dakota on culinary maps. But there, it would seem, the similarities end.

Nonagenarian Marilyn Hagerty is a sensible old-school small-town journalist. Born in 1926 in Pierre, South Dakota, she followed husband Jack Hagerty to Grand Forks, where he became editor of the local newspaper, the *Grand Forks Herald*, in 1957. Through Jack she got hired on as a *Herald* reporter. Determined to gain respect as a woman in a male-dominated profession, she resisted writing the gossip columns to which female writers typically were assigned. After her three children were grown, Marilyn became a regular columnist for the *Herald*. One long-running column, That Reminds Me, contains historical reminiscences of the Grand Forks area she came to call home. Another, Eatbeat, describes her experiences dining in local restaurants. It was through a characteristically matter-of-fact 2012 Eatbeat column describing experiences eating in Grand Forks' newest chain restaurant that Marilyn Hagerty "went viral." Overnight, Marilyn Hagerty and her adopted hometown accidentally became world famous, and the "Olive Garden Lady" was born.

Molly Yeh is in many ways the antithesis of the "Olive Garden Lady." While Marilyn Hagerty comes from Danish immigrant stock and spent her entire life in small towns on the northern Great Plains, Yeh's background is cosmopolitan.[1] She grew up in a suburb of Chicago, where her father played in the symphony orchestra. Both of Yeh's parents are Julliard-trained clarinetists. Her mother is of Ashkenazi Jewish heritage, while her father is Chinese American. Like her mother

[1] Although Pierre is the capital of South Dakota, according to US Census bureau data, its population has never topped 15,000. When Yeh was born in Glenview, Illinois, in 1989, its population actually was smaller than that of Grand Forks, which Hagerty had already called home for three decades. But while Grand Forks is a regional commercial hub, Glenview is a suburb of the large city of Chicago.

and father, Molly moved to New York City to study music at the Julliard School of Performance Arts. Living in New York City, Molly embraced the culturally diverse local food scene. She began writing a food blog, where she honed her cheery, informal writing style and sunshine-laden photography. Then she married fellow Julliard student Nick Hagen, and moved with him to his family's farm in northwestern Minnesota. Yeh used her move to "just south of nowhere" to transform herself into a food media star, initially blogging full-time before publishing a cookbook and scoring her own show on the Food Network.

Where Marilyn Hagerty is elderly and down-to-earth, Molly Yeh is young and hip. (Indeed, although she continues to contribute columns to the *Herald*, officially Hagerty retired while Yeh was still in diapers.) Hagerty's writing and persona are simple and unsentimental, while Yeh's sunny and self-deprecating. Hagerty is a bastion of small-town Midwestern practicality, while Yeh's work is awash in Pinterist-ready perfection. Nonagenarian Marilyn Hagerty wonders what all the fuss is about her down-to-earth reporting, while millennial Molly Yeh's specialty is making a fuss over everyday events. But both became media darlings in recent years thanks to the collision of urban and rural cultures in an online world. In her own way, each woman performs a savvy version of rustic femininity that reinforces community ties and belies the interconnectedness of twenty-first-century American foodways.

The Olive Garden Lady

Marilyn Hagerty is nothing if not earnest. She was 85 years old when her long-running Eatbeat column in the *Grand Forks Herald* went viral in 2012.[2] Within three days, her column received 400,000 hits—twenty times more than the next most popular story.[3] That number soon reached 1 million hits.[4] Urbanites across the United States pounced with snarky criticism, while other readers wrongly assumed that her review of a major Italian-style restaurant chain was a clever piece of satire. Why else would the newspaper in the state's third-largest city, home to its flagship research university, publish a piece earnestly describing the experience of dining at a chain restaurant that had become shorthand for lowbrow culture?

"The Olive Garden Lady," as she became known, quickly became a media phenomenon. Readers across the country delighted or scoffed at her reviews of Ruby Tuesday and McDonalds. She appeared on Anderson Cooper and *The Today Show*, and judged a competition round on *Top Chef*. Celebrity chef Anthony Bourdain scored her a reservation at three-Michelin-star-rated Manhattan restaurant Le Bernardin, and then contributed a forward to a new book-length compilation

---

[2] "Woman's Olive Garden Review Goes Viral," HuffPost, 39:30 500, https://www.huffingtonpost.com/2012/03/08/marilyn-hagerty-olive-garden_n_1332753.html.

[3] A. B. C. News, "Olive Garden Review Gets Celeb Attention, Receives More than 400K Views," ABC News, accessed April 30, 2020, https://abcnews.go.com/US/marilyn-hagertys-north-dakota-olive-garden-review-celebrity/story?id=15893217.

[4] Norah Kleven, "Marilyn Hagerty Remembers Anthony Bourdain," *Grand Forks Herald*, June 8, 2018, /community/4457711-watch-marilyn-hagerty-remembers-anthony-bourdain.

of Hagerty's past Eatbeat columns, *Grand Forks: A History of American Dining in 128 Reviews*. Suddenly, after more than fifty years of writing her characteristically matter-of-fact reports on every dining establishment within a fifty-mile radius of Grand Forks—from the local "anniversary restaurant" to truck stops and fast food joints—Hagerty was able to use her new New York City connections to enjoy fifteen minutes of fame.

So why did Marilyn Hagerty "go viral" after more than fifty years writing for the same small newspaper with approximately 30,000 subscribers? While New Yorkers might have assumed Marilyn Hagerty's Olive Garden review was a work of satire, her lively description of her first visit to Grand Forks' newest restaurant was very much in earnest. Her readers in that town of 50,000—and particularly those in surrounding rural areas—might never have set foot in an Olive Garden before the Grand Forks location opened in 2012. And its opening was eagerly awaited by many local residents who were familiar with its reliably tasty food, because the best-known Grand Forks restaurant serving Italian food at the time also specialized in burritos, broasted chicken, and barbeque ribs. Indeed, prior to its opening, my husband and I would sometimes dine at the nearest Olive Garden location when we were visiting the larger city of Fargo (population 120,000) some 75 miles away. Whenever we did, we would run into people we knew from Grand Forks. So popular was Grand Forks' eatery when it finally opened that Hagerty waited several weeks before checking it out for herself and her loyal readers.

Hagerty's review of the Grand Forks Olive Garden struck a cultural chord because the chain had become a touchstone in early-twenty-first-century American popular culture. According to Erin Gloria Ryan, "Expressing a preference for dining at Olive Garden in 2012 … prove[d] a lack of cultural awareness to people who define themselves by being culturally aware."[5] It appeared on a popular blog listing of Stuff White Trash People Like, and a reality show competitor on *The Bachelor* lost her chance to marry the wealthy Firestone tire heir after identifying Olive Garden as her favorite restaurant.[6]

Marilyn Hagerty's guilelessness sets her apart from big-city culinary reviewers. Hagerty insists that she is a restaurant reporter, *not* a food critic. She intentionally avoids criticizing restaurants' food, lest she damage the establishment's business (or, one suspects, hurts the owner's feelings). While this might seem absurd to foodies in New York City or Los Angeles, it makes a great deal of sense for a woman who grew up on the northern Plains during the Great Depression.

People in the Upper Midwest—and particularly rural women—have long valued strengthening community ties above individual fame. Neighborliness represents a core cultural value for rural Midwesterners like Hagerty. Farmers and farm women have long exchanged labor with the neighbors, weaving tight community webs. Those communitarian values persist today, even as high-priced high-tech equipment replaces physical labor in the fields and farm households increasingly rely on women's off-farm labor to provide needed income and health in-

[5] "We Are All the Olive Garden Lady," accessed April 30, 2020, https://jezebel.com/we-are-all-the-olive-garden-lady-5892028.

[6] "We Are All the Olive Garden Lady."

surance. After all, a neighbor's assistance still might be the only thing that enables you to survive an unexpected blizzard. Moreover, as rural communities struggle to survive amid outmigration and the rise of big-box stores and Amazon.com, their remaining residents hold fast to traditional cultural values. To publish a critical review of a local restaurant would be dangerously akin to Big City back-stabbing. Rural women might gossip amongst themselves, but they are expected to plaster on a friendly smile for outsiders. They must maintain a cheerfully united front in the face of an attack from the outside world. Thus for the Olive Garden Lady to critique the fruits of a chef's labors would undermine not only her communitarianism but her femininity.

Hagerty's report on her visit to the new Grand Forks Olive Garden was typical of her long-running Eatbeat column. In the piece that made her famous, as in so many other columns she has written over the years, Hagerty described the restaurant setting, summarized the food and beverage offerings, and her interaction with her server. One notable exception: on her first visit to that new Olive Garden, Hagerty apparently dined alone.

In most Eatbeat entries, she reports with whom she dined and what they ate, hinting at the social role expected of rural women of her generation. In this, she sometimes treats her food column as if it were a social page, explaining who she was dining with and why. Reading the Eatbeat and her four other weekly columns thus reveals much about her social network. This is ironic, because Hagerty has told her neighbors that she wanted to do food reporting for the *Herald* so that she would not be relegated to the society pages of her husband's newspaper. But in her carefully factual reporting, Hagerty informs her readers who dined with her on that particular occasion, and what each person ordered. While she occasionally breaks bread with prominent local figures, far more often she dines with friends or her college-aged grandchildren. Thus her inclusion of their names serves to expand the number of dishes that she can comment on, and also helps to paint the scene of their shared dining experience. It also reinforces the nostalgic tone and celebration of local community connectedness that she depicts in her regular columns reporting on local happenings. For fifty years those accounts appeared under the guise of letters to her sister Shirley. After Shirley died, Hagerty continued writing her popular column, simply redirecting them to Shirley's friend Sandy.[7]

As a female journalist operating in a man's world, Hagerty adopted a straightforward writing style. She came to rely on short, simple declarative sentences that exert expertise without directly challenging the authority of male publishers and restauranteurs. Yet for Hagerty to write as a true food critic would come across as overly harsh and unwomanly. Instead, she has carved out for herself a safer role as a "food reporter," describing her experiences without critiquing them. When readers asked to identify her favorite restaurant in 2008, Hagerty insisted she was

> at a loss to name any one favorite place. It depends on what I am seeking. I like the light breakfast at Perkins. I would go to Al's for meatloaf and to North

[7] Bob Collins, "After 50 Years, the Letters to Shirley Stop," NewsCut, accessed April 30, 2020, https://blogs.mprnews.org/newscut/2016/03/after-50-years-the-letters-to-shirley-stop/.

Side Cafe for egg rolls. I think the liver pâté at Whitey's is very good. I like the waiters at Sanders [the only fine dining establishment in Grand Forks at the time]. Very proper, you know. 'l Bistro [sic] at Canad Inn has some very nice items. I could go on and on.[8]

The personal connections she shares with her dining companions influence—indeed, are just as newsworthy as—the quality of the dining experience on which Hagerty builds her columns.

Hagerty's Eatbeat column also represents a valuable service to her larger community of readers. While Grand Forks boasts far more, and more diverse, dining options than it did even a decade ago, its offerings are still limited. And those in the surrounding farming regions are even more sparse. Hagerty's accounts of her visits to scattered rural restaurants encourage residents of the local commercial hub to explore its hinterlands, and might attract more patronage of far-flung diners and truck stops. And amid the current COVID-19 crisis, Hagerty and her colleagues at the *Herald* are working hard to publicize those local establishments that are "weathering the storm" and finding creative ways to serve customers while practicing social distancing.[9]

Hagerty evokes both Scandinavian and Depression-era frugality in her Eatbeat columns. She consistently lists the price for the dishes she and her dining companions order, as well as other top-selling menu items. She rarely orders higher-priced entrees, and often reports carrying home leftovers. She insists on visiting the restaurants on which she reports at her own expense. To do otherwise "would not be professional and would not leave me feeling free to write what I think."[10] Despite this admirable devotion to professionalism, Hagerty remains loath to criticize the restaurants she visits, for to do so would be unseemly—particularly for a rural woman—and it wouldn't be "North Dakota nice."

Of course Hagerty recognizes the difference between a McDonald's Big Mac (her "secret sin"[11]) and a four-hour fine dining experience at Le Bernardin. In fact, celebrity chef Anthony Bourdain, who arranged for her to dine at Le Bernardin, wrote in his forward to her book, "She misses nothing. I would not want to play poker with her for money."[12] Her son James, who writes for the *Wall Street Journal*,

[8] Marilyn Hagerty, "Greater Grand Forks Offers Diners a Variety of Restaurants," *Grand Forks Herald* March 26, 2008, reprinted in Hagerty, *Grand Forks*, 196. Perkins is a major American casual dining chain. Al's, North Side Cafe, Whitey's, and Sanders were all well-established local eateries at the time. 'L Bistro had opened the previous year.

[9] Marilyn Hagerty, "Restaurants keep going even during the hard times," *Grand Forks Herald* April 18, 2020, A3.

[10] Marilyn Hagerty, "Greater Grand Forks Offers Diners a Variety of Restaurants," *Grand Forks Herald* March 26, 2008; reprinted in *Grand Forks*, 196.

[11] Marilyn Hagerty | Jan 21st 2015 - 6am, "THE EATBEAT: Greater Grand Forks McDonald's Restaurants Offer Fun Fast Food," Grand Forks Herald, accessed April 30, 2020, https://www.grandforksherald.com/lifestyle/food/3660368-eatbeat-greater-grand-forks-mcdonalds-restaurants-offer-fun-fast-food.

[12] Anthony Bourdain, "Foreward," "Grand Forks - Marilyn Hagerty - Paperback," HarperCollins Publishers: World-Leading Book Publisher, ix, accessed April 30, 2020, https://www.harpercollins.com/9780062228895/grand-forks/.

explained to Minnesota Public Radio what regular *Grand Forks Herald* readers already knew: that if Hagerty devotes most of her column to describing the décor rather than the food, it indicates that she found little to compliment about the food.[13] So if Marilyn Hagerty's next Eatbeat column devotes more space to the quality of the napkins than she does the cuisine, you might want to consider dining elsewhere. If you're a foodie who embraces more exotic flavors, you will know to skim over her careful quotations from her culinary dictionary yet again defining the term "sushi," and will read between the lines about just how authentic the cuisine is at the popular Mexican restaurant where Hagerty assures her readers that the salsa is never too spicy. Readers of all culinary persuasions would do well to read carefully her reporting on the region's best knoephla soup and tater tot hotdish (Sharpless, Ch. 3, this volume). Whether you find her food reporting laughable or charming, you know that Marilyn Hagerty will remain true to her rural community values.

City Girl Meets Beet Farm

Since 2012, both nonagenarian Midwesterner Marilyn Hagerty and twenty-something Manhattanite Molly Yeh cleverly built their food fame on a foundation of generational and urban-rural cultural tensions. As we have seen, Hagerty was charmingly befuddled by "going viral," but it was her brave forays into the Manhattan food scene that made her a media darling. Likewise, Molly Yeh highlights her journey from Julliard-trained percussionist and Manhattan ethnic restaurant aficionado to Midwestern food blogger in her blog and cookbook, *Molly on the Range*. Yeh's creative melding of East Asian and eastern European culinary traditions and knack for vivid photography launched her career as a food writer. Her informal, self-deprecating tone describing her adventures decorating an elaborate mousse cake with a marzipan moose made many millennials aspire to be like her.[14] But it is her choice to abandon that cosmopolitan culture and remake herself as a rural farmwife updating traditional Midwestern cuisine that made Molly Yeh a star.

Millennial Molly Yeh brings a very different set of cultural norms to her version of rural Grand Forks food writing. In contrast to Hagerty's short, choppy sentences, Yeh writes in a personable, flowing style uninterrupted by formalities such as capital letters. In her friendly blog accompanied by unbelievably beautiful photographs of her cooking, Yeh bubblingly reports loving her newfound access to farm-fresh eggs, her in-laws' own apple trees, and plenty of time to perfect her recipes while her husband works 17 hours a day during harvest time. Since arriving on the northern Plains, Yeh has brought new meaning to farm-to-table cuisine in creative ways. After a miserable first attempt at making her farmer husband's great aunt's lefse recipe, she has embraced rural Midwestern recipes like those that Mar-

[13] "A Son on What It's like When Mom Goes Viral," MPR News, accessed April 30, 2020, https://www.mprnews.org/story/2012/03/14/a-son-on-what-its-like-when-mom-goes-viral.

[14] "I Like This Bitch's Life: Molly Yeh," The Cut, accessed April 30, 2020, https://www.thecut.com/2015/01/i-like-this-bitchs-life-molly-yeh.html.

ilyn Hagerty finds most comforting. But just as she has long sought to merge her Chinese and Jewish culinary heritage, Yeh produces Midwestern comfort foods with a twist.[15] Yeh even published a new cookbook of upscale Midwestern recipes fit for foodies, like Yemeni-spiced chicken pot pie.

Whereas her early blog writing emphasized her cosmopolitanism and ethnic diversity, since arriving in the Upper Midwest Yeh has embraced rurality. In her new Food Network show, *Girl Meets Farm*, Molly Yeh portrays herself as a food expert, but she chooses to frame herself as the (newly arrived) girl next door raising her own chickens, rather than a big city chef—or the highly successful food blogger and TV star she willed herself into being. Just as Hagerty's overnight fame took her to Manhattan, Julliard-trained musician Molly Yeh followed her trombonist husband Nick Hagen from New York City to his family's sugar beet farm outside Grand Forks. Seeking a way to fill her time on the farm "just south of nowhere," Yeh threw herself into blogging, quickly transforming her cooking and photography hobbies into a career.[16] She was named *Saveur*'s "Blogger of the Year" and to Forbes' "30 Under 30" list, appeared on *The Today Show*, published a cookbook, and launched her own television show on the Food Network, which is now in its sixth season. Yeh is now rapidly rising in the ranks of Food Network celebrities. Yet despite all of her success, a good part of Yeh's appeal is her lighthearted determination not to take herself too seriously.

Just as Marilyn Hagerty plays up her small-town background in her newspaper columns, Molly Yeh emphasizes her transplanted rural roots. In her television show, which premiered in 2018, Yeh leaves behind her big city image, presenting herself as exquisitely at home on a farm in the middle of nowhere. *Girl Meets Farm* opens with B-reel of the rural Minnesota landscape and family farm and a voice-over from Yeh herself talking about her home "on the North Dakota–Minnesota border." In the pilot episode, Molly declares, "I grew up in a city, but I *love* living in the middle of nowhere. Life is simple here, it's cozy—especially in the winter—and everybody here is just so sweet and welcoming."

Yeh's home is not really in the middle of nowhere. While Yeh tends to play up her connection to North Dakota because it sounds so remote to most Americans, she actually resides in Minnesota. She and husband do now live on farmland that has been in his family for generations. But local residents know that Hagen and Yeh's farm actually sits just outside East Grand Forks, Minnesota, which is separated by a slow-flowing river from downtown Grand Forks. Although Grand Forks is certainly smaller than Chicago or New York City, it is a regional commercial hub, with a hospital, events center, and big-box stores that attract visitors from throughout the region and busloads of tourists from Canada (or at least it did until the COVID-19 pandemic closed the border). The University of North Dakota attracts faculty and students from all over the world. And while it only scored an

---

[15] For an interesting point of comparison, see Virginia Scharff's discussion of her Jewish mother's cooking in St. Louis, Missouri, in an earlier generation (Scharff, Ch. 53, this volume).

[16] "How Molly Yeh Baked Her Way Home," Midwest Living, accessed April 30, 2020, https://www.midwestliving.com/food/desserts/bread-muffins/how-molly-yeh-baked-her-way-home/.

Olive Garden restaurant relatively recently and its dining options remain more limited than in larger cities, it is now home to an impressive array of exotic eateries and quirky shops. Indeed, later episodes of *Girl Meets Farm* show her eating in local Grand Forks restaurants (though noticeably not the now-famous local Olive Garden location) with suitably glamorous hipster friends. Yeh and husband Nick Hagen told the *Grand Forks Herald* they are pleased with how the series depicts their community: "They've captured Grand Forks in its true best light," Hagen said. "It's a great opportunity for non-Midwesterners to see what a mid-size Midwestern city is all about."[17] But the fish out of water element of a big city girl landing in the middle of nowhere is the hook that sells her newfound celebrity.

Girl Meets Farm revolves around family life in her adopted Midwestern community. She repeatedly emphasizes her role as adoring and supportive farmwife and daughter-in-law who is at home in—indeed deeply embedded in—her extended family (by marriage) and the local rural community. In her first episode, she makes crunchy paprika potato salad, on-trend wilted Brussel sprouts in bacon, and spicy Shakshuka with feta (a Middle Eastern simmered tomato dish topped with perfectly poached eggs) for her extended farm family. But rather than emphasizing the cosmopolitanism of her chosen menu, she sells these as yummy, Midwestern dishes: lots of mayo and bacon, and not too spicy. No talk of North African or Israeli cuisine here. And don't worry: "If you need to let this simmer on the stove for a little bit because maybe YOU have a farmer husband who says he's going to be in in 20 minutes, but an hour later he's just bringing the tractor on in, it's perfect for this." She's sure that your farmer husband will love her tomatoey egg dish just as much as hers does.

Each episode of *Girl Meets Farm* follows a similar trajectory intended to depict Molly Yeh as a typical rural farmwife. Our TV friend Molly welcomes us into her sun-drenched kitchen as she demonstrates how to make one of her favorite homey dishes. Her turquoise retro refrigerator (with its designer brand name carefully disguised), butcher block counters, and white farmhouse sink evoke 1950s rural domesticity. She prepares one exquisitely beautiful dish, then cleverly pauses her cooking long enough to go out to visit her husband, Nick Hagen, hard at work in the barn or fields. Playing the supportive housewife, she serves Nick a snack or meal from her latest creation, such as an upscale grilled cheese inspired by a New York everything bagel, or brings a sample of her latest baking creations and asks him to build a cabinet to display them. Wifely duties attended to, she returns to the kitchen to complete preparations for her next fabulous party. A cute little pink toy tractor often appears to deliver or remove servings of completed dishes on display on her kitchen counter.

Each episode builds up to some kind of community celebration. In the pilot, Yeh prepares an elaborate brunch for their extended family to celebrate Nick and Molly's anniversary. Later episodes highlight other special events, such as a baby

[17] Pamela D. Knudson | Jun 7th 2018 - 4pm, "Molly Yeh Show on Food Network Debuts This Month," Grand Forks Herald, accessed April 30, 2020, https://www.grandforksherald.com/news/4457426-molly-yeh-show-food-network-debuts-month.

shower, her father's birthday, or the fall harvest. Each episode features Yeh demonstrating how to prepare several courses that she then serves to guests from her community or more worldly family or friends visiting from out of town.

Throughout the television series Yeh emphasizes her husband's role as a farmer. For example, in season 4, episode 5, we see Nick, his father, and neighboring farmers on enormous combines harvesting wheat. Far less attention gets paid to their farm's primary product: sugar beets. Yeh can mill her own whole-wheat flour from Nick's wheat berries, but sugar beet processing is far less romantic, just earning Yeh's comment that the "bazillion tons" of sugar beets that the men harvest will be "processed into the kind of table sugar you and I eat every day" (season 2, episode 2). Presumably Yeh's penchant for home baking spares her family and friends from the sugar and corn syrup added to many processed foods. But Molly makes up for it by adding special desserts to each featured meal, often decorated with her signature sugary sprinkles.

Yeh maintains a delicate balance between food expert and home cook, and between producer and consumer. Inviting outsiders to their farm allows Molly to simultaneously play hostess and cast herself as an insider. She puts West Coast food blogger friends to work picking apples (season 2, episode 5), and serves visiting college friends fresher falafel than they ate from their favorite food stand in New York (season 4, episode 6). While her father takes a relatively active role engaging their shared ethnic heritage and musical training to celebrate the Chinese New Year (season 1, episode 4 and season 2, episode 11) and even performs a local concert on the UND campus (season 6, episode 7), most guests appear as assistants lending a hand—or simply their appetites—to Molly's food achievements.

Girl Meets Farm emphasizes Yeh's ability to "go native" in the rural Midwest. In the pilot episode, she reminisced that "When I first moved to town, Aunt Elaine was always teaching me about recipes of the region and different berries she has growing in her garden, some of which I'd never even heard of." That episode showed Molly driving across a bridge linking Minnesota to North Dakota (carefully editing out the hip downtown area that belies the rurality the episode seeks to emphasize) to visit her aunt-by-marriage Elaine to pick up some homemade berry preserves.

Molly's ethnically diverse background, her elite training and big-city childhood should make her an outsider in an area where century-old ethnic tensions between Swedish and Norwegian immigrants are laughingly maintained and newcomers are viewed with suspicion. For example, I am a Caucasian Midwesterner who has lived in Grand Forks for thirteen years. Both my children are born and raised in Grand Forks and attend our neighborhood elementary school, where my husband and I serve in the Parent-Teacher Organization. I am a local Girl Scout troop leader and active in my local church. But as a college professor who moved here from out of state—and an outspoken feminist to boot—I will probably always be held at arms' length by my neighbors. In contrast, biracial Manhattanite Molly Yeh has been embraced precisely because she married into a local farming family, even though she has found fame and fortune by manipulating local customs.

Even as she asserts her authority as a uniquely situated food expert, in *Girl Meets Farm* Yeh presents herself as a proper rural female contributing member of a broader, timeless farming community. Regarding the wheat harvest (season 4, episode 5) she declared:

> So wheat harvest is kind of a community effort. Every year Nick and his dad will go and help a neighboring farmer with their wheat harvest, and then when they are done with that, the neighboring farmers come on over to help with our harvest, and whoever's harvesting will traditionally host a dinner. So I'm doing my part.

She served them a ham and potato pizza that, she claims, has everything those farmers need. Then she tops it off with a dessert made from "my little harvest" of rhubarb from a charmingly timeless rhubarb patch: "Everybody on the farm can't remember a time when the rhubarb patch wasn't there" (season 4, episode 5). Over time, Yeh abandoned the "fish out of water" shtick that drove the show's first season, Yeh instead claiming her rightful place grafted into the Hagen family tree and their rural community.

Where once Yeh emphasized her artistry in her blog, today she emphasizes her newly adopted homespun hostess role. But she does so with a decidedly small-town Midwestern flair. In contrast to celebrity chef Alex Guarnaschelli, who battled her way to the title of "Iron Chef" in Food Network's primetime shows, Molly Yeh models herself after more conventionally feminine Food Network stars like Giada De Laurentiis and Ree Drummond, whose shows are filmed in their own kitchens and are broadcast in the network's daytime lineup. Yeh's story in many ways echoes that told by fellow blogger-turned-television star "Pioneer Woman" (Drummond), the "sassy former city girl" who married a "hunky rancher" and now "shares her special brand of home cooking" from her ranch kitchen (Prescott, Conclusion, this volume).[18] Like De Laurentiis and Drummond, Yeh's hyper-femininity permits her to embrace her culinary expertise, because it keeps her safely within her home kitchen. But where Drummond's show emphasizes solitary ranch life out on the open range of the southern Plains accompanied by her trusty basset hound, Yeh's little farmhouse on the Minnesota prairie is soundly embedded in her newly adopted Midwestern community. *Girl Meets Farm* episodes balance social events featuring local hipsters or visiting trendy coastal friends against regular extended farm family gatherings.

Constructing Rural Femininity

Hagerty and Yeh live, work, and write about the same college town and highlight similar upper Midwest communitarian values. Yeh's TV show celebrates the kind of supportive rural community that Marilyn Hagerty embodies. Hagerty identifies her dining companions and what they ordered in each Eatbeat column, because

[18] "Ree Drummond," Food Network, accessed April 30, 2020, https://www.foodnetwork.com/profiles/talent/ree-drummond.

who doesn't like to see their name in print in the hometown paper?[19] Similarly, *Girl Meets Farm* closes each episode with a gathering of family or friends to enjoy Yeh's creations. But while Hagerty seeks out home cooking in truck stops throughout the Red River Valley, Molly makes food far fancier than Marilyn's favorite local restaurants could even imagine. Rather than being apprenticed to her farmwife mother-in-law to learn how to make local favorites like knoephla and lefse, Yeh teaches her mother-in-law to make pistachio-white-chocolate pastry pockets and reinvents tater tot hotdish (made with homemade creamed soup and tater tots produced in Grand Forks' potato-processing plant marching across the top "in perfect rows and columns"[20]) to make it worthy of a Manhattan bistro.

Marilyn Hagerty and Molly Yeh make an unlikely pair. Hagerty brings traditional rural values to a college town restaurant beat, while Yeh brings hipster foodie culture to beet farming. Hagerty continues to report earnestly on her experiences eating at local truck stops and fast food restaurants, taking her newfound fame in stride. Her short, declarative sentences leave little room for adding "a bit of sparkle and fun" to dining in the Upper Midwest. But Molly Yeh insists there's room for foodies even in Grand Forks, highlighting the fried cheesy pickles at the town's eclectic bar/restaurant The Toasted Frog on Cooking Channel's *The Best Thing I Ever Ate* (season 8, episode 13). Hagerty was impressed by the Tuscan farmhouse styling at the bright and airy new Olive Garden restaurant. Meanwhile, Yeh built a model of her in-laws' working beet farm out of gingerbread, complete with molded gingerbread Quonset hut and grain bins, a pink tractor, and blue raspberry hot tub.[21] Yeh used styling language straight out of TLC's *What Not to Wear*, suggesting that "small pops of red and gold … add a bit of sparkle and fun to the farm."[22]

It was the collision of these two women's cultural and culinary worlds that took the internet by storm nearly a decade ago. But despite being separated by two generations and coming from such seemingly different worlds, if we peel back their carefully constructed public personas, we discover that Hagerty and Yeh are far more alike than they may initially appear. Both are shrewd writers turned celebrities who skillfully play up their own "fish out of water" plot lines to endear themselves to both native North Dakotans and more worldly viewers across the country and around the world. The elderly Hagerty shrewdly acts intensely befuddled on her well-publicized visits to New York City and her repeated references to accidentally "going viral," all the while claiming not to know what that meant, let alone how it came to be. Meanwhile Yeh presents effortless perfection, and deftly plays up the incongruity of her big city persona and her new home on a sugar beet

[19] *Made to Stick: Why Some Ideas Survive and Others Die*, 1st edition (Random House, 2007).

[20] Molly Yeh, "Classic Tater Tot Hotdish," molly yeh, accessed May 16, 2020, http://mynameisyeh.com/mynameisyeh/2017/10/classic-tater-tot-hotdish.

[21] "How to Make a Gingerbread House, Step by Step - Part 1," accessed April 30, 2020, https://food52.com/blog/11857-how-to-build-a-gingerbread-farm-part-1.

[22] "How to Make a Gingerbread Farm, Part 3," Food52, 45:00 500, https://food52.com/blog/11913-how-to-make-a-gingerbread-farm-part-3.

farm to attract attention to her sugary-sweet food blog and television show. Aging but hardly geriatric, as a Scandinavian daughter of the Depression, Hagerty hides her media savvy behind a baffled façade. Meanwhile, millennial Molly masks hers with similarly self-deprecating cheerfulness.

More importantly, the foundation of each woman's fame is her careful construction of a generation-specific form of rustic femininity. Marilyn Hagerty personifies a daughter of the Great Depression raised on the sparsely-populated northern Great Plains. She knows the value of a dollar, and thus is more at home treating herself to a McDonald's Big Mac than to a multi-course meal at three-Michelin-star Le Barnardin. She rejects the frivolity and gender-role expectations of gossip columns, yet relies on reporting the opinions of other members of her vast social network in Eatbeat. Hagerty embodies Scandinavian–Midwestern feminine self-effacement even as she shrewdly promotes her unexpected fame.

Just as she chose to marry a Julliard-trained sugar beet farmer, Molly Yeh skillfully marries her cosmopolitan background and communitarian behavior. Although her "fish out of water" story made her a rising media star, it is her "girl next door" persona that maintains and grows her appeal. In other words, Yeh's simultaneous embrace of modern rural femininity and Midwestern community life skyrocketed her to stardom.

Decades and ostensibly worlds apart, Marilyn Hagerty and Molly Yeh each built solid careers on the strength of their carefully crafted food writing styles. But over the past two decades, Hagerty and Yeh have skillfully manipulated their public personas to achieve surprising degrees of fame (if more limited fortune) by playing up their seeming discomfort in one another's worlds. By embracing generation-specific versions of rustic femininity, Marilyn Hagerty and Molly Yeh have become media darlings, and brought fame to their adopted hometown that is not so much the middle of nowhere as it might appear.

—50—

Convenience Cooking: Seven-Layer Casserole

Catharine Wilson
Recipe of Jean Wilson
Kemptville, Ontario, 1950s

Casseroles may not be so hip today, but they are a classic American dish and were very popular in the 1950s and 1960s. Women liked them because they were easy to prepare, inexpensive, and nutritious. My mother, living on the edge of a small town in Ontario, liked the Seven-Layer Casserole because she could assemble it in the morning and set her oven to come on before Dad arrived home from work, so it was piping hot and wafts of bacon filled the air on his arrival. Meanwhile she was free throughout the day to sew curtains, wax the floor, volunteer at the library, and drive my sister and me to Brownies and piano lessons after school. Casseroles were aimed at busy women like my mother who wanted convenience cooking. Many involved simply opening a series of cans: canned vegetables, canned chow mein noodles and, of course, the ubiquitous Campbell's Soup which acted as the binder. Some of you may even remember the potato chip casserole! Things could get very salty.

This Seven-Layer Casserole, however, was made with simple, clean ingredients and still holds sway with the health conscious today. It's a meal-in-one-dish: all your meats, grains, and vegetables can be assembled right in the baking/serving dish. I find that our extended family, with all its special dietary needs—gluten free, diabetic, potato free—can all enjoy it without anyone being left out. Kids enjoy layering the ingredients too, just like I did years ago, "helping" Mother in the kitchen. Her recipe is below in italics and captures some of the food conveniences of the 1950s.

Seven-Layer Casserole

1 cup Minute Rice (I use brown rice)
1 cup corn niblets
1 large onion, sliced
1 large green pepper slivered
salt and pepper
1 7-oz. can Hunts tomato sauce + ½ can water
1 ½ lbs. chuck (ground beef)
salt & pepper
1 7-oz. can Hunts tomato sauce + ¼ can water
Bacon slices to cover (substitute prosciutto as a healthier choice)

In a greased 7x12 Pyrex dish, layer ingredients in the order mentioned. Cover and cook for 1 hour at 375°F. Then uncover and bake until bacon is crisp (about 30 minutes).

—51—

Kalua Pork

Cynthia C. Prescott

Kalua Pork is one of the most common dishes served at Hawaiian luaus. It is a traditional recipe of indigenous Hawaiians. Authentic Kalua Pork is prepared in an imu oven. A fire is built at the bottom of a large pit. The fire is used to heat porous lava rocks, which are lined with banana and ti leaves to provide moisture and flavor. A whole pig is cooked over the hot rocks in the pit all day.[1]

Kalua Pork is also a standard option in Hawaiian plate lunches. Hawaiian plate lunches are believed to have originated on sugar and pineapple plantations in the 1880s. Plantation laborers—many of them of Chinese or Japanese descent—brought lunches consisting of leftovers from the previous evening meal packed in bento boxes. Meat or fish were combined with rice to make the lunches more filling (rather than traditional Hawaiian taro). Over time, food carts and trucks began visiting the fields to sell inexpensive plates of similar foods. Macaroni salad made with pasta, mayonnaise, salt and pepper, was adapted from mainland United States culture and became a popular addition to the "plate lunch."[2]

In the 1950s, Hawaii's plantation era ended, as the islands' economic activity shifted increasingly toward tourism. But plate lunches remained a popular item at diners, drive-ins, and now fast food restaurants. Popular plate lunches today reflect Hawaii's cultural diversity. Several dishes are updated versions of traditional indigenous Hawaiian dishes: kalua pork, laulau (pork, chicken, or beef, butterfish, and taro leaves steamed in ti leaves), and poke (raw tuna mixed with seaweed

---

[1] Kalena McElroy, "A Brief History of Hawaii's Famous Kālua Pork Dish," Culture Trip, accessed April 13, 2020, https://theculturetrip.com/north-america/usa/hawaii/articles/a-brief-history-of-hawaiis-famous-kalua-pork-dish/.

[2] "Chinese Laborers in Hawai`i - Hawaii History - Short Stories," accessed April 13, 2020, http://www.hawaiihistory.org/index.cfm?fuseaction=ig.page&PageID=292&returntoname=Short%20Stories&returntopageid=483; "Japanese - Hawaii - Immigration...- Classroom Presentation | Teacher Resources - Library of Congress," webpage, accessed April 13, 2020, http://www.loc.gov/teachers/classroommaterials/presentationsandactivities/presentations/immigration/japanese2.html; "A Brief History of Plate Lunches in Hawaii—Hawaii Ocean Project," *Hawaii Ocean Project* (blog), July 6, 2018, https://hawaiioceanproject.com/a-brief-history-of-plate-lunches-in-hawaii/.

and onions). But equally popular are Japanese-inspired chicken katsu (breaded, fried chicken cutlet served with sweet soy-based tonkatsu sauce) and loco moco (a hamburger patty topped with an over-easy fried egg and brown gravy).[3]

Another cheap, filling, and ethnically diverse popular Hawaiian dish for which I personally have never acquired a taste is Spam musubi. It is an adaptation of Japanese *onigiri*—a snack made of compacted rice wrapped in nori, a black seaweed paper, and often seasoned with fish. Spam Musubi utilizes the canned ham product that the U.S. military introduced to Hawaiian civilians during World War II.[4]

I first tasted Kalua Pork on my honeymoon in Kauai in 2005. Eating even greatly adapted versions of it take me back to the first meal that I ate on that very special vacation (which also happened to be my birthday dinner): Kalua Pork and Pineapple pizza, which I enjoyed along with a Mai Tai cocktail with my new husband overlooking the beach at the resort where we were staying. The Kalua Pork was even tastier at the luau that we attended our final night in Kauai.

I first sought out recipes for Kalua Pork as a way for my husband and me to relive our honeymoon. While I still cherish those memories, these days I value the recipe that I have developed even more because it is an easy way to feed my family. As a working mother of two, I appreciate that this is an easy meal to prepare in my slow cooker, and that the leftover meat is easily adapted for use in various other recipes.

I adapted these recipes from various recipes that I found online, using only ingredients readily available in a small city in the Midwest. I serve the meat over rice on the first day, and then utilize the leftover meat in various other ways throughout the week. The leftover meat also freezes well for future use.

Amid the COVID-19 pandemic in spring 2020, I received requests from various friends and relatives to participate in a Quarantine recipe exchange:

> Going back to old times with a recipe exchange! As the world is social distancing right now, many of us are experimenting in our kitchens to help pass the time. So you have been invited to be a part of a #QuarantineCooking recipe exchange!

My thoughts immediately went to this combination of recipes, which rely on readily available ingredients, most of which are pantry staples. In the early days of stay-at-home orders, many grocery stores were sold out of long-grain rice and flour tortillas. And virus outbreaks at meat processing plants are likely to make pork roasts more difficult to find in the coming days. When I have managed to acquire these normally readily available ingredients, these recipes have provided

---

[3] "A Brief History of Plate Lunches in Hawaii—Hawaii Ocean Project"; meghan, "Top 5 Favorite Hawaii Plate Lunch Foods," Text, Hawaii Magazine, January 15, 2014, https://www.hawaiimagazine.com/blogs/hawaii_today/2014/1/15/top_five_favorite_Hawaii_plate_lunch_menu_foods.

[4] "The WWII Origins of Spam in Asian American Cuisine | Time," accessed April 13, 2020, https://time.com/5593886/asian-american-spam-cuisine/; Bruddah Ron, "What the Heck Is Spam Musubi!?," *The Hawaii Plan* (blog), March 8, 2019, http://www.thehawaiiplan.com/what-is-spam-musubi/.

a degree of comfort and culinary variety to our mundane existence at home. The simplicity of these recipes is also welcome as I seek to balance working from home and full-time childcare.

Notice that my preferred combination of recipes reflect the diverse culinary not only of Hawaii but of twenty-first-century Midwestern American culture.

Day 1: Serve finely-shredded pork over freshly-cooked long grain rice.
Day 2: Hawaiian fried rice (see recipe below).
Day 3: Pulled pork burritos
Day 4: Baked potatoes topped with cheese, pork, BBQ sauce, and green onions

Note: I freely adapted these recipes over time through experimentation, and never measure ingredients as I add them. I offer here my best guess as to how I typically prepare these dishes.

"Kalua" Pork

6-10 lbs bone-in pork shoulder roast (formerly called Boston Butt roast)
2-4 Tbsp Liquid Smoke
1-2 Tbsp coarse sea salt
2 cups cooked long-grain rice (8 cups total if also making fried rice—see recipe below)

Trim visible fat from the pork roast. Pierce the remaining meat 10-20 times with the tip of your knife. Then rub Liquid Smoke and salt into the meat. Transfer to a slow cooker, and cook on Low until the meat is fully cooked and falling off the bone, and can be easily shredded with a large fork. An 8-lb roast will take approximately 9 hours on Low.

Remove the bone and discard. Use meat shredding claws or a pair of large serving forks to shred the meat to your desired consistency—finely shredded for eating by itself over rice; coarse for fried rice. (You can do this right in the slow cooker crock.) Stir the meat to combine with the pan juices. Return to the slow cooker for an additional 15-30 minutes on low to allow the meat to absorb the juices.

Hawaiian Fried Rice

2 Tbsp + 1 tsp vegetable oil
1 tsp sesame oil
2 cloves garlic, minced
0.5 tsp fresh ginger, minced
2 eggs
6 cups cold, dry long grain rice (day old rice works best)
2-4 Tbsp soy sauce
1 cup frozen peas & diced carrots, thawed and drained
1 cup Kalua pork (coarsely shredded works best)
1 15-oz. can pineapple tidbits, drained well
3 green onions, sliced (green parts only)

Heat the 1 tsp oil in a small skillet. Lightly scramble the eggs and cook in the skillet over medium heat until mostly done, but still very soft. Set aside.

Meanwhile, heat the 2 Tbsp vegetable oil and 1 tsp sesame oil in a wok or large skillet over medium-high heat. Add the garlic and ginger and cook, stirring constantly, for 1 minute. Add the rice and stir fry until lightly brown. Add soy sauce to taste and continue to stir until the brown color of the soy sauce is evenly distributed.

Warm the shredded pork gently in the microwave and drain off juices. Add the pork, peas & carrots, and scrambled egg to the rice, and stir fry until well combined. Remove from heat, and stir in the drained pineapple and green onions.

Notes:
This is one of my elder daughter's favorite recipes. A friend who emigrated from China as a child also often prepares fried rice for his family. His version uses medium-grain sushi rice and whatever proteins and vegetables he has on hand, often including an ingredient more typical of twenty-first-century American life: leftover rotisserie-roasted chicken from the local grocery store. His eldest daughter objected to my inclusion of ginger in my version, and she and her sisters were not impressed by the presence of pineapple that is my daughters' favorite part. Feel free to adapt to your own family's tastes. I leave off the green onions for my kids, and offer extra soy sauce and extra pork at the table.

My seven-year-old recently decided she does not like kalua pork, and will only eat the rice, vegetables, and pineapple out of this dish. To provide an easy substitute protein for her, I fry up 1 or 2 extra eggs when I make Hawaiian fried rice, and melt lots of Colby-Jack cheese over the top.

—52—

Breadfruit Stew

Diana Chen

Republic of the Marshall Islands and Springdate, Arkansas, USA, 21st Century

The unassuming town of Springdale, Arkansas, temperate and landlocked, has recently become home to thousands of migrants from the Republic of the Marshall Islands (RMI). As the Islands are increasingly inundated by the rising Pacific, more Marshallese are expected to resettle in Springdale, with their foodways and other traditions in tow. Three thousand miles from Springdale, the RMI's major population centers have undergone a nutritional transition from the ancestral diet after centuries of colonialism, war, and nuclear testing. However, on the more rural coral atolls many people still live a mostly subsistence lifestyle based on breadfruit agroforestry and fishing. The following recipe is adapted from one gifted to me during fieldwork conducted in Springdale, where breadfruit (alas, from the Caribbean) is seasonally available at niche grocery stores. Note that ripe breadfruit will have a white residue on its skin. This recipe appropriately blends breadfruit and coconut milk, traditional Marshallese staples, with certain Asian seasonings (the Islands were at one time colonized by Japan), and the chicken bouillon and processed vegetables more characteristic of home cooking in the Midwest. This stew can easily be veganized by substituting faux chicken bouillon. Enjoy it the Marshallese way – with family and friends!

Breadfruit Stew

5 cups of water
2 bay leaves
3 cups of breadfruit, peeled and cut into small pieces
1 tbsp. vegetable oil
1 small onion, cut into small pieces
5 cloves minced garlic
2 tbsp. grated ginger
2 tsp. curry powder
2 tbsp. chicken bouillon
1 can of red kidney beans, drained and rinsed
1 can of white kidney beans, drained and rinsed

2 cups of frozen peas, corn, or mixed vegetables
2 cups of cabbage or other vegetables, cut into small pieces
1 cup of coconut milk

1. Bring water to a boil in a large pot. Add breadfruit and bay leaves and boil for 20 minutes.
2. Meanwhile, cook onion in vegetable oil on medium-high heat for five minutes. Add garlic and ginger and cook for one more minute.
3. Add the onion, garlic, ginger, curry powder, bouillon, and beans to the breadfruit. Return to a boil. Then reduce to medium heat and cook for another 10-15 minutes.
4. Add cabbage and peas. Cook for 5 more minutes or until vegetable are tender.
5. Remove from heat and stir in coconut milk. Remove bay leaves, then serve.

—54—

North Fareway Visit, March 23, 2020

Pamela Riney-Kehrberg

This is my account of a visit to a grocery store in Ames, Iowa, in the midst of the COVID-19 pandemic. It had been more than a week since I shopped, and both my mother and I needed food. She's over 80, diabetic, and on lockdown with everyone else at her senior living facility, so I was shopping for both of us. Most of what I wanted was basic food: fruit, vegetables, *ingredients*. I had no need of meat—we buy our protein in bulk from local farmers. I cook from scratch nearly every day, and am an avid baker, so having to do my own cooking holds no terrors for me. Weeks on weeks of my own cooking may get boring for me and for my family, but we will definitely eat well. After reading other people's FaceBook accounts of bare shelves, I was, however, nervous about what I would find at my usual grocery store, part of a small chain that operates in Iowa, Minnesota, and Illinois.

The store was much busier than it normally would have been on a Monday morning at 9:00. The store had opened up at 8:00 for the elderly and others at higher risk. I arrived just as the store opened to everyone else. There was plenty of fruit and vegetables, although it was clear something had to be missing. I didn't figure out what, but the produce had been artfully re-arranged. A few kinds of canned soup were gone, like classic tomato and chicken and noodle, but there was still a lot of soup. There were plenty of canned beans—plenty of pop. The deli meat was sparse, and had, again, been artfully arranged to hide what was missing. There were, for example, no large tubs, but lots of smaller, more expensive packages. The tortillas had been ransacked, but there were still a few packages. There was no ramen or cup noodles. All the spaghetti was gone, but there were still other kinds of pasta. There was very little flour—and none of the good stuff (meaning King Arthur) was available. No yeast for baking. Someone had put out a product I had never seen before—instant sourdough starter. There was no t.p., and hadn't been since late last week. The cheese was a little sparse, but not bad. Eggs were limited to one carton per person, but there were plenty. The poor checker looked exhausted, and told me he had been working 12 hour days. He also told me that the company normally loads 80 truckloads to send out each day, but today they were sending out 180. The man who wheeled my groceries out had worked the day before to stock shelves, even though the store is normally closed on Sunday. There was plenty of food, just not exactly what some people may have wanted.

Figure 54.1: Baking bread by Pamela Riney-Kehrberg. We are baking regularly. My son needs sourdough bread, and it is hit or miss if we can find it. So, we bake.

And off I went with an expensive load of groceries, some of which I left by my mother's back door. I had bought a couple extra items—say, two jars of spaghetti sauce, just in case. I had also purchased some treats, like jellybeans, M & Ms, and cashews, so we wouldn't feel deprived. Our refrigerator is full, the basement pantry likewise: two weeks of food on hand, and ready for consumption, as we wait out the virus.

—53—

Doing the Heavy Lifting: Gender Roles and Consumption in the Age of COVID-19

Virginia Scharff

As I sit writing this, we are into our fourth month of pandemic self-isolation. A novel coronavirus, known as COVID-19, came to the United States at the beginning of the year, and all signs point to many more months of widespread infection and death. In the wave of business closures that followed, forty million people have filed for unemployment—so far. Eight days ago, a Minneapolis police officer named Derek Chauvin murdered an African American man, George Floyd, setting off a week of protests and disorder across the nation, with no end in sight. Every night brings fresh outrage, and renewed pain. Meanwhile, Donald Trump, purportedly President of the United States, tweets and cowers, poses and spews incoherent words decipherable only as hate messages. We are in a hell of a mess.

Hundreds of thousands have taken to the streets. But even as they confront the racist history of our nation, and some smaller element seeks to use this moment of horror to spark chaos, millions of Americans, I think, continue to stay mostly at home. Amid all the fear and tension, we are trying to work, trying to tend our families, trying to hold it together. I cannot help but imagine the pain of trying to survive when you've lost your job, or experienced violence, or cannot afford food or health care. I cannot imagine the terror of being without shelter at this time.

I try to contemplate what has changed, and what persists. For me, and I suspect for many other middle class, white women, feeding our families is an essential task, and a significant source of self-worth. But getting, processing, and preparing food has changed. Trying to minimize our risk of catching the virus, middle-class Americans like me are shopping less often for more things, making do with what we have. Between ventures out into grocery stores, dealing with the haphazardness and frustration of online orders, and cleaning, cleaning, cleaning, the work of consumption has become more fraught. From stocking up on essentials to midnight vigils pursuing a lucky click for a delivery, to disciplined hand-washing and disinfecting, we have become hyper-conscious of the supply chain in novel ways.

While I am ambivalent about how useful it might be to compare what we are going through with war, the metaphor keeps popping up. Way back in March, anticipating months of self-isolation (we are both over 60), my husband, Chris, and I jokingly cast ourselves in the roles of the Union stalwarts who ramped up the volunteer efforts that did so much to deliver victory in the Civil War. I declared myself household Quartermaster. Chris appointed himself founder of the Sanitary Commission. I told him he was made for the part of Dorothea Dix. He responded that he was made to reenact Frederick Law Olmsted. Gender fluidity goes only so far on this home front. Turns out, that has been the case in households and villages living through rapid social and technological change, in many, many places and times.

At this strange moment in history, I have thought often of my late friend and feminist mentor, Kathy Jensen. I've wondered what she would think and do, how she would adjust, what insights she would have. Jensen came to know how stubborn gender could be, in the course of her remarkable career as a sociologist, working with rural women across the world, from Chinle, Arizona, to Katmandu, Nepal, by way of St. Onge, Riverton, Cairo and Laramie. Kathy grew up on a ranch in the shadow of Bear Butte, in the Black Hills of South Dakota. She went on to become one of those pioneering feminist scholars of the 1970s and '80s, part of a stunningly original community of thinkers, many of them working in the American West. They showed us why we needed to understand women's work, and their insights reconfigured our understanding of technology, of production and reproduction, of the relation of the domestic world to public life.[1] Jensen's 1983 article, unforgettably titled, "Mother Calls Herself a Housewife, But She Buys Bulls," was based not only on her personal history, but on dozens of oral history interviews conducted in 1979 and 1980 for the Wyoming Heritage and Contemporary Values Project. Jensen and her colleagues found that rural women developed "a higher level of skills and more diverse technological competence than is usually expected of urban women (and most urban men)." Rural women perpetually crossed those economic and ideological boundaries between domestic and public production, between men's and women's work. Their labor was essential to the family's ability to survive and thrive, to communities, and to larger social entities. But even as such work was valued, ranch families, like other families, maintained gendered identities, and mostly sustained gender inequality.[2]

Jensen studied women's work in rural settings ranging from the Navajo reservation in Arizona and the Wind River Reservation of Wyoming, to the Powder River Basin and the Black Hills, to the Nile Delta in Egypt and the rural villages of Nepal. She was always attentive to cultural histories, sensitive yet unsentimental. Jensen often collaborated with her husband, sociologist Audie Blevins, working on poverty in Native communities in Wyoming, investigating microfinancing of women's enterprises in Nepal. Her 1994 article about Egyptian women in agriculture, in *Frontiers: A Journal of Women's Studies*, opened with an unforgettable im-

[1] For pathbreaking work, see Judy Smith, *Something Old, Something New, Something Borrowed, Something Due: Women and Appropriate Technology* (Butte, Montana and Washington, D.C.: National Center for Appropriate Technology, 1978); *Women and Technology: Deciding What's Appropriate* (Missoula, MT: Montana Committee for the Humanities, 1979); Joan Rothschild, ed., *Machina ex Dea: Feminist Perspectives on Technology* (New York: Pergamon Press, 1983).

[2] Katherine Jensen, "Mother Calls Herself a Housewife, But She Buys Bulls," in Jan Zimmerman, ed., *The Technological Woman* (Westport, CT: Praeger Press, 1983), 136-144.

age. A man in western dress drove a combine, while two women wearing *galabiyas* stood on the back of the combine, filling fifty-kilo sacks with wheat. The women tied and lifted the full sacks onto the head of another traditionally dressed woman, who then carried the grain out of the field. That piece was titled, "Who Carries the Load? Who Carries the Cash? Work and Status among Egyptian Farm Women." Jensen had a gift for noticing and naming the stickiness of gender in the face of technological change.[3]

In addition to being a founding mother of women's studies at the University of Wyoming, Kathy was entirely undaunted by hanging sheetrock, doing home plumbing, and of course, loading sacks of feed, herding cows and dealing with chickens in all their glory. As a child on the ranch, she had learned to be ready to tackle any job. Her mother had been stricken with childhood polio, an illness that had lifelong consequences. Jensen children knew that they were expected to step in and help out with every job on the farm. Kathy cooked huge meals for harvesting crews when she was just old enough to heft heavy pots, and drove to town for supplies before she had reached the legal age to get a license.

We lost Kathy to breast cancer in 2010, and I miss her all the time. I have wished for her company often, in these early months of the COVID-19 pandemic, wondering what she would think about the new ways in which we are producing and provisioning and processing and consuming the things we eat. In addition to being ready for any kind of work, she was an inspired and resourceful cook and passionate gardener and an accomplished seamstress, all valuable skills in times of crisis, and three traditional areas of women's work. She would be thinking in structural terms about what she was doing, every time she patched a pair of jeans, planted a seed, turned yet another pot of beans into cassoulet.

Many of us are approaching the tasks of household production and consumption with new focus in the age of COVID-19. Some friends and family seem to relish the kind of labor-intensive work that housewives did before mass production. I do wonder how household members parcel out this intensified domestic work. History tells us that in times of national crisis, women do a disproportionate share of noncommodified work (often called, simply, "consumption," or "reproduction"). Home sewing, for example, has made a big comeback; women and girls I know (no men, at least in my circle) are sewing masks for their friends and family, and cranking out dozens more to be sent to essential workers. I'd be willing to bet that everyday meal planning and cooking remains mostly women's work, but I would like to know for certain. Bread baking, especially with homegrown sourdough starter, has become a national obsession, and I'd love to know who's doing most of the kneading.

Gardening surges. Everyone who has a little bit of dirt, and even some who have only a couple of pots and a balcony, seems to be doing their version of urban or suburban homesteading. I've grown organic vegetables for more than forty years, and have never been gladder that I started my journey into adulthood as a back-to-the-land hippie. Still, I temper my sweet memories of gardening in the

[3] Katherine Jensen, "Who Carries the Load? Who Carries the Cash? Work and Status among Egyptian Farm Women," *Frontiers: A Journal of Women's Studies* 15, no. 2 (1994): 133-152.

Figure 53.1: Raised garden beds. Author's private collection.

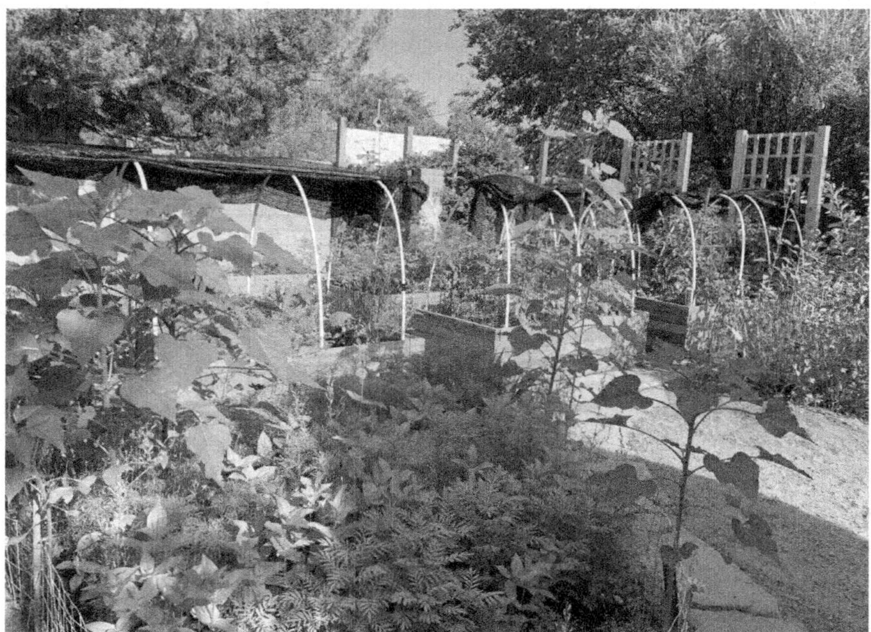

Figure 53.2: Hoop houses. Author's private collection.

golden mists of dawn and dusk with a healthy dose of irony. Back in the days of commune living, our house had a hand mill to grind wheat berries for bread baking. At least one of those loaves proved equal to the task of driving a nail through a wooden counter. There was goat milk so rank that cheese made from it could not really be kept in the house. One member of the household thought we should keep not only a compost bucket for vegetable trimmings, but also a "soup bucket" for refuse that he considered edible. Other house members referred to the products of his culinary innovation as "compost soup."

In that communal household, there was plenty of gender sentimentality. Women often played the part of Earth Mothers in long skirts and peasant blouses, men flaunting their masculinity as they built cabins in the fields, their own little Waldens. At the same time, counterculture stereotypes frayed at the edges as incipient feminist consciousness inched its way in. As historian Gretchen Lemke-Santangelo reminded us, women in the counterculture were pivotal in sustaining community at the time, ambivalent about or openly critical of the sexism they encountered, and crucial in bringing some countercultural values into the mainstream, from body positivity to environmentalism.[4]

I didn't really buy the Earth Mother thing even then, though I did enjoy a good prairie skirt. I was always skeptical of the nostalgia for the pre-industrial, labor-intensive household production that usually falls on the shoulders of women. I remember very well when, a few years after my time on the farm, Ivan Illich published *Gender*, a manifesto to return to the "natural," pre-feminist order of things. Illich celebrated the delights of each family raising and slaughtering its own pigs, each woman joyfully rendering lard.[5] It didn't sound like fun to me. Twenty years later, I reflected on the ways in which the industrial order fails to account for women's unpaid consumption work, in an article about the persistence of gender blindness in environmental history. As evidence that not all work in our world is rationalized, mechanized, and commodified, I weighed my groceries and calculated the monthly tonnage of the repetitive lifting I did, getting things off the supermarket shelf, and taking them to where they would reside in my house. Turned out to be a lot of hefting, before the first egg was scrambled, or the first counter wiped off. It was third grade math, but I think I made the point.[6]

Just as invisibility underscores inequality, sentimentality is another tool of patriarchal power. When I wrote about Thomas Jefferson's perpetual celebration of "the tender and tranquil amusements of domestic life," I made it my business to point out what kind of heavy work was actually going on back at Monticello,

[4] Gretchen Lemke-Santangelo, *Daughters of Aquarius: Women in the Sixties Counterculture* (Lawrence: University Press of Kansas, 2009).

[5] Ivan Illich, *Gender* (New York: Pantheon Books, 1983)

[6] Virginia Scharff, "Man and Nature: Sex Secrets of Environmental History," in Virginia J. Scharff, ed., *Seeing Nature through Gender* (Lawrence, KS: University of Kansas Press, 2003), 3-20.

Figure 53.3: Tomato. Author's private collection.

while Jefferson was off writing the Declaration of Independence and dancing at the court of Louis XVI and inventing a country. His wife, his daughters, his sons, his enslaved concubine and all the enslaved people upon whom he depended, were doing everything from slaughtering scores of hogs and chickens to planting and hoeing and harvesting his celebrated garden and his less famous tobacco, carting water, brewing beer, spinning and weaving, manufacturing nails, caring for and burying and mourning each other.[7]

Decades of reflecting on and struggling over the gendering of domestic work have made me hyper-aware of the politics of housework. Race and class and gender matter. Our 2020 quarantine house in Albuquerque is well stocked, almost too comfortable, a prosperous home for Anglo cis-hetero geezers-in-training. We are both retired professors, working part-time for others. Nobody around here needs homeschooling, nobody is going out to work a shift in a hospital or a grocery store. Everybody has a pension and health insurance. We are white. That makes all the difference in a culture where black and brown and Native people are always, always at risk.

So, we are pretty calm and secure, and we have time to grow things, obtain supplies, and process and prepare food more meticulously than ever before. For the first time in all these decades, I'm sprouting tomatoes, celery, eggplants and peppers from seed, in flats of plastic pots saved from years of trips to local nurseries for plant starts. After thirty years of gardening in this yard, last year we worked with our kids to build raised beds in wooden boxes, with gorgeous trellises, designed by my daughter's woodworker boyfriend. We called the project a "climate

[7] Virginia Scharff, *The Women Jefferson Loved* (New York: HarperCollins, 2010).

Figure 53.4: Skororat Commune, 1974-75. Author's private collection.

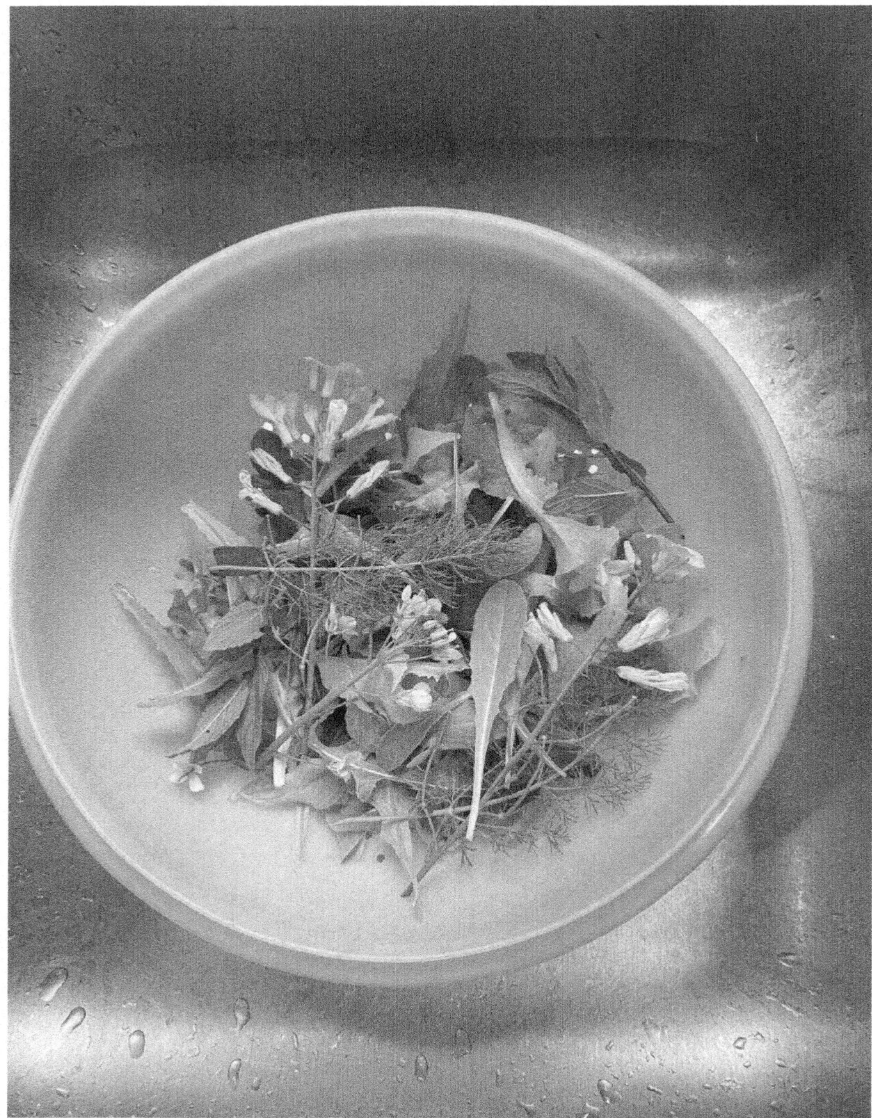

Figure 53.5: Salad Greens. Author's private collection.

and life cycle adaptation," because we couldn't keep water in the ground level beds any more, with summers increasingly too hot and dry to grow tomatoes and peppers. My annual bean-harvesting backache had become too high a price to pay for those perfect *haricots verts*. We got serious about shade cloth, which made a big difference. This year, we cranked things up early in the years with plastic covered hoop houses over two beds, with the result that we were, for a couple of months, the Albuquerque Lettuce Repository. We have been sharing our embarrassing abundance of lovely salads by leaving bags of greens on our front porch for pickups. As lettuces begin to bolt and get too bitter to eat, I yank them up and put in tomato and pepper plants currently waiting their turn on the back wall. Some of last year's crops have re-seeded in the beds. When I found a couple of volunteer Brandywine tomato seedlings, I nearly wept. Kathy Jensen would understand.

I've known for most of my life that growing your own food is hugely satisfying both to the taste buds and to the sense of self-esteem. But let's face it. The hobby horticulture we practice is not cheap. Somebody once offered the opinion that each of their home-grown tomatoes cost $5.00. Ours may be a little more expensive, given how much we spend, making sure they get enough water here in the desert. Some of them are heirloom varieties, notoriously tricky and susceptible to disease. All of them demand drip irrigation, at a time when we know that climate change is making our part of the world hotter and drier. Those delicious homegrown tomatoes come with a side of guilt. The flowers that I love so much are probably even less entitled to their share of the region's beleaguered aquifer. Nevertheless, I persist, trying to use water ever more efficiently, and likely failing.

As devoutly as I've gardened, I've also cooked. My mother was a brilliant, passionate, adventurous cook. We used to brag that she was the first Jewish lady in St. Louis to buy a wok. I learned by watching and helping in the kitchen, by helping her type out many of her best loved recipes, and by being lucky enough to inherit her hundred cookbooks. By now, I don't use recipes much, believing that I have enough experience and skill to know how to substitute what I have for what I might otherwise use. Sometimes, the experiments go a little awry, but most of the time, I am able to balance the bitter, the sweet, the salty, and the sour, and throw in a little umami. I've followed my mom in always having a pantry that borders on hoarder status. But now, finding a can of not-quite-expired tomatoes or olives at the back of a shelf, or a not-too-freezer-burned bag of some bygone garden produce or supermarket protein in the depths of the freezer, feels a little like a treasure hunt. For someone who's long cooked with what's on hand, and kept a lot of stuff on hand, this is a moment that offers potential for satisfaction in making delicious meals, adaptable leftovers, things to leave on the porch for family and friends.

What luxury. Here in our cocoon, amid political rage, the need for truth and justice about our racist past and present, pandemic stress and all, we are endlessly aware of our extraordinary good fortune, built on the backs of those with far less. As I sit here lamenting the canceled travel plans and postponed celebrations, I know that my problems are those of a very lucky few. The consequences for many Americans, those who have lost health, lost loved ones, lost jobs and businesses, lost so much in so many ways, are mounting fast. The dreadful repercussions of national incompetence, malevolence and mendacity, will last for years. The injustice we see around us demands to be addressed, and redressed.

While we sit at home cultivating our own garden, we aren't by any means self-sufficient. We are more and more mindful of the people risking their lives to keep us safe, to care for us when we cannot care for ourselves, to produce what we want and need. Industrial agriculture and corporate food processing and grocery retail, lavishly fertilized with government subsidies, offer artificially cheap commodities, produced at every turn by horribly underpaid and exploited workers. Every night brings more stories about the hazardous conditions farm-workers face, and fresh hellish news of virus outbreaks in meatpacking plants, which Trump has declared to be "essential businesses." Growers and plant managers insist that sick workers are not entitled to stay home to get well, that their illnesses do not qualify as "work-related," that workers who refuse to put themselves at risk cannot collect unemployment. Racism and xenophobia horribly compound the injury. Those vicious forces underwrite my comfort.

So here I sit, making out a grocery list for the next brave foray into the anxious marketplace, omitting the pork shoulder I was thinking would make great carnitas. There is no need for someone to get sick because I want to make tacos. I'm thinking about Florence Kelley, and her effort, through the National Consumers' League, to unite housewives with workers laboring in unsafe conditions, back at the turn of the twentieth century. I'm thinking of Caesar Chavez and Dolores Huerta, organizing the United Farmworkers and getting consumers all over the nation to boycott table grapes until the growers gave in. If ever there was a moment for such an alliance between producers and consumers, this is that moment. Never let a crisis go to waste.

As I rummage through my refrigerator, my pantry, my garden beds, I'm contemplating putting together something that will be, I hope, a step up from compost soup. I'm thinking about Kathy Jensen talking to rural women the world over, trying to understand their essential work, in houses and fields and factories, in good times and bad. Even in isolation, I feel the connection to Kathy and all those who broke the trail for me, and to the women and men whose labor enables my comfort, my health, my survival. This impulse to connect, I think, must be the beginning of a new way of thinking in a perilous world made more dangerous still by those who would tear us apart. The Age of Aquarius isn't going to get out there and dawn, all by itself.

Postscript, January 1, 2021

As we enter a second year of coping with the COVID-19 pandemic, I am stunned by what has changed since last May, and what has not. I found a stash of heirloom beans and chicos (dried corn), grown in San Luis by Chris's friend Arnie Valdez, in a bag in our pantry. I took this as a good omen, discovering them just in time to cook them up for our first huevos rancheros of the year. I'd like to think that this lucky surprise was the Nuevo Mexico equivalent of New Year black-eyed peas.

Though we greet 2021 with hope, we are also still divided, fearful, resentful and beleaguered. We will get a new President, and for the first time, a woman Vice President, who believe in science and justice and equality and civil society. Vaccines make their way out onto the supply chain, painfully slowly. Millions more people are out of work, facing eviction, scared and increasingly desperate. The summer brought a bit of respite, some socializing with family and friends in the backyard, even a couple of visits to restaurant patios. The latter, it turned out, felt a little too risky to us, especially as the case numbers began to climb, then skyrocket, over the fall. I realize that my May musings only began to touch on masks. Now, when we venture forth from the bunker, we mask up, try to keep our distance from anyone we encounter, work to keep our cortisol levels from spiking when we're a little too close to anyone whose nose or, god forbid, mouth, we can see. People's very faces have been politicized.

And yet, what hasn't changed, but has in fact become increasingly clear, is that we will not have the means to recover from this global calamity if we succumb to barefaced toxic individualism. Isolated as we are, we have learned to connect in new ways, and to see those connections for the lifeline that they are. We have to know the histories that underlie present conflict, misery, contradiction. We need an awareness of how inequality of gender, race, class and nation have exacerbated our collective crisis. The very concept of a pandemic—a distant threat that becomes local, and cannot be mitigated without both global and local actions—challenges us to link our well-being to others, near and far.

In my little part of the world, our family and friends still exchange farm produce, cooked dinners, notes of encouragement, on our porches. Two new rescue dogs and a cat have joined the family. We're learning the art of patience. We're trying to take responsibility amid privilege. We're failing a lot, but this is a long game.

We dream of a life beyond isolation, a time of gathering together again. I imagine a potluck dinner at a long table, each contributing in their own way, all welcome. There will be something to eat for everyone. I will finally stop re-watching seasons of "The Great British Baking Show," and get to taste some of the epic sourdough bread an ambitious friend has been perfecting and sharing on social media, all self-deprecation and mouth-watering photos.

I pray that we'll know how to make sure there's enough, and everyone will get a taste. But it won't be soon. The year has shown us that we can take nothing for granted, that we have to act with purpose and bravery. That's something my baking friends understand. Everything takes time to rise.

—55—

Pam's Pandemic Soup

Pamela Riney-Kehrberg
Iowa, USA, 2020s

This soup is an adaptation of a recipe that appears in Martha Engstrom's *Grandma's Farm Country Cookbook,* which reprints a collection of recipes from *The Farmer's Wife*, dating to the nineteen-teens, twenties and thirties.[1] I have taken a bean chowder recipe, and updated it to fit our tastes and what was sitting in my cupboards and freezer.

The soup grew out of the realization that my son, not in school and stranded at home with mom and dad, vastly prefers homemade soup and bread for lunch to sandwiches and other lunch fare. The soup also took advantage of bacon from the whole hog in our freezer, and beans I had purchased but never used. The soup would be equally good made with ham. I have chosen to use navy beans because they were what I had at hand, but any kind of dried bean would work. Navy beans are particularly nice because they are small, and cook more quickly than most dried beans. The Sriracha was a definite change to the original recipe, but an adaptation suited to modern taste buds that go for a bit more spice.

Pam's Pandemic Soup

2 cups dried navy beans
1 large onion
1 large can (28 oz.) diced tomatoes
1 pound bulk bacon, cubed
Black pepper, salt, Sriracha, to taste

Navy beans require soaking. Place 2 cups navy beans in six cups hot water, and allow to soak for at least two hours. Then drain the beans, put in a large pot, cover with water, adding an inch or two of water above the level of the beans. Bring to a boil, and then reduce to a simmer, and cook for at least an hour. After an hour, fry the bacon, and add the onion (diced), cooking until the bacon is to your taste, and the onion translucent. Drain thoroughly, and add to the water and beans in the pot. Add the can of tomatoes. Add additional water if the soup is too thick for your taste. Cook for at least an hour. Season with pepper, salt, and Sriracha to taste. I used 1-2 tablespoons of Sriracha, for a moderately spicy soup.

---

[1] "Bean Chowder," in Martha Engstrom, *Grandma's Farm Country Cookbook* (Stillwater, MN: Voyageur Press, 1996), 13.

—56—

COVID Reflection

Sara Egge

Most days I work on our kitchen table next to my five-year-old daughter. COVID transformed our kitchen table into my home office because my husband works in the spare-bedroom-turned-office. Before my two-year-old son went back to daycare mid-summer, my daughter and I usually worked side-by-side in the afternoons because then he napped. By August, my daughter transitioned to working on a Chromebook lent to us by her school district. Virtual kindergarten was relentless, convening six hours a day with only a few short breaks.

When naptime was worktime, I got an hour-and-a-half on a good day. The rest I cobbled together in pieces, snatching a few minutes in the evenings or on weekends. The bulk of my worktime happened after dark, when the three other members of my family slept soundly upstairs. Late into the night I plodded, revising syllabi for hybrid learning or grading papers once classes began in the fall.

It was no secret before the pandemic how precious childcare is, but the pandemic has forced many caregivers into desperation. My small central Kentucky town already had garnered the label "childcare desert" by a local childcare taskforce, and securing a spot in one of the few facilities was cause for celebration. When daycares and schools shut down in March, parents had to make difficult choices. I was three weeks away from traveling to archives in three cities, part of a sabbatical research plan that I had anticipated for three years. Instead of pouring through naturalization records, I became the only caregiver to our two kids opposite my "essential worker" husband. For four months, I labored at home, the routine changing only when daycare reopened in July. I prepped all my fall classes in a mad rush.

What saved me was not an institutional resource, policy change, or community initiative. This pandemic splintered and distanced us, and like so many others, our household became an impenetrable fortress. Within mine, my husband contributed as best he could despite grueling work expectations, but it soon became clear that he couldn't give enough. I wasn't alone. Two colleagues and I began texting plans to form a "pod school," taking a day or two each week to host our trio of kids while they completed virtual school. Our close contacts became theirs, and my daughter soon sat with her Chromebook not only at my kitchen table but at the kitchen tables of these two women.

"Pod school" was a privilege, one for which I am grateful. It was also messy and chaotic. It allowed me to complete the basic functions of my job, but the pandemic—and the burden it places on working parents—continues to cut deep. I often hear people say how grateful they are that the pandemic forced them to slow down and break away from the hustle-and-bustle. I do not share their sentiments. I have never labored more with fewer resources. And I did not have to face institutional racism, economic hardship, or healthcare inequalities.

The absence of regular and reliable school and childcare created the most upheaval in our pandemic lives, so I found comfort in the familiarity of cooking meals for my family. Even before COVID, we ate most of our meals at home because our small town lacks abundant restaurant options. Over the last few years, we've practiced our culinary techniques, improving our abilities as home cooks. We like to eat a variety of dishes, a wider array than we did as a midwestern kids, but at the heart of our cuisine is our shared rural upbringing.

Both our families had large deep freezers, extensive pantries, and sizeable kitchens. Gender divided the labor of each family member, and we never really questioned it. Our mothers planted massive gardens each year, canning, freezing, drying, and otherwise preserving all the produce they raised. Our fathers hunted and fished, and we either raised ourselves or purchased from neighboring farmers most of the pork, beef, and poultry that we ate. I often sheepishly say that I was in high school before I realized that not every family prepared their daily meals by grabbing jars full of home-canned produce from basement shelves and packages of home-raised meat from deep freezers.

My husband and I have continued the foodways of our families. Every year we bring back a quarter of beef raised on my parent's farm, carefully stacking the roasts, steaks, and other cuts in our deep freeze. Kentucky's growing season allows us to enjoy spinach, kale, lettuce, radishes, and peas in spring and again in the fall. My raised beds then shift to summer plantings and tomatoes, peppers, squash, cucumber, carrots, and okra, which begin from seeds that sprout in cartons in my laundry room. These are annual routines, ones that COVID did not dictate. But I appreciated them more this year, in part because they took my mind off the uncertainty of the virus and the tedium of home isolation.

COVID did not dramatically change the home cooking we did. We shopped weekly, as we did before, but I went alone, with a mask on my face and hand sanitizer applied in the car. Sometimes we cooked recipes honed over the years, full of flavor and fancy ingredients. But since the arrival of our two young kids, we often kept our meals simple. After quickly clearing the kitchen table of the papers, books, and devices used only minutes before mealtime, we sat down to the chorus that accompanies a meal with small children—"Mama, can I have ketchup on my rice?" … "I dropped my fork!" … "Eat your peas!" … "Please don't lick the table."

After washing the last dish and putting away any leftovers, I moved the papers, books, and devices back to the kitchen table.

—57—

Life Amid a Pandemic

Cynthia C. Prescott

"Normal" Life

In "normal" life I am a university professor married to another university professor. We have two daughters, who normally attend an afterschool program at their elementary school. Both girls are passionate about the performing arts, so we squeeze in piano lessons, dance classes, gymnastics lessons, and play rehearsals, in addition to church and Girl Scout activities, in the evenings and weekends. I squeeze in grocery shopping on weekends, in between dropping the girls off and picking them up from their various extracurricular activities. Or I take my younger daughter shopping with me, which is one of the few times we are alone together. Being at the end of the supply chain in a smaller city in northern North Dakota, our grocery options are limited. I plan meals and shopping trips carefully, alternating between my local grocery chain and the SuperTarget big box store, usually adding a stop at the warehouse club that is the only store in town with consistently fresh produce.

Most days, the girls eat breakfast and lunch in their school cafeteria/gymnasium. While I'm not thrilled about the nutritional value of the highly processed cold cereal, chicken nuggets, and the like that they eat at school, I love the convenience of not needing to prepare and serve them those two meals each day, and not having to argue with them about what I will serve or pack them. Dinnertime is harried enough. We all return home shortly before 6 p.m. tired and "hangry" (hungry and cranky), so my husband does his best to entertain the girls and ease their transition from school to home as I rush to get a meal on the table. After dinner, one of us supervises the girls' piano practice while the other does the dishes. So far we've managed to maintain a family dinner table, but I know that is likely to fall by the wayside as my girls reach middle and high school.

Preparing and serving meals is stressful on top of a full-time job. During the week, my husband and I largely fend for ourselves on breakfast and lunch. I typically throw a Lean Cuisine® frozen entrée and a snack or two (plus my beloved soda) into an insulated lunch sack on my way out the door. I heat it in the microwave I keep in my campus office, then catch up on emails or Facebook as I eat. I live for my weekly "date lunches" with my husband. Although the number of both chain and local ethnic restaurants have increased dramatically in the past decade, we still periodically get bored with the dining options. But the opportunity to eat food I haven't had to plan or prepare, food that appeals to me rather than my picky children, and the hour of uninterrupted conversation with my spouse is priceless.

COVID-19 Crisis

Enter a global pandemic. The reality of the COVID-19 crisis began to take hold across the United States just as we were packing our bags for a long-awaited spring break trip to visit my husband's family in Arizona. While COVID hit San Francisco, California, and the Pacific Northwest hard by early March, there were only a handful of reported cases of the virus in Arizona, and none in North Dakota, so we felt safe enough embarking on a trip we had been planning for nearly a year. For the first few days, our vacation proceeded more or less as planned. On Saturday, we visited a crowded playground, and squeezed into long tables with hundreds of strangers to enjoy dinner and a show at Organ Stop Pizza. By Monday, the pizza lunch buffet at our favorite arcade was served by their kitchen staff, and we took lots of breaks for hand-washing. But the next day, things changed radically. Across the nation, state and city officials ordered restaurants and bars to close—or switch to carryout or delivery—rather than serve their anticipated St. Patrick's Day crowds. By the end of the week, grocery store shelves had been stripped of staples such as bread and pasta, and even of baking basics like flour and sugar.

Just before we left for Arizona, our university announced it was moving all classes online for two weeks following spring break. Our daughters' school district closed for a few days. By the time we returned a week later, the university had ordered most staff to work from home, and moved instruction online through the summer. It became apparent that our children would be home for the remainder of their school year. My husband and I suddenly had become full-time caregivers to our children, even as we had to work twice as hard to redesign all of our courses on the fly.

Stuck at home with bored children, food became one of our few forms of entertainment, even as it became increasingly difficult to acquire. Rather than eating most of their meals at school, and contentedly munching the same peanut-free snacks I packed each day to protect classmates with food allergies, now my children were eating three meals and two snacks a day at home. And because so many other parts of our lives were disrupted or less interesting, our usual go-to recipes suddenly felt tedious. But even acquiring our usual foods became challenging. Because we had traveled out of state, we were asked to "self-quarantine" at home for 14 days, meaning I couldn't even hunt our increasingly bare grocery store shelves. Instead, I began to order groceries online from the one store in town that offered that option, hoping that the items I requested would be available by my appointed pickup window four days later. I scoured the local newspaper and social media to find local restaurants offering "no-contact" delivery. We did our best to support our local eateries, and occasionally even convinced our children to sample more exotic cuisine. Once out of quarantine, I returned to grocery shopping in person. I shopped on weekday mornings to avoid crowds and wearing a cloth mask sewn

Figure 57.1: Pandemic Oreo macarons. Photo by Cynthia C. Prescott

for me by a friend using quilting fabric and elastic I had leftover from hobbies I pursued before I began balancing a full-time job and parenting. I visited only one store once a week by myself with a carefully organized shopping list to minimize time spent in the store, rotating among the three stores I used to frequent, stockpiling nonperishable items available at each one in turn. Two months into self-distancing, the local checkouts all installed Plexiglas shields to prevent spread of the virus. Scanning and paying for groceries on my smartphone grew suddenly appealing as another means to reduce contact with others.

With basics like bread and hotdog buns—not to mention hand sanitizer and toilet paper—increasingly scarce, and dramatically more time spent at home, many people turned to baking. The stress of offering my courses online while managing my kids' online learning left me with little time or energy to experiment with sourdough starter and the like. But my kids and I did embark on elaborate baking projects each weekend, projects for which we never would have found the time otherwise. Homemade soft pretzel twists—my first attempt at kneaded yeast dough—were a stunning success. Cutting out and decorating homemade conversation candy hearts and sugar cookies kept my kids busy for hours. Surprise deliveries of those candies and cookies to friends' doorsteps throughout the town took some of the sting out of canceling our annual Easter egg hunt. We even attempted finicky French Oreo *macarons*. Three hours of work to produce a lopsided almond flour meringue sandwich cookie that tastes a good bit like the manufactured treat from which it was made. And my daughters only liked the ones we rolled in leftover Oreo crumbs. Why didn't we do this sooner? (Figure 57.1)

As I stayed in touch with friends via Facebook and an occasional Zoom happy hour gathering, I was struck by how many of these changes have fallen to women. While we may aspire to egalitarian marriages, traditional gender role expectations persist. Whether they previously worked from home or not, most of our husbands did their best to replicate their previous work lives from home. Meanwhile, their wives ended up perching their laptop computers at the kitchen table, surrounded by their children's schoolwork, or squeezed temporary desks into closets. While some of my friends reported that their laundry has never been cleaner, those trips to the laundry room and to the pantry to fix yet another snack for hungry or bored children are yet more interruptions preventing them from focusing on their own careers. When encouraged to ask their fathers for assistance while Mom is in yet another Zoom meeting, our children whine, "But Dad is *working*."

And we were the lucky ones who are able to (attempt to) work from home. Millions of doctors, nurses, first responders, and food producers were on the front lines. Indeed, major breakouts of COVID-19 at meat processing plants cost lives of workers who could not afford the luxury of working from home with their children safely underfoot. Resulting plant closures began to disrupt supply chains throughout the US and beyond. And millions more Americans were unemployed, as their workplaces were forced to shut down to accommodate social distancing. Although statistics were not yet readily available, it became increasingly apparent that women were disproportionately being affected, because women disproportionately worked in the kinds of service-industry jobs most impacted by the shutdowns.

Learning to Adapt

Nine weeks into social distancing, my family settled into something of a routine. I even found time to hide out in my bedroom and reflect on our experiences as my children enjoyed yet more screen time. Because COVID-19 numbers remained relatively low in our area, our children were able to return to school in person when the new school year began in late August. But we pulled them out of afterschool programming and extracurricular activities to reduce contact, reducing our available workday from ten hours to less than seven, and leaving our kids looking to us to fill their evenings and weekends with exciting activities. Meanwhile, my husband and I scrambled to adapt some of our courses to entirely online delivery, while learning to teach others in a socially-distanced hybrid format. Students attending class face-to-face had to wear masks and remain six feet apart, making the debates and small-group work at the heart of my pedagogical methods extremely challenging. As the virus spread through our college town, growing numbers of students were forced to isolate or quarantine, and a growing percentage joined our classes remotely, testing the limits of our teaching creativity.

We found ways to make it work. I set up an office in our basement, and managed to squeeze in some research and writing time. Conferences I looked forward to attending were canceled, but the increasing reliance on web conferencing enabled me to participate in others that ordinarily would have been out of reach. I simplified our meals to accommodate disrupted supply chains, and we ordered more takeout food—primarily "family style" meals from locally-owned restaurants struggling to survive. I shopped online, and turned weekly trips to pick up groceries and library books "curbside" into what passed for adventures with my children by tacking on a run through a fast food drive-thru window for a treat. I enrolled our children in online music, craft, and gymnastics lessons, and ran biweekly Girl Scout troop meetings via Zoom. We filled our house with gym equipment to provide physical activity for energetic children confined to desks for six hours each day. I invented family outdoor adventures to fill our weekends. When we did not feel comfortable allowing our ten-year-old to attend her closest friend's birthday party at an indoor water park, I arranged an outdoor playdate to placate them. I rearranged a weekly meeting to carve out time for weekly date lunches with my husband—even braving disease exposure to dine *al fresco* at two local restaurants before dropping temperatures forced us back to eating takeout at home.

We made it work, but I found myself growing increasingly exhausted. I faced what Christina Bieber Lake calls "early onset winter."[1] As weeks turned into months, the light at the end of the tunnel grew dim. Decision fatigue set in as we had to adjust every aspect of our lives. Each of the many hats I ordinarily wore simultaneously became more difficult. Girl Scout troop supplies had to be ordered, sorted into packets for each individual scout, and delivered to their homes. Each precious playdate required extensive planning and negotiation with other mothers (but never fathers, who seemed content to just leave their children to play more video games alone in their rooms). Online enrichment activities had to be researched, their registrations managed, and required me to remain within earshot to resolve technical difficulties and fetch missing supplies. My children adapted to the changing circumstances, but at significant cost to their emotional well-being. Besides my usual roles of cook, chauffeur, maid, and social coordinator, I found myself serving as their therapist and primary playmate. And each of those roles was made more difficult and complicated by the pandemic.

I also sought to support friends who were struggling even more than I was. As much as I was struggling, the gamble we made on our family's health by sending our children to school in person bought us valuable time. Friends and colleagues facing greater physical risks found themselves supporting their children through distance learning or even began homeschooling their youngsters. Meanwhile, those without partners or children found themselves stuck at home alone, desper-

[1] Christina Bieber Lake, *The Flourishing Teacher* (InterVarsity Press, 2020), chap. 4.

ate for social interaction. I fought the fog of "pandemic brain" to coordinate online gatherings for several different groups of friends, seeking to offer a lifeline to loved ones who were drowning in various ways.

Nine months into this global pandemic, our lives were once again turned upside down. Just as I began to feel like I was regaining some semblance of sanity, the pandemic hit our community in earnest. North Dakota's COVID-19 deaths per capita were the worst in the nation.[2] Growing numbers of nurses and teachers were forced to quarantine, leaving those who remained on the job stretched to a breaking point. Our public schools returned to distance learning, leaving families scrambling to arrange care. I found myself once again supervising my children's distance learning even as I struggled with end-of-semester grading, moving three courses to online delivery in time for the start of spring semester, and revising this book manuscript. Instead of racing through each day's lessons in under an hour, as they had done in April, I had to coordinate my children's four or five live Zoom lessons each day, and ensure they completed other lessons in between them. Uninterrupted work time, a precious commodity throughout the fall, disappeared overnight. I responded to emails to the sound of first-grade reading lessons. Date lunches were replaced by increasingly tense negotiations over the nutritional content of my children's frequent snacks. And each time I escaped to my basement office to try to concentrate for an hour or two, I paid for it with my children's resentment and feelings of abandonment.

As much as my family's and friends' lives have been turned upside down by this pandemic, we have been insulated by our privilege. We had the career flexibility to stay home with our children and limit our exposure to the disease. We enjoyed relatively reliable high-speed internet access to enable all those Zoom meetings. We could afford to pay for online academic enrichment and social engagement. Meanwhile, front-line workers relied on whatever form of childcare they could find so that they could continue tending to an increasingly ill population. Children struggled (or neglected) to complete online assignments without guidance and supervision, or lacking the necessary materials when their parents were unable to get off work during the appointed pickup window.

Both initial research and anecdotal evidence suggest that, amid each of these transitions and the ongoing hardships of the pandemic, women have borne the brunt of the labor. Nine months into the crisis, fathers continue to work away in their home offices while mothers perch in shared living space with their children, juggling their offspring's online schedules as well as their own. Even after moving all of my classes online, I continued going into my office on our increasingly deserted campus on my two teaching days each week to ensure an adequate internet connection for my class Zoom meetings that conflicted with my children's—and to get away from the girls' never-ending demands on my attention. A sociologist friend and her colleague at another university are carving out a few hours each week from their own teaching and parenting responsibilities to interview univer-

[2] Prashansha Maharjan, "Six more COVID-19 deaths reported Sunday in North Dakota," *Grand Forks Herald* November 22, 2020, https://www.grandforksherald.com/newsmd/coronavirus/6773885-Six-more-COVID-19-deaths-reported-Sunday-in-North-Dakota.

sity faculty about how they are managing work and family during the pandemic (Ammons and Minnotte, Ch. 62, this volume). The interviews are ongoing, but preliminary analyses suggest many women faculty struggle to support their children, spouses/partners, and extended family amid this global crisis. Yet some men faculty report enjoying increased research time, improved family relationships, and better mental clarity as the pandemic has restricted other activities.[3] Quantitative studies—most of them performed by men—confirm that women are bearing the brunt of lost research productivity.[4]

The experts reassure me that what my children will remember is the family togetherness as we went for daily walks around our neighborhood and played endless board games. I suspect they also will remember hours and hours playing online games and socializing via video chat. But my ten-year-old has gotten pretty good at staying on task and logging onto her four or five daily Zoom meetings on time without my assistance. Both my girls have embraced learning simple household tasks that had always seemed easier just to do ourselves: to prepare a few basic foods independently, and to do simple chores like loading the dishwasher or washing machine. So for all their clinging to Mom, I think they'll come out with this a little more prepared to become independent adults. Whether they grow up to build more egalitarian divisions of those household tasks with their future partners remains to be seen.

---

[3] Krista Lynn Minnotte and Samantha K. Ammons, Personal communication, December 15, 2020.

[4] Flaminio Squazzoni et al., "No Tickets for Women in the COVID-19 Race? A Study on Manuscript Submissions and Reviews in 2347 Elsevier Journals during the Pandemic," SSRN Scholarly Paper (Rochester, NY: Social Science Research Network, October 16, 2020), https://doi.org/10.2139/ssrn.3712813; Minnotte and Ammons, Personal communication.

—58—

Clay, COVID, and Matzah Balls: An [Im]Perfect Passover in a New Home

Rebecca Shimoni Stoil

The Calendar

To say our life has been normal over the past year might be a stretch, even without a global pandemic. Admittedly I mark my own time by academic year. It's a habit I suppose I got into in grad school almost a decade ago, but as a mother whose older children bracket summer break with a Memorial Day birthday and a Labor Day birthday (yes, bring on the jokes), my years turn over some time between those two events.

I got my PhD in May 2019. When you're a student-parent, the entire family's life seems to be shaped by the parameters of your studies. My research trips were our summer vacation. My daughter was two months old when my PhD began, and finishing second grade when I was hooded. Our life—my life—became amorphous, lost its clear trajectory. The job market. Interviews. A hire.

We moved—the third major cultural move in less than a decade—from a small agrarian community in the Judean Hills to Baltimore to Atlanta, where I took up life as a semi-absentee mother, commuting 230 miles three times each week to Clemson. The children started a new school. My oldest started middle school. My husband struggled to understand southern culture. My kids struggled to define themselves. A basketball coach asked my son if he was Jamaican (he looks like the Kite Runner). My daughter broke her arm before she knew her classmates' names, before my employee health insurance kicked in, and, of course, while I was a two-hour drive away. It was a rocky start.

And then COVID.

I also count time by the Jewish calendar. I've always found it to be logical. Months are calculated by lunar cycles. Holidays are set around harvests. There are multiple new years in the Jewish calendar. The new year for the world begins, like the academic year, in the fall, and it is a stately, solemn new year, with none of the frivolity of December 31. A second before the fall harvest, it reminds us, to quote *Game of Thrones*, that winter is coming. That the richness of the fall is also a reminder of the barrenness of winter. There is an early spring new year – that one is for the trees – and a late spring new year that coincides with the barley harvest, a sign in ancient times that you would get those dense, storable carbohydrates that were the anchor of ancient farming communities. Perhaps un-coincidentally, that holiday is also the new year of the Jewish people, Passover, the Biblical story of the Exodus that traditionally marked the transition from slavery to freedom.

The Jewish calendar shaped our COVID as well.

Purim, a holiday of frivolity and mayhem, serves as our memorial of the "lasts." The last time we socialized. The last time the children were in school. The last time we happily participated in public assembly—a cheerful street parade in our new hometown of Atlanta. The last time we had people over in our house—to make the traditional hamentaschen cookies. The last time things were normal.

The Bricks

The next week began our long process of social distancing. First, my mother announced that she was self-isolating. Then my university moved to online. Then the children's school. My daughter stopped riding horses. My son's spring football season ended after two practices. My mother realized she couldn't come for Passover. My brother and sister-in-law realized that, given my husband's high risk factors, we couldn't host them either.

My children, increasingly isolated, realized that the long-awaited visit of the Whole Family to our new Atlanta house, the thing that seemed like it would finally certify that this was, in fact, our home, the center of their new universe, was not going to happen.

Don't worry, I told them. We'll do Zoom. I wrote a COVID–Haggaddah, the book that narrates the Exodus as the Passover Seder is conducted. I included hand-washing jokes. I made it into a PDF so that everybody could print it in Maryland, Virginia, Missouri. I made an elaborate menu. Sent it to my mother so that we could have the same foods on the table.

The food shortages began. I found matzah for sale in my Costco. My mother and brother couldn't. Unused to practicing traditional Judaism outside of a major center of Jewish life, I failed to anticipate the absence of key ingredients. My menu fell away. No gefilte fish terrine. No brisket. I called Costco day after day to locate an egg shipment, because in the absence of leavening required by Jewish law on the eight days of Passover, stiffly beaten egg whites are central to, well, everything. I got a giant box of brown eggs, but then realized that over half of them were fertilized, rendering them unkosher. I looked into local chicken ordinances.

I tried to distract. I doubled down on digging my vegetable garden, but our new home provided me with further obstacles as I began to remove basketball-sized chunks of soggy, slimy marine clay from the chosen spot. I doubled down again, teaching my younger children how to use slurry to separate dirt from clay. The clay that came out of the buckets was pure, deep orange. I told the children to make bricks. I told them they could understand now what the Haggadah was talking about. That they could feel a tiny second of history in their soft, smooth hands. I told them about the enslaved children here in their new home who had made bricks like these, day after day, year after year. I told them about the ghostly fingerprints of one enslaved child that were recently discovered on a brick in the tony historical district of Charleston, SC. I told them that their bricks could take a proud place as our Seder centerpiece, to remind us that we were slaves in Egypt, and that there were slaves here, and (I suppose in the back of my COVID-home-schooling brain, although I never said it) that there were worse things than not having gefilte fish or being able to hug grandma.

The Matzah Balls

The first night of Passover came. We were running late. I had only printed out two copies of my Haggadah, hardly sufficient for the five people sitting around the table. I had forgotten to send the PDF to my brother altogether. There was a chicken, not a brisket, in the oven. There was no chopped liver or gefilte fish, but a hard boiled egg sat proudly on the Seder plate. The traditional lamb shank wasn't there—but surely a scorched chicken neck could also remind us of the offerings made in the Temple? The kitchen of the new house was hot. And—I peeked in the pot—the matzah balls. Were. Sinking.

This is where I should tell you that I told my brother and sister in law about this project. And they said: talk about how COVID changed the division of kitchen labor.

You see, our family has unwritten laws. When my grandparents were alive, as was the case six years ago, my grandmother cooked the Seder dinner. My mother was the sous chef. My grandfather made three things: the chicken soup, the matzah balls, and the *charoset*, a sort of a finely chopped relish of apples, cinnamon, wine and walnuts or pecans that represents the mortar by the Hebrew slaves. This was the hierarchy from the time I was at least in middle school. It remained unchanged until 2014, when my grandfather died and my grandmother moved to a senior home. I once added a salad to the menu, and that was revolutionary. The Seder moved to my house in Baltimore, because it was easier for my grandmother's walker. My grandmother became a guest rather than a cooking participant. But did I cook, determine the menu? No. I cleaned the kitchen and made it kosher, and then my mother would come and take over. I slid into my mother's former role, and my sister-in-law into mine.

I leveraged my newfound power into minor menu changes. I added a delectable toffee snack known affectionately in corners of the internet as "matzah crack," since I hate, please note, hate, traditional Passover desserts. After attending a family Passover how-to lesson with my rabbi, I introduced the pre-Seder sweet-and-sour meatball hors d'oeuvres, a nod to octogenarian grandmothers and preschool children who would be hopelessly hungry and grumpy during the hour-long Seder ceremony before we actually got to eat the festive meal. I added the spread-like *charoset* that my Kurdish and Persian husband's family made, a thick but oddly airy paste made of dried fruits soaked and then ground together with nuts into a uniform texture somewhere between apple butter and peanut butter. And I took over my grandfather's role entirely. I became in charge of everybody's favorite course—the soup course.

I had learned to make my family's chicken soup in massive quantities, because it was an infinitely expandable and adaptable recipe that froze easily and offered myriad ways to stretch a grad-student-family's budget. You put a chicken, or just necks and backs, parsnips (when I remember), onions, carrots, and celery in a giant pot. Cut the celery and the onions big, because you're not going to eat them and they're easier to fish out that way. Cut the carrots and parsnips into thick coins, thick enough to hold up for hours. Do not cover the pot. Do not allow it to boil. Let it simmer that way for as long as you can. I like at least 4 hours. Once, exhausted from work and grad school. I left the pot on all night. I wouldn't do it again for fear of starting a conflagration, but the chicken soup that came out looked like clear liquid gold, an intense elixir that glistened in a bowl, awaiting noodle cooked separately so as not to cloud the soup with starch. Maybe you've heard of "Jewish chicken soup?" This is it.

I took over the process of making the matzoh balls. I already knew how to make them, because I discovered in college that there was no statute of limitations restricting matzah balls to Passover and then I went a little bit *kneidel*-crazy, cooking up giant pots of them for friends. But my grandfather's were his pride. He would run discussions on their texture, color, consistency, a generally overly modest man bathing in praise of his creation. They were light but not too airy. Never dense – he used to rail about a friend (otherwise an excellent cook) whose matzah balls were "cannonballs." He attributed his secret to "not using the mix, just matzoh meal," the large cardboard containers of, well, pulverized matzah. He also replaced the teaspoons of vegetable oil in the recipe with an older, secret ingredient that horrified his cholesterol-counting friends: chicken schmaltz, the lard of the Jewish kitchen.

People liked, maybe even loved, my matzah balls. My kids and my brother alone would eat multiple recipes' worth over the two Seder nights. I counted my output, rolling the raw dough into balls and dropping them into a boiling pot of soup (but not THE soup, because that would have ruined it) by the dozens. But here's the thing. I used the "box," the equivalent of Duncan Hines brownies, adding the eggs, and yes, chicken schmaltz, to the packaged mix. It worked well.

Until, of course, this year. I don't know if it is because of Coronavirus or because there are limited places and limited quantities here in Atlanta (yes, not as limited as if I were to live, say, in Clemson or even nearby Greenville, but the devil's in the comparison so to speak), but by the time I timidly ventured out with a three-page-long list to buy the myriad Passover products (there was no online interface for delivery or in-store pickup of these seasonal items), there was no matzah ball mix on the shelves. I improvised, quickly, and bought the matzoh meal.

Hours before the Seder, my soup was coming together, creating a heat island of chicken humidity in the crisp Georgia spring air. I started on the matzah balls, following the directions on the back of the matzoh meal container (my grandpa's "secret" recipe) assiduously. The dough was mushy. I corrected it. It was too dry. I corrected it. I put it into the fridge to chill, and prayed (metaphorically) that it would work out.

It didn't. Like my elaborate homeschooling schedules, my plan to spend isolation gradually working up to running a 5k route, my plans to let Corona subside and then do an NEH in New York, a conference in Italy (ok, that one faded early), my matzah balls sunk into the well of expectations. They were both asymmetric and globular, hard as rocks, dense as, dare I say it, cannonballs.

I told myself they would be ok, like the chicken-neck-shank-bone and chicken masquerading-as-brisket.

The Seder

This is the part I'm supposed to write about. The part where I tell you how the food on the table and the way we conducted our thousand-years-old Passover Seder was changed by a globular microbe, not visually unlike my ill-fated matzah balls.

First, the numbers. Kitchen disasters notwithstanding, this Seder was supposed to be big. We had invited other awkward Atlantans, multinational Jewish families caught in this strange always expanding boom town without the multigenerational circus that usually defines Jewish family celebrations. As of the week before Purim, my father (divorced from my mother) announced that he was joining too, bringing the total number of attendees on either night of the Seder to approximately 20. Instead, it was just the five of us, two frustrated parents and three exhausted kids who sat down at the elaborately arranged Seder table with a white flowered table cloth that had graced my grandparents' table in New Jersey back in the ancient days of 2014, before I became the sous chef or the only chef.

As you can imagine, the Zoom was initially a disaster, because the Seder involves everybody singing stuff together and this is something that Zoom does poorly at best. But the children were dressed in clean, festive clothes and my cousin Phyllis, a family member long lost due to (I am not joking) an 80-year-old debate over Marxism between her mother and my family, managed to log in and join us for the first hour or so of festivities. There was political humor about plagues and such, asynchronous singing so awful that we descended into laughter, and the moment in which our dog and my dog-in-law failed to understand that the other dog barking was on Zoom, and so they both had to spend time in other rooms after they tried to have their own Zoom dialogue.

My sister-in-law, usually the sous-sous-chef, made a successful Passover dinner for the first time, including recipes from our family that she had never cooked. My brother had even found matzah in the end, and drove from Baltimore to Virginia to drop some off in proper contactless delivery style to the small table set up on my mother's front porch. My mother couldn't read the print on my Haggadah, so I now had the only viable copy, but I'd jump in to add some little tidbit on Zoom every time we got to a good section that deviated from the centuries-old-text.

We took turns reading from the thousands-years old text, just as we would around the table. The youngest children split the Four Questions just as they have in our family for centuries. Some things change and some things stay the same. The sameness offers comfort, stability, a reminder that some things can remain constant in a world of so much uncertainty. The change reminds us that we can adapt and be flexible without losing ourselves.

And dinner? It was great. I made a recipe I introduced a few years ago for a matzah farfel (broken up pieces of matzah)-cranberry-pineapple casserole and everybody ate it like it was cake (practically was). The chicken was great. The matzah balls may have been a disaster, but the soup was perfect. The traditional tzimmes, a sort of a compote of dried fruit, sweet potatoes, white potatoes, with hints of orange tasted like my past and like every Passover I could remember.

The next night, I slowly, delicately reheated my chicken soup. A few hours before the second Seder started, I took out my mixing bowls and started over on the matzah balls. This time I worked slowly, intentionally, making sure everything was the right quantity, the right temperature. And that night, when we sat down for our second Zoom, we were even better. We learned how to not grimace at the singing, and changed the tunes a bit to accommodate more responsive song. And when we got to the soup course, the matzah balls floated like little light clouds in their golden broth. My grandfather would have approved.

Maztah Ball (Kneidlach) Soup

Submitted by Rebecca Shimoni Stoil
Atlanta, Georgia, USA 2020
[provenance: northeastern US, early-mid 20th Century based on Lithuania, 19th Century]

(This will make 8-10 servings, but the soup freezes exceptionally well. Throughout the year, I make big pots of the soup and freeze it into meal size containers, as well as into ice cubes for use instead of commercially made bullions/broths) This recipe takes a long time because of the soup, but is fairly un-labor intensive.

For Soup:
2.5 lbs Chicken (any combination of parts; I've done necks and backs, thighs – I like using a whole chicken and then saving it for coronation chicken salad the next day)
10 carrots, peeled and sliced into rounds approx. ¾ inch thick
5 parsnips, peeled and sliced into rounds approx. 1 inch thick
4 onions, quartered

I bunch celery, washed and chopped into pieces about 1 in long (I frequently leave out the celery and/or the parsnips; given the choice, I'd keep the parsnips and skip the celery.)
Salt to taste.

For Matzah Balls:
4 large eggs (but actually large; if not large, get 5)
4 tbsp rendered chicken fat (You could use oil. People do. It doesn't come out nearly as good.)
1 cup matzah meal
½ cup chicken broth (Have a cup on hand, though, just in case.)
1 tsp salt

Chicken Soup
Place all of the items in a large soup pot, making sure that they are covered by at least three inches of water. Cook uncovered, over low heat, so that the soup never exceeds a gentle simmer, for AT LEAST 4 hours. Add salt to taste.

Matzah Balls (make while soup is cooking):
In a medium bowl, beat eggs and fat together until well mixed (I like to think slightly bubbly)

Stir in 1 cup matzah meal, salt, and then ½ cup broth

Chill for AT LEAST 25 minutes. It should be cold and relatively solid with no residual liquid.

Working with wet hands, roll into balls between 1"-1.5" in diameter.

Drop balls into a large pot of lightly boiling soup (NOT INTO YOUR SERVING SOUP. I just make a pot full of chicken bullion soup to cook the kneidlach in). Cover and cook for approximately 30 minutes. Balls will sink initially and then float upwards ... if you're lucky.

To Serve:
Place 2-3 Matzah balls into a bowl. Ladle soup broth over them. Fish out some carrots, parsnips and celery and place in bowl. Soup should be golden and translucent.

Tzimmes (Slow-Baked Fruit Compote)

3lbs Potatoes, mixed white and sweet or just sweet, peeled and cut into bite sized chunks
2lbs Carrots, peeled and cut into chunks (not rounds).
½ lb Pitted prunes
½ lb Dried apricots
¼ c Honey
¼ c Brown sugar
1 c Warm water
1c Orange juice at room temperature
3t Cinnamon sticks (or more if you like a more cinnamon taste) - You can use 2t ground cinnamon, if you don't have sticks.
Margarine

Equipment
Large casserole with lid or ovenproof bowl with aluminum foil.
Mixing bowl, measuring cups

Directions
Preheat oven to 350° F (If you need to cook it at 325° F so you can cook brisket or chicken at the same time, you can. It will just take longer to cook through.)

Grease a large ovenproof bowl or casserole with the margarine

Clean, peel, and cut the potatoes and carrots. Place in the baking bowl.

Add dry fruit and cinnamon sticks, tossing everything together so it is nicely mixed and the fruit is somewhat evenly distributed.

In a separate bowl, mix together the honey, brown sugar, warm water, and ½ c orange juice. Mix until the sugars are dissolved. (If you are using ground cinnamon, add it here.)

Pour the sugar mix over the potato mix.

Bake, covered, for 1 to 1 ½ hours. Stir every 20 minutes or so. Add a mix of ½ OJ, ½ water if it appears to be too dry. It is done when the potatoes and carrots are tender and the liquid is syrupy.

—59—

Quarantine Baking

Nikki Berg Burin

I've always enjoyed baking. Cookies, muffins, bread—pretty basic stuff. So when the COVID-19 quarantine began, baking seemed a likely activity to fill the long days that lay ahead, especially with two children at home. However, what began as a familiar activity with my 9-year-old daughter, soon became a culinary adventure. There was something in the realization that we were stuck at home for an extended period and that we were quite literally in it together that led my daughter and I to tackle baking challenges that we would have likely passed over as too tricky, too messy, too indulgent, or too time-consuming in normal circumstances. Why not heat up a giant pot of oil, make our house smell like a fast food kitchen, and try making our own glazed doughnuts, then beignets, then doughnuts again? Why not shell two cups of pistachios that seemed determined to stay closed so as to make that decadent Norwegian brownie cake we've been eyeing for some time? Why not make a raspberry white chocolate cheesecake on a Wednesday morning just because? Why not give French macarons a try and maybe even croissants (clearly we were starting to go mad by this time). We measured. We mixed. We kneaded. We shaped. We waited. We baked. We cooled. We tasted. We did ok most of the time. We failed sometimes (blasted macarons!) (Prescott, Ch. 57, this volume). Occasionally, we amazed ourselves. No matter the result, when we were in the kitchen together and when we enjoyed our treats with the rest of our family, the worries of quarantine were nowhere in sight.

As time passed and the pandemic raged on, it became increasingly clear how fortunate and privileged our family was to go on such culinary adventures. Baking was an effective form of temporary escapism for us, because we had the necessary leisure time and resources to indulge in it. Meanwhile, parents across the country were losing their jobs and worrying about how to feed and house their children. Kids everywhere were finding themselves home alone and forced into a new independence as their parents had no option to work remotely or to take time off. Hundreds of thousands of families were faced with illness, hospitalization, and death. Seeing the positive side of the pandemic and making the most of it was not simply a matter of attitude, but also and largely one of status. It was relatively easy for me to escape into the world of baking with my daughter knowing that our family was financially secure and that we would be able to weather the storm within the safety of our home. I am grateful for the fulfilling experiences shared with my daughter in our kitchen. I am distressed that such experiences were not an option for most families. I am hopeful that as a society we will collectively reflect on the socioeconomic inequalities illuminated by the pandemic (even in our own kitchens) and work to make meaningful and lasting change.

Figure 59.1: Baking macarons with my daughter. Photo by Nikki Berg Burin.

—60—

"... Time enough for that": A Recipe for Comfort in the Pandemic

Pamela J. Snow Sweetser

My mother, 89 year old Janet Riley Snow, lives in Presque Isle, Maine, east central Aroostook County, population 66,792 and declining. Her house is in town, mine on our farm just outside city limits. We are 300 miles north of the city of Portland, and our near neighbor, New Brunswick, Canada, is eight miles due east. On April 14, 2020, Aroostook had two known cases of COVID-19, the Portland area had 484, and New Brunswick had 53. Democratic governor, Janet Mills, extended our state shut-down through May 15. The virus stayed away all summer and much of Aroostook County convinced itself it wasn't coming. Though scientists and medical professionals counseled restrictions and safety measures, many resisted with "Impeach Mills" and pro-Trump signs sprouting side-by-side on lawns. Men showed up in the auto parts store sporting no masks and pistols on their hips. We coped with community divisiveness by staying close to home and following CDC safety protocols. We took a hard look at what truly matters to us.

The first matter for me was to quit procrastinating and start preserving my mother's life story. She is a fiery second-wave feminist who loves her kitchen as a distinctly female gendered space, which is deceptive. Her old-fashioned granny aprons should carry a warning: "Danger! Do not push my feminist buttons!" She is independent and creative, resilient and empathetic. A year ago she and I undertook "Swedish death cleaning" to spare our survivors the burden of too much "stuff." COVID-19 trivialized our "death cleaning." What my mother keeps in her memory is all that matters. The illusion of "There'll be time enough for that later on" evaporated. On January 25, 2021, my spicey little mother turns 90. Resurrecting her recipes for *Backstories: The Kitchen Table Talk Cookbook* was the first step back through her life. She has stories to tell. Among them lies her long affair with food.

The summer she was nine, Janet began learning to cook with her hot-tempered, French-speaking grandmother, Delena (Lena) Nadeau Wakefield. Although Lena learned to speak English when she married, she did not read it and never owned a cookbook. She was, nonetheless, an extraordinary cook.[1] She showed Janet how

---

[1] She learned bread making from her father who was a hotel chef in Sheridan, Maine, in the early 20th century.

to work without written recipes, memorizing essential ingredients and ways to experiment with them, gauging amounts using taste, sight, smell and touch to judge when a dish, pastry, or bread was ready for the pot or oven. By the time she reached high school my mother had developed a genius for cooking. She married at seventeen and took over her own kitchen table. Cookbooks were optional.

During the 1950s and '60s, Janet's Parker House dinner rolls made her famous in her small town of Masardis, Maine. She mixed triple batches in a twelve-quart, hand-cranked bread dough bucket and baked them by the hundreds for church and Grange suppers, Extension and Women's Club fund raisers, and for Christmas presents. Decadently delicious, made with fresh whole cow's milk, hen house eggs, and home churned butter from the family's farm, they were, by today's nutritional standards, a heart attack waiting to happen. In the days when wives and mothers dutifully fed their husbands and children fat and sugar for strength and energy, they were an ideal food. You could never eat just one roll. This was a bread for special occasions and for comfort in times of duress.

Comfort has many forms, among them, good food and happy memories. 2020 has been bad, though so far our losses have just been traditions and indoor face-to-face gatherings. The first to go was my mother's weekly "Candlelight Supper" for the family. Complete with brocade tablecloth, linen napkins, full place settings, and silver candlesticks, it was always a feast of plenty that we ate with gusto and sincere gratitude. We stayed distanced and waited through the summer. September ended with no active covid cases, but at Halloween we decided to forego November and December holiday celebrations. Then came Thanksgiving. The virus had found Aroostook County. On December 27, 2020, identified cases stood at 497 and climbing. Five victims had died.

Though still involved at the university and active in the community, my mother placed herself under house arrest six months ago. My stepfather took over weekly grocery shopping, while she goes out only for essential purposes. She cooks delicious meals, has plenty of ways to occupy herself, and enjoys virtual visits with family. Although she mixes her now vegan Parker House Rolls in an electric bread maker, the smell of them baking is the same. It stirs memories of home and family and with them reassurance we can get through this pandemic. The best recipe for coping is not comfort food itself, but rather appreciation for the hands that make it.

Parker House Rolls

Janet Riley Snow, Circa 1950s[2]

Preparation Time

3 hours; total cooking time: 12-15 minutes; makes about 3 dozen.[3]

Ingredients

1 ½ cups whole milk

1 cup butter divided in half

½ cup sugar

1 lg. yeast cake (2 oz.) or 3 packets dry yeast

½ cup warm water

3 large eggs

1 teaspoon salt

6 cups all-purpose flour

Instructions

1. Heat milk to simmer in a sauce pan, remove from heat, add one half of the butter and sugar, stir and cool to lukewarm.
2. Dissolve yeast in the half cup warm water. Allow to sit until it becomes foamy.
3. Lightly beat the eggs.
4. In a large bowl combine milk mixture with the eggs, salt, and yeast water.
5. Add half the flour and mix until smooth.
6. Using ½ cup increments, mix in all but about ¼ c of the remaining flour until dough forms a ball.
7. On a floured bread board knead the dough for about 10 minutes until it feels smooth and elastic. It should not feel stiff or sticky. Let it rest while you clean and grease the bowl.
8. Return the dough to the bowl, cover and set in a warm place to rise until double (1-2 hours). Make sure to use a cover that will prevent the dough from drying out.
9. Grease one or more large baking pans. Melt the other half cup of butter.
10. Punch down and remove raised dough from bowl. Knead briefly to form a smooth ball.
11. Divide the ball in half. Roll one at a time to about ⅓" thickness.
12. Use a 2 ½-3 inch biscuit or cookie cutter to cut out rolls. Set the leftover dough aside.
13. Make a deep crease across the top half of each circle, a little above the center.

[2] Since their 19th century origin in the kitchen of Boston's famous Parker House Hotel restaurant, the eponymous rolls, with their many variations, are identified by their rich, delicious and mostly unhealthy ingredients, and by their distinctive shape. Any basic yeast bread dough can become Parker House rolls.

[3] Recipe can be doubled or tripled. In the 1950s Janet mixed large batches in a hand-crank bread maker pail.

14. Brush each roll with the melted butter, then lift to gently stretch into an oval.
15. Press the longer side over the shorter side to make a layer that comes down over the edge of the shorter side.
16. Place the rolls about 1 inch apart in the baking pan. Brush tops with more butter.
17. Cover with wax paper or clean cloth. Put in a warm place to rise until double in size.
18. Roll out the second ball and repeat steps 11-17.
19. Form one or two small loaves from the trimmed dough, place in a loaf pan, cover, allow to rise until doubled.
20. Preheat oven to 375 degrees, bake for 12-15 minutes. Bread is done when it sounds hollow if you tap it.
21. Serve warm. Store cooled rolls in an airtight container, or freeze.

—61—

Recipes for the Pandemic

Dee Garceau

Missoula, Montana, USA, 2020s

Kitchen Improv

I used to buy takeout on evenings when I opened the fridge and nothing appealed. I'd go to my favorite deli and spend too much money on a grilled chicken breast with lemon and a side of garlic-sautéed asparagus, to go. Maybe some chocolate ribbon gelato for dessert. Or I'd go to the local organic food emporium, which had a hot-food bar, and pick up their sausage polenta casserole with green chiles and black olives. Or maybe just pile up a salad-to-go from their inordinately healthy, organic, non-GMO, free-range, gluten-free, hormone-free, locally sourced, fair trade, vegan-friendly, paleo-friendly salad bar. And then meet friends at Big Dipper for homemade ice cream. I loved green tea ice cream with hot fudge. No really. It's good. These habits were hard on the wallet, but they were balm to the spirit.

Covid-19 changed all that. I followed the pandemic protocols, sheltering at home, wearing a mask to get groceries, and opting for in-person visits outdoors with friends and family. The virus was insidious. You could become infected and not know it. You might be asymptomatic and pass it to those around you. You might walk past a healthy-looking person at the supermarket who unknowingly breathed viral droplets into the air. The same air you were breathing. The virus was frightening in its ease of transmission, its stealth. So we put our heads down and stuck to the protocols, hoping to stem the tide of cases, hoping to stay well, hoping against hope to save lives.

The Era of Deprivation. That is the title in my mind's eye, of this episode. We are deprived of the things we do in person with loved ones, like hug, play cards, shoot hoops, do puzzles, tell stories, banter with each other, and taste from each other's plates. Deprived too, of ordinary, friendly contacts that lit each day—the barista, the guy on the quad-lift next to me at the gym, the student who stopped by my office. Deprived of movies on the big screen, window shopping at the mall, or going to the batting cages with my sweetheart. But I'm alive and fortunate, grateful for my health, for a roof over my head and for food on the table.

Still, I cannot do Pollyanna. I have a friend who works hard to see the blessings in everything. Too hard sometimes. Last week I got word that two classes I was slated to teach were cancelled. In response to the COVID crisis, the legislature froze funding at the university. Suddenly I had no job in the coming academic year. That day, my friend posted cheerily on Facebook that COVID-19 was really "a blessing in disguise." I lost it. I shot back a reply: "Covid-19 is neither a blessing nor a curse; it simply is. People are losing jobs, losing their lives, and losing loved ones. I cannot gloss that over." The dangers, the worry about loved ones in other states, the fears about your next paycheck, and the restrictions wear like a shoe that causes blisters on a long walk. You walk the line and it's painful.

All this is to say, we had to get creative at home. I remembered a story from my father's boyhood in the Great Depression. One Sunday his Mom invited the local Catholic priest over for dinner. She wanted to bake him a cake but lacked the usual ingredients for frosting. Determined to favor the priest with a cake, she used leftover beet juice to flavor and color the frosting, but admonished the children not to tell.

That made my Dad and his siblings want to spill the beans, or rather the beets. All through dinner, they asked questions like, "What are we having for dessert?" (Cake). "Does it have frosting?" (Yes). "What kind?" Dad's mother deflected the most pointed questions until the cake appeared, resplendent in pink frosting. Then Dad couldn't resist: "Wow, look at the color of that frosting! It's pink!" His sister Charlotte picked up the cue: "How does someone make frosting so pink?" His Mom cut the cake with no reply. Dad waited until a piece of cake was passed to him. The priest was already eating his slice. Dad dug into his first bite and could hold back no longer: "Gee, this frosting tastes an awful lot like … beets!" His mother, my grandmother, turned beet pink.

I don't remember the rest of the story, only that I shared my father's boyhood glee as he recounted trying to bust my grandmother about the beet juice while she tried to impress *le Père.* And I was impressed with my grandma's ingenuity.

I followed her example. No longer buying takeout, scaling down my budget, and avoiding the grocery for as long as possible, I looked for ways to use up whatever food I had: Three overripe bananas, this close to being rotten. A smidgen of flax flour. A remnant of whole wheat flour. A bag of pecans. Congealed honey at the bottom of a plastic bear. Half a bag of chocolate chips. My neurons started firing. From that asteroid storm came this recipe:

Banana-Chocolate-Chip Muffins

Mix together the following ingredients:
¼ cup flax flour
¼ cup white flour
½ cup whole wheat flour
1 cup wheat bran
¼ cup pecan "flour" (Start with whole pecans, and pound into a pulp. Walnuts work well too).
1 tsp baking powder
1 tsp baking soda
¼ cup honey
2 tbsp vegetable oil
2 eggs
3 soft bananas, mashed
½ bag chocolate chips.
If the batter is too thick, add ¼ cup milk, any kind (soy, almond, oat, cows, 2%, skim, rice milk).
Pour batter into greased muffin tin. Bake at 400° F for 15-20 minutes.

Other inventions followed. Below are two that can be adapted to the foods you have at hand:

Vegetable Mayhem

To use up remnant fresh vegetables: Sauté in olive oil, fresh garlic, and black pepper. To wit:
½ head of cauliflower, rinsed and chopped
1 yellow onion, chopped
All the cloves in half a garlic bulb, peeled and crushed in a garlic press
Leftover baked red potatoes, sliced into "home fries" size
If you want protein in the meal, scramble two eggs with the veggies.

Sauté all of the above in olive oil. Add black pepper to taste.
Serve with a side of ketchup laced with a few drops of hot sauce.

Pandemic Safety Sandwich

2 slices whole grain bread, toasted.
Add mayo.
Radish sprouts; or raw baby spinach, baby chard, or arugula.
If no fresh greens add sliced pickles, dilly beans, or pickled okra.
Tomatoes, sliced, and sprinkled with black pepper.
Sliced red onion if you have it.
If you want protein, add hummus, or cheese, or deli-sliced meat.

—62—

Labor, Loss, and Joy: COVID-19 and Food among Faculty Parents

Samantha K. Ammons and Krista Lynn Minnotte[1]

The COVID-19 pandemic has changed the fabric of life. One of the most significant changes has been increased permeability of the boundaries between work and family, particularly among those in high-status occupations.[2] Perhaps nowhere has this been truer than in academia, where substantial work-to-family blurring already existed in a pre-pandemic world.[3] The structure of academic jobs, bringing together heavy job demands, high autonomy, and few location constraints, means that work can happen nearly anywhere at any hour of the day.[4] For many academic parents, COVID-19 intensified this blurring, with the home becoming a classroom and their primary workplace, along with the place where family life unfolds.

In this essay, we use the lens of food to discuss how COVID-19 altered work and home for this occupational group. Food and food-related rituals have long been central to work and family life, providing structure and opportunities for connection, as well as sustenance.[5] As such, they offer a unique vantage point for understanding how these core domains intersect in pandemic times. To explore this topic, we draw heavily from interviews we conducted with 26 tenure-system faculty parents at two universities about work-family stressors during COVID-19. Although interviews are still ongoing for our study, we have reached the point in which informal observations, including preliminary emergent themes, are possible for this essay. At times, we also include our own lived experiences since both Krista Lynn and Sam are faculty parents. Although both of us have abandoned our

---

[1] Authors contributed equally to this work, and they are listed alphabetically.

[2] Phyllis Moen, Jack Lam, Samantha Ammons, and Erin L. Kelly, "Time Work by Overworked Professionals: Strategies in Response to the Stress of Higher Status," *Work and Occupations* 40, no. 2 (May 2013): 79-114; Scott Schieman, Paul Glavin, and Melissa A. Milkie, "When Work Interferes with Life: Work-Nonwork Interference and the Influence of Work-Related Demands and Resources," *American Sociological Review* 74, no. 6 (December 2009): 966-988.

[3] Katerina Bodovski, "Why I Collapsed on the Job," *The Chronicle of Higher Education*, February 15, 2018.

[4] Joy Misra, Jennifer Hickes Lundquist, and Abby Templer, "Gender, Work Time, and Care Responsibilities Among Faculty," *Sociological Forum* 27, no. 2 (June 2012): 300-323.

[5] Marjorie L DeVault, *Feeding the Family: The Social Organization of Caring as Gendered Work* (Chicago, IL: University of Chicago Press, 1991).

university offices and work solely from home, Krista Lynn's and Sam's family lives differ. Krista Lynn and her husband, who is also a faculty member, have three children (ages 6, 7, and 9) who they are homeschooling this academic year. Sam's partner transitioned his inflexible 8:30 A.M. to 5:00 P.M. job from a cubicle to their sunroom, while their two daughters (ages 10 and 13) are remote learning from home. From these diverse voices and households, we find these initial themes: food operates as a source of labor, loss, joy, meaning, and escape.

COVID-19 has expanded the labor associated with food for many faculty parents. Our study participants told us that the provisioning of food became more labor-intensive, and that the amount of time devoted to meal preparation also tended to increase. This was largely due to more meals being consumed at home with most family members being home for all meals, along with fewer take-out/restaurant meals. Time devoted to clean-up from preparing and cooking food also grew due to the sheer increase in the number of meals consumed at home. In the Minnotte household, trips to the grocery store take place about every 2 to 3 weeks, which means each trip is carefully planned. Selective eaters in the Minnotte household also create the challenge of obtaining preferred foods in the face of grocery-store shortages, while the tedium of eating all meals at home increases the cognitive labor of searching for new recipes and snack foods that can bring novelty and excitement.

Another way that COVID-19 has increased food-related labor is through the collision of work and school schedules. Unfortunately for Sam's household, COVID-19 has brought three slightly different timetables under the same roof for months on end. With her oldest daughter in remote learning middle school, her youngest daughter in remote learning elementary school, and her partner working from home (with a 10 second commute instead of 15 minutes), meal misalignments are a constant source of friction. Their household breakfast window has expanded and lasts from 6:45 to 8:30 A.M., while lunch spans from 11:30 A.M. to 2:00 P.M. During these times, there is a constant flow of people in and out of the kitchen and a general reshuffling of people in their small house. To alleviate isolation and foster some sense of shared temporal order, Sam helps her daughters with their breakfast and lunch prep, and visits with each one while they are eating. Mercifully, the evening meal brings everyone's schedules in sync for a few short hours. In Krista Lynn's household the timing of meals is organized around when her children are the most productive with homeschool activities, meaning early breakfasts and late lunches coupled with an afternoon snack. Overall, COVID-19 has made households very busy places, especially for parents who shoulder more of the cooking responsibilities.

Unsurprisingly, it is women who tend to pick up the extra food-related labor (cooking, meal planning and clean up) that COVID-19 has created. For example, men were more likely to have full-time homemaking partners who continued to take care of meal preparation during this challenging time. In these interviews, the food-related labor of their partners was nearly invisible. Among this highly educated occupational group, this gender pattern was not always uniform. Some participants described a gendered division of labor in which men took on the risk-taking associated with going into the outside world to purchase food and other goods for the family (but even then, the lists men took with them on their foraging trips were often drawn up by their partners). Additionally, in some households, whichever partner had the more flexible schedule did the meal planning, preparation, and cooking, regardless of gender.

Food was also connected to a larger sense of loss over not being able to connect with others in the same ways as prior to COVID-19. Some participants missed meeting up with friends at bars, while others missed date nights with their partners at favorite local restaurants. Food could also no longer serve as social glue bringing people together in the same space—potlucks, weekly dinners with friends, and parties had long been abandoned. Others missed food-related traditions that were also discarded with the pandemic, such as Eddie's[6] tradition of grocery shopping with his children for their family's weekly meals. Eddie would often draw this out for hours to give his wife some much-needed alone time, but also to maximize time with just his children, something he treasured. Krista Lynn's family missed hosting holiday dinners that had become a pre-pandemic substitution for extended family who were many miles away. Zoom celebrations with friends, while fun and better than nothing, cannot fully substitute for the joy of sharing a meal together.

While food increased labor and reminded participants of COVID-19 related isolation, some participants spoke of food as a source of joy and respite in otherwise dark times. Participants found revitalization through the pursuit of food-related hobbies, such as Hugh's ongoing goal of crafting the perfect croissant. Others enjoyed spending more time experimenting with cooking and baking than they had previously. The work conditions of partners often came into play, sometimes leading to changes in who was responsible for meal preparation. Men were more likely to fall into this category than women. Ted, for example, took over most of the cooking, while his wife, a frontline worker, increased her work hours. This toying with the allocation of the division of household labor, including meal preparation, was described as an enjoyable experiment.

Food also served as a way of maintaining cherished rituals during turbulent times. For example, Rachael and her family continued dining at local restaurants—a weekly family routine—to ensure a sense of normalcy. For others, nightly dinners consumed as a family created a sense of togetherness, something that seemed more important than ever given the uncertainties associated with the pandemic. In Sam's household, the evening meal is the only one that they all share together, which is ironic since no one leaves the house all day. At least one participant (John) described striving for efficiency in food preparation, such as cooking large batches of food to use for multiple meals, to maximize time spent together as a family, while still allowing for work productivity. In contrast, a shift to homeschooling in the Minnotte household, meant that family breakfasts and dinners were abandoned, and instead Krista Lynn would use this time to catch up on work tasks that could not be completed during normal hours, returning to these tasks

[6] With the exception of Krista Lynn and Sam, all first names are pseudonyms.

when the children were in bed and on the weekends. Other food-related rituals were established, such as Sunday morning bacon and waffles, that brought the Minnotte family together for at least one meal per week.

Ways of building meaning and giving back were also connected to food for some study participants. Many faculty parents mentioned that although they were experiencing some food-related hardships, others in their communities were far worse off. Stable jobs with good benefits and pay gave our participants more options. They could afford to pay more for hard-to-find items, were able to grow produce on their property, and simply did not have to worry about dire food insecurity. For Sam, her community garden plot and backyard raised beds took on added importance. She doubled her plantings, canned all summer long, and donated many pounds of organic produce to frontline essential care workers and low-income residents in her neighborhood. Likewise, Ralph doubled down on his community work done within a religious context to help many who were suffering due to job loss and potential homelessness, bringing a sense of meaning to his daily activities.

Lastly, we also heard faculty parents mention how food venues offered a sense of escape, and a much-needed change of scenery. Since many of our participants rarely left their homes, a trip to the market became a special occasion. Shopping trips were doubly precious, not only because they were an outing that pulled them out of the house every few weeks, but also because provisioning afforded them time to themselves. Jackie, for example, described getting a latte about once a week and drinking it slowly in a grocery-store parking lot. Our participants said they craved and treasured this time spent away from pets, children, and spouses. Relatedly, several of our interviewees mentioned feeling disappointed that they could no longer work from coffee shops. Home, and all the additional roles and responsibilities that COVID-19 has shoved into it, did not always feel like a haven or a productive workspace.

Although we did not set out to use the lens of food to understand the work-family pandemic toll, nevertheless it ties together many of our participants' experiences. Meals have always operated as temporal anchors, marking the start, middle, and close of the workday. They continue to do so in the context of COVID-19, but they also introduce new challenges given the altered terrain of work and family. Food provisioning, preparation, and consumption, often shared activities with close companions and loved ones, take new shape as families adjust to the ramifications of a global pandemic. Our participants' experiences highlight how food is laborious, taking time and energy to find, prepare, and plan, and yet this time investment can feel like leisure or a much-needed diversion. This labor also brings joy and continuity during a time that feels uncertain and threatening, while also offering a venue to build meaning by giving back to others. In many respects, then, food, quite simply, is a chameleon that morphs with changing surroundings and circumstances. The same animal everywhere, but with unique markings as it blends into every household context.

—Conclusion—

Community Potlucks and Global Markets

Cynthia C. Prescott

Like our relationship with food, this book defies easy classification. Edited academic volumes typically focus on a specific topic or theme, carefully masking the personal views of contributors behind a critical tone and third-person verbiage. Cookbooks collect recipes, but traditionally provide little analysis of their cultural context. Each of these literary forms resembles a specialty store, offering a specific form and function. Yet readers often approach these volumes as they might hit a supermarket on the way home from work: the readers enter the volume, select what they need, and move on. This volume, in contrast, came together like a community potluck or covered dish dinner. Each contributor shared what she wished, with some effort from the editors to ensure a balanced meal. Some contributions are rich and meaty, while others are sweet and comforting. We invite our readers to sample widely from this collection, but to also feel free to savor your favorites.

This smorgasbord particularly seeks to satisfy our desire to understand the backstory behind the foods that we eat. Traditional cookbooks provided information and advice, but little warmth behind the recipes that they share—though, as the scholarship of Rebecca Sharpless (Sharpless, Ch. 3, this volume), Kathryn Harvey (Harvey, Ch. 5, this volume), and Erna van Duren (Van Duren, Ch. 8, this volume) demonstrate, applying a scholar's critical eye to these publications can reveal volumes. Community cookbooks, as Mary Murphy (Murphy, Ch. 14, this volume) and Rachel Snell (Snell, Ch. 12, this volume) skillfully show us, were aspirational, offering more insight on how their contributors wanted to be viewed than about the daily realities of their lives. Contemporary cookbooks tend to focus on a particular style of cuisine or to celebrate cultural fusion, such as Molly Yeh's Jewish/Chinese/Midwestern-farm fusion cookbook. Our hunger for backstory helps explain the popularity of Yeh's blog, cookbook, and now hit television show (analyzed by Cynthia Prescott, Ch. 48, this volume): through skillful camera work, Yeh invites us into her home filled with warmth and strikingly beautiful food. *Backstories: The Kitchen Table Talk Cookbook* similarly invites you to share cozy family memories. But where Food Network's new millennial Martha Stewart ultimately presents herself as a charming food authority and the newly-rural "hostess with the mostest," *Backstories* encourages you to take a step back and recognize not only the women who created and refined these heirloom recipes but also the cultural forces that shaped the work involved in crafting those beloved dishes.

Community Potlucks

A century ago, as Catharine Wilson highlights (Wilson, Ch. 4, this volume), community meals were a central part of work bees. Today, only the Old Order Amish continue to hold work bees on a regular basis. Other ethnic communities have moved away from holding barn raisings or corn husking bees. As middle-class women entered the paid workforce in the late twentieth century, they were no longer available to host elaborate dinner parties to support their husband's advancement in his workplace. High-power meetings moved to restaurants; office parties increasingly rely on catered or commercially produced baked goods. But many communities still hold occasional potluck suppers. These might serve as fellowship gatherings following worship services not so dissimilar to biweekly Amish church dinners, or as fundraisers for a family in need. Most of these community meals tend to be social gatherings divorced from shared physical labor. Yet these potlucks still rely on a common thread of domestic work. These food offerings provide skilled cooks with an opportunity to display their skill. But that display is constrained by gendered social expectations.

Potluck suppers typically offer an ample meal by combining the efforts of the community's women. Ironically, community-oriented women typically prepare their covered dishes in the isolation of their individual kitchens, then deliver them to the community in a covered dish. Once at the event, women typically work together to host the event, bustling around to reheat and serve the food as needed, while men and children focus on consuming their offerings. Men are more likely to contribute to community meals that are centrally organized within a community kitchen. Such large-scale productions require a more hierarchical command structure that parallels that of professional chefs—a career path that remains blocked to most women, no matter how skilled they might be in the kitchen. Or men might contribute to a community barbecue by grilling meat—thus ensuring they remain safely outdoors, away from the feminized space of the kitchen, and that they are contributing the highly valued main course. They can almost imagine themselves to be hunters providing for their community. In so positioning themselves, they erase the lower-status labor, likely provided by women, required to acquire the burger patties and buns from a warehouse club or food service supply company—let alone to slaughter the cattle and bake the buns, likely performed by even lower status immigrant men and women at large factories somewhere in the rural Midwest. These hard-working chefs likely look forward to enjoying the potluck of home-baked desserts contributed by the less visible female worker bees.

For all the variety of a potluck meal, there are limits to the diversity we are likely to find there. As we have seen, culinary traditions vary regionally. Furthermore, the religious or fraternal organizations that host such events tend to attract populations with similar racial, ethnic, and class backgrounds, and these gatherings serve to reinforce such divisions. The preferred flavors of these similarly oriented populations tend to align. Sometimes this conformity is intentionally coordinated. Humorist Dave Barry reported that when he visited the "Grand Cities" of Grand Forks, North Dakota, and East Grand Forks, Minnesota (the region now home to the Olive Garden Lady, millennial food celebrity Molly Yeh, and this author), the local newspaper assigned residents "to bring one of the three basic potluck food groups: (1) Hotdish; (2) Jell-O salad; and (3) Bars, which are desserts cut into bars." But that "potluck supper was almost a disaster, because … for a while there, there were hardly any hotdishes."[1] The potlucks at my Grand Cities church are less closely scripted, but when I moved to Grand Forks from Los Angeles, California, a decade after Barry's 2002 visit, I was appalled to discover that all of the "salads" at church potlucks contained either Jell-O or ground beef.

I soon learned that there is substantial pressure to produce a familiar dish for these church potlucks, because anything that is too exotic is likely to scare off potential diners. Few enjoy such a culinary reputation that people jockey for line position to ensure a taste of our contribution like Diane McKenzie's neighbors did to nab one of Nana's Buns (McKenzie, Ch. 39, this volume). But no cook looks forward to packing up rejected leftovers at the end of such an evening. I initially resisted this cultural conformity. I only grudgingly agreed to prepare a slow cooker full of "sloppy joe" mix to help feed the church's college-aged fellowship group, because I had never cared for that dish, and had not consumed red meat in over a decade. But the organizers scoffed at my urging that we provide a vegetarian alternative. So I dusted off my trusty Betty Crocker cookbook (Prescott, Ch. 39, this volume) and prepared the beef-and-tomato concoction to fill commercially-produced hamburger buns. I had trouble hiding my frustration and embarrassment when young adults passed over the sloppy joe mix I prepared because I had included foreign-looking pieces of green bell pepper along with the ground beef and tomato sauce. The students apparently feared that the resulting sandwiches would be too spicy for their midwestern palates. Learning from this experience, I soon yielded to local cultural expectations and began contributing readily recognizable dishes that, like so many other dishes at these events, substituted cheese for seasoning. I learned to save my (admittedly not very authentic) Mexican, Chinese, and even Italian repertoire for book club gatherings attended by fellow transplanted academic women who shared my yearning for healthier dishes featuring more flavor and, yes, a dash of spice.

Marketing Rural White Femininity

For all that urbanites (myself included) scoff at rural people's discomfort with foreign flavors and laugh with Dave Barry at the sameness of potluck suppers, they nonetheless display a yearning for the rituals and flavors associated with rural kitchens. As skilled consumers, some rely on Yelp reviews, the Olive Garden Lady's expertise, or my father's strategy of looking for parking lots filled with local vehicles to identify the truck stops and small-town restaurants with the best traditional country fare. Others trust national chains like Cracker Barrel to serve up reliable "home cooking." For Thanksgiving dinner, Chinese New Year (Prescott, Ch. 49, this volume), or their family's Passover Seder (Stoil, Ch. 58, this volume),

[1] Dave Barry, "Isn't It Grand? While Ice-Fishing, Dave Catches Schnapps," *Baltimore Sun*, March 3, 2002, https://www.baltimoresun.com/news/bs-xpm-2002-03-03-0203030367-story.html.

they dust off recipes passed down through generations, struggling to make sense of bare-bones recipes like contestants in a Technical Challenge on the hit television show *The Great British Baking Show.*

Moreover, urban North Americans demonstrate an enormous appetite for constructions of rural womanhood. Millions of people tune in to watch Molly Yeh (Prescott, Ch. 49, this volume), Joanna Gaines, and Ree Drummond display their household achievements. Yet no matter how many watch their television shows, buy their recipe books or housewares, or dine at their restaurants, these celebrities are not domestic divas. They aspire to Martha Stewart's level of market saturation, but seek to distance their brand images from the very market that made them famous. Instead, they evoke nostalgic rural values and wholesome forms of white femininity even as they skillfully commercialize that image.

Chip and Joanna Gaines became household names through their popular home renovation television show *Fixer Upper*. Building on that success, they have amassed a commercial following. Though their renovation show, restaurant, home accessory and gardening store, vacation rental homes, and media network are based in the city of Waco, Texas (population 144,015[2]), much of their brand's appeal is centered on their family farmhouse and Joanna's rustic chic design. They moved their Magnolia Market into converted grain silos. On their website, Joanna proclaims that she "appreciates the old way of living, simple and hard-working with home at the center."[3] Episodes of *Fixer Upper* typically open with scenes of their children frolicking with farm animals, and also feature their sons playing baseball or helping their dad move furniture, while the girls drop in to help Joanna put the finishing touches on staging each renovated property. Just as Molly Yeh chooses to soft-pedal her Jewish-Chinese ethnic fusion with a growing emphasis on a very white Midwestern farm image, Joanna Gaines downplays her Korean and Lebanese heritage to portray herself as pure Texas farm girl.[4]

Blogger Ree Drummond took this rural chic marketing a step further, branding herself as "The Pioneer Woman." Her wildly successful blog featuring photos of her rancher husband and recipes for "cowboy-friendly dishes" launched her lifestyle brand, which now incorporates housewares and even a fashion line. Her website promises, "Anyone can embody the pioneer woman way of life—and we're here to show you how!"[5] Yet nowhere does Drummond actually define what constitutes a "pioneer woman" lifestyle. Her newest book is titled *Frontier Follies: Adventures in Marriage and Motherhood in the Middle of Nowhere*, and she announced the redesign of her website with the greeting, "Welcome to my new frontier!" But Drummond's brand has little connection to the Old West. That

---

[2] "Waco, Texas Population 2020 (Demographics, Maps, Graphs)," accessed December 17, 2020, https://worldpopulationreview.com/us-cities/waco-tx-population.

[3] "Chip and Joanna Gaines from Fixer Upper Our Story," *Magnolia* (blog), accessed December 17, 2020, https://magnolia.com/about/.

[4] "Things You Didn't Know about Chip and Joanna Gaines of 'Fixer Upper' - Insider," accessed December 17, 2020, https://www.insider.com/fixer-upper-chip-and-joanna-gaines-facts-2020-4#joanna-gaines-is-one-quarter-german-one-quarter-lebanese-and-half-korean-1.

[5] "Welcome to The PioneerWoman," The Pioneer Woman, May 26, 2020, https://www.thepioneerwoman.com/about-pioneer-woman/a32672345/about-us/.

"pioneer" label seems to bear little connection to the European-descended settlers who settled lands taken from Native inhabitants near Pawhuska, Oklahoma, where Drummond's family now runs cattle, let alone those who farmed and published community cookbooks in Montana (Murphy, Ch. 14, this volume) and Oregon (Mayer, Ch.18. this volume) a century ago. No sunbonnets, calico dresses, or other symbols of nineteenth-century frontier life appear on her blog. Instead, Drummond presents herself as a thoroughly modern ranch wife, dressed in gauzy blouses over form-fitting blue jeans and fancy cowboy boots.

To Drummond, "pioneer" seems to be a generic term designed to evoke rural nostalgia and to highlight how far she has come from urban life. But just how rural is Ree Drummond now, and how urbane was she before? Whereas Molly Yeh can legitimately claim big city roots—she grew up in a suburb of Chicago, and launched her blogging career in New York City—Ree Drummond was born in Bartlesville, Oklahoma, with a population at that time of less than 30,000.[6] She did grow up next to a country club and attend college in Los Angeles, California, and she abandoned plans to move to Chicago to marry her rancher husband. Though she loves to post strongly gendered images of her husband resembling the famed Marlboro Man advertising image alongside photos of dogs and horses, Drummond's own image and expertise more closely resemble other white middle-class lifestyle brands than traditional rural stereotypes.[7] Her recent announcement of her family's "bonus kid," an African-American teenager, provided an opportunity to play up the rurality of her family, telling amusing stories about Jamar learning to appreciate their distance from specialty food stores and Ree's mistaken purchase of fly-fishing gear to support his newfound interest in fishing in Oklahoma ranch ponds. As hard as Drummond worked to emphasize her excitement at welcoming Jamar to her family, the photos that illustrate her "adventures … in the middle of nowhere" also served indirectly to reinforce the rest of the family's whiteness. Charming photos of a smiling Jamar in football gear appear alongside images of him in family photos, where he appears to be clinging to the edges of an otherwise incredibly close-knit white family.[8] For all the ethnic diversity that Drummond, Gaines, and Yeh bring to the table, their increasingly visible brands all rely on gleaming white farmhouse kitchens, and highly polished, modernized forms of white rural cuisine. They rely on nostalgia and the proclaimed wholesomeness of life on the farm or ranch to sell products that are every bit a product of the twenty-first-century electronic media marketplace.

[6] U.S. Bureau of the Census, "1990 Census of Population and Housing: Population and Housing Unit Counts: Oklahoma," 1992, https://www.census.gov/prod/cen1990/cph2/cph-2-38.pdf.

[7] Ree Drummond, "About Pioneer Woman," The Pioneer Woman, July 26, 2010, http://https://thepioneerwoman.com/about-pioneer-woman/a5039/about/.

[8] Ree Drummond, "Bonus Kid," The Pioneer Woman, November 9, 2020, https://www.thepioneerwoman.com/ree-drummond-life/a34305465/ree-foster-son-jamar/.

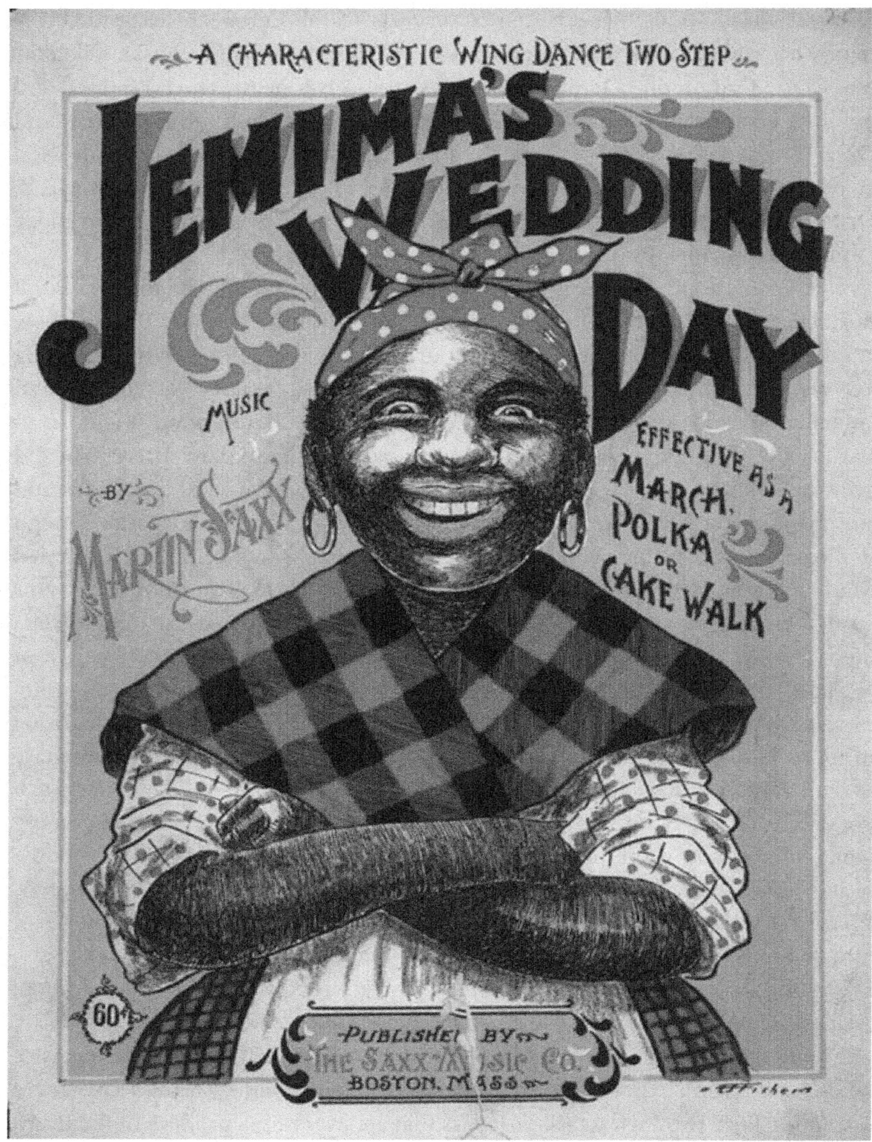

Figure 1: Jemima character on cakewalk sheet music. "Jemima's Wedding Day: Cake Walk. Martin Saxx (words by Jere O'Halloran). Boston, MA: Saxx Music Co., 1899 sheet music cover. https://commons.wikimedia.org/wiki/File:JemimasWeddingDay.jpg

Marketing a Rural "Slave in a Box"

Juxtaposing Yeh, Gaines, and Drummond against popular images of rural African American women reveals how race and class have operated in marketing rural nostalgia over the past century. In June 2020, as antiracist movements spread across the United States and around the world in the wake of the death of a Black man, George Floyd in the custody of a white police officer in Minneapolis, Minnesota, Quaker Oats Company announced that it would retire its 130-year old Aunt Jemima brand and logo. The history of that Aunt Jemima brand elucidates many of the themes that this volume explores: the economic and cultural power of food, the gendered labor of food preparation, social class distinctions in foodways, and the globalization of processed foods and American-based corporations. But the story of Aunt Jemima also elucidates particularly clearly a theme that receives less attention in the rich stories and scholarly essays within this volume: the realities of white cultural dominance in North America.

Aunt Jemima Pancake Flour was the first ready-made pancake mix. It was the brainchild of two investors, Chris Rutt and Charles Underwood, who purchased a defunct flour mill in St. Joseph, Missouri, in 1893. Seeking a new market for their Pearl Milling Company flour, Rutt and Underwood experimented until they had developed a self-rising pancake mix. The pair had difficulty selling their novel product until Rutt came up with a brand image with which to market it. Rutt named it "Aunt Jemima," after a popular minstrel show character (Figure 1).

The Aunt Jemima character played on racialized Mammy imagery that thrived amid early-twentieth-century romanticization of the antebellum rural US South. That Mammy stereotype evoked a simple-minded, dark-skinned, obese, and desexualized Black woman who was content to be enslaved on a southern plantation.[9] The minstrel character Aunt Jemima (or "Jemimy" or "Mandy") was a headstrong and superstitious character who was often duped by modern technology, but who was an expert in the plantation kitchen. She represented the enslaved Black women who loyally labored to produce the good food and support the genteel leisure of delicate white women in the Old South. By focusing on her role as skilled cook, moreover, she downplayed the even harsher reality of thousands of enslaved women forced to chop cotton and labor to produce the foodstuffs that the mistress served to her family. Aunt Jemima produced good food and relieved white women from both labor and guilt over their reliance on others' labor.

R.G. Davis purchased the company and recipe in 1890, and soon turned it into a national brand. Davis tapped into the turn-of-the-century production, consumption, and marketing revolution in a rapidly urbanizing nation. While Rutt and Underwood had come up with the idea of a ready mix to ease pancake making, Davis utilized a wider range of industrial food products to improve the product. He added rice and corn sugar to the mix to improve its taste and flavor. By

[9] Mick McElya, "Commemorating the Color Line: The National Mammy Monument Controversy of the 1920s," in Cynthia J. Mills and Pamela H. Simpson, eds., *Monuments to the Lost Cause: Women, Art, and the Landscapes of Southern Memory* (Knoxville: University of Tennessee Press, 2003), 203–18.

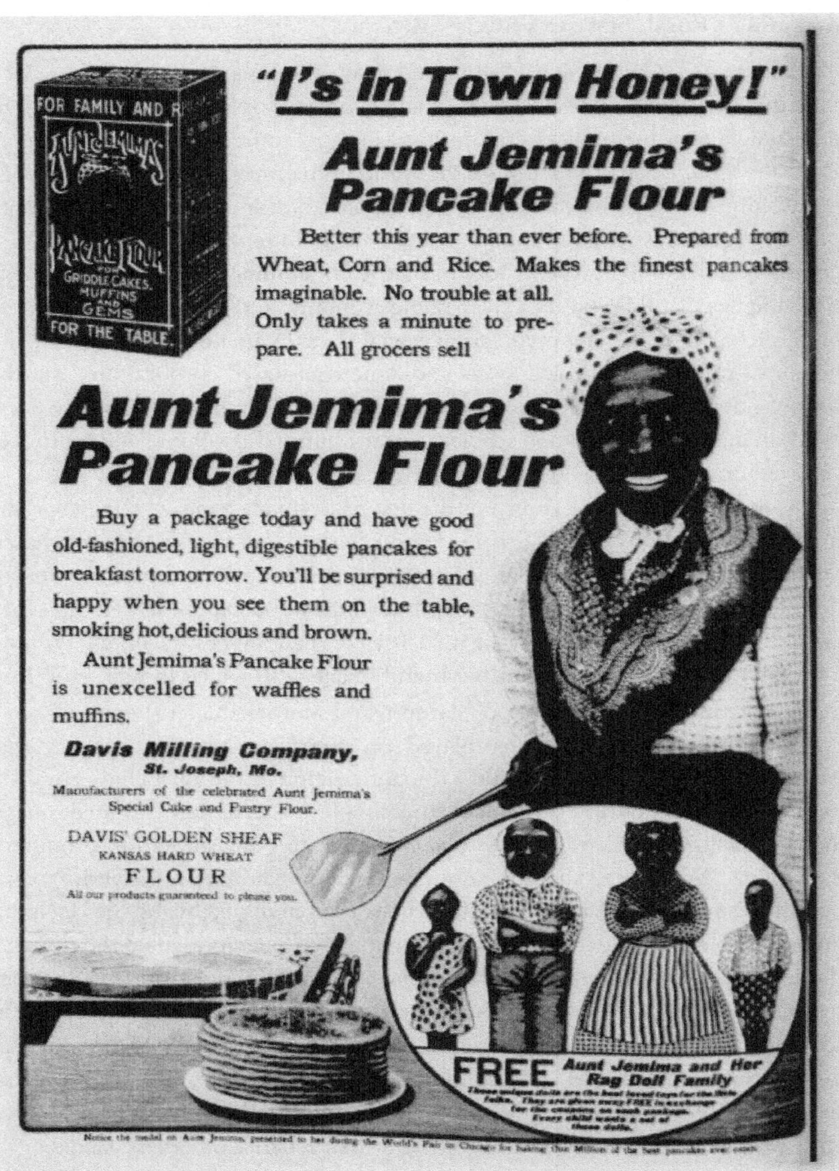

Figure 2: Davis Milling Company, "'I's in Town Honey!' Aunt Jemima's Pancake Flour" advertisement. New-York tribune. [volume] (New York [N.Y.]), 07 Nov. 1909. Chronicling America: Historic American Newspapers. Lib. of Congress. <https://chroniclingamerica.loc.gov/lccn/sn83030214/1909-11-07/ed-1/seq-44/>

adding powdered milk to the product, he ensured that housewives need only add water to the mix to produce tasty pancakes. And he began packaging the improved product in individual boxes printed with an increasingly recognizable brand.[10]

Most importantly, Davis utilized changing trademark laws and modern advertising techniques to promote the brand. He hired former slave Nancy Green to portray the "Aunt Jemima" character in public appearances, beginning at the 1893 Chicago World's Fair, where Green sang and told stories about plantation life—only some of them true—while cooking pancakes for (predominately white) fair guests. Purd Wright invented a legend tracing the product to a loyal former slave's beloved pancake recipe that she served on a mistress-less rural plantation; the packaged product made her skilled Southern rural cooking available to urban northerners. The veritable J. Walter Thompson advertising company fleshed out the colorful Aunt Jemima myth, broadening her appeal both to white southerners at the height of "Lost Cause" memory making and middle-class white northerners' "servant problem"—a shortage of live-in domestic servants as young women were attracted to factory work and "new immigration" from southern and eastern Europe was sharply curtailed. As middle-class housewives throughout the nation turned to labor-saving devices and products to fill in for household help, Aunt Jemima offered the perfect blend of technological convenience and nostalgia linking that industrial product with mythic cheerful, loyal servants far removed from modern urban life. Between 1910 and the 1930s—as white southerners erected monuments to Confederate generals and the film adaptation of the novel *Gone With the Wind* reinforced the Mammy stereotype—the pancake company published numerous full color, glossy advertisements featuring romanticized images of the rural Old South, hired a white actress with a history of performing in blackface to play the character in a radio series, and distributed highly popular Aunt Jemima and family rag dolls (Figure 2). Advertisements reassured white housewives that they would be able to please their men in the absence of their own Mammy. The Aunt Jemima brand thus played on older ideas about race, gender, social class, and rurality to market a modern manufactured food product to urbanites. White suburban housewives were, as historian Maurice M. Manring argued, buying the idea of a "slave in a box," when they bought a box of pancake mix to feed their families.[11]

Quaker Oats (whose logo also evoked a fictional historical figure) acquired the brand in 1925, initially doubling down on the racist imagery that had made the brand so successful. Quaker operated "Aunt Jemima's Pancake House" (later "Aunt Jemima's Kitchen") in Disneyland's Frontierland from 1955 to 1970. Not until the Civil Rights Movement protests against segregation of public spaces gave way to critiques of cultural racism did the company back down from marketing their product through the Mammy image. Protests and boycotts by African American

[10] Maurice M. Manring, *Slave in a Box: The Strange Career of Aunt Jemima* (Charlottesville, Virginia: University of Virginia Press, 1998), 72–78.

[11] Manring, chaps. 3–4; See also: Tiffany Hsu, "Aunt Jemima Brand to Change Name and Image Over 'Racial Stereotype,'" *The New York Times*, June 17, 2020, sec. Business, https://www.nytimes.com/2020/06/17/business/media/aunt-jemima-racial-stereotype.html.

activists persuaded the company to adapt Aunt Jemima character's image in 1968 to try to distance it from the racial stereotypes that underpinned it. They replaced her Mammy headscarf (which had served to contain Black "natural" hair, hiding it from the white gaze) with a thinner headband and chose a younger, slimmer model. At the brand's centennial in 1989, Quaker removed her headgear and added earrings and a lace collar to evoke a modern, possibly urban, Black woman, but the new grandmotherly image was not enough to prevent growing criticism of the brand, whose name and logo still served up Black female subservience to white consumers.[12]

Multinational snack, food, and beverage company Pepsico acquired Quaker Oats—including the Aunt Jemima brand—in 2001. Black Lives Matter protests sparked by George Floyd's death and hardships associated with a pandemic disease that closed many public spaces and disrupted the food industry's supply chain (a topic we will return to in a moment) finally persuaded Pepsico to retire the Aunt Jemima brand in June 2020. Candy titan Mars soon followed suit, renaming Uncle Ben's rice brand "Ben's Original." The new name removed the title "Uncle," which—like "Aunt"—was used by Southern whites to avoid applying the honorifics "Mr." and "Mrs." to Blacks. Mars also plans to remove the image of a white-haired Black man in a bow tie—designed, like Aunt Jemima, to evoke subservience—from the logo, and announced several diversity initiatives.[13] Cream of Wheat, Land O'Lakes, Eskimo Pie, and others also announced plans to remove racial imagery and change brand names, though seeking to maintain other aspects of the rural nostalgia central to their brands. And, direct Aunt Jemima competitor Mrs. Butterworth's syrup—sold in bottles shaped like a Black woman that invited white customers to grab her at her midsection in a way that evoked white men's historic sexual access to Black women's bodies as well as her subservience—announced that they, too, would review their brand and packaging.[14] Pepsico renamed the Aunt Jemima brand "Pearl Milling Company," a return to its nineteenth-century roots. Their corporate website celebrated this move to honor the "'pearl' inside

[12] Manring, *Slave in a Box*, chap. 6; Hsu, "Aunt Jemima Brand to Change Name"; "Aunt Jemima Syrup Bottle," National Museum of American History, accessed December 11, 2020, https://americanhistory.si.edu/collections/search/object/nmah_1297790; Alina Selyukh, "Aunt Jemima Will Change Name, Image As Brands Confront Racial Stereotypes," NPR.org, June 17, 2020, https://www.npr.org/sections/live-updates-protests-for-racial-justice/2020/06/17/879104818/acknowledging-racial-stereotype-aunt-jemima-will-change-brand-name-and-image.

[13] "Uncle Ben's Rice Officially Changes Its Name and Packaging," PEOPLE.com, accessed December 10, 2020, https://people.com/food/uncle-bens-rice-officially-rebrands-as-bens-original/; "Inside the Cottage Industry Trying to Revive Aunt Jemima and Other Brands with Racist Roots," Fortune, accessed December 10, 2020, https://fortune.com/2020/12/08/aunt-jemima-uncle-bens-eskimo-pie-brands-racist-roots-revived-black-lives-matter-movement-trademarks/.

[14] The Associated Press, "Mrs. Butterworth, Uncle Ben's, Colgate, More Brands Consider Changes after Aunt Jemima," *Syracuse Post-Standard*, June 19, 2020, sec. Business, https://www.syracuse.com/business/2020/06/mrs-butterworth-uncle-bens-colgate-more-brands-consider-changes-after-aunt-jemima.html.

the familiar red box,"[15] apparently missing the irony that this attempt at cultural inclusion and authenticity served to replace a Black caricatured figure with an overwhelmingly white image that also emphasized the artificially whitened flour in this highly processed industrial food product.

As the Aunt Jemima story and the many other stories shared in this volume make clear, food may be a basic requirement for human life, but it plays many other functions in human society. It serves as a social instrument that nourishes both body and soul. Food serves as a conduit to collaboration, whether sharing meticulously prepared dainty refreshments at ladies' aid society meetings or a mug of bad coffee or overpriced glass of wine at a downtown restaurant during an academic conference. Yet food and recipes are commodities that serve economic purposes. Recipes can economize, offering substitutions for expensive or scarce ingredients. Recipes also can promote certain products, such as General Mills' incredibly successful Betty Crocker brand and the now defunct Aunt Jemima.

Food can display one's social status or disguise hardship (see Murphy, Ch. 14, this volume). And, as Sara Egge (Egge, Ch. 40, this volume) and Jenny Barker Devine (Barker Divine, Ch. 44, this volume) show us, and Aunt Jemima has shown the world this year, food also bears political meaning. As the stories and recipes included in this volume make clear, certain foods also evoke powerful memories. These memories serve as a social binding agent in families and communities. Yet as Aunt Jemima also teaches us, some foods' cultural meanings—like their bleached flour and other highly processed ingredient lists that are linked to obesity and chronic disease—are manufactured and potentially harmful to our nation's wellbeing.

Pandemic Foodways

This volume came together amid national and global turmoil. The SARS-COV-2 virus shaped this volume in many ways. Archives closed, forcing us to pivot our research efforts. Kathryn Harvey (Harvey, Ch. 5, this volume) and Erna van Duren (van Duren, Ch. 8, this volume) creatively substituted online resources for the rich cookbook collections that remained inaccessible at the Archival and Special Collections libraries at the University of Guelph. Regrettably, the global crisis also disrupted our efforts to produce a truly global cookbook. We had hoped to include recipes, stories, and scholarship from RWSA members who reside in Africa, Asia, Europe, and Oceania. We envisioned highlighting the foodways of the Global South and peoples of color within North America. But, many who intended to contribute to this volume were unable to do so as they struggled simply to feed their families. Time constraints on the editors also prevented us from recruiting more contributions from scholars and communities beyond RWSA's current membership.

The pressures of social distancing and making do during the pandemic contributed to the nostalgic tone in many of the more personal stories that do appear

[15] "Aunt Jemima Our History," Aunt Jemima, accessed March 13, 2021, http://www.auntjemima.com/our-history.

in these pages. Indeed, some of our contributors set out to write analytical essays about their families' foodways, but struggled to achieve such critical distance amid the ongoing crisis. With our lives so disrupted by COVID-19, it is hardly surprising that nostalgia colored many of the personal reflections that appear throughout this volume, and especially those in Part III: Nostalgia and Foodways (Prescott, Ch. 19, this volume). As our neighbors—now visible to us only via social media—turned from microwaving convenience foods to nurturing their own sourdough starter, and from farm-to-table fine restaurants to home cooking, it makes sense that our thoughts turned to our mothers' and grandmothers' baking. While many of the rural cookbooks that we studied were aspirational, the family recipes and stories that appear in this volume tend toward comfort food and comforting memories of love expressed through food—including in our contemplations on the COVID crisis.

If we were honest, many of our contributors' passion for studying rural life is itself motivated at least in part by nostalgia for a time when families and communities gathered around the kitchen table to share the fruits of their labor. Where others might scoff at that golden haze, the Rural Women's Studies Association seeks to celebrate the strengths of rural families and communities. Yet we do so with the critical eyes of scholars who consciously choose to remove our rose-colored glasses and examine how rural women's work functioned within society in different places and time periods. We reach out our hands to scholars and activists—albeit figuratively and electronically, especially during this pandemic—around the world, hoping that our scholarship can inform and enrich the lives of people of all genders, ethnicities, and cultures.

—Contributors—

Linda Ambrose is Professor of History at Laurentian University in Sudbury, Ontario. She writes about women's organizations, biography, and women and religion, especially Pentecostalism.

Samantha K. Ammons is Associate Professor of Sociology at the University of Nebraska at Omaha. She specializes in occupations and the work-family intersection.

Jenny Barker Devine is Professor of History at Illinois College. She was recently usurped as the family baker by her teenage daughter, Liz.

Nikki Berg Burin is a historian, spouse, mother of two, and an increasingly adventurous home baker from Grand Forks, ND.

Lynne Byall Benson is a Senior Lecturer in Women's, Gender, and Sexuality Studies at the University of Massachusetts Boston. Her research interests include the history and development of the field of home economics.

Eli Bosler is an adjunct history instructor at Eastern Gateway Community College, who specializes in the rural Midwest.

Carla Burgos is an MA student in Art History at the University of Texas as San Antonio.

Joseph Cates is Curator of Education/Public Programming at Vermont's Sullivan Museum and History Center. He grew up in rural Alabama watching his Grandmama cook.

Diana Chen loathes cooking. She is more interested in researching the biocultural aspects of urban ethnic foodways in the US. She lives in Northwest Arkansas.

Myrtle Dougall (1896-1991) was wife, mother, and homemaker who was a good cook, good neighbor, and sang alto in the church choir.

Sara Egge is the Claude D. Pottinger Professor of History at Centre College in Danville, Kentucky. She has two kids and enjoys hiking and running.

Margaret Thomas Evans is Associate Professor of English at Indiana University East. She teaches writing and researches rural women's organization's use of social media.

Dee Garceau is a professor of history who makes documentary films. She loves fresh coffee, piping hot, at the kitchen table with family and friends.

Tracey Hanshew is an assistant professor of history at Washington State University Tri-Cities. Her research focuses on ranching women and cowgirls in the rural American West.

Kathryn Harvey is an archivist at the University of Guelph, having *recently* served 11 years as Head of its Archival and Special Collections.

Mazie Hough is Associate Professor of History and Women's, Gender, and Sexuality Studies at the University of Maine. Inspired by the women in her family she continues to do research in women's history.

Sarah Kesterson is an undergrad Communication student at University of Wyoming and employee of the American Heritage Center.

Marie Kenny of Brackley, Prince Edward Island, Author, Artist and former president of the Federated Women's Institutes of Canada. An Advocate for Empowering Women, a dedicated Wife, Mother and Grandmother of 20.

Hannah Peters Jarvis (1763-1845) was an English immigrant to Canada and member of the upper class.

Katherine Jellison is Professor of History at Ohio University. Her research centers on issues of gender and U.S. consumer culture.

Joan M. Jensen is Professor Emerita of History at New Mexico State University. She is a founding mother of the Rural Women's Studies Association.

Cherisse Jones-Branch is Professor of History and Dean of the Graduate School at Arkansas State University. Her research focuses on rural black women's activism.

Katie Mayer is the technical services librarian at the Oregon Historical Society Research Library and an avid baker.

Amy L. McKinney is an associate professor of history at Northwest College in Powell, Wyoming. The great-granddaughter of Norwegian immigrants, she enjoys making lefsa.

Diane McKenzie is a graduate student at the University of Lethbridge. Her research focus is women who farm and the intergenerational transfer of family farms.

Krista Lynn Minnotte is Professor of Sociology at the University of North Dakota. Her scholarship explores the interconnections between gender, work, and family.

Elizabeth H. Morris is a former Cooperative Extension Home Economist turned farm wife, gardener, mother of two, and grandmother of two.

Sara E. Morris is a librarian at the University of Kansas. For fun she researches rural women, cooks and bakes, and works out to mitigate the calories.

Mary Murphy is Distinguished Professor of History at Montana State University, where her research and teaching focuses on the history of gender and food.

Stephanie Noell is Special Collections Librarian at the University of Texas at San Antonio.

Cynthia C. Prescott is Professor of History at the University of North Dakota and an occasional baker. Her research focuses on portrayals of rural women in cultural memory.

Pamela Riney-Kehrberg is Distinguished Professor of History at Iowa State University and a Fellow of the Agricultural History Society. She teaches a variety of courses, including America Eats.

Virginia Scharff is Distinguished Professor Emerita of History at the University of Wyoming and Senior Scholar at the Autry Museum of the American West.

Rebecca Sharpless is Professor of History at Texas Christian University. Her research focuses on women in the American South, Texas, food, and labor.

Rachel Snell's research focuses on recipes as sources of collective biography for nineteenth-century women. She lives in Maryland with her family.

Joan Speyer is a retired K-16 educator in Maine. Interests include traveling, photography, reading, and cooking, all best when connected to family and friends.

Pamela Snow Sweetser is a retired educator. She now farms, and as an independent scholar does historical research on rural women's household work.

Rebecca Shimoni Stoil is a history professor at Clemson University and mid-20th-century recipe aficionada who recently added Georgian to her already extensive list of identities.

Maureen Sherrard Thompson is a Ph.D. candidate at Florida International University. Her dissertation focuses on business, environmental, and gender perspectives associated with the late-nineteenth and early-twentieth century seed industry.

Erna van Duren is a professor in the University of Guelph Lang Business School. Her research encompasses food business, value chains, food security and cookbooks.

Audrey Williams (nee Syme) (1926 – 2019), was a teacher, homemaker, and farmer who lived in the Alston District in southern Alberta, Canada.

Catharine Anne Wilson is the Redelmeier Professor in Rural History, University of Guelph, Canada. Her research focuses on rural households in Ontario 1800-1960. Her manuscript, "Bee-ing Neighbours," is currently under review by McGill-Queen's University Press.

Jean Wilson is mother and homemaker extraordinaire who has a great love of family, family heirlooms, and family traditions.

Made in the USA
Coppell, TX
12 May 2021